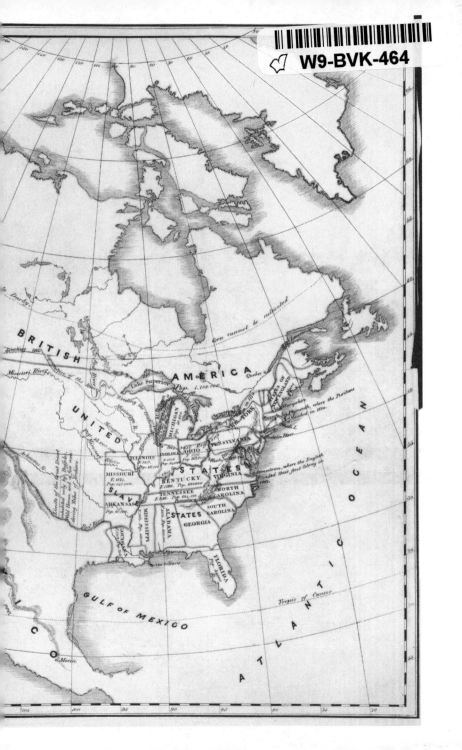

Alexis de Tocqueville

Democracy in America

The Arthur Goldhammer Translation

VOLUME II

EDITED AND WITH AN INTRODUCTION BY

Olivier Zunz

LIBRARY OF AMERICA PAPERBACK CLASSICS

Distributed to the trade in the United States by Penguin Group (USA) Inc.
and in Canada by Penguin Books Canada Ltd.

Library of Congress Control Number: 2011944892
ISBN: 978-1-59853-152-7

Library of America Paperback Classics are printed on acid-free paper.

FIRST LIBRARY OF AMERICA PAPERBACK CLASSIC EDITION
February 2012

Manufactured in the United States of America

OLIVIER ZUNZ
WROTE THE CHRONOLOGY AND
OLIVIER ZUNZ AND ARTHUR GOLDHAMMER
WROTE THE NOTES FOR THIS VOLUME

Contents

PART I
INFLUENCE OF DEMOCRACY ON THE
EVOLUTION OF THE AMERICAN INTELLECT

PART II

INFLUENCE OF DEMOCRACY ON
THE SENTIMENTS OF THE AMERICANS

PART III

INFLUENCE OF DEMOCRACY ON

MORES PROPERLY SO-CALLED

PART IV

ON THE INFLUENCE THAT DEMOCRATIC IDEAS
AND SENTIMENTS EXERT ON POLITICAL SOCIETY

INTRODUCTION

by Olivier Zunz

After two and a half years of sometimes anguished effort, Alexis de Tocqueville published the first volume of *Democracy in America* in 1835. The book, drawing on both Tocqueville's experiences during his nine-month stay in America (April 1831–February 1832) and his subsequent readings in American political and legal writings, found an immediate audience in France among readers eager to learn of the American political system from such a keen observer. The political class studied it. The press celebrated the author as a new Montesquieu. Historian François Guizot was delighted. Chateaubriand introduced Tocqueville to the right literary salons. The French Academy rewarded Tocqueville with its Montyon prize (he and Gustave de Beaumont had already won it for their penitentiary report). Best of all, Tocqueville was elected a member of the Academy of Political and Moral Sciences, an institution that became a platform for promoting his new political science.

Among the admirers was Pierre-Paul Royer-Collard, a powerful supporter of the constitutional monarchy and well-known public speaker. Although he discouraged Tocqueville from becoming a politician himself, citing the new author's lack of oratorical gifts, Tocqueville launched his political career anyway. He was elected to represent his ancestral district in Normandy in the national assembly. In the Chamber, Tocqueville chose to sit just left of center. He described himself as a "liberal of a new kind." What that meant was clear to anybody who had read his book. Other French liberals, Guizot first among them, had looked to England for an alternative to the French constitutional monarchy. Tocqueville had gone instead to America to see a democracy. He had found there what he had hoped: a way to promote equality without threatening liberty. His newly-acquired knowledge seemed especially valuable to him given the fragile nature of French governments. Louis Bonaparte's unsuccessful coup in Strasbourg in 1836 was only the latest menace to the July Monarchy. But if Tocqueville saw his political career as a means of implementing some of his ideas, he remained too independent and unwilling to compromise to find allies.

Tocqueville's effectiveness as a politician was also limited by his commitment to his intellectual work. He felt the need to explain more fully "the influence of equality of conditions and [of] democratic government on civil society in America: on habits, ideas, and mores." In the first footnote of the 1835 volume, he had suggested that Beaumont's documentary novel, *Marie*, would be such a book, but Beaumont dealt specifically with race, and so the larger task remained.

Tocqueville's active public life caused him to change his approach to his project. Gone were the days where he could lock himself in an attic room and forget the world around him. He had mounted two political campaigns to gain his electoral seat. After 1838, he was busy in the Chamber, where he reported on slavery in the French colonies; he actively participated in the debates at the academy; he was also a married man and proprietor of a large inherited estate in Normandy. There were moments when he thought it was all too much. "I cannot go on living like this," he wrote to Beaumont.[1]

In the end, Tocqueville chose to use volume 2, published in 1840, as an occasion to synthesize the observations he reported in volume 1. He no longer transcribed entire conversations with informants from his American notebooks and letters. Instead, he sought a new level of generalization about democracy. He adopted a more abstract tone.

IDEAL TYPES

Tocqueville thought carefully about the art of political classification, which originated with Plato. Where Montesquieu, his model, had looked into the nature of republican, monarchical, and despotic governments, Tocqueville focused on two forms of society: aristocracy and democracy. Although he kept *Democracy in America* as the book title, he was no longer describing a particular place but distinct "social states" that possessed unique combinations of characteristics. Later Max Weber would call such combinations "ideal types."

For Tocqueville, this approach reflected a choice as intensely personal as it was conceptual. An aristocrat at heart who had become a democrat by reason, Tocqueville was in effect reflecting on the two sides of his personality. Aristocracy was the lost world he had grown up in and democracy the new one he had embraced. "I am aristocratic by instinct," he said, but "I have an intellectual preference for democratic institutions."[2] In volume 2, Tocqueville spelled out his inner conflict as an exemplar of the larger one of his day.

Ever critical, Tocqueville came down hard on both worlds. He exposed aristocrats as living in soundproof chambers away from the noise of everyday people. As a result, they showed no empathy for people not of their class. Madame de Sévigné, who saw hanging as a diversion, "had no clear notion of what it meant to suffer when one was not a nobleman." This was the kind of callousness that justified revolutions. Conversely, Tocqueville saw democratic men and women dangerously neglecting particular human beings around them in favor of some vague notion of the larger collective, perhaps generous in spirit but void of specific commitments. In democratic times, Tocqueville saw an "excessive weakening of the parts of society against the whole." "This is one of my central opinions," he wrote to Henry Reeve, when the young lawyer from London was putting the final touches on the first English translation of volume 2.[3]

THEORETICAL ACROBATICS

Tocqueville rearranged the organization of volume 2 several times. In what became its second part, Tocqueville rephrased most forcefully his theory of the relationship between equality and liberty already proposed in 1835. It went as follows: "One can imagine," he wrote, "an extreme point at which liberty and equality touch and become one. Suppose that all citizens take part in government and that each has an equal right to do so. Since no man will then be different from his fellow men, no one will be able to exercise a tyrannical power. Men will be perfectly free, because they will all be entirely equal, and they will all be perfectly equal because they will be entirely free. This is the ideal toward which democratic peoples tend." Tocqueville envisioned a perfect society where liberty and equality were one and the same. If you were everybody's equal, you were obviously free. If you were truly free, you would be everybody's equal. But in the real world, he observed, people desired equality so much that they were willing to sacrifice their political liberty for it. The French people under Napoleon's tyrannical regime were the perfect example of that. Tocqueville argued also that new forms of despotism such as that of the crowd or public opinion had to be feared as much as the old absolutism. Despotism, regardless of its source, promoted equality in powerlessness, an unenviable condition. This is why one had to work constantly at keeping liberty alive. Tocqueville expressed forcefully his sense that liberty was fragile and all too easily sacrificed to the drive for equality. This was the axiom on which he built his new political science. As a politician, he would work towards solutions.

In these central chapters, Tocqueville gave his tightest theoretical statements contrasting aristocracy and democracy. He explained how democracy broke asunder the aristocratic chain of solidarity among men and replaced it with an excessive dose of what he called individualism, a word Tocqueville was among the first authors to use, and may in fact have coined.

America was the perfect field for individualism. Where else had the fixed positions of traditional societies so completely disappeared? The American was an individualist, whose obsession with wealth was beginning to be heralded as a national trait. Tocqueville suggested his busyness may instead have been a means of avoiding the moral misery Pascal ascribed to restlessness.

Yet the same American saved himself from the danger of imprisoning himself "in the loneliness of his own heart" by his long practice of liberty. Associations, in Tocqueville's great theoretical scheme, were engines of liberty. Tocqueville labeled the art of association "the fundamental science." By coming together, like-minded Americans exercised their freedom of action. By regrouping "into a multitude of small private societies," they mustered means not available to any individual. In small groups, they better achieved their personal as well as collective goals. Thanks to their associational habits, Americans might also avoid the dangers of homogenization.

Tocqueville found a name for democracy's ability to turn individualism into an asset. He labeled the mechanism "self-interest properly understood." It took Tocqueville some time to establish a positive connection between "self-interest" and collective betterment. In his travels, he at first saw people fending only for themselves everywhere he turned. "Private interest rears its head here constantly, reveals itself openly, and proclaims itself to be a social theory," Tocqueville wrote disparagingly to his friend Ernest de Chabrol from New York in 1831.[4] But he later changed his mind and posited instead an "enlightened love" of oneself that led Americans to "sacrifice a portion of their time and wealth" to the common good. Using language he borrowed from Montesquieu, Tocqueville speculated that in America, "interest" had replaced "virtue" as the motivation for working for the community. Turning self-interest into a benefit for all, Tocqueville argued, was a positive development for civilization because as an impulse, it was in much greater supply than virtue.

THE TERMS OF COMPARISON

As part of his effort to define a new political science, Tocqueville meant to go beyond the French-American encounter that informed volume 1. A good comparison between two places required the introduction of a third one—the "tertium quid." Tocqueville naturally took another look at England, the country where liberals of the old kind—Montesquieu and Guizot especially—had taken their inspiration. Tocqueville had visited England briefly in 1833. He had focused his observations on its landed aristocracy, but he had not integrated them into his account of American democracy in the first volume.

Tocqueville returned to England, this time with Beaumont in 1835, and they went to Ireland as well. During this journey, Tocqueville studied closely the problems of industrial wealth and poverty (he had met the economist Nassau Senior, who was revising the Poor Laws, in 1833), a topic he was also beginning to investigate in France. The same year, he presented an essay on pauperism to the local learned society in Normandy.

In America, Tocqueville had not observed industrial life. Although he had developed extensive connections in New

England, he had not visited the Lowell textile mills. By contrast, the Saint-Simonian economist Michel Chevalier had reported on them in detail.[5] Nonetheless, Tocqueville speculated in volume 2 on the threat a new industrial aristocracy could pose to American democracy.

Tocqueville's thinking on industrialization continued to evolve. In 1840, he focused on the industrial aristocracy yet made no analytical connection between the spread of industrialization and the coming of socialism. By 1848, however, he had reached the conviction that socialism was the enemy of freedom, hence irreconcilable with democracy. To make the point, he printed in the 13th edition of *Democracy in America* (in 1850, the last one published in his lifetime), as an appendix, a speech he had given in the chamber early in 1848 warning of the impending social revolution.

As he worked on the 1840 volume, Tocqueville let his "liberalism of a new kind" overtake his "new political science." He altered his reflection on America according to his priorities as a politician in the French Chamber.[6] As he admitted later to his cousin Louis de Kergorlay, "Although I very seldom spoke of France in that book, I did not write a page without thinking about France or without having France in a manner of speaking before my eyes."[7] He gave much space in the new volume to the dysfunctions of administrative centralization, attacking the stifling effects the search for material comfort had on his contemporaries and predicting that few great revolutions would occur in an age of individualism if the only thing people cared about were modest improvements in well-being.

Mind and Mores

In the first part of the 1840 volume, Tocqueville applied his method of contrasting the effects of aristocratic and democratic social states on the life of the mind of Americans (and other democrats) and devoted the third section to mores. On the intellect, Tocqueville developed a theory that Americans believed only in their own reason—they were products of a *de facto* Cartesianism. You could detect it easily in reading their books or listening to their speeches. Poets turned to personal introspection—"I have only to consider myself"—to represent mankind. Historians relied on general causes and neglected superior individuals they would have recognized in hierarchical societies. Orators used generic words. While an aristocratic society dealt in specifics, a democratic one spread the belief in the universality of the species. At times, Tocqueville assigned to "social state and political constitution" more than they were likely to be responsible for. He admitted having "personified equality in several places," having said "that equality did certain things or refrained from doing certain others." In doing so, he had turned "equality into a living being."

Here as elsewhere in the book, Tocqueville was at pains to leaven his catalogue of democratic defects by pointing out that democracy contained the seeds of its redemption. For men of action, no matter how they expressed themselves, had to pay attention to detail in their daily activities. Attention to detail more than made up for "the weak points in the theory."

On mores, Tocqueville was especially interested in gender roles. He saw that the same great "social movement that is bringing son and father, servant and master, and in general, inferior and superior closer to the same level is raising woman and will make her more and more the equal of man" albeit fulfilling different roles. In her widely-read *A Treatise on Domestic Economy for the Use of Young Ladies at Home, and at School*, published in 1842, Catherine Beecher approved effusively of Tocqueville's specific understanding of the division of labor between American men and women. It helped that Tocqueville had concluded that the "superiority" of American women was "primarily responsible for the singular prosperity and growing power of this people."

Democracy Is Best

Toward the end of his 1840 volume, Tocqueville stopped equivocating between his two worlds. He came down, at last, on the side of democracy. Insisting again, as in volume I, that the communal point of departure determined the course of American history, Tocqueville explained to the French that they had to work doubly hard to make democracy work, for they had started out on the wrong foot. In France, equality, "introduced by absolute power and under the eye of kings," had already penetrated the habits of peoples "long before liberty figured among their ideas." Equal only in their lack of liberty, the French "had to overthrow or coerce the old powers. This led them to make revolutions and inspired in many of them the unbridled taste for disorder." The opposite was true of Americans where "liberty was old and equality comparatively new." Tocqueville insisted on these opposite historical sequences as a means of warning his countrymen that they had to reverse course. Only if the French changed their ways could equality lead to "liberty" rather than "servitude."

To drive the point home, Tocqueville returned to the issue of mediocrity in democracy. It was a very important question, for all critics of democracy tended to agree that democracy was rarely conducive to outstanding achievement. In democracy, it seemed to many as though middle class values brought out only middling ideas. Not much of great significance was likely when plain materialism prevailed. Tocqueville decried the lesser quality of arts and sciences in a utilitarian democracy. He reminded his readers that he obviously admired great works across the ages. Archimedes, as portrayed by Plutarch, was a model to emulate. Archimedes was "so high-minded" that his work was purely theoretical; "he never deigned to write any treatise on the construction of war machines." By contrast, Americans committed themselves only to practical work. They did not risk scientific abstractions. They were too busy making money. Pascal was another cautionary example. "Had Pascal only some great profit in mind," Tocqueville insisted, "I cannot believe that he would have been able to concentrate the powers of his mind as he did to uncover the Creator's best-kept secrets."

Having conceded that much, Tocqueville reconsidered the meaning of success. In a democracy, he argued, people found true greatness not in crowning achievements that benefited only a few but in progress for most. Tocqueville had intimated as much throughout the volume only to restate this conviction most forcefully in his conclusion: "Equality is less lofty, perhaps, but more just, and its justice is the source of its grandeur and beauty."

THE OUTCOME

In sharp contrast to volume 1, which had met with enormous acclaim five years earlier, volume 2 received a rather cold reception in 1840. Soon after publication Tocqueville confided to John Stuart Mill: "It is likely there is a considerable flaw in the book. I believe the defect lies in the book's own premise, which contains something obscure and problematical not grasped by the masses. . . . Starting from ideas about American and French society, I meant to depict the general features of democratic societies, for which there is not yet a complete model. This is where I lose the ordinary reader. Only men very accustomed to looking for general and speculative truths like to follow me in this direction. I think the comparatively lesser impact of my book comes from this original sin of the subject matter much more than from the ways in which I have dealt with this or that part of the topic."[8] Tocqueville may also have suspected that his contemporaries resented his American prescription.

Yet *Democracy in America*, as an artful mix in the reader's mind of the 1835 and 1840 volumes, has endured to this day. It has become a founding document of how we think of democracy, not just in America but throughout the modern world. Readers have emphasized different points with the passage of time. Shortly before his untimely death at fifty-three, likely from tuberculosis, Tocqueville had written to the Russian mystic and Parisian society figure Madame Swetchine, "Long practice has taught me that the success of a book is much more due to the ideas the reader already has in mind than to what the author writes."[9] Witness the American case: Ante-bellum readers respected the work, which they put in a category altogether different from condescending travelogues by other Europeans. They especially appreciated Tocqueville's treatment of self-government as the institutional base of democracy. During the Civil War, Americans read *Democracy in America* with new eyes, realizing that they could no longer take for granted the mutual reinforcement of liberty and equality on American soil if blacks were not integrated into the polity. The existential question that animated Tocqueville had come to the fore in America. The American readership finally grasped

Tocqueville's anxiety. In the years following the Civil War, Senator Charles Sumner, who had befriended Tocqueville, did much to cement the author's reputation as a visionary in his 1874 *Prophetic Voices Concerning America.*

Tocqueville's readership receded in the inequality of the Gilded Age. The Progressives had little use for his work in their criticism of capitalism and rhetoric of social conflict. They neglected it even as some of them dusted off Madison's "Federalist 10" to devise a new theory of interest-group politics. But when the Progressives' countervailing powers blossomed into the New Deal, and an enlarged state was perceived as a Leviathan, Tocqueville returned as the theoretician of independent voluntary associations for "a nation of joiners." From there, Tocqueville became a champion of the American consensus in the 1950s.[10] Postwar Americans intellectuals relied on Tocqueville for defining the national character, but they downplayed his reflections on race and significant appreciation of cultural diversity that have made his work endure to our own day.

Tocqueville's work has known many revivals and even late discoveries. *Democracy in America* was translated, first in fragments and then in full, into all the East European languages in the 1990s, after the collapse of the Soviet Union. Eastern European intellectuals, like Americans before them, highlighted Tocqueville's praise of voluntary associations and his attack on centralization. With Tocqueville, they embraced the idea that liberty, and the responsibilities that go with it, required boundless energy on the part of civil society. Tocqueville never anticipated that his powerful formulations would continue to find an echo in such radically different circumstances. But his decision to write about America as the first fully realized example of the democratic "social state" has liberated his work from a particular time or place.

Thanks to my friends Charlie Feigenoff, Arthur Goldhammer, Christopher Loomis, and Max Rudin for important suggestions when writing this introduction.

[1]Tocqueville to Gustave de Beaumont, October 8, 1839, Alexis de Toc-

queville, *Œuvres Complètes* (Paris: Gallimard, 1951–) [hereafter *O.C.*], Tome 8, volume I, 380.

[2]Circa 1841, see Olivier Zunz and Alan Kahan, eds., *The Tocqueville Reader: A Life in Letters and Politics* (Oxford: Blackwell, 2002) [hereafter *Tocqueville Reader*], 219.

[3]Tocqueville to Henry Reeve, February 3, 1840, in *Tocqueville Reader*, 158.

[4]Tocqueville to Ernest de Chabrol, June 9, 1831, in Olivier Zunz, ed., *Alexis de Tocqueville and Gustave de Beaumont in America: Their Friendship and Their Travels*, trans. Arthur Goldhammer (Charlottesville: University of Virginia Press, 2010) [hereafter *Tocqueville/Beaumont*], 38.

[5]Michel Chevalier, *Lettres sur l'Amérique du Nord* (Paris, 1836), letters XII and XIII.

[6]Seymour Drescher, "Tocqueville's Two *Démocraties*," *Journal of the History of Ideas* 25 (April–June 1964), 201–16.

[7]Tocqueville to Louis de Kergorlay, October 18, 1847, in *Tocqueville/Beaumont*, 587.

[8]Tocqueville to John Stuart Mill, December 30, 1840, in *Tocqueville Reader*, 213–14.

[9]Tocqueville to Madame Swetchine, January 7, 1856, *O.C*, Tome 15, volume 2, 269.

[10]Olivier Zunz, "Tocqueville and the Americans: *Democracy in America* as Read in Nineteenth-Century-America," in *The Cambridge Companion to Tocqueville* ed. Cheryl B. Welch (Cambridge: Cambridge University Press, 2006), 377, 379–80.

DEMOCRACY IN AMERICA
VOLUME II

PREFACE

THE democratic social state of the Americans has naturally suggested certain laws and certain political mores.

The same social state has also given rise to a multitude of sentiments and opinions unknown to the old aristocratic societies of Europe. It has destroyed or modified previously existing social relations and established new ones. The aspect of civil society has been altered no less than the physiognomy of politics.

I dealt with the first subject in the work I published on American democracy five years ago. The second is the topic of the present book. These two volumes complement each other and together constitute a single work.

I must warn the reader at once against an error that might lead to serious misunderstanding.

Because I attribute such a variety of effects to equality, the reader might conclude that I regard it as the sole cause of everything that happens nowadays. But to do so would be to assume that I hold a very narrow view indeed.

There are today any number of opinions, sentiments, and instincts whose origins can be traced to factors unrelated to equality or even contrary to its nature. If I were to take the United States, for example, I could easily prove that the nature of the country, the origin of its inhabitants, and the religion, acquired learning, and prior habits of its original founders all exerted, and continue to exert, independent of democracy, an immense influence on the way in which people think and feel. In Europe, causes of a different kind but also distinct from the fact of equality may be at work and explain much of what is happening there.

I recognize the existence and influence of all these various causes, but they are not part of my subject. I did not set out to demonstrate the reasons for all our inclinations and ideas. I simply wanted to point out the ways in which equality has modified both.

Since I am firmly of the opinion that the democratic revolution to which we are witness is an irresistible fact, and one that it would be neither desirable nor wise to oppose, some

3

readers may be surprised to discover how often I find occasion in the book to be quite severely critical of the democratic societies created by this revolution.

My answer is simple: it is because I am not an enemy of democracy that I sought to deal with it in a sincere manner.

People do not receive the truth from their enemies, and their friends seldom offer it. That is why I have told it as I see it.

My premise is that many people will take it upon themselves to proclaim the new goods that equality promises to mankind but few will dare warn of the perils that it holds in the offing. I have therefore focused primarily on those perils, and being convinced that I had clearly made them out, I was not so cowardly as to hold my tongue about them.

I hope that readers will judge this second work to be as impartial as they seem to have judged the first. Amid the swirl of divisive and contradictory opinions, I have tried for a moment to forget the sympathies and antipathies that each of them may inspire in me. If any of my readers finds a single sentence whose purpose is to flatter one of the great parties that have stirred up passions in our land or one of the petty factions that have lately irritated the country and sapped its energy, let him speak out and accuse me.

The subject that I have sought to embrace is vast, for it includes most of the feelings and ideas to which the new state of the world has given rise. Such a subject surely exceeds my strength, and I am by no means satisfied with what I have accomplished.

But if I have not achieved the goal I set myself, I hope that readers will at least do me the justice of granting that I conceived and carried out my project in a spirit that might make me worthy of success.

PART I

*Influence of Democracy
on the Evolution of
the American Intellect*

Chapter 1

ON THE PHILOSOPHICAL METHOD
OF THE AMERICANS

THERE is not, I think, a single country in the civilized world where less attention is paid to philosophy than in the United States.

Americans have no philosophical school of their own, and the schools that divide Europe are of precious little concern to them. They scarcely even know their names.

Yet it is easy to see that nearly everyone who lives in the United States shares a similar cast of mind and conducts his thinking according to a common set of rules. In other words, Americans possess a common philosophical method, even though they have never taken the trouble to define its rules.

To be free of the systematic spirit, the yoke of habit, family maxims, class opinions, and, up to a point, national prejudices; to treat tradition only as a source of information and existing facts as useful to study only in order to do things differently and better; to seek on one's own and in oneself alone the reasons for things, to strive for results without becoming wedded to the means of achieving them, and to aim beyond form at substance: these are the principal features of what I shall call the philosophical method of the Americans.

If I were to take this one step further and search these traits for the chief among them, the one that most nearly epitomizes all the rest, I would say that in most activities of the mind the American relies solely on the unaided effort of his own individual reason.

America, then, is one of the countries in which Descartes is studied least but his precepts are respected most. This should come as no surprise.

Americans do not read Descartes, because their social state discourages speculative studies, but they respect his maxims because that same social state leaves them naturally disposed to adopt them.

In the constant state of flux that prevails in a democratic

society, the bond that ties generation to generation is loosened or broken. People easily lose track of the ideas of their ancestors or cease to care about them.

Nor can the inhabitants of such a society derive their beliefs from the opinions of the class to which they belong, because in a sense there are no longer classes, and those that do still exist are so variable in their composition that the body can never exert any real power over its members.

As for the possibility of one intelligence influencing another, it is necessarily quite limited in a country whose citizens, having become more or less identical, can observe each other at close range. Seeing that no one possesses any incontestable mark of greatness or superiority, each person is forced back on the most obvious and accessible source of truth, his own reason. What is destroyed as a result is not only confidence in any particular individual but also the readiness to believe anyone solely on the basis of his word.

Each person therefore retreats within the limits of the self and from that vantage ventures to judge the world.

The American custom of deriving the rules of judgment solely from within fosters other habits of mind as well.

Because Americans see that they can, unaided, overcome all the petty difficulties of practical life, they readily conclude that everything in the world can be explained and that nothing surpasses the limits of intelligence.

Hence they are quick to deny what they cannot comprehend: this leaves them with little faith in the extraordinary and an almost insuperable distaste for the supernatural.

Because they are accustomed to trusting only in what they witness for themselves, they like to examine very carefully any matter that concerns them. To that end they will strip away as much of the outer husk as they can, remove anything that stands between them and the object of their attention, and eliminate whatever is hiding the thing and preventing them from getting a good, close look. This habit of mind soon leads them to despise all outward forms, which they regard as useless and inconvenient veils placed between themselves and truth.

Americans therefore had no need to draw their philosophical method out of books; they discovered it in themselves. I would say the same about what happened in Europe.

There, the same method took hold and gained wide acceptance only as conditions became more equal and men grew more alike.

Let us briefly review the sequence of events.

In the sixteenth century reformers submitted to the judgment of individual reason some of the dogmas of the ancient faith but continued to bar discussion of all others. In the seventeenth century, Bacon in the natural sciences and Descartes in philosophy rejected received formulations, destroyed the empire of tradition, and overthrew the authority of the master.

Finally, generalizing the same principle, the philosophers of the eighteenth century set out to subject all beliefs to the scrutiny of each individual.

Who does not see that Luther, Descartes, and Voltaire all employed the same method and differed only as to the breadth of applicability they claimed for it?

What accounts for the fact that the reformers confined themselves so narrowly to the realm of religious ideas? Why did Descartes, seeking to limit the employment of his method to certain subjects even though he had developed it to apply to all, state that only philosophical and not political questions should be subject to individual scrutiny? How did it come about that in the eighteenth century people suddenly derived from the same method general applications that Descartes and his predecessors had either not noticed or refused to see? Finally, what accounts for the fact that in this period the method we are discussing suddenly found its way out of the schools and into society, where it became the common rule of intelligence, and after becoming popular in France was either openly adopted or secretly followed by all the peoples of Europe?

The philosophical method we are discussing was born in the sixteenth century and developed and generalized in the seventeenth. But it could not be widely adopted in either. The political laws, the social state, the habits of mind that derive from these two primary causes worked against it.

It was discovered in an epoch when men were beginning to be more equal and more alike. It could be generally followed only in centuries when conditions had finally become all but identical and men almost the same.

The philosophical method of the eighteenth century was therefore not only French but democratic, which explains why it was so readily accepted throughout Europe, whose face it did so much to change. The French turned the world upside down not because they shed their old beliefs and modified their ancient mores but because they were the first to generalize and elucidate a philosophical method with which it became easy to attack everything old and clear the way for everything new.

If someone were now to ask me why this same method is today adhered to more rigorously and applied more often by the French than by the Americans, among whom equality is nevertheless as complete and of longer standing, I would answer that it is due in part to two circumstances that must be understood before proceeding further.

It was religion that gave birth to the Anglo-American societies. This must always be borne in mind. Hence religion in the United States is inextricably intertwined with all the national habits and all the feelings to which the fatherland gives rise. This gives it a peculiar force.

This powerful fact is coupled with another no less powerful, namely, that religion in America has, as it were, set its own limits. The religious order there remained entirely distinct from the political order, so that it was possible to change old laws easily without undermining old beliefs.

Christianity has therefore retained a powerful hold on the American mind, and — this is the point I particularly want to emphasize — it reigns not simply as a philosophy that one adopts upon examination but as a religion in which one believes without discussion.

In the United States, Christian sects come in an infinite variety and are constantly changing, but Christianity itself is an established and irresistible fact, which no one seeks to attack or defend.

Having accepted the principal dogmas of the Christian religion without examination, Americans are obliged to receive in the same way a large number of moral truths derived from and dependent on those dogmas. This sets narrow limits to individual analysis and removes from consideration several of the most important matters of human opinion.

The other circumstance I spoke of is this:

Americans have a democratic social state and constitution, but they have not had a democratic revolution. They came to the land they occupy more or less as we now see them. This is a fact of quite considerable importance.

There is no such thing as a revolution that does not disturb ancient beliefs, sap authority, and obscure common ideas. Hence, to one extent or another, every revolution has the effect of leaving men to their own devices and forcing each individual to confront a yawning void of almost limitless proportions.

When, in the wake of a prolonged struggle between the various classes of which the old society was composed, conditions become equal, envy, hatred, and scorn of one's neighbor, together with pride and exaggerated confidence in oneself, invade the human heart, as it were, and for a time hold sway there. This, independent of equality, acts as a powerful influence that tends to divide men and make them mistrust one another's judgment and seek enlightenment only in themselves.

Each man then seeks to be self-sufficient and prides himself on subscribing to his own peculiar beliefs about all things. Henceforth men are united only by interests and not by ideas, and it almost seems as if the opinions of mankind are nothing more than intellectual dust, blown about by every wind and unable to coalesce into any fixed shape.

Thus, the independence of mind that equality presupposes is never so great, and never appears so excessive, as when equality first begins to take hold, in the throes of labor attending its birth. One should therefore distinguish carefully between the kind of intellectual liberty that equality can provide and the anarchy that revolution brings. Each of these two things must be considered separately if we are to avoid exaggerated hopes or fears about the future.

I believe that the people who live in the new societies will often make use of their individual reason, but I am far from believing that they will often abuse it.

The reason for this is something that applies in general to all democratic countries, something that will restrain individual independence of mind within fixed and at times narrow limits.

I shall take this up in the next chapter.

Chapter 2

ON THE PRINCIPAL SOURCE
OF BELIEFS AMONG
DEMOCRATIC PEOPLES

DOGMATIC beliefs are more common at some times than at others. They arise in various ways and can change in both form and content. It is, however, impossible to eliminate the existence of dogmatic beliefs, by which I mean opinions that men accept on faith and without discussion. If each individual took it upon himself to form all his own opinions and to pursue the truth in isolation, exploring only avenues he himself had opened up, it is unlikely that a substantial number of people would ever unite in any common belief.

Now, it is easy to see that no society can prosper without such beliefs, or, rather, that none can survive that way, for without common ideas, there is no common action, and without common action, men may still exist, but they will not constitute a social body. If society is to exist and, *a fortiori*, to prosper, the minds of all citizens must be drawn and held together by certain leading ideas. And that cannot happen unless each of them draws his opinions from the same source and is prepared to accept a certain number of ready-made beliefs.

If I now consider man in isolation, I find that dogmatic beliefs are no less indispensable for living alone than for acting in common with one's fellow men.

If man were forced to prove for himself all the truths of which he daily avails himself, his work would never end. He would exhaust himself in preliminaries and make no progress. Since he has neither the time — because life is short — nor the ability — because his mind is limited — to act this way, he is reduced to accepting as true a host of facts and opinions that he has had neither the time nor the power to examine and verify for himself, but which cleverer men have discovered and the multitude has adopted. It is on this basic foundation that he erects the edifice of his own thoughts. It is not his will that brings him to proceed in this manner; the inflexible law of his condition compels him to do so.

No philosopher in the world is so great that he does not believe on faith a million things that he learns from others, or that he does not assume the truth of a far greater number of propositions than he demonstrates.

This is not only necessary but desirable. Anyone who undertook to examine everything for himself would be able to devote but little time and attention to each particular thing. His mind would be kept in a state of perpetual agitation that would prevent him from delving deeply into any truth or settling on any firm conviction. His intelligence would be at once independent and feeble. He must therefore choose among the various matters of human opinion and adopt many beliefs without discussing them so as to delve more deeply into the small number he has singled out for scrutiny.

It is true that any man who accepts an opinion on the basis of someone else's word subjects his mind to slavery, but it is a salutary servitude, which allows him to make good use of his freedom.

In any event, there must always be a place in the intellectual and moral world where authority exists. This place may vary, but it must exist somewhere. Individual independence may be great or small, but it cannot be boundless. Thus the question is not whether some form of intellectual authority exists in democratic ages but only where it resides and what its extent may be.

In the previous chapter I showed how equality of conditions fosters a sort of instinctive incredulity about the supernatural and a very high and often quite exaggerated idea of human reason.

Men who live in ages of equality are therefore not inclined to locate the intellectual authority to which they submit outside and above mankind. Usually they seek the sources of truth in themselves or in their fellow men. This is sufficient, perhaps, to prove that no new religion can be established in such ages, and that any attempt to do so would be not just impious but ridiculous and unreasonable. We may anticipate that democratic peoples will not find it easy to believe in divine missions, that they will be quick to mock new prophets, and that they will want to locate the principal arbiter of their beliefs within the limits of mankind and not beyond.

When conditions are unequal and men dissimilar, a few individuals will be very enlightened, very learned, and very powerful on account of their intelligence, while the multitude will be very ignorant and quite limited. People who live in aristocratic ages are therefore naturally inclined to take the superior reason of a man or class as a guide for their opinions, while they are disinclined to recognize the infallibility of the masses.

The contrary is the case in ages of equality.

As citizens become more equal and more alike, each individual's penchant to believe blindly in a certain man or certain class diminishes. The disposition to believe in the mass increases, and the world comes increasingly under the sway of public opinion.

Not only is common opinion the only guide left to individual reason in democratic nations, but its power there is infinitely greater than it is elsewhere. In times of equality, men have no faith in one another because of their similarity, but that same similarity gives them almost unlimited confidence in the judgment of the public, because it seems unlikely to them that, everyone being equally enlightened, truth should not lie with the greater number.

When a man who lives in a democratic country compares himself individually to the people around him, he feels with pride that he is equal to each of them, but when he contemplates his fellow men as a group and sees himself in relation to that great body, he is immediately overwhelmed by his own insignificance and weakness.

The same equality that makes him independent of each of his fellow citizens in particular leaves him isolated and defenseless against the actions of the majority.

In democratic nations the public therefore possesses a singular power, of which no aristocratic nation can even conceive. Rather than persuade people of its beliefs, it imposes them, it permeates men's souls with them through the powerful pressure that the mind of all exerts on the intelligence of each.

In the United States, the majority takes it upon itself to provide individuals with a range of ready-made opinions and thus relieves them of the obligation to form their own. People there adopt a large number of theories in philosophy, morality, and politics without examination, on faith in the public at large. Indeed, if one looks into the matter closely, it becomes apparent that religion itself reigns there far less as revealed doctrine than as common opinion.

I know that American political laws are such that the majority is sovereign in its rule over society. This greatly increases its inherent influence over the intellect, for there is no more inveterate habit of man than to recognize superior wisdom in his oppressor.

In fact, the political omnipotence of the majority in the United States increases the influence that the opinions of the public would otherwise have on the mind of each citizen, but it is not the basis of that influence. One must look for the sources in equality itself and not in the more or less popular institutions that equal men may establish for themselves. There is reason to believe that the intellectual ascendancy of the majority would be less absolute in a democratic nation subject to a king than in a pure democracy, but it will always be quite absolute, and regardless of what political laws men are subject to in ages of equality, we may anticipate that faith in common opinion will become a sort of religion, with the majority as its prophet.

Thus intellectual authority will be different, but it will be no less potent. Far from believing that it is destined to disappear, I predict that it may easily become too powerful and may ultimately impose limits on the action of individual reason narrower than is appropriate to the grandeur and happiness of the human race. I see two very clear tendencies in equality: one impels each individual toward new ways of thinking, while the other would induce him to give up thinking voluntarily. And I see how, under the sway of certain laws, democracy might snuff out the intellectual freedom that the democratic social state encourages, so that the human spirit, having smashed all the shackles once placed on it by classes or individuals, would tightly chain itself to the general will of the majority.

Had democratic peoples merely substituted the absolute power of a majority for all the various powers that formerly hindered or retarded to an unusual degree the flourishing of individual reason, only the character of the evil would have changed. Men would not have found the way to live independently. They would only have discovered — no easy task — a new face of servitude. In this, I cannot repeat too often, there is matter for deep reflection on the part of those who see freedom of the intellect as a sacred thing and who hate not just the despot but despotism itself. As for me, when I feel the hand of power weigh upon my brow, it scarcely matters who my oppressor is, and I am not more inclined to submit to the yoke because a million arms are prepared to place it around my neck.

Chapter 3

WHY THE AMERICANS SHOW MORE APTITUDE AND TASTE FOR GENERAL IDEAS THAN THEIR ENGLISH FOREFATHERS

GOD does not contemplate the human race in general. At a single glance he takes in every human being separately, and in each he sees the resemblances that make him like all the others and the differences that set him apart.

God therefore has no need of general ideas; that is, he never feels the need to subsume a very large number of analogous objects under a single form in order to think about them in a more convenient way.

This is not the case with man. If the human mind undertook to examine and judge individually all the particular cases that came to its notice, it would soon become lost in a sea of detail and cease to see anything. In this extremity it has recourse to an imperfect but necessary procedure that is as much a proof of its weakness as a compensation for it.

After giving cursory consideration to a certain number of objects and remarking that they resemble one another, it ascribes a single name to all of them, sets them apart, and proceeds on its course.

General ideas attest not to the strength of the human intellect but rather to its insufficiency, for in nature no beings are exactly alike; no facts are identical; no rules are applicable indiscriminately and in the same way to several objects at once.

General ideas are admirable in one respect, namely, that they allow the human mind to make rapid judgments about a great many things at once, but the notions they provide are always incomplete, and what they gain in breadth they lose in exactitude.

As societies age, they acquire knowledge of new facts and every day, virtually unwittingly, grasp some number of particular truths.

As man grasps more truths of this kind, he naturally discovers new general truths. One cannot look at a multitude of particular facts separately without ultimately discovering the common thread that ties them together. Out of a number of individuals comes the notion of species, and out of a number of species, inevitably, comes the notion of genus. Hence the longer a people has been enlightened, and the more varied the forms of its enlightenment, the more accustomed it will be to general ideas, and the greater its taste for them.

But there are also other reasons why men are impelled to generalize their ideas or dissuaded from doing so.

Americans make much more frequent use of general ideas than do the English, and relish them more. This seems quite remarkable at first glance, given that the two peoples share the same origin, lived for centuries under the same laws, and are still in constant communication in regard to opinions and mores. The contrast seems even more striking when one focuses on Europe and compares that continent's two most enlightened peoples.

The English seem to suffer pangs of regret whenever they are forced to tear themselves away from the contemplation of particular facts in order to trace their causes; and when they do generalize, it is only in spite of themselves.

By contrast, the French taste for general ideas seems to have become a passion so unbridled that it must be satisfied at every turn. Every morning, upon awakening, I find that somebody has just discovered some general and eternal law I had never heard of before. There is no writer so mediocre that he is content to test his wings by discovering truths applicable to a great kingdom, and who does not feel unhappy with himself if his subject does not encompass the entire human race.

Such dissimilarity between two highly enlightened peoples astonishes me. When I think, moreover, about what has happened in England over the past half century, I feel justified in saying that the country's taste for general ideas has increased as its ancient constitution has grown more tenuous.

Hence the more or less advanced state of enlightenment is not in itself enough to explain what leads the human mind to love general ideas or to avoid them.

When conditions are highly unequal, and inequalities are permanent, individuals gradually become so dissimilar that there seem to be as many distinct forms of humanity as there are classes. We never observe more than one of these at a time, and, losing sight of the common thread that ties them all together in the vast bosom of the human race, we always see only certain men and never man as such.

Hence people who live in aristocratic societies never conceive highly general ideas about themselves, and because of this they are habitually mistrustful of such ideas and feel an instinctive distaste for them.

By contrast, a person who lives in a democratic country sees around him only people more or less like himself, so he cannot think of any segment of humanity without enlarging and expanding his thought until it embraces the whole of mankind. Any truth applicable to himself seems applicable in the same way to all his fellow citizens and fellow human beings. Having become accustomed to using general ideas in the field of studies that takes up the better part of his time and interests him most, he carries the habit over into other fields, and in this way the need to discover common rules everywhere, to subsume large numbers of objects under a single form, and to explain a set of facts by adducing a single cause becomes an ardent and often blind passion of the human intellect.

There is no better proof of this than the opinions of Antiquity in regard to slaves.

The most profound geniuses of Greece and Rome, the most comprehensive of ancient minds, never hit upon the very general yet at the same time very simple idea that all men are alike and that each is born with an equal right to liberty. They did their utmost to prove that slavery was inscribed in nature and would always exist. What is more, all available evidence suggests that even those ancients who were born slaves and later freed, several of whom have left us very beautiful texts, envisioned servitude in the same light.

All the great writers of Antiquity belonged to the slave-owning aristocracy, or, at any rate, saw that aristocracy as society's undisputed master. They stretched their minds in many directions, but in this one respect they proved limited, and it took the coming of Jesus Christ to make people understand that all members of the human race are by nature similar and equal.

In ages of equality, all men are independent, isolated, and weak. The actions of the multitude are not permanently subject to any man's will. In such times, humanity invariably seems to chart its own course. In order to explain what is happening in the world, one is therefore reduced to looking for a few great causes, which, by acting in the same way on each of our fellow men, induce all of them to follow the same route voluntarily. This again naturally favors general ideas and fosters a taste for them.

I showed earlier how equality of conditions leads each man to seek the truth for himself. It is easy to see that such a method subtly encourages the mind to formulate general ideas. If I repudiate traditions of class, profession, and family and throw off the weight of precedent in order to seek my way by the light of reason alone, I will tend to base my opinions on the very nature of man, which inevitably leads me, almost without my knowledge, to large numbers of very general notions.

All this explains why the English show much less aptitude and taste for generalization of ideas than their American progeny or — even more — their French neighbors, and why the English in recent years have shown more of both than did their forebears.

The English were for a long time a highly enlightened as well as a highly aristocratic people. Their enlightenment made them consistently receptive to very general ideas, while their aristocratic habits caused them to cling to highly particular ones. Out of this came the philosophy — at once audacious and timid, broad and narrow — that until recently was the dominant one in England and still claims the allegiance of any number of narrow and inflexible English minds.

Apart from the causes explored above, there are others, less apparent but no less effective, that foster a taste and often a passion for general ideas in nearly all democratic peoples.

Ideas of this sort must be carefully distinguished. Some are the product of slow, detailed, and conscientious intellectual effort, and these expand the sphere of human knowledge.

Others spring easily from a first brief exertion of the mind and lead only to highly superficial and dubious notions.

Men who live in ages of equality have much curiosity and little leisure. Their lives are so practical, so complicated, so agitated, and so active that little time remains for them to think. Men in democratic centuries love general ideas because they eliminate the need to study particular cases. General ideas pack a lot into a small volume, so to speak, and yield a great deal in a short period of time. So when, upon cursory and superficial examination, such men come to believe that several objects share some feature in common, they call a halt to their research and, without considering in detail how the objects in question may be similar or different, hasten to subsume them all under a single formula so as to move on to something else.

One of the distinctive characteristics of democratic centuries is a taste for easy successes and instant gratification. This can be seen in intellectual pursuits as well as other areas of life. Most people who live in ages of equality are bursting with an ambition which, while keen, is also lackadaisical. They want to achieve great success instantaneously, but without great effort. These contradictory instincts lead directly to a search for general ideas, with which they flatter themselves that they can paint vast subjects with little effort and command the attention of the public without difficulty.

I do not know, moreover, whether they are wrong to think this way, for their readers are as afraid of delving into things as they are and usually look to works of the mind only for facile pleasures and effortless instruction.

If aristocratic nations make insufficient use of general ideas and are often thoughtlessly contemptuous of them, democratic peoples are by contrast always ready to abuse such ideas and become indiscreetly passionate about them.

Chapter 4

WHY THE AMERICANS HAVE NEVER
BEEN AS PASSIONATE AS
THE FRENCH ABOUT GENERAL
IDEAS IN POLITICS

I SAID previously that Americans exhibit a less lively taste for general ideas than do the French. This is especially true of general ideas relating to politics.

Although Americans do infuse their legislation with general ideas infinitely more than do the English, and although they are far more concerned than the English are to bring practical affairs into line with theory, political bodies in the United States have never been as enamored of general ideas as the Constituent Assembly and Convention were in France. The American nation as a whole has never been passionate about these kinds of ideas in the way the French were in the eighteenth century, nor did Americans ever display so blind a faith in the correctness and absolute truth of any theory.

This difference between us and the Americans stems from several causes, but primarily from this:

The Americans are a democratic people who have always taken charge of public affairs themselves, and we are a democratic people who for a long time could only dream about the best way to conduct public business.

Our social state led us to conceive very general ideas about government at a time when our political constitution still prevented us from correcting those ideas through experience and gradually discovering their inadequacies, whereas in America these two things constantly balance and naturally correct each other.

At first glance this statement might seem to contradict what I said earlier, that democratic nations draw from the very tumult of their practical life the love they display for theory. Closer examination reveals that there is no contradiction.

People who live in democratic countries are very avid for general ideas because they have relatively little leisure and such ideas make it unnecessary to waste time delving into particular cases. This is true, but only with respect to matters that do not occupy their minds on a regular and necessary basis. Merchants will eagerly seize upon any general ideas one may wish to lay before them concerning philosophy, politics, science, and the arts, and they will not examine those ideas very closely. But they will not entertain ideas having to do with business until they have examined them, and will accept them only tentatively.

The same thing happens to statesmen when it comes to general ideas about politics.

On any subject about which it is particularly dangerous for democratic peoples to embrace general ideas blindly and over-enthusiastically, the best corrective is to make sure that they deal with that subject in a practical manner on a daily basis. Then they will have no choice but to delve into the details, and the details will reveal the weak points in the theory.

The remedy is often painful, but its effect is certain.

In this way, democratic institutions, which force each citizen to be concerned with government in a practical way, moderate the excessive taste for general theories in political matters that equality encourages.

Chapter 5

HOW RELIGION USES DEMOCRATIC INSTINCTS IN THE UNITED STATES

I N an earlier chapter I showed that men cannot do without dogmatic beliefs and, indeed, that it was most desirable for them to have such beliefs. I would add here that dogmatic beliefs in regard to religion seem to me most desirable of all. This can be deduced quite clearly even if we wish to consider only the interests of this world.

There is virtually no human action, no matter how particular we assume it to be, that does not originate in some very general human conception of God, of his relations with the human race, of the nature of the human soul, and of man's duties toward his fellow man. Inevitably, these ideas are the common source from which everything else flows.

Men therefore have an immense interest in developing very definite ideas about God, the soul, and their general duties toward their Creator and their fellow man, for doubt about these fundamental points would leave everything they do vulnerable to chance and in a sense condemn them to disorder and impotence.

Hence this is the subject about which it is most important for each of us to have definite ideas, and unfortunately it is also the subject about which it is most difficult for each of us by ourselves, relying solely on our own reason, to formulate our ideas clearly.

Only minds truly emancipated from life's ordinary preoccupations, deeply penetrating, extraordinarily agile, and highly practiced, can break through to such necessary truths, and then only with a great investment of time and care.

What is more, we find that even philosophers such as these are almost always plagued by uncertainties. With every step they take, the natural light that illuminates their path grows dim and threatens to disappear, and despite all their efforts they have thus far been able to discover only a small number of contradictory notions. For thousands of years the human mind has been tossed from one to another of these without ever managing to grasp the truth firmly or even to uncover new errors. Such studies are well beyond the average capability of man, and even if most men were capable of pursuing them, they clearly would not have the leisure to do so.

Definite ideas about God and human nature are indispensable to people's everyday activities, yet their everyday activities prevent them from acquiring such ideas.

This, I think, is without parallel. Among the various branches of knowledge, some are not only useful to the multitude but within their reach. Others are accessible to relatively few people and are not cultivated by the majority, whose needs are limited to their ultimate applications. When it comes to knowledge of God and human nature, however, daily practice is indispensable to all, even though the cultivation of such knowledge is inaccessible to most.

General ideas pertaining to God and human nature are therefore, of all ideas, the ones most appropriately shielded from the usual action of individual reason, and in which there is most to gain and least to lose in recognizing an authority.

The primary purpose of religion, and one of its principal benefits, is to provide an answer to each of these primordial questions that is clear, precise, intelligible to the multitude, and eminently capable of withstanding the test of time.

Some religions are palpably false and patently absurd. Nevertheless, it is fair to say that any religion that remains circumscribed within the limits I have just indicated, and which does not seek, as several have done, to halt the growth of the human mind wherever it may occur, imposes a salutary discipline on the intellect; and it must be acknowledged that, if religion does not save men in the other world, it may yet contribute greatly to their happiness and grandeur in this one.

This is especially true of men who live in free countries.

When a people's religion is destroyed, doubt takes hold of the highest regions of the intellect and half paralyzes all the others. Individuals become accustomed to making do with confused and fluctuating notions about the matters of greatest interest to themselves and their fellow men. They defend their opinions badly or give them up altogether, and because they despair of resolving on their own the greatest problems with which human destiny confronts them, they cravenly cease to think about such things at all.

Such a state inevitably enervates the soul; it weakens the springs of the will and prepares citizens for servitude.

Not only will citizens then allow their liberty to be taken from them; in many cases they surrender it voluntarily.

When no authority exists in matters of religion, any more than in political matters, men soon become frightened in the face of unlimited independence. With everything in a perpetual state of agitation, they become anxious and fatigued. With the world of the intellect in universal flux, they want everything in the material realm, at least, to be firm and stable, and, unable to resume their former beliefs, they subject themselves to a master.

For my part, I doubt that man can ever tolerate both complete religious independence and total political liberty, and I am inclined to think that if he has no faith, he must serve, and if he is free, he must believe.

I am not certain, but it may well be that the great utility of religion is even more apparent in nations where conditions are equal than it is elsewhere.

One has to admit that while equality brings the world much that is good, it also opens the door to some highly dangerous instincts, as will be shown later. It tends to isolate people from one another, so that each individual is inclined to think only of himself.

It also leaves their souls inordinately vulnerable to material pleasures.

The greatest advantage of religions is that they inspire quite contrary instincts. There is no religion that does not place the object of man's desires beyond and above the goods of the earth, and that does not naturally raise man's soul toward regions far superior to those of the senses. Nor is there any religion that does not impose on each individual certain duties toward, or in common with, the human race and that does not therefore turn him away now and then from contemplation of himself. Even the falsest and most dangerous of religions do this.

Religious peoples are therefore naturally strong precisely where democratic peoples are weak, which shows clearly how important it is that men retain their religion when they become equals.

I have neither the right nor the desire to examine the supernatural means by which God inspires religious belief in the heart of man. For the moment I am looking at religions from a purely human standpoint. What I want to know is how they can most easily maintain their power in the democratic centuries we are just now embarking on.

I have pointed out how reluctant the human mind has been to entertain dogmatic beliefs in ages of enlightenment and equality, and how the need for such beliefs is keenly felt only in regard to religion. This suggests first of all that in such times more than others, religions should remain discreetly within their proper limits and not seek to venture beyond them, for if they try to extend their power beyond religious matters, they run the risk of not being believed about anything. Hence they must carefully circumscribe the limits within which they claim to mold the human mind, and beyond those limits they should leave the mind entirely free to set its own course.

Mohammed professed to derive from heaven, and placed in the Koran, not only religious doctrines but also political maxims, civil and criminal laws, and scientific theories. By contrast, the Gospels deal only in a general way with man's relation to God and men's relations with one another. Beyond that, they teach nothing and oblige one to believe in nothing. Among countless other reasons, that alone is enough to show why the first of these two religions cannot rule for long in ages of enlightenment and democracy, whereas the second is destined to reign in such times as in all others.

Continuing this same line of inquiry, I find that if religions are to be able, humanly speaking, to maintain themselves in democratic centuries, it is not enough that they confine themselves strictly to religious matters. Their power also depends in large part on the nature of the beliefs they profess, on the external forms they adopt, and on the obligations they impose.

What I said earlier about equality leading men toward very general and very vast ideas is to be understood principally with respect to religion. Men who are similar and equal readily conceive of the notion of a single God who imposes the same rules on each of them and grants them future happiness at the same price. The idea of the unity of the human race continually brings them back to the idea of the unity of the Creator, whereas, by contrast, men who are widely separated from one another and highly dissimilar are apt to devise as many deities as there are nations, castes, classes, and families and to discover a thousand private roads to heaven.

There is no denying the fact that Christianity itself has in some ways been affected by this influence of the social and political state on religious beliefs.

Before the Christian religion first appeared on earth, Providence, no doubt in preparation for its coming, had gathered much of mankind like a vast flock under the scepter of the Caesars. Although the men who made up this multitude differed greatly from one another, they had this much in common: all were obedient to the same laws, and each of them was so weak and small relative to the greatness of the prince that all seemed equal when compared to him.

Clearly, this new and peculiar state of mankind must have disposed men to receive the general truths taught by Christianity, and it explains why the Christian religion was able to captivate the human mind so easily and rapidly.

Confirmation of this came after the destruction of the Roman Empire.

As the Roman world shattered, as it were, into a thousand pieces, each nation regained its original individuality. Within these nations, an infinite gradation of ranks soon developed. Races stood out, and castes divided each nation into several peoples. In the midst of this common effort, which seemed to encourage human societies to subdivide themselves into as many fragments as it was possible to conceive, Christianity did not lose sight of the principal general ideas it had brought to light. Nevertheless, it appeared to lend itself, insofar as its nature allowed, to the new tendencies to which the fragmentation of mankind gave rise. Men continued to worship one God, the creator and keeper of all things. But each people, each city, and, as it were, each man believed it possible to obtain some special privilege and to win the favor of private protectors capable of intervening with the master sovereign. If Divinity could not be divided, it could nevertheless be multiplied, and its agents could be magnified beyond all measure. For most Christians, homage to angels and saints became an almost idolatrous cult, and for a time there was reason to fear that the Christian religion would regress toward the religions it had vanquished.

It seems obvious to me that the more the barriers that divide the nations of mankind and the citizens of each nation disappear, the more the human mind tends, as if by its very nature, to embrace the idea of a single, all-powerful being imposing the same laws in the same way on everyone equally. Hence it is especially important in democratic times not to allow the homage paid to secondary agents to become confused with the reverence due solely to the Creator.

Another truth seems quite clear to me: that religions should burden themselves less with external practices in democratic ages than in other times.

In discussing the philosophical method of the Americans, I showed that nothing is more repugnant to the human mind in ages of equality than the idea of submitting to forms. Men who live in such times are impatient of figurative images. Symbols strike them as puerile artifices used only to veil or embellish truths that it would be more natural to present plainly and openly. Ceremonies leave them cold, and they are naturally inclined to look upon the details of religious worship as a matter of secondary importance.

Those responsible for regulating religion's external form in democratic times should pay close attention to these natural instincts of human intelligence so as not to struggle against them unnecessarily.

I firmly believe in the necessity of forms. I know that they enable the human mind to contemplate abstract truths with a steady gaze and, by helping it grasp such truths firmly, allow it to embrace them ardently. I do not imagine that religion can be maintained without external practices, yet I also think that in the centuries on which we are now embarking, it may be particularly dangerous to allow such practices to proliferate unduly. Indeed, they should be restricted, keeping only those absolutely necessary for the perpetuation of dogma itself, which is the substance of religion,[1] as opposed to ritual, which is only the form. A religion that became more obsessive about details, more inflexible, and more concerned with petty observances at a time when men were becoming more equal would soon find itself reduced to a band of fanatical zealots surrounded by an incredulous multitude.

I anticipate the inevitable objection that since all religions are concerned with general and eternal truths, they cannot give in to the fickle instincts of each century without forfeiting the character of certainty in men's eyes. My response is once again that a careful distinction must be made between the principal opinions that constitute a belief — what theologians call articles of faith — and subsidiary notions associated with these. Religions are obliged always to hold firm in regard to the former, regardless of the particular spirit of the times, but they should refrain from constraining themselves in the same way as to the latter in centuries when everything is constantly in flux and when the mind, accustomed to the shifting spectacle of things human, resists being pinned down. Immobility in external and secondary matters seems to me to offer hope of endurance only when civil society is itself immobile; in any other circumstance, I am inclined to believe that it is a danger.

Of all the passions that equality brings into being or encourages, there is, as we shall see, one that it causes everyone to feel with particular ardor, namely, the passion for well-being. The passion for well-being is a striking and indelible feature of every democratic age.

There is reason to believe that a religion that set out to destroy this most basic of passions would in the end be destroyed by it. If it sought to dissuade men from contemplating the goods of this world entirely so that they might think solely

---

[1] In all religions, there are some ceremonies that are inherent in the very substance of the faith, and these should be kept without changes. This is particularly clear in the case of Catholicism, where form and substance are often so closely intertwined that they are one and the same.

of the goods of the other, it is to be anticipated that their souls would slip through its fingers and, rejecting religion altogether, plunge headlong into material and present pleasures.

The chief business of religions is to purify, regulate, and restrain the overly ardent and exclusive desire for well-being that men feel in ages of equality, but I think it would be a mistake for them to try to subdue it completely and destroy it. They will not succeed in dissuading men from love of wealth, but they may yet persuade them not to enrich themselves by other than honest means.

This leads me to one last consideration, which in a sense includes all the others. As men become more alike and more equal, it becomes increasingly important for religion not only to remain studiously aloof from the daily course of business but also to avoid unnecessary conflict with generally accepted ideas and with the enduring interests of the masses, because common opinion seems increasingly to be the foremost of powers, and the most irresistible. Outside it there is no base of support powerful enough to withstand its blows for long. This is no less true in a democratic nation subject to a despot than in a republic. In centuries of equality, kings often command obedience, but it is always the majority that inspires belief. Hence it is the majority that must be satisfied in all that is not contrary to faith.

I showed in the first part of this book how American clergymen stay out of public affairs. This is the most striking, but not the only, example of their restraint. In America, religion is a world apart in which the clergyman reigns but which he is careful never to leave. Within its confines he guides men's minds. Beyond those limits, he leaves them to their own devices and abandons them to the independence and instability intrinsic to their nature and to the times. I know of no country in which Christianity is less cloaked in forms, rituals, and symbols than in the United States, or in which it lays clearer, simpler, or more general ideas before the mind of man. Although Christians in America are divided into a multitude of sects, they all see their religion in the same light. This applies to Catholicism as well as to other faiths. Nowhere else are Catholic priests less interested in small, individual observances or extraordinary and particular methods of seeking salvation, and nowhere else are they more devoted to the spirit of the law and less to the letter. Nowhere else is the doctrine of the Church that prohibits worshiping saints and limits worship to God more clearly taught or more strictly obeyed. Nevertheless, American Catholics are very docile and very sincere.

Another remark concerns the clergy of all faiths: American clergymen do not seek to divert and focus all of man's attention on the life to come. They are quite willing to allow his heart to dwell in part on the concerns of the present. They seem to regard the goods of this world as important, though secondary. Although they do not take part in productive labor, they are interested in its progress and applaud it, and, even as they hold out the other world to the faithful as the great object of their hopes and fears, they do not forbid the honest pursuit of prosperity in this one. Rather than show how these two things are distinct and contrary, they seek instead the point of contact and connection between them.

All American clergymen are aware of the intellectual power of the majority, and respect it. They support conflict with it only when necessary. They do not involve themselves in partisan disputes, subscribe readily to the general opinions of their country and time, and put up no resistance to the tide of feelings and ideas that carries everything before it. They strive to correct their contemporaries but do not part company with them. Public opinion is therefore never their enemy. Rather, it supports and protects them, and their beliefs prevail partly through their own strength and partly through the strength that the majority lends them.

Thus religion, by respecting all democratic instincts not hostile to it and by enlisting some of them in its own behalf, successfully struggles against the spirit of individual independence, which is for it the most dangerous.

Chapter 6

ON THE PROGRESS OF CATHOLICISM
IN THE UNITED STATES

AMERICA is the most democratic country on earth, and it is at the same time the country where, according to reliable reports, the Catholic religion is progressing most rapidly. At first sight this is surprising.

Two things must be carefully distinguished: equality encourages men to want to judge for themselves, but it also gives them a taste for, and an idea of, a single social power that is both simple and the same for all. Men who live in democratic centuries are therefore highly inclined to shun all religious authority. If they do consent to submit to an authority of this kind, they want it to be unified and uniform. Religious powers that do not all converge toward a single center are inherently an affront to their intelligence, and it is almost as easy for them to conceive of a situation in which there is no religion as of one in which there are several.

Now more than in the past we see Catholics becoming unbelievers and Protestants turning Catholic. If we look at Catholicism internally, it seems to be losing. If we look outside it, it is winning. There is an explanation for this.

People today are by nature not particularly inclined to believe, but if they accept religion at all, they soon discover in themselves a hidden instinct that propels them unwittingly toward Catholicism. Any number of the doctrines and customs of the Roman Church astonish them, but they harbor a secret admiration for the way it is governed, and its great unity attracts them.

If Catholicism were ultimately to escape from the political animosities it has stirred up, I have virtually no doubt that the spirit of the age, which now seems so hostile to it, would become quite favorable, and that it would suddenly make great conquests.

One of the most familiar weaknesses of the human mind is the wish to reconcile contrary principles and buy peace at the expense of logic. Hence there have always been and will always be men who, after submitting certain of their religious beliefs to some authority, will seek to exempt other beliefs from that same authority, and who will allow their minds to fluctuate erratically between obedience and liberty. But I am inclined to think that the number of such people will be smaller in democratic centuries than at other times, and that our progeny will tend increasingly to fall into one or the other of two categories: those who abandon Christianity entirely, and those who join the Roman Church.

Chapter 7

WHAT MAKES THE MIND OF
DEMOCRATIC PEOPLES
RECEPTIVE TO PANTHEISM

LATER I will show how the prevailing taste for very general ideas among democratic peoples manifests itself in politics, but for now I want to call attention to its principal effect on philosophy.

There is no denying that pantheism has made great progress in recent years. Writings from a portion of Europe visibly bear its stamp. The Germans have introduced it into philosophy and the French into literature. Most works of the imagination published in France contain opinions or illustrations borrowed from pantheistic doctrine or reveal a tendency on the part of their authors to entertain such doctrines. This, it seems to me, is no accident, but the effect of a persistent cause.

As conditions become more equal and each man in particular becomes more similar to all others, weaker and smaller, one stops looking at citizens and becomes accustomed to considering only the people; one forgets individuals and thinks only of the species.

In such times, the human mind is keen to embrace a host of diverse objects simultaneously. It invariably aspires to associate a multitude of consequences with a single cause.

The mind becomes obsessed with the idea of unity and looks for it everywhere, and when it thinks it has found it, there it is content to dwell. Upon discovering in the world but one creation and one Creator, it finds even that primary division of things troubling and deliberately seeks to enlarge and simplify its thought by subsuming God and the universe in a single whole. If I encounter a philosophical system which holds that everything in the world, material or immaterial, visible or invisible, is merely part of one immense being, which alone remains eternal amid constant change and continuous transformation of all its component parts, I may conclude straightaway that even though such a system destroys human individuality — or, rather, because it does — it will hold a secret charm for men who live in democracy. All their intellectual habits prepare their minds for it and pave the way for them to adopt it. It naturally draws and captivates their imagination. It feeds their intellectual pride and flatters their intellectual sloth.

Among the various systems that philosophy employs to explain the universe, pantheism seems to me one of the most apt to seduce the human mind in democratic centuries. All who are still enamoured of man's true greatness should join forces to combat it.

Chapter 8

HOW DEMOCRACY SUGGESTS TO THE AMERICANS THE IDEA OF MAN'S INFINITE PERFECTIBILITY

E QUALITY suggests a number of ideas that would not otherwise occur to the human mind and modifies most of the ideas it already holds. As an example I will take the idea of human perfectibility, because it ranks among the chief ideas of which the mind is capable of conceiving and is in itself a major philosophical theory whose consequences for practical affairs are constantly in evidence.

Although man resembles the animals in several respects, one feature is peculiar to him alone: he perfects himself and they do not. Mankind could not help noticing this difference from its inception. The idea of perfectibility is therefore as old as the world. Equality did not bring it into being but did give it a new character.

When citizens are classed by rank, profession, or birth and everyone is forced to follow the path chosen for him by chance, each individual thinks that the limits of human potential are not far off from wherever he happens to find himself, and no one tries to fight against a destiny that seems inevitable. Not that aristocratic peoples absolutely deny man's capacity to perfect himself, but they do not think of it as unlimited. They think in terms of amelioration, not change. They imagine the condition of the societies of the future as better but not different. And while they acknowledge that humanity has made great progress and may still make more, they believe that certain unsurpassable limits are laid down in advance.

Hence they do not believe that they have arrived at the sovereign good and the absolute truth (has any man or people ever been foolish enough to imagine such a thing?), but they do like to persuade themselves that they have attained more or less the degree of grandeur and knowledge that our imperfect nature allows, and since nothing is stirring in their vicinity, they easily imagine that everything is in its place. Legislators then pretend to lay down eternal laws; peoples and

38

kings build nothing but monuments for the centuries; and the present generation takes it upon itself to save future generations the trouble of controlling their own destiny.

As castes disappear; as classes come together, and change is evident in men subjected to tumultuous mixing as well as in usages, customs, and laws; as new facts emerge and new truths are brought to light; as old opinions disappear and others take their place; the image of an ideal and always fleeting perfection presents itself to the human mind.

Every man then becomes a witness to constant change. Some changes make his position worse, and he understands only too well that no nation or individual, no matter how enlightened, is ever infallible. Others improve his lot, and he concludes that man in general is endowed with an infinite capacity to perfect himself. His reverses make him see that no one can claim to have discovered absolute good; his successes inflame his desire to pursue it unremittingly. Thus, always searching, falling, picking himself up again, often disappointed, never discouraged, he marches indefatigably on toward the immense grandeur that he can but dimly make out at the end of the long road that mankind has yet to travel.

It is impossible to believe how many consequences flow naturally from the philosophical theory that man is infinitely perfectible or to imagine what a prodigious influence it exerts even on people who, because they have always been concerned exclusively with action and not with thought, seem to act in keeping with that theory without knowing what it says.

I once met an American sailor, and I asked him why his country's ships are not built to last. Without hesitation he answered that the art of navigation was making such rapid progress that the finest ship would soon be useless if its existence were prolonged for more than a few years.

In these words, spoken off the cuff by a coarse fellow in response to a specific question, I recognized the general and systematic idea that guides a great people in everything it does.

Aristocratic nations are by nature inclined to restrict the limits of human perfectibility unduly, whereas democratic nations sometimes stretch those limits more than they should.

Chapter 9

HOW THE EXAMPLE OF THE AMERICANS DOES NOT PROVE THAT A DEMOCRATIC PEOPLE CAN HAVE NO APTITUDE FOR SCIENCE, LITERATURE, OR THE ARTS

THERE is no denying the fact that, among civilized nations today, few have made less progress in the higher sciences or produced a smaller number of great artists, illustrious poets, and celebrated writers than the United States.

Struck by this, any number of Europeans have drawn the conclusion that it is a natural and inevitable result of equality and held that if a democratic social state and democratic institutions were ever to prevail throughout the world, the light that illuminates the mind of man would gradually go dim, and human beings would sink back into darkness.

Those who reason in this way are confusing a number of ideas that are best kept apart and examined separately. They unintentionally mix what is democratic with what is merely American.

The religion preached by the earliest immigrants and bequeathed to their descendants — a religion simple in its forms of worship, austere and almost savage in its principles, and hostile to outward signs and ceremonial pomp — naturally offers little encouragement to the fine arts and is only reluctantly tolerant of literary pleasures.

The Americans are a very old and very enlightened people who came upon a vast new country where they were free to spread out as much as they wanted and which they found easy to make fertile. Nothing like this has ever occurred anywhere else in the world. Hence everyone in America enjoys unparalleled opportunities to make or increase his fortune. The possibilities open to greed are endlessly breathtaking, and the human mind, constantly distracted from the pleasures of the imagination and the works of the intellect, is engaged solely by the pursuit of wealth. The United States, like all other countries, has industrial and commercial classes, but it also has something not found anywhere else: everybody in the country is engaged in both commerce and industry.

I am nevertheless convinced that if the Americans had been alone in the world with the freedoms and enlightenment acquired by their fathers and their own passions, they would soon have discovered that one cannot make progress in the practical application of science for long without cultivating theory, and that the arts serve to perfect one another. No matter how absorbed they might have been in pursuing the principal object of their desires, they would soon have recognized that the best way to attain one's goal is not to head unwaveringly toward it.

Indeed, so natural is the taste for the pleasures of the mind in the heart of civilized man that a certain number of people always share it even in the civil nations least disposed to indulge such pursuits. Once felt, this intellectual need would soon have been satisfied.

At a time when Americans were naturally inclined to ask nothing of science but its particular applications to the practical arts and ways of making life more comfortable, learned and literary Europe set out in search of the general sources of truth, while at the same it worked to perfect anything that might contribute to man's pleasures or serve his needs.

Among the enlightened nations of the Old World, the Americans singled out one in particular as paramount, a nation with which they were closely united by common origins and similar habits. Among the people of that nation they found celebrated scholars, skillful artists, and great writers, and they were able to gather up treasures of the intellect without needing to work to accumulate them.

I cannot accept the idea that America is separate from Europe, despite the ocean that divides them. I regard the people of the United States as the portion of the English people charged with exploiting the forests of the New World, while the rest of the nation, granted more leisure and less preoccupied with life's material cares, can indulge in thought and develop the human mind in every way possible.

Thus the situation of the Americans is entirely exceptional, and there is reason to believe that no other democratic people will ever enjoy anything like it. Their wholly Puritan origin; their markedly commercial habits; the very country they inhabit, which seems to discourage study of science, literature, and the arts; the proximity of Europe, which allows them not to study these things without lapsing into barbarism; and a thousand more specific causes, of which I have been able to discuss only the most important — all of these things must have concentrated the American mind in a singular way on purely material concerns. Passions, needs, upbringing, and circumstances all seem to have conspired, in fact, to focus the attention of Americans on this earth. Only religion causes them to cast a fleeting and distracted glance heavenward from time to time.

Let us therefore cease to see all democratic nations in the guise of the American people and try at last to see them as they really are.

It is possible to conceive of a people without castes, hierarchies, or classes; whose law, recognizing no form of privilege, would provide for equal division of all inheritances; and which would, at the same time, be deprived of enlightenment and liberty. This is not an idle hypothesis: a despot might deem it in his interest to establish equality among his subjects and leave them ignorant the more easily to keep them enslaved.

Not only will a democratic people of this kind exhibit neither aptitude nor taste for science, literature, or the arts, but there is reason to believe that it will never acquire them either.

The law of inheritance itself would demolish the fortunes of each generation, and no one would create new ones. The poor man, deprived of enlightenment and liberty, would not so much as conceive of the idea of raising himself to the level of the wealthy, and the wealthy man would not know how to defend himself against being dragged down into poverty. A complete and invincible equality would soon come to exist between the two. No one would then have the time or taste to indulge in the labors and pleasures of the intellect. Everyone would sink into a numb state of identical ignorance and equal servitude.

When I try to imagine a democratic society of this kind, I immediately feel trapped in a low, dark, and airless place where any light from outside soon fades away and vanishes. A sudden heaviness weighs me down, and I grope in the surrounding darkness for a way back to air and daylight. None of this description applies, however, to the case in which already enlightened men, having done away with the particular and hereditary rights that previously left all property in the hands of certain individuals and corporations in perpetuity, remain free.

When people living in a democratic society are enlightened, they see readily that there is nothing to limit them or hold them back or force them to be content with their present fortune.

Hence the idea of adding to it occurs to all of them, and if they are free, they will attempt to do so; but not all will succeed in the same way. To be sure, the legislature no longer grants privileges, but nature does. Natural inequality being very great, unequal fortunes will result as soon as each individual turns all his faculties to the task of making himself rich.

The law of inheritance still stands in the way of founding wealthy families but no longer prevents the existence of wealthy individuals. It constantly pulls citizens back toward a common level from which they constantly escape. Property becomes more unequal as enlightenment increases and liberty grows.

There has recently arisen a sect celebrated for its genius and its extravagance, which has proposed that all property be concentrated in the hands of a central power that would then be charged with distributing it to individuals on the basis of merit. This would offer an escape from the complete and eternal equality that seems to threaten democratic societies.

There is a simpler and less dangerous remedy, which is to grant privilege to no one, to give everyone equal enlightenment and equal independence, and to leave it to each individual to make a place for himself. Natural inequality will soon declare itself, and wealth will shift on its own to the most highly skilled.

Free and democratic societies will therefore always include in their midst a multitude of opulent or well-to-do individuals. These wealthy individuals will not be as closely bound to one another as were the members of the old aristocratic class;

their instincts will be different, and they will almost never be as secure and complete in their possession of leisure, but they will be infinitely more numerous than the aristocracy could have been. These men will not limit themselves strictly to material concerns, and to one degree or another they will be able to indulge in the labors and pleasures of the mind. Hence they will do so, because while it is true that a part of the human mind is drawn to that which is limited, material, and useful, another part is naturally drawn upward to the infinite, the immaterial, and the beautiful. Physical needs tether the mind to the earth, but once it is held back no longer, it resumes its course without outside assistance.

Not only will the number of people capable of taking an interest in works of the mind be greater, but the taste for intellectual pleasures will gradually filter down to those who, in aristocratic societies, seem to have neither the time nor the ability to enjoy them.

When hereditary wealth, class privilege, and prerogatives of birth no longer exist and each person draws his strength only from himself, it becomes clear that the principal cause of disparities in the fortunes of men is intelligence. Anything that serves to fortify, expand, or adorn the intellect immediately takes on great value.

Even the crowd, in its own special way, recognizes the conspicuous usefulness of knowledge. Those who do not savor its charms prize its effects and make some effort to acquire it.

In enlightened and free democratic centuries, there is nothing to separate men or keep them in their place. They rise or fall with singular rapidity. All classes have one another constantly in view because they live in close proximity. They communicate and mingle every day and emulate and envy one another. To the people this suggests a host of ideas, notions, and desires they would not have if ranks were fixed and society immobile. In nations such as these, the servant never considers himself entirely a stranger to the pleasures and labors of the master, nor the poor man to the pleasures and labors of the rich. The rural man seeks to resemble the city dweller, and the provinces strive to be like the metropolis.

Thus no one allows himself to be reduced easily to life's merely material concerns, and the humblest of artisans will on occasion cast an eager and furtive glance at the higher world of the intellect. People do not read in the same spirit or in the same way as in aristocratic nations, but the circle of readers expands constantly until ultimately it encompasses all citizens.

Once the multitude begins to take an interest in the labors of the mind, it discovers that a good way to acquire fame, power, or wealth is to excel in one or another of them. The restless ambition to which equality gives rise immediately avails itself of this as of all other opportunities. The number of people who cultivate the sciences, literature, and the arts becomes immense. The world of the intellect becomes prodigiously active, as each individual seeks to blaze a new trail and attract the attention of the public. What happens is similar to what is happening to political society in the United States: the works produced are often imperfect, but their number is countless, and while the results of each individual effort are usually quite insignificant, the overall result is always very substantial.

It is not true, therefore, to say that men who live in democratic centuries are by nature indifferent to science, literature, and the arts. It must be acknowledged, however, that they cultivate these fields in their own way and bring to the endeavor their own qualities and deficiencies.

Chapter 10

WHY AMERICANS DEVOTE THEMSELVES MORE TO THE PRACTICAL APPLICATIONS OF SCIENCE THAN TO THE THEORY

ALTHOUGH the democratic social state and democratic institutions do not arrest the growth of the human mind, there can be no doubt that they steer it one way rather than another. Even limited in this regard, their effects are still very great, and I beg the reader's indulgence if I pause for a moment to dwell on them.

In discussing the philosophical method of the Americans, we made a number of observations that are pertinent here.

Equality fosters in each individual the desire to judge everything for himself. It inspires in him a taste for the tangible and the real in all things as well as contempt for traditions and forms. These general instincts are particularly evident in regard to the subject of this chapter.

People who cultivate the sciences in democratic nations are always afraid of losing their way in utopian ideas. They distrust systems and like to stick very close to the facts, which they prefer to study for themselves. Since they are not easily impressed by the mere name of any of their fellow human beings, they are unlikely to swear by the teachings of authority. Indeed, they are always looking for the weak side of any doctrine deemed to be authoritative. Scientific traditions have little hold on them. They never dwell for long on the subtleties of any school and are not comfortable with bandying about big words. They delve to the heart of any subject that interests them, insofar as their abilities allow, and they love to explain what they find out in plain language. Science therefore has a freer and surer but less lofty style.

The mind, it seems to me, can divide science into three parts.

The first contains the most theoretical principles and most abstract notions, those whose applications are either unknown or highly remote.

The second comprises those general truths which, though still derived from pure theory, nevertheless lead by a straight and short path to practical applications.

Methods of application and means of execution make up the third.

Each of these different aspects of science can be cultivated separately, although reason and experience teach us that none of the three can prosper for long if completely divorced from the other two.

In America, the purely practical part of the sciences is admirably cultivated, and care is taken with those theoretical aspects of science that are immediately necessary for the application at hand. In this respect the American mind has invariably shown itself to be clear, free, original, and fertile. But almost no one in the United States devotes himself to the essentially theoretical and abstract aspects of human knowledge. In this the Americans carry to excess a tendency that can, I think, be found in all democratic peoples, though to a lesser degree.

Nothing is more necessary to the cultivation of the higher sciences, or of the loftier aspects of the sciences, than meditation, and nothing is less suited to meditation than the circumstances of democratic society. In such a society one does not find, as in aristocratic nations, a numerous class that enjoys repose because it finds everything to its liking, and another that does not stir because it has abandoned hope that things will ever improve. Everyone is restless: some want to attain power, others to achieve wealth. In the midst of this universal tumult, this constant clash of conflicting interests, this unending quest for fortune, where is the calm necessary to the deeper strategies of the intellect to be found? How is one to ponder some specific point when everything is in flux and one is daily swept along and buffeted about by the impetuous current that carries all things before it?

One must be careful to distinguish the kind of permanent agitation that exists in a peaceful, established democracy from the tumultuous revolutionary movements that almost always accompany the birth and development of a democratic society.

When a violent revolution takes place in a highly civilized nation, it cannot fail to impart a sudden impetus to feelings and ideas.

This is especially true of democratic revolutions. Because such revolutions stir all classes of the nation at once, they fill every citizen's heart with vast ambitions.

Although the French made remarkable progress in the exact sciences at the exact moment they were finishing off what was left of feudal society, that sudden burst of creativity must be attributed not to democracy but to the unprecedented revolution that attended its growth. What happened then was a special case; it would be imprudent to take it as indicative of a general law.

Great revolutions are no more common in democratic nations than in other countries; I am even inclined to believe that they are less so. What is common in democratic nations, however, is a somewhat troubling restlessness, a constant turnover of people, which disturbs and distracts the mind without stimulating or elevating it.

Not only is meditation difficult for men who live in democratic societies, but they are inclined by nature to hold it in relatively low esteem. The democratic social state and institutions encourage most people to be constantly active, and the habits of mind appropriate to action are not always appropriate to thought. The man who acts is often forced to settle for approximations, because he would never achieve his goals if he insisted on perfection in every detail. He must constantly rely on ideas that he has not had the leisure to delve into, for what helps him is far more the timeliness of an idea than its rigorous accuracy. All things considered, it is less risky for him to invoke a few false principles than to waste time trying to show that all his principles are true. Long and learned proofs do not determine how the world is run. Quick assessments of specific facts, daily study of the shifting passions of the multitude, momentary chances and the skill to grasp them — these are the things that decide how affairs are dealt with in democratic societies.

In centuries in which nearly everyone is active, there is thus a general tendency to place too much value on quickness of mind and superficial concepts and too little on deeper but slower exertions of the intellect.

This opinion of the public influences the judgment of those who cultivate the sciences. It either persuades them that they can succeed in scientific study without meditation or dissuades them from studying those sciences that require it.

There are many ways of studying the sciences. Countless people are drawn to the discoveries of the mind for selfish, commercial, or industrial reasons having nothing to do with the disinterested passion that burns in the hearts of a few. There is a desire to use knowledge, and a pure desire to know. I have no doubt that, from time to time, small numbers of people do conceive an ardent and inexhaustible love of truth, which feeds on itself and is a source of constant pleasure though it never is fully gratified. It is this ardent, proud, and disinterested love of what is true that leads straight to the abstract sources of truth from which such people draw fundamental ideas.

Had Pascal only some great profit in mind, or had he been moved solely by the desire for glory, I cannot believe that he would have been able to concentrate the powers of his mind as he did to uncover the Creator's best-kept secrets. Seeing him, as it were, wrest his soul from life's concerns so as to devote himself entirely to this research, only to die of old age at forty, having prematurely ruptured the bond between soul and body, I stand amazed in the knowledge that no ordinary cause could have produced such extraordinary efforts.

Time will tell whether these passions, so rare and so fruitful, can originate and develop in democratic societies as readily as in aristocratic ones. I confess that I find this hard to believe.

In aristocratic societies, the class that shapes opinion and takes the lead in public affairs enjoys a permanent and hereditary place above the multitude and naturally forms a high idea of itself and of man in consequence. It loves to hold out to mankind the prospect of glorious satisfactions and to set magnificent goals for man's desires. Aristocracies often act in ways that are highly tyrannical and highly inhuman, but they rarely conceive base thoughts and exhibit a certain haughty disdain for petty pleasures even as they indulge them: every soul is thereby raised to a very high pitch. In aristocratic times, vast ideas of the dignity, power, and grandeur of man are widely entertained. These opinions influence those who cultivate the sciences along with everyone else. They facilitate the mind's natural yearning for the highest realms of thought and naturally foster a sublime and almost divine love of truth.

In such times, men of learning are therefore drawn to theory, and it is even common for them to feel a rash contempt for practice. "Archimedes," says Plutarch, "was so highminded that he never deigned to write any treatise on the construction of war machines, and because he regarded the whole science of inventing and building machines and, in general, any craft of practical value as vile, base, and mercenary, he put his mind and his studies to use only in writing things whose beauty and subtlety were in no way tinctured with necessity." This is the aristocratic objective of the sciences.

It cannot be the same in democratic nations.

Most people in such nations are quite intent on immediate material gratifications, and since they are always unhappy with the position they occupy and always free to abandon it, they think only of ways to change or improve their fortunes. To minds so disposed, any new method that shortens the road to wealth, any machine that saves labor, any instrument that reduces the costs of production, any discovery that facilitates or increases pleasures seems the most magnificent achievement of the human mind. It is primarily for these reasons that democratic peoples devote themselves to science, understand it, and honor it. In aristocratic centuries men turn to science particularly to gratify the mind; in democratic centuries they do so to gratify the body.

We may take it for granted that the more democratic, enlightened, and free a nation is, the more rapidly the number of people with a self-interested appreciation of scientific genius will increase, and the greater the profit, fame, and even power authors of discoveries immediately applicable to industry will earn, for in democracies the class that works takes part in public affairs, and those who serve it must look to it for honors as well as money.

It is easy to imagine that in a society organized in this way, the human mind is subtly encouraged to neglect theory and to devote unparalleled energy to applications or, at any rate, to those aspects of theory most necessary to the people who apply it.

Though the mind may yearn instinctively for the higher

realms of the intellect, it does so in vain, for interest focuses its attention on the middle range. There it exerts its strength and brings its restless energy to bear and works miracles. The same Americans who did not discover a single one of the general laws of mechanics have introduced into navigation a new machine that is changing the face of the world.

Of course I by no means wish to imply that today's democratic nations are fated to witness the extinction of the transcendent lights of the human spirit or even that they will never kindle new lights of their own. At the stage the world is now in, with so many literate nations constantly goaded by the ardor of industry, the connections among the various branches of science cannot fail to strike the eye, and the very taste for practice, if it is enlightened, should discourage neglect of theory. With so many applications being tried, so many experiments being repeated every day, it is almost impossible that very general laws should not frequently emerge, so that great discoveries may be common though great inventors be rare.

I believe, moreover, that science is a high calling. Although democracy does not encourage men to cultivate science for its own sake, it does vastly increase the number who do cultivate it. It is inconceivable that from such a vast multitude there should not on occasion arise a speculative genius impassioned solely by the love of truth. One can rest assured that such a genius will strive to penetrate nature's deepest mysteries regardless of the spirit of his country and his times. There is no need to aid his development; it is enough to stay out of his way. All I mean to say is this: permanent inequality of conditions encourages men to limit themselves to the proud and sterile search for abstract truths, whereas the democratic social state and institutions encourage them to look to science only for its immediate and useful applications.

This tendency is natural and inevitable. It is interesting to note and perhaps necessary to point out.

If those who are called to lead nations in our time had a clear and prescient grasp of these new instincts, which will soon be irresistible, they would understand that with enlightenment and liberty men who live in democratic times cannot fail to perfect the industrial aspects of science, and that henceforth the social power should direct all its efforts to supporting advanced studies and fostering great scientific passions.

Nowadays the human mind needs to be forced to concentrate on theory. Left to itself, it veers in the direction of practice, and rather than allow it to indulge repeatedly in detailed examination of secondary effects, it is good to distract it from these on occasion in favor of something loftier, the contemplation of primary causes.

Because Roman civilization perished in the wake of barbarian invasion, we are perhaps too inclined to believe that civilization can perish in no other way.

If the sources of our enlightenment were ever to die out, they would dwindle gradually, like a flame left unattended. If we were to limit ourselves to applications, we might lose sight of principles, and when we had forgotten principles entirely, we would make poor use of the methods derived from them. We would no longer be capable of inventing new methods and would make unintelligent and artless use of learned procedures we no longer understood.

When Europeans first landed in China three hundred years ago, they found that nearly all the arts had achieved a certain degree of perfection and were surprised that people who had come so far had not gone further. Later they discovered vestiges of certain advanced bodies of knowledge that had been lost. The nation was industrial; it had preserved most scientific methods, but science itself no longer existed. Europeans took this as the explanation for what they found to be the singularly static character of the Chinese mind. The Chinese, following in the footsteps of their forebears, had forgotten the reasons that had guided them. They continued to use formulas without seeking to fathom their meaning. They held on to instruments though they had lost the art of modifying or reproducing them. Hence the Chinese could not change anything. They had to give up making improvements. They were forced always to imitate their forebears in every respect lest the slightest deviation from the path laid out for them in advance plunge them into impenetrable darkness. The source of human knowledge had almost dried up, and though the river still flowed, its waters could no longer increase in volume or change direction.

China had nevertheless lived in peace for centuries. Its conquerors had adopted its mores. Order prevailed. Material prosperity of a sort was everywhere apparent. Revolutions were rare, and war was all but unknown.

Hence we must not reassure ourselves with the thought that the barbarians are still far from our gates, for if there are peoples who allow the torch of enlightenment to be snatched from their grasp, there are others who use their own feet to stamp out its flames.

Chapter 11

IN WHAT SPIRIT AMERICANS
CULTIVATE THE ARTS

I WOULD be wasting my readers' time as well as my own, I think, if I were to attempt to show how a generally modest level of wealth, an absence of excess, and a universal desire for well-being and constant striving to achieve it result in a situation in which the taste for the useful takes precedence over the love of the beautiful in the heart of man. Democratic nations, where all these things are found, will therefore cultivate those arts that enhance the convenience of life rather than those whose purpose is to embellish it; they will usually prefer the useful to the beautiful, and they will want the beautiful to be useful.

I intend, however, to press the argument further, and, having made this first point, I shall sketch a number of others.

It is commonly the case that, in centuries of privilege, the practice of virtually every trade becomes a privilege, and each profession is a world apart to which not everyone has access. Even when entry to the trades is free, moreover, the natural immobility of aristocratic nations tends to make a distinct class of all the practitioners of a particular trade, a class always composed of the same families, all of whose members know one another and soon come to share common opinions and a sense of corporate pride. In an industrial class of this kind, each artisan has not only his fortune to make but also his reputation to keep. His behavior is governed not by his own self-interest or even the interest of his customer but by the corporate interest, and the corporate interest is that each artisan produce masterpieces. In aristocratic centuries, therefore, the aim of the arts is to do the best possible work, not the quickest or the cheapest.

By contrast, when each profession is open to all comers, and large numbers of practitioners are constantly entering and leaving, so that they become strangers to one another, each indifferent and almost invisible to all the rest owing to their number, the social bond is destroyed, and each worker, left to rely solely on himself, seeks only to earn as much as he can at the lowest possible cost. The only constraint on his activity is what his customer wants. Now, it so happens that even as the workman is undergoing this transformation, a corresponding revolution is taking place in the customer.

In countries where wealth, like power, is permanently concentrated in the hands of a few, those few — always the same — enjoy the benefit of most of the goods of this world. Necessity, opinion, and moderation of desire exclude everyone else.

Since the size of this aristocratic class remains fixed, neither contracting nor expanding, its needs are always the same, and it always experiences them in the same way. The men who occupy this hereditary position of superiority naturally derive from it a taste for things that are well made and highly durable.

This shapes the nation's ideas about the arts in general.

It is often the case in such nations that even peasants would rather do without things they covet than make do with anything less than perfect.

In aristocracies, therefore, workers toil for a limited number of very hard-to-satisfy customers. Their hope of profit depends primarily on the perfection of their workmanship.

This is no longer the case when all privileges have been abolished, ranks mingle, and everyone moves constantly up and down the social ladder.

In democratic nations there are always many citizens whose patrimonies are divided and whittled away. In better times they acquired certain needs that stay with them after the ability to satisfy them no longer exists, and they anxiously search for some roundabout way of achieving the same satisfaction.

In democracies one also finds large numbers of people whose fortunes are on the rise but whose desires nevertheless outpace them, and who covetously ogle whatever goods money can buy long before they can afford them. Such people are constantly on the lookout for the shortest routes to nearby pleasures. These two factors combine to ensure that in any democracy there is always a multitude of citizens whose needs outstrip their resources and who, rather than give up the things they covet altogether, are quite prepared to settle for less than complete satisfaction.

The workman easily understands these passions because he shares them. In aristocracies he sought to sell very expensive products to a small number of customers. Now he realizes that there may be a quicker way to get rich by selling cheaply to everyone.

Now, there are only two ways to lower the price of merchandise.

The first is to find better, faster, more ingenious ways of making the product. The second is to turn out a larger number of roughly similar products but of lower quality. In democratic nations, all the workman's intellectual faculties are directed toward these two ends.

He tries hard to come up with methods that will allow him to work not just better but faster and more economically, and, if he cannot manage this, he will attempt to reduce the product's intrinsic quality without rendering it totally unfit for its intended use. When only rich men had watches, nearly all watches were of excellent quality. Now, few are better than mediocre, but everybody has them. Thus democracy not only tends to turn the human mind toward the useful arts but also encourages craftsmen to produce inferior goods in large numbers very rapidly and persuades consumers to settle for such wares.

Not that the arts are incapable of working wonders, if need be, in democracies. This becomes apparent when customers are willing to pay craftsmen for their time and effort. In a climate of unlimited industrial rivalry, intense competition, and endless experimentation, excellent workers do emerge, men at the forefront of their professions. Seldom are they given the opportunity to show what they can do, however. They carefully husband their efforts, settling for shrewd, self-critical mediocrity, knowing that they can do better but aiming no higher than mediocrity allows. In aristocracies, by contrast, workmen always bring all their know-how to bear, and when they stop, it is because they have reached the limits of what they know.

When I see in my travels that a country's artisans produce

admirable things, this tells me nothing about that country's social state or political constitution. But if the products of the arts are generally inferior in quality, plentiful in quantity, and low in price, I can be certain that the country is one in which privileges are on the wane and classes are beginning to mingle and soon to coalesce.

Artisans who live in democratic centuries aim not only to make useful things that everyone can afford but also to endow those things with outstanding qualities they do not really possess.

In the confusion of classes everyone hopes to appear to be something he is not and goes to great lengths to succeed at this. Democracy is not the source of this sentiment, which is all too natural a product of the human heart, but democracy applies it to material things: hypocrisy of virtue is common to all ages, but hypocrisy of luxury belongs more particularly to democratic centuries.

To satisfy human vanity's new needs the arts have recourse to every kind of imposture. Industry sometimes goes so far in this direction as to do itself harm. Diamonds have already been imitated so perfectly that it is easy to mistake fake ones for real. Once a technique for making fake diamonds that cannot be distinguished from real ones has been invented, people will likely abandon both, and they will once again become mere pebbles.

This brings me to what people call, by way of supreme compliment, the fine arts.

I do not believe that a democratic social state and institutions have as a necessary effect a decrease in the number of people who cultivate the fine arts, but they do exert a powerful influence on how those arts are cultivated. Because most people who already had a taste for the fine arts become poor while many who are not yet rich begin, by imitation, to develop such a taste, the quantity of consumers generally increases, while the number of very wealthy and very refined consumers decreases. What happens then in the fine arts is similar to what I already pointed out in discussing the useful arts. The number of works grows rapidly, while the merit of each diminishes.

Since it is no longer possible to aim for greatness, one seeks elegance and prettiness instead. One strives not so much for reality as for appearance.

Aristocracies produce a small number of great paintings, whereas democratic countries produce a multitude of minor ones. The former raise statues of bronze; the latter make plaster casts.

The first time I arrived in New York, by way of that part of the Atlantic Ocean known as the East River, I was surprised to see lining the bank at some distance from the city a number of small white marble palaces, several of which boasted an antique architectural style. The next day, I went to take a closer look at one that had particularly attracted my eye, and I discovered that its walls were of whitewashed brick and its columns of painted wood. The same was true of all the monuments I had admired the night before.

The democratic social state and institutions also impart certain distinctive tendencies to all the imitative arts, tendencies that are easily pointed out. They commonly discourage portraits of the soul and encourage portraits of the body, and they substitute representation of movement and sensation for that of feelings and ideas. Finally, in place of the ideal, they put the real.

I doubt that Raphael produced as elaborate a study of the intricate workings of the human body as do the draftsmen of today. He did not attach the same importance as they do to rigorous exactitude in this respect because he aspired to surpass nature. He sought to make of man something superior to man. He undertook to embellish beauty itself.

By contrast, David and his pupils were as good anatomists as they were painters. They produced marvelously good representations of the models they had before them, but seldom did they imagine anything more. They followed nature exactly, whereas Raphael searched for something better. They left us an exact portrait of man, but he showed us glimpses of divinity.

What I have said applies to the choice of subject as well as to the manner of treating it.

The painters of the Renaissance generally looked for great subjects that would either transcend themselves or allude to the remote past in such a way as to provide a vast scope for their imagination. Our painters often use their talent to reproduce exactly the details of private life that are constantly before them, and copy from every conceivable angle petty objects of which nature provides only too many originals.

Chapter 12

WHY AMERICANS BUILD SUCH INSIGNIFICANT AND SUCH GREAT MONUMENTS AT THE SAME TIME

IN the previous chapter I said that in democratic centuries monuments of the arts tend to become more numerous and less grand. I now hasten to point out the exception to this rule.

In democratic nations individuals are very weak, but the state, which represents them all and holds them in its grasp, is very strong. Nowhere do citizens seem more insignificant than in a democratic nation. Nowhere does the nation itself seem greater or make a vaster impression on the mind. In democratic societies man's imagination shrinks when he thinks of himself as an individual and expands without limit when he thinks of the state. Hence the same men who live cramped in scant quarters often nurse gigantic ambitions when they turn their attention to public monuments.

The Americans have traced the outlines of a vast city on the site chosen to be their capital. Today its population is barely larger than that of Pontoise, but they say that some day it will be home to more than a million people. They have already uprooted trees for ten leagues around lest they inconvenience the future citizens of this imaginary metropolis. In the center of the city they have erected a magnificent palace to serve as the seat of Congress and have given it the pompous name "Capitol."

Every day the several states themselves conceive and carry out prodigious undertakings that would astonish the engineers of the great nations of Europe.

Thus democracy encourages men not just to produce a host of trifling works but also to erect a small number of very great monuments. Between these two extremes, however, there is nothing. The scattered traces of a few huge edifices therefore tell us nothing about the social state or institutions of the people that built them.

At the risk of departing from my subject, I might add that

such traces leave us no better informed about that people's grandeur, enlightenment, or true prosperity.

Any time any power whatsoever is capable of inducing an entire nation to cooperate in a common enterprise, it will, with little knowledge and much time, be able to make something huge from the accumulation of so much strenuous effort, yet there is no reason to conclude from this that the nation in question was very happy, very enlightened, or even very strong. The Spanish found Mexico City full of splendid temples and vast palaces, but this did not prevent Cortez from conquering the Mexican empire with six hundred foot soldiers and sixteen horses.

If the Romans had known the laws of hydraulics better, they would not have built all the aqueducts that surround the ruins of their cities; they would have made better use of their power and wealth. If they had invented the steam engine, perhaps they would not have extended to the ends of their empire those long, artificial heaps of stone known as Roman roads.

Things such as these stand as magnificent testimony to their ignorance as well as their grandeur.

A people that left no vestiges of its passage other than a few lead pipes in the ground and a few iron rails on its surface might have achieved greater mastery over nature than the Romans.

Chapter 13

THE LITERARY ASPECT OF DEMOCRATIC CENTURIES

W HEN one enters a bookshop in the United States and peruses the American books that fill its shelves, the number of books seems very large whereas the number of familiar authors seems quite small.

First one finds a multitude of elementary texts intended to impart the rudiments of human knowledge. Most of these works were written in Europe. The Americans reprint them in a form adapted for their use. Then there is an almost endless number of religious books, Bibles, sermons, pious anecdotes, controversies, and reports published by charitable societies. Finally, there is the lengthy catalog of political pamphlets: American parties do battle not with books but with pamphlets, which circulate with incredible rapidity, survive for a brief time, and then die.

Amid all these obscure products of the human mind appear the more remarkable works of but a small number of authors whose names are or ought to be known to Europeans.

Although America is today perhaps less concerned with literature than any other civilized country, one does meet many individuals there who are interested in things of the mind and who, if they do not devote their lives to studying such things, nevertheless savor their charms in their hours of leisure. Most of the books these people want are supplied by England, however. Nearly all the great English works are reproduced in the United States. The literary genius of Great Britain still shines its rays into the depths of the New World's forests. There is hardly a pioneer hut in which the odd volume of Shakespeare cannot be found. I remember reading the feudal drama *Henry V* for the first time in a log cabin.

Not only do Americans draw upon the treasures of English literature every day, but one can truly say that they find the literature of England on their own soil. Of the few people engaged in writing works of literature in the United States, most are English in substance and especially in form. To the democratic milieu they thus bring literary ideas and usages current in the aristocratic nation they have chosen as their model. They paint with colors borrowed from foreign mores. Since they almost never represent the reality of the country in which they were born, they are seldom popular there.

The citizens of the United States themselves seem so convinced that books are not published for their benefit that, before deciding what one of their writers is worth, they usually wait until the English have sampled his work. It is the same as in painting, where the painter of the original is deemed to have a right to judge the merits of the copy.

Properly speaking, therefore, Americans still have no literature. The only recognizably American authors I know are journalists. They are not great writers, but they speak the country's language and make themselves heard. The rest strike me simply as foreigners. To Americans they are what the imitators of the Greeks and Romans were to us during the renaissance of letters: an object of curiosity rather than of general sympathy. They divert the mind and have no effect on mores.

As I said earlier, democracy is far from the sole cause of this state of affairs, and one must look to any number of particular circumstances independent of democracy to find the reasons for it.

If Americans had come from a different background and been transplanted to another country yet maintained the social state and laws they have now, I do not doubt that they would have a literature. As they are, I am certain that eventually they will have one, but it will have a character different from that to be found in American writing today, a character all its own. It is not impossible to map out that character in advance.

Imagine an aristocratic nation in which literature is cultivated. Works of the intellect, like affairs of government, are controlled by a sovereign class. Literary life, like political existence, is almost entirely concentrated in that class or in those closest to it. This suffices to give me the key to everything else.

When a small number of men are concerned with the same things at the same time and form a group whose membership does not change, it is easy for them to agree on certain primary rules, which each of them must then take for his guide.

If the subject that concerns these men is literature, strict laws will soon be applied to works of the mind, and no deviation from these laws will be tolerated.

If the position these men occupy in the country is hereditary, they will naturally be inclined not only to adopt certain fixed rules for themselves but also to abide by rules imposed by their forebears. Their laws will be both strict and traditional.

These men have never been obliged to concern themselves with material things, any more than their fathers, hence their interest in works of the mind may well extend back over several generations. They have grasped the technique of literature and ultimately come to love it for its own sake and to take an informed pleasure in seeing its rules adhered to.

And that is not all: the men I am speaking of begin and end their lives in comfort or wealth, hence they naturally entertain a taste for exquisite satisfactions and a love of refined and delicate pleasures.

More than that, a certain delicacy of mind and heart, which is often the result of such long and peaceful enjoyment of so many goods, leads them to banish from their very pleasures anything that might be too unusual or too intense. They would rather be amused than intensely aroused; they want their interest stimulated but have no desire to be swept away.

Now imagine a large number of literary works produced by or for the people I have been describing. It is easy to see that this literature will conform to rules laid down in advance. The slightest work will be polished down to the last detail. Technique and effort will not be spared anywhere. Each genre will have its own special rules setting it apart from all the others, and no deviation from those rules will be permitted.

Style will seem almost as important as ideas and form almost as important as substance. Tone will be polite, measured, and even. The mind will invariably move at a stately pace, seldom with haste, and writers will devote more effort to perfecting their works than to producing them.

Should members of the lettered class fall into the habit of frequenting only themselves and writing only for one another, they may lose sight of the rest of the world entirely and thereby lapse into affectation and falsity. They will impose small-minded rules on literature for their own exclusive use, gradually alienating themselves from common sense and leading ultimately to a loss of contact with nature.

Their desire to express themselves in terms other than the vulgar may lead them into a sort of aristocratic jargon hardly less remote from fine style than the dialect of the people.

Such are the natural perils that literature must confront in aristocracies.

Any aristocracy that sets itself entirely apart from the people becomes impotent. This is true in literature as well as in politics.[1]

Let us now look at the picture from the other side.

Let us imagine ourselves transported to the heart of a democracy in which ancient traditions and present enlightenment have fostered a sensitivity to the pleasures of the mind. Ranks in this society have mingled and combined. Knowledge, like power, is infinitely divided and I daresay widely dispersed.

It is thus a confused multitude whose intellectual needs are to be satisfied. Not all the new enthusiasts of the pleasures of the mind have received the same education. Not all are enlightened in the same respects. They do not resemble their fathers, and at any given moment they are different from what they were themselves the moment before, for among them places, feelings, and fortunes are constantly changing. Hence no common traditions or habits exist to forge intellectual bonds among the people, who have never had the power, the will, or the time to achieve a common understanding.

Yet it is from this incoherent and agitated multitude that authors spring, and it is the same multitude that parcels out the profits and the glory.

I have no trouble understanding that in such circumstances I should expect to find in the literature of such a people only a few of the rigorous conventions that readers and writers

---

[1] All this is especially true in aristocratic countries long subjected to peaceful monarchical rule.

When liberty prevails in an aristocracy, the upper classes are obliged to call constantly on the services of the lower classes, and in calling on their services they draw closer to them. As a result, they often become imbued with something of the democratic spirit. When a privileged corps governs, moreover, it develops an energy and a habit of enterprise, a taste for action and excitement, that inevitably influence works of literature of every description.

recognize in aristocratic centuries. If the people of one period did happen to agree on certain conventions, it would still be impossible to deduce anything about subsequent periods, for in a democratic nation, each new generation is a new people. In such a nation, it is therefore difficult to subject literature to strict rules and almost impossible to subject it to permanent ones.

In democracies, it is by no means the case that everyone who is concerned with literature has received a literary education, and most of the people who do acquire some tincture of belles-lettres go into politics or embrace a profession that allows them only stolen moments to savor the pleasures of the mind. Hence they regard these pleasures not as the principal charm of their existence but as a fleeting if necessary relaxation from the serious business of life. Such men can never acquire a knowledge of the literary art deep enough to appreciate its delicacies; the little nuances escape them. Having only a very limited time to devote to literature, they want every moment to be profitable. They like books that can be obtained easily and read quickly and that do not require scholarly research to be understood. They insist on facile beauties that yield of their own accord and can be enjoyed immediately. Above all they require surprise and novelty. Habituated to practical life, to competition and monotony, they have need of intense and rapid emotions, sudden illuminations, and glaring truths or errors to wrench them out of their own lives and plunge them instantly and almost violently into the heart of the subject.

Need I say more? Who cannot guess what is to follow?

Taken as a whole, the literature of democratic centuries cannot present the image of order, regularity, knowledge, and art that literature exhibits in aristocratic times. Form will usually be neglected and occasionally scorned. Style will frequently seem bizarre, incorrect, exaggerated, or flaccid and almost always seem brazen and vehement. Authors will aim for rapidity of execution rather than perfection of detail. Short texts will be more common than long books, wit more common than erudition, and imagination more common than depth. An uncultivated, almost savage vigor will dominate thought, whose products will frequently exhibit a very great variety and singular fecundity. Authors will seek to astonish rather than to please and to engage the passions rather than beguile taste.

Some writers will no doubt want to try a different path now and then, and if their gifts are superior, neither their faults nor their qualities will stand in the way of their attracting readers. But these exceptions will be rare, and even those whose work on the whole departs from common usage will always return to it by way of certain details.

The two conditions I have just described are extremes, but nations do not jump suddenly from one to the other. The transition is gradual, with infinite gradations. When a literate people makes this switch, there is almost always a moment when the literary genius of democracy encounters that of aristocracy and the two seem to want to reign in harmony over the human spirit.

Such periods are fleeting but very brilliant. They are fertile without exuberance and dynamic without confusion. French literature was like this in the eighteenth century.

I would say more than I mean to if I were to state that a nation's literature is always subordinate to its social state and political constitution. I know full well that there are other causes apart from these that impart certain characteristics to literary works, but to me these seem the most important.

There are always numerous relations between the social and political state of a people and the genius of its writers. He who knows the one is never completely ignorant of the other.

Chapter 14

ON THE LITERARY INDUSTRY

D EMOCRACY not only instills a taste for literature in the industrial classes but also introduces the industrial spirit into the heart of literature.

In aristocracies, readers are demanding and few in number. In democracies, they are less difficult to please, and their number is prodigious. In aristocratic nations, therefore, there is no hope of success without immense effort, and such effort may yield considerable glory but not much money, whereas in democratic nations, a writer may boast of achieving a modest renown and a substantial fortune at little cost. He does not need to be admired to accomplish this; it is enough if people have a taste for his work.

The ever-growing multitude of readers and their constant need for novelty ensure that even books that readers hold in low esteem will sell.

In democratic times, the public often treats its authors as kings commonly treat their courtiers: it makes them rich but holds them in contempt. What more is needed by the venal souls born in courts or worthy of living in them?

Democratic literatures are always crawling with authors who see literature as nothing more than an industry, and for every great writer there are thousands of retailers of ideas.

Chapter 15

WHY THE STUDY OF GREEK AND LATIN IS PARTICULARLY USEFUL IN DEMOCRATIC SOCIETIES

WHAT used to be called "the people" in the most democratic republics of Antiquity bears little resemblance to what we refer to by that name. In Athens all citizens took part in public affairs, but only 20,000 out of a population of more than 350,000 were citizens. All the rest were slaves, who carried out most of the functions today assigned to the people and even the middle classes.

Thus Athens, with its universal suffrage, was only an aristocratic republic in which all nobles enjoyed an equal right to government.

The struggle between the patricians and plebeians of Rome should be seen in the same light, as an intestine quarrel between elder and younger branches of a single family. All in effect valued aristocracy and partook of its spirit.

Bear in mind, too, that books were rare and expensive throughout Antiquity, and it was very difficult to reproduce and distribute them. Owing to these circumstances, literary tastes and habits were concentrated in a small number of men, so that something like a small literary aristocracy developed within the elite of a larger political aristocracy. In keeping with this, there is no indication that the Greeks and Romans ever treated literature as an industry.

These peoples were not just aristocracies; they also constituted highly disciplined and very free nations, so that they inevitably imparted to their literary productions the particular defects and special qualities characteristic of literature in aristocratic centuries.

Indeed, a glance at texts left us by Antiquity is enough to reveal that although ancient writers sometimes lacked variety and imagination in their choice of subjects and boldness, energy, and generality in their thought, they always demonstrated admirable mastery of technique and care in rendering details. Nothing in their work seems hasty or accidental.

Everything is written for connoisseurs, and the search for ideal beauty is always apparent. No literature brings out the qualities that writers in democracies naturally lack better than that of the Ancients. Hence there is no literature more appropriate for study in democratic centuries. Such study is more apt than any other to combat the literary defects inherent in such ages; as for their natural qualities, these will spring up on their own, so there is no need to teach people how to acquire them.

One point needs to be clearly understood.

A study may be useful to a people's literature yet not appropriate to its social and political needs.

To insist on teaching only belles-lettres in a society where everyone was habitually driven to increase or maintain his wealth by the most vigorous of means would be to produce very polite and very dangerous citizens. On account of their social and political state they would daily experience needs that their education never taught them how to satisfy, and they would therefore invoke the Greeks and Romans to sow trouble in the state rather than cause it to bear fruit through their industry.

It is obvious that in democratic societies individual interest as well as the security of the state requires that the education of the majority be scientific, commercial, and industrial rather than literary.

Greek and Latin should not be taught in all schools, but it is important that those destined by nature or fortune to cultivate literature, or predisposed to savor it, find schools where it is possible to gain complete mastery of ancient literature and steep oneself in its spirit. A few excellent universities would do more to achieve this result than a host of bad schools in which superfluous subjects taught poorly stand in the way of teaching necessary subjects well.

Everyone who aspires to excel in literature in a democratic nation should feast often on the works of Antiquity. There is no more salutary hygiene.

Not that I consider the classics beyond reproach. I believe only that their special qualities can serve as a marvelous counterweight to our peculiar deficiencies. They prop us up where we are most likely to fall.

Chapter 16

HOW AMERICAN DEMOCRACY
HAS CHANGED
THE ENGLISH LANGUAGE

I F the reader has fully grasped what I have said thus far about literature in general, he will have no trouble imagining the kind of influence that a democratic social state and democratic institutions can exert on language itself — and language is thought's primary instrument.

To tell the truth, American authors live more in England than in their own country, since they study English writers constantly and use them every day as models. This is not true of the population itself, which is much more immediately affected by factors peculiar to the United States. Attention should therefore be focused not on the written but on the spoken language if one hopes to observe the changes that the idiom of an aristocratic people may undergo when it becomes the language of a democracy.

Educated Englishmen, better able to appreciate these delicate nuances than I, have often assured me that the language spoken by the enlightened classes in the United States is notably different from that spoken by the same classes in Great Britain.

Their complaint was not only that Americans had introduced many new words — the difference and the distance between the two countries would have been enough to explain that — but that those new words were borrowed especially from the jargon of the parties, the mechanical arts, or the language of business. They added that old English words were often given new meanings by Americans. Finally, they said that the inhabitants of the United States frequently mixed styles in a singular manner, sometimes putting together words that in the mother country were customarily kept apart.

These remarks, which were made to me on several occasions by people who struck me as worthy of belief, induced me to reflect on this subject myself, and my reflections led me, by way of theory, to the same conclusion they had reached through practice.

In aristocracies, language inevitably partakes of the general ambience of repose. Few new words are created, because few new things come to pass. If anyone did anything new, moreover, they would try to describe it using familiar words whose meaning had been fixed by tradition.

If, in such societies, the human mind at length succeeds in rousing itself, or if enlightenment comes to it from without, people will begin to coin new expressions, and these will tend to have a learned, intellectual, and philosophical character indicating that they do not owe their birth to a democracy. When the fall of Constantinople turned the tide of science and literature toward the West, the French language was almost immediately invaded by a multitude of new words, all of which had their roots in Greek or Latin. Erudite neologisms came into use in France at this time, but only by the enlightened classes, and the people never felt the effect of this, or did so only in the long run.

The same phenomenon can be observed in every nation in Europe. Milton alone introduced more than six hundred words into the English language, nearly all of them derived from Latin, Greek, or Hebrew.

By contrast, the perpetual fluidity that is so prominent a feature of democracy is forever reshaping the face of language as well as of business. The general agitation and intellectual competition elicit a large number of new ideas. Old ideas may vanish or reappear or ramify to produce countless subtle variants.

Consequently, some words must be retired from use, while others have to be introduced.

Furthermore, democratic nations love change for its own sake. This can be seen in language as well as in politics. They sometimes feel a desire to change words even when there is no need.

The genius of democratic peoples is revealed not only by the large number of new words they introduce but also by the nature of the ideas those new words represent.

With such peoples, the majority makes the law in regard to language as in regard to everything else. Now, the majority is more concerned with business than with studies and more concerned with political and commercial interests than with philosophical speculations or belles-lettres. Most of the words it coins or accepts will bear the hallmark of these habits. They will serve primarily to express the needs of industry, the passions of the parties, or the details of public administration. This is the direction in which language will expand constantly, whereas it will gradually abandon the terrain of metaphysics and theology.

As for the source from which democratic nations draw their new words and the way in which they go about fabricating them, both are easily described.

Men who live in democratic countries have little notion of the languages spoken in Rome and Athens and see no need to search back all the way to Antiquity for the expressions they need. If they resort on occasion to learned etymologies, it is usually vanity that causes them to rummage about in dead languages and not erudition that calls ancient words to mind as a matter of course. Sometimes it is the most ignorant among them who use such words most often. The very democratic desire to move beyond one's proper sphere often leads them to embellish a quite menial calling with a Greek or Latin name. The lower the craft, the more remote from learning, the more pompous and erudite the name. Thus, for example, our tightrope walkers have turned themselves into acrobats and funambulists.

Instead of borrowing from dead languages, democratic peoples prefer to borrow from living ones, for they are in constant communication with one another, and men from different countries readily imitate one another because they become more alike with each passing day.

Democratic peoples do most of their innovating in their own tongues, however. On occasion they will restore a forgotten expression to prominence or take a term peculiar to a particular class of citizens and introduce it in a figurative sense into the common tongue. A host of expressions that initially belonged to the specialized language of a party or profession have thus come into general circulation.

The most common expedient employed by democratic peoples for the purpose of linguistic innovation is to bestow an unusual meaning on an expression already in use. This method is very simple, very quick, and very convenient. No knowledge is necessary for its use, and ignorance may even facilitate it. But it subjects the language to great perils. By doubling the sense of a word in this way, democratic peoples sometimes cast doubt on both the retained meaning and the acquired one.

An author begins by slightly bending the original meaning of a known expression, and, having altered it in this way, he does his best to adapt it to his subject. Another author comes along and bends the meaning in another direction. A third takes it down yet another path, and since there is no common arbiter, no permanent tribunal that can fix the meaning of the word once and for all, the situation remains fluid. As a result, it seems as if writers almost never stick to a single thought but always aim at a group of ideas, leaving it to the reader to judge which one has been hit.

This is an unfortunate consequence of democracy. I would rather see the French tongue bristle with Chinese, Tartar, or Huron words than allow the meaning of words to become uncertain. Harmony and homogeneity are only secondary beauties of language. These qualities are largely matters of convention, and if necessary one can do without them. But good language is impossible without clear terms.

Equality necessarily changes language in several other ways.

In aristocratic centuries, during which each nation tends to hold itself apart from all others and prefers to present a distinctive face to the world, it is common for peoples that share a common origin to become quite alien to one another, so that even though each continues to understand the others, they cease to speak in the same way.

At such times, too, each nation is divided into a certain number of classes, which see little of one another and do not mix at all. Each of these classes adopts and clings to certain intellectual habits peculiar to itself and prefers certain words and terms that are passed on from generation to generation, like an inheritance. Thus out of the common idiom comes a language of the poor and a language of the rich, a language of commoners and a language of nobles, a language of the learned and a language of the uninitiated. The deeper the divisions and the more insuperable the barriers, the truer this becomes. I am willing to bet that in India language varies enormously from caste to caste and that there is almost as much difference between the language of a pariah and that of a Brahmin as there is between their styles of dress.

By contrast, when men, no longer bound to their place in society, see and communicate with one another constantly, when castes are abolished and classes are replenished with new recruits and become indistinguishable, all the words of the language get mixed together. Those that do not suit the majority perish. The rest form a common stock, from which everyone chooses more or less at random. Nearly all the dialects that used to fragment the idioms of Europe are clearly on their way out. In the New World there is no patois, and the patois of the Old World are daily disappearing.

This revolution in the social state influences style as well as language.

Not only does everyone use the same words, but they become used to employing words indiscriminately. The rules laid down by style are all but abolished. Seldom does one encounter expressions that seem, by their very nature, either vulgar or refined. Because individuals of various ranks bring with them wherever they go expressions and terms they are accustomed to using, the origins of words are lost, like the origins of men, and confusion develops in language as in society.

In the classification of words, there are of course some rules that are not associated with one form of society rather than another but derive instead from the very nature of things. Some expressions and turns of phrase are vulgar because the sentiments they are supposed to express are really low, and others are lofty because the objects they seek to depict are naturally quite high.

The mixing of ranks will never eliminate such differences. But equality cannot fail to destroy what is purely conventional and arbitrary in forms of thought. I am not even sure whether the necessary classification that I indicated above will not always be less respected by democratic peoples than by others, because in a democratic people one does not find men who, by virtue of their education, enlightenment, and leisure, are permanently disposed to study the natural laws of language and to enforce respect for those laws by observing them themselves.

I do not want to abandon this subject without mentioning one last feature of democratic languages that may be more characteristic of them than all the others.

I showed earlier that democratic peoples have a taste and often a passion for general ideas. This is a consequence of their inherent virtues and defects. This love of general ideas manifests itself in democratic languages through the constant use of generic terms and abstract words and by the way in which these are used. Therein lies the great merit of these languages as well as the great weakness.

Democratic peoples are passionate about generic terms and abstract words because such expressions magnify thought and aid the work of the intelligence by allowing a large amount of material to be compressed into a small space.

A democratic writer will speak easily of "capacities" in the abstract rather than of "capable men" and will avoid going into detail about the things to which those capacities may be applied. He will speak of "actualities" to describe at one stroke everything he sees going on before his eyes at that very moment, and he will use the word "eventualities" to encompass anything that might henceforth take place anywhere in the universe.

Democratic writers are forever coining abstract words of this sort, or else they use the abstract words of the language in increasingly abstract senses.

To invigorate their discourse, moreover, they personify these abstractions and set them in action as though they were real individuals. They will say things like, "Circumstances require that capacities must govern."

I can best illustrate what I mean by my own example.

I have frequently used the word *equality* in an absolute sense. I have, moreover, personified equality in several places, and so I have said that equality did certain things or refrained from doing certain others. The men of the age of Louis XIV would not have spoken this way. It would never have occurred to them to use the word equality without applying it to something in particular, and they would sooner have given up the word than consent to turn equality into a living being.

Such abstract words, which are so common in democratic languages and which are used constantly without being linked to any particular fact, both magnify thought and cast a veil over it. They make the expression more rapid and the idea less clear. When it comes to language, however, democratic peoples prefer obscurity to effort.

I am not sure, moreover, that vagueness does not possess a certain secret charm for the people who speak and write in democratic nations.

Because the people who live in these countries are often left to rely on their own unaided intelligence, they are almost always wracked by doubt. Furthermore, since their situation is constantly changing, they are never held fast to any of their opinions by the very immobility of their fortune.

Men who live in democratic countries will therefore often have vacillating thoughts; they need very broad expressions to contain them. Since they never know whether the idea to which they are giving voice today will fit the new situation in which they may find themselves tomorrow, they naturally develop a taste for abstract ideas. An abstract word is like a box with a false bottom: you can put in any ideas you please and take them out again without anyone being the wiser.

Generic and abstract terms are the basis of all language. Hence I am not claiming that such words are found only in democratic languages. All I am saying is that men in ages of equality tend to increase the number of words of this type in particular; they tend to take them always in isolation, in their most abstract sense, and to use them incessantly, even when the occasion does not require it.

Chapter 17

ON SOME SOURCES OF POETRY
IN DEMOCRATIC NATIONS

Several quite diverse meanings have been given to the word "poetry."

It would be tiresome to explore here which of these is best. I would rather just say straightaway which I have chosen.

Poetry in my eyes is the search for and depiction of the ideal.

The poet is one who completes and amplifies nature by eliminating part of what exists, enhancing the picture with touches supplied by his imagination, and blending together certain circumstances that, while real, are not ordinarily found in combination. Thus the aim of poetry is not to represent what is true but to embellish it, and to supply the mind's eye with a superior image.

I take verse to be ideal beauty in language. As such, it may be eminently poetical, but verse in itself does not constitute poetry.

I want to inquire whether, among the actions, sentiments, and ideas of democratic peoples, there are not some that lend themselves to the imagination of the ideal and therefore ought to be considered natural sources of poetry.

It must first be acknowledged that the taste for the ideal, and the pleasure that people take in seeing it depicted, are never as intense or widespread in a democratic people as they are in an aristocracy.

In aristocratic nations, the body sometimes acts on its own, while the soul remains absorbed in burdensome repose. In such nations even the common people often exhibit poetic tastes, and their spirit will at times soar above and beyond their surroundings.

In democracies, however, the love of material pleasure, the idea of betterment, competition, and the lure of imminent success are like spurs driving each man as quickly as he can go down his chosen career path and barring so much as a moment's deviation from his course. Most of his spiritual effort is aimed in this direction. His imagination, though not suffocated, is almost exclusively preoccupied with conceiving the useful and representing the real.

Equality not only discourages portrayal of the ideal but also reduces the number of objects to be portrayed.

Aristocracy, by keeping society from changing, fosters stead-fastness and permanence in positive religions as well as stability in political institutions.

Aristocracy not only maintains the human mind in faith but disposes it to adopt one faith rather than another. An aristocratic people will always be inclined to establish intermediate powers between God and man.

In this respect it makes sense to say that aristocracy shows itself favorable to poetry. When the universe is populated with supernatural beings that, rather than being apprehended by the senses, are discovered by the mind, the imagination feels at home, and poets, with a thousand diverse subjects to portray, are met with countless readers ready to take an interest in their work.

In democratic centuries, by contrast, beliefs can fluctuate as much as laws. Doubt then pulls the poet's imagination back down to earth and confines him to the visible and real world.

Even when equality does not undermine religions, it simplifies them. It distracts attention from secondary agents and focuses it primarily on the sovereign master.

Aristocracy naturally leads the human mind to contemplate and dwell on the past. By contrast, democracy inspires in men a kind of instinctive distaste for all that is old. In this respect, aristocracy is far more favorable to poetry, because distance usually magnifies things and shrouds them in obscurity and thus on both counts renders them more suitable for depiction of the ideal.

Having deprived poetry of the past, equality then strips away part of the present.

In aristocratic nations, certain privileged individuals enjoy an existence that is in a sense outside the human condition, and above it. Among their seemingly exclusive prerogatives are power, wealth, glory, wit, delicacy, and distinction of every sort. The multitude never see them up close or have any detailed knowledge of what they do. It takes little effort to portray such men in a poetic way.

In the same nations, however, one also finds ignorant, humble, and subjugated classes who lend themselves to poetry by the very extremity of their coarseness and wretchedness, quite as much as the others do by virtue of their refinement and grandeur. Furthermore, the various classes that make up an aristocratic people are so distant from one another, and know so little of one another, that the imagination in representing them can always add something to or subtract something from reality.

In democratic societies, where all men are insignificant and very much alike, each person looks at himself and instantly sees everyone else. Hence poets who live in democratic centuries can never take a particular individual as the subject of their work, for a mediocre object that one sees distinctly from every possible angle can never lend itself to representation of the ideal.

Thus equality, in establishing itself on earth, dries up most of poetry's former sources.

Let us try to show how it reveals new ones.

When doubt had depopulated heaven and the progress of equality had reduced each man to smaller, more familiar proportions, poets, as yet unable to imagine what they might put in place of those great figures that had receded from view along with aristocracy, turned their gaze upon inanimate nature. As they lost sight of heroes and gods, they sought first to depict rivers and mountains.

This gave rise, in the previous century, to what was called descriptive poetry par excellence.

Some people believe that this embellished depiction of the material and inanimate things that cover the earth is the poetry peculiar to democratic centuries, but to my mind this is a mistake. It represents, I think, only a passing phase.

I am convinced that in the long run democracy will deflect the imagination from everything external to man in order to focus it exclusively on man himself.

Democratic peoples may well amuse themselves briefly by contemplating nature, but the only thing that really inspires them is the sight of themselves. There alone do their natural sources of poetry lie, and we may assume that any poet who chooses to forgo those sources will lose all power over the souls he hopes to charm, and the sight of his raptures will leave his readers cold.

I have shown how the idea of progress and of the indefinite perfectibility of the human race was intrinsic to ages of democracy.

Democratic peoples scarcely trouble themselves about what was but dream readily of what will be, in which respect their imagination knows no bounds. It stretches and grows beyond all measure.

This offers poets a vast array of possibilities and allows them to take a long view. Democracy, which closes the past to poetry, opens the future.

Because all the citizens who make up a democratic society are roughly equal and alike, poetry cannot fasten on any single one of them, but the nation as a whole becomes a fit subject for portraiture. The similitude of individuals, which makes each of them an unsuitable subject for poetry when taken separately, enables poets to embrace all in a single image and ultimately to contemplate the people as such. Democratic nations see themselves more clearly than other nations, and the imposing figure they exhibit lends itself marvelously to portrayal of the ideal.

I am quite prepared to admit that the Americans have no poets but not that they have no poetic ideas.

Europe is much concerned with the American wilderness, but Americans themselves hardly give it a thought. The wonders of inanimate nature leave them cold, and it is hardly an exaggeration to say that they do not see the admirable forests that surround them until the trees fall to their axes. Another spectacle fills their eyes. The American people see themselves tramping through wilds, draining swamps, diverting rivers, populating solitudes, and taming nature. Americans do not reserve this magnificent image of themselves for rare occasions. It accompanies the most trivial as well as the most important actions of each and every one of them and is always present to the mind's eye.

It is impossible to imagine anything as insignificant, dull, or encumbered with petty interests — in a word, as antipoetic — as the life of an American. Among the thoughts that guide such a life, however, one is invariably pregnant with poetry, and that one is like the hidden sinew that gives vigor to all the rest.

In aristocratic centuries, each people, like each individual, is inclined to remain fixed in place and separate from all others.

In democratic centuries, people are extremely mobile and impatient in their desires, hence they are constantly changing places, and inhabitants of different countries mingle with, see, listen to, and borrow from one another. So it is not only the members of a single nation who become more alike. Nations themselves grow more similar until they seem, in the eye of the beholder, to merge into one vast democracy, each citizen of which is a people. For the first time in history, the features of the human race become clearly visible.

Everything connected with the existence of the human race as a whole, with its vicissitudes and its future, becomes a very rich vein for poetry.

The poets of aristocratic times created admirable works by taking as their subject certain incidents in the life of a people or a man, but none ever dared to embrace the destinies of all mankind, whereas poets who write in democratic ages may undertake to do just this.

As individuals look beyond their own country and at last begin to perceive humanity as such, God reveals ever more of himself to the human spirit in his full and entire majesty.

If faith in positive religions often wavers in democratic centuries, and if belief in intermediate powers, whatever they be called, fades, men are nevertheless apt to form a far vaster idea of Divinity itself and to see its intervention in human affairs in a new and brighter light.

Seeing the human race as a single whole, they find it easy to conceive that a single design presides over its destinies, and in the actions of each individual they come to recognize signs of the general and fixed plan whereby God conducts the species.

This, too, may be considered a very abundant source of poetry, which democratic centuries make available.

Democratic poets will always seem petty and cold if they venture to bestow corporeal form on gods, demons, and angels and bring them down from heaven to vie for the earth.

But if they seek to link the great events they narrate to God's general designs for the universe, and to reveal the sovereign master's thought without showing his hand, they will be admired and understood, because the imagination of their contemporaries naturally follows this same route.

One may anticipate as well that poets who live in democratic ages will depict passions and ideas rather than persons and actions.

The language, dress, and daily activities of men in democracies are refractory to the idealizing imagination. Such things are not poetic in themselves, and even if they were, they would cease to be so because they are too well known to anyone to whom the poet might speak about them. Thus the poet is forced constantly to delve beneath the surface revealed by the senses to catch a glimpse of the soul itself. Nothing lends itself more to portrayal of the ideal than man seen in just this way, by sounding the depths of his immaterial nature.

I have no need to scour heaven and earth to find a marvelous subject rich in contrasts and abounding in examples of grandeur and pettiness, deep darkness and striking clarity, and capable of inspiring simultaneous pity, admiration, contempt, and terror. I have only to consider myself: man emerges from nothingness, journeys through time, and ultimately vanishes forever into the bosom of the Lord. Only for a moment do we see him roaming the outer reaches of the two abysses that otherwise consume his existence.

If man knew absolutely nothing about himself, he would not be poetic, for no one can portray a thing he has no idea of. If he saw himself clearly, his imagination would remain idle, having nothing to add to the picture. Man is sufficiently exposed, however, to see something of himself, yet sufficiently veiled that the rest remains shrouded in impenetrable darkness, into which he makes repeated forays in the vain hope of understanding himself fully.

Hence one should not expect the poetry of a democratic people to live on legends, to feed on traditions and ancient memories, to try to repopulate the universe with supernatural beings in which readers and poets themselves no longer believe, or to serve up cold personifications of virtues and vices that can be seen in their own right without such devices. It lacks all these resources, but man remains, and man is enough. Human destinies — man, taken apart from time and country and set before nature and God, with his passions, doubts, unprecedented good fortune and incomprehensible misery — will become the chief, if not the sole, subject of poetry for such peoples, as is already apparent when one considers what has been written by the greatest poets to have emerged since the world turned toward democracy.

The writers who in recent years have so admirably portrayed Childe Harold, René, and Jocelyn did not pretend to be recounting the actions of an individual; their purpose was to illuminate and magnify certain still-obscure aspects of the human heart.

Such are the poems of democracy.

Hence equality does not destroy all the subjects of poetry; it reduces their number but enlarges their scope.

Chapter 18

WHY AMERICAN WRITERS AND ORATORS ARE OFTEN BOMBASTIC

I HAVE often noted that Americans, who generally conduct business in clear, incisive language devoid of all ornament and often vulgar in its extreme simplicity, are likely to go in for bombast when they attempt a poetic style. In speeches their pomposity is apparent from beginning to end, and, seeing how lavish they are with images at every turn, one might think they never said anything simply.

The English are prone to a similar flaw, but more rarely.

The reason for this can be stated without much difficulty.

In democratic societies, each citizen is usually preoccupied with something quite insignificant: himself. If he lifts up his eyes, he sees only one immense image, that of society, or the even larger figure of the human race. He has either very particular and very clear ideas or very general and very vague notions; there is nothing in between.

Once drawn out of himself, therefore, he invariably expects that someone is going to set before him some prodigious thing to behold. This is the price he demands to tear himself briefly away from the myriad small concerns that keep him busy and lend charm to his existence.

This, I think, explains fairly well why men in democracies, whose affairs are generally so slight, ask their poets for works conceived on such a vast scale and portraits so extravagant in their proportions.

Writers, for their part, are hardly likely to resist these instincts, which they share. They are always pumping up their imaginations until they become so unreasonably inflated that they forsake the great for the gigantesque.

They hope in this way to attract the immediate attention of the crowd and focus it on themselves, and in this they are often successful. For the crowd, which looks to poetry only for very vast subjects, lacks the time to take the precise measure of all that are laid before it and lacks as well a sure enough taste to discern readily in what respects those subjects are disproportionate. Author and public mutually corrupt each other.

We have seen, moreover, that in democratic peoples the sources of poetry are beautiful but relatively rare. They are soon exhausted. Finding no more material for the ideal in what is real and true, poets give up on truth and reality altogether and create monsters.

I have no fear that the poetry of democratic peoples will prove timid or quite mundane. I worry, rather, that it will constantly be losing itself in the clouds and end up depicting worlds that exist only in the imagination. I fear that the works of democratic poets will often be replete with immense and incoherent images, exaggerated portraits, and bizarre composites, and that the fantastic creatures that spring from such poets' minds may at times make one long for the real world.

Chapter 19

SOME OBSERVATIONS
ON THE THEATER OF
DEMOCRATIC PEOPLES

WHEN a revolution that has changed the social and political state of an aristocratic people begins to affect literature, it generally manifests itself first in drama and remains conspicuous there long afterward.

The theatergoer is in a sense taken unawares by the impressions he receives. He has no time to quiz his memory or consult the experts. It does not occur to him to resist the new literary instincts he has begun to feel. He yields to them, not knowing what he is yielding to.

Authors are quick to divine which way the taste of the audience is secretly leaning, and they shape their work accordingly. Drama, having given the first signs of a literary revolution in the making, soon brings that revolution to completion. For a foretaste of what the literature of a people making the transition to democracy will be like, study its theater.

Even in aristocratic nations, plays constitute the most democratic part of literature. No literary pleasures are more accessible to the crowd than those that come from seeing a play. To experience them requires neither study nor preparation. They grip you in the midst of your preoccupations and your ignorance. When a class of citizens first begins to feel for the pleasures of the mind a love still half-uncivilized, it immediately takes to drama. The theaters of aristocratic nations have always been filled with non-aristocrats. Only in the theater did the upper classes mingle with the middle and lower classes and agree, if not to accept their opinion, then at least to suffer them to express one. It is in the theater that scholars and men of letters have always had the greatest difficulty establishing the supremacy of their taste over that of the people and resisting the influence of the people's taste on their own. The pit has often imposed its law on the boxes.

If it is difficult for an aristocracy to keep the people from invading the theater, it is easy to see that the people will reign over the theater as masters when, democratic principles having seeped into laws and mores, ranks blend and intellects as well as fortunes become comparable, and the upper class loses not only its hereditary wealth but also its power, traditions, and leisure.

The natural literary tastes and instincts of democratic peoples will therefore manifest themselves first in theater, and we may anticipate that they will do so in a violent manner. In written works, aristocratic literary canons will be amended little by little, by gradual and so to speak legal means. In the theater, they will be overturned by riot.

The theater brings out most of the qualities and nearly all the vices inherent in democratic literatures.

Democratic peoples hold erudition in very low esteem and care little about what happened in Rome and Athens. What they want to hear about is themselves, and what they ask to be shown is a picture of the present.

So when ancient heroes and mores are frequently reproduced on stage, and great care is taken to remain faithful to the traditions of Antiquity, it is safe to conclude that the democratic classes do not yet rule the theater.

Racine, in his preface to *Britannicus*, very humbly excuses himself for making Junia a vestal virgin, because according to Aulus-Gellius "no one under the age of six or above the age of ten was accepted." Were he writing today, he surely would never dream of accusing himself of such a crime or of defending himself against such an allegation.

An action of this kind sheds light not only on the state of literature at the time it occurred but also on the state of society itself. A democratic theater does not prove that a nation is a democracy, because, as we have just seen, democratic tastes can influence the drama even in aristocracies. But when the spirit of aristocracy reigns alone in the theater, that is incontrovertible proof that the entire society is aristocratic, and one can make so bold as to conclude that the same erudite and literate class that guides authors also commands citizens and takes the lead in public affairs.

When the aristocracy rules the theater, its refined tastes and arrogant penchants seldom fail to result in a rather selective view of human nature. The aristocracy is primarily interested in certain social conditions, and it likes to see these portrayed on stage. Certain virtues and even certain vices seem, in its eyes, particularly worthy of being reproduced. It applauds representations of these qualities while averting its eyes from all others. In the theater, as elsewhere, it does not wish to encounter any but great lords and is stirred only by kings. So, too, with styles. An aristocracy deliberately imposes on dramatic authors certain ways of saying things. It wants to set the tone for how everything is said.

Thus drama often portrays only one side of man and at times even depicts traits not found in human nature. It rises above human nature and goes beyond it.

In democratic societies, audiences have no such preferences and rarely display antipathies of this kind. What they like to see on stage is the same confused mixture of conditions, sentiments, and ideas that they find in life. Theater becomes more striking, more vulgar, and more true.

Sometimes, though, the people who write for the theater in democracies also go beyond human nature but in a different way from their predecessors. Aiming to reproduce the little singularities of the present moment in minute detail and to describe the peculiar physiognomies of certain individuals, they forget to delineate the general features of the species.

When the democratic classes rule the theater, they introduce freedom not only in the choice of subjects but equally in the manner in which those subjects are treated.

Since love of the theater is, of all literary tastes, the most natural in democratic peoples, the number of dramatic authors, the size of the audience, and the number of theatrical productions all increase steadily in democracies. Such a multitude, composed of such diverse elements and spread about so many different locations, cannot be subject to one set of rules or one body of laws. No agreement is possible among such a large number of judges, who, because they have no way of meeting, render their verdicts independently. If the effect of democracy is in general to cast doubt on literary rules and conventions, in the theater it abolishes them entirely only to replace them with nothing more than the whim of each author and each audience.

The theater also offers an excellent example of what I said earlier about style and art in democratic literature in general. In reading criticism inspired by the dramatic works of the age of Louis XIV, one is surprised to discover that audiences set great store by plausibility and attached considerable importance to consistency of characterization, so that no character in a play ever does anything that cannot be easily explained and understood. It is also surprising to see how much value was attached in those days to forms of language and what nit-picking criticisms were made of dramatic authors for their choice of words.

Apparently, people in the age of Louis XIV greatly exaggerated the value of such details, which can be perceived in private but go unnoticed on the stage. After all, the chief purpose of a play is to be performed, and its chief merit is to move its audience. If the theatergoers of that time exaggerated the value of details, it was because they were also readers. After leaving the performance, they expected to renew their acquaintance with the writer at home in order to round off their judgment of him.

In democracies, people listen to plays, but they do not read them. Most people who attend plays go in search of intense emotions of the heart rather than pleasures of the intellect. They expect to find not a work of literature but a show, and provided that the author speaks the language of the country correctly enough to make himself understood and his characters arouse curiosity and awaken sympathy, they are happy. Immediately thereafter, they return to the real world, without asking anything more of the fiction. Hence style is less necessary on the democratic stage, where the breaking of rules is more likely to pass unnoticed.

As for the rules of plausibility, it is impossible to respect them while at the same time rapidly turning out novel and unexpected work. So authors neglect them, and audiences are forgiving. If you touch the audience, you can be sure that it will not worry about the route you took to get it there. It will never reproach you for breaking the rules in order to move it.

When Americans go to the theater, they clearly exhibit all the instincts I have been discussing. Note, however, that to date only a small number of them do in fact go. Although both the size of the audience and the number of plays have increased prodigiously in the United States over the past forty years, most of the population is still extremely reluctant to participate in this kind of amusement.

There are specific reasons for this with which the reader is already familiar, so that a brief reminder will suffice.

The Puritans, who founded the American republics, were not only enemies of pleasure but professed a special abhorrence of the theater. They looked upon it as an abominable diversion, and as long as their spirit reigned uncontested, dramatic performances remained wholly unknown. The views of the founding fathers of the colonies on this subject left a deep imprint on the minds of their descendants.

Furthermore, the extreme regularity of habit and the great rigidity of mores that one finds in the United States have thus far done little to encourage the development of dramatic art.

Drama wants for subjects in a country that has never witnessed a great political catastrophe and in which love always leads directly and easily to marriage. People who spend every weekday making their fortunes and every Sunday in prayer do not lend themselves to the comic muse.

One fact by itself is enough to show how unpopular the theater is in the United States.

Americans, whose laws authorize freedom and even license of speech in all matters, have nevertheless imposed a kind of censorship on dramatic authors. Plays can be performed only when town officials allow. This shows clearly that peoples are like individuals. They indulge their principal passions to the hilt and then take care lest they yield more than they should to tastes they do not possess.

No part of literature is more closely or more abundantly linked to the present state of society than the theater.

The theater of one period will never suit the next if a major revolution has changed mores and laws in between.

People still study the greater writers of previous centuries, but they do not go to plays written for another audience. The dramatic authors of the past live only in books.

Traditional tastes in certain individuals, vanity, fashion, an actor's genius — each of these things may sustain or revive aristocratic theater in a democracy for a while, but before long it will collapse of its own weight, not overthrown but abandoned.

Chapter 20

ON CERTAIN TENDENCIES PECULIAR TO HISTORIANS IN DEMOCRATIC CENTURIES

HISTORIANS who write in aristocratic centuries generally attribute everything that happens to the will and humor of certain individuals, and they are likely to impute the most important revolutions to the merest of accidents. They shrewdly elucidate the smallest of causes and often fail to notice the greatest.

Historians who live in democratic centuries exhibit quite opposite tendencies.

Most of them attribute almost no influence over the destiny of the species to the individual and no influence over the fate of the people to citizens. On the other hand, they ascribe great general causes to the most insignificant particular facts. These opposing tendencies can be explained.

When historians in aristocratic centuries contemplate the world stage, they see all the leading roles filled by a very small number of prominent actors. The august personages standing in the limelight monopolize their full attention, and while busy unveiling the hidden motives behind what the principals say and do, they neglect everything else.

Because of the importance of what these few leading actors do, the historians in question develop an exaggerated idea of the influence that a single individual can exert, and this naturally leads them to believe that the activities of the multitude must always be traced back to the specific action of an individual.

By contrast, when all citizens are independent of one another and each of them is weak, none exerts a very great, much less a very durable, power over the masses. At first sight, individuals seem to have absolutely no power over the masses, and society seems to proceed on its own owing to the free and spontaneous cooperation of all its members.

This naturally prompts the mind to look for the general

reason that could have struck so many intellects at once and simultaneously reoriented them all.

I am firmly convinced that, even in democratic nations, the genius, vices, and virtues of certain individuals can delay or hasten the fulfillment of a people's natural destiny. But these kinds of fortuitous and secondary causes are infinitely more varied, more hidden, more complicated, less powerful, and consequently more difficult to sort out and trace in ages of equality than in centuries of aristocracy, where the only problem is to analyze the particular action of one man or a small number of men within a general context.

The historian soon tires of such labor. His mind loses itself in a labyrinth, and, unable to see individual influences clearly or to elucidate them adequately, he denies their existence. He prefers to speak of the nature of races, of the country's physical constitution, or of the spirit of civilization. This reduces his toil and gives the reader greater satisfaction with less effort on the historian's part.

M. de La Fayette says somewhere in his memoirs that the exaggerated system of general causes is a wonderful source of consolation for mediocre public men. I would add that it is also an admirable source of consolation for mediocre historians. It invariably provides them with a few grand explanations useful for quickly extricating themselves from any difficulties they encounter in their works, and it favors weak or lazy minds by allowing them to garner a reputation for profundity.

My own view is that in every period some of the events of this world must be ascribed to very general causes, others to very particular ones. Causes of both kinds are always encountered; the only thing that differs is their relative importance. General facts explain more things in democratic centuries than in aristocratic ones, and particular influences explain less. In ages of aristocracy, the opposite is true: particular influences are stronger, and general causes are weaker, unless inequality of conditions itself is considered a general cause, which allows certain individuals to thwart the natural proclivities of all others.

Historians who seek to describe what goes on in democratic societies are therefore right to pay a great deal of attention to general causes and to devote their primary effort to uncovering them, but they are wrong to deny the particular actions of individuals simply because it is not easy to find these out or trace their effects.

Not only are historians who live in democratic centuries inclined to ascribe a great cause to every fact, but they are also apt to connect facts to one another and derive a system from them.

In aristocratic centuries, the attention of historians is always focused on individuals, and they therefore miss the connections among events, or, rather, they do not believe that such connections exist. To them it seems that the fabric of history is constantly being rent by the passage of one individual or another.

In democratic centuries, by contrast, the historian is far more aware of acts and far less of actors, hence he can easily relate one act to another and establish a methodical order among them.

Although ancient literature has left us some very fine histories, it offers no great historical system, whereas the most miserable of modern literatures abound with such systems. Classical historians apparently made insufficient use of those general theories that our historians are prepared to abuse at the drop of a hat.

Those who write in democratic centuries have another, more dangerous tendency.

When all trace of the action of individuals on nations is lost, it is common to see change in the world without being able to discover any driving force behind that change. Since it becomes quite difficult to identify and analyze the various factors which, acting separately on the will of each citizen, cause an entire people to undergo change, it is tempting to believe that the change in question is not voluntary and that societies are unwittingly obedient to a superior force, which dominates them.

Even if one should discover on earth the general fact that controls the particular will of each individual, this would not preserve human freedom. A cause vast enough to apply to millions of people at once and strong enough to move them all in the same direction might easily seem irresistible. After surrendering to it, one is quite prepared to believe that it was impossible to resist.

Thus historians who live in democratic times not only deny certain citizens the power to act on the fate of the people but also deny peoples themselves the ability to shape their own destiny, thereby making them subject to either inflexible providence or a sort of blind fatality. According to such historians, the destiny of every nation is irrevocably fixed by its position, origin, antecedents, and nature, and nothing it does can change that. They see each generation as firmly linked to the preceding one, and in this way they proceed backward in time, from era to era and necessary event to necessary event, all the way back to the origin of the world, forging a long, closely linked chain that encompasses and binds the entire human race.

Not content to show how things happened, they also like to show that they could not have happened otherwise. They contemplate a nation that has reached a certain point in its history and contend that it was obliged to follow the path that took it there. This is easier than showing how it might have chosen a better route.

Perusing the historians of aristocratic ages, and particularly those of Antiquity, one often has the impression that man can become master of his own fate and govern his fellow man if only he can bring himself to heel. A glance at the histories written nowadays would suggest that man has no power over either himself or his surroundings. The historians of Antiquity taught men how to command; today's historians teach little but how to obey. In their texts, the author often looms large, but humanity is always small.

If this doctrine of fatality, which is so attractive to those who write history in democratic times, were to spread from writers to readers and thereby infiltrate the citizenry en masse and take hold of the public mind, it would soon paralyze the new societies and reduce Christians to Turks.

I would add, moreover, that such a doctrine is particularly dangerous at the present time. Our contemporaries are only too ready to doubt the existence of free will because as individuals they feel frustrated by their weakness no matter which way they turn, yet they are still quite prepared to recognize the strength and independence of men joined together in a social body. One should be careful not to obscure this idea, because the goal is to exalt men's souls, not to complete the task of laying them low.

Chapter 21

ON PARLIAMENTARY ELOQUENCE
IN THE UNITED STATES

I N aristocratic peoples, all men are connected with and dependent on one another. All are linked by a hierarchical bond, which helps to keep each individual in his place and enforce obedience in the body as a whole. Something analogous to this can always be found in the political assemblies of such peoples. The parties naturally line up behind certain leaders, whom they obey by a sort of instinct that is only the result of habits contracted elsewhere. They carry the mores of the larger society over into the smaller one.

In democratic countries it is common for large numbers of citizens to make for the same point, but each one does so — or at any rate flatters himself that he does so — wholly of his own accord. Accustomed to subjecting his movements to no rule other than his personal impulses, he finds it difficult to bend to rules imposed from outside. The taste for independence, and the habit of using it, accompany him into the nation's councils. If he consents to join with others in pursuit of a common goal, he wants at least to remain his own master, cooperating in the common success as he sees fit.

That is why parties in democratic countries are so impatient of direction and accept a subordinate role only in times of great peril. Even so, the authority of leaders, which may in such circumstances be great enough to compel action and speech, is almost never great enough to compel silence.

In aristocratic nations, the members of political assemblies are also members of the aristocracy.

Each of them possesses a secure high rank of his own, and the place he occupies in the assembly is often less important in his eyes than the place he fills in the country. This consoles him for his lack of a role in the discussion of public affairs and dampens his ardor for seeking to play a mediocre one.

In America it is common for a representative to owe his position entirely to his seat in the assembly. Hence he is constantly spurred by the need to play an important role there and feels an irrepressible desire to keep his ideas perpetually in the public eye.

He is driven in this direction not only by his own vanity but also by that of his constituents and the constant need to please them.

In aristocratic nations, a member of the legislature is rarely under the strict mandate of his constituents. Often he is in some sense their only possible representative. Sometimes they are his strict dependents, and if at any point they refuse to vote for him, he can easily win election elsewhere, or he can give up his public career and retire to a life of idleness that retains a splendor of its own.

In a democratic country like the United States, a representative seldom gains a lasting hold over the minds of the voters. No matter how small the electorate, its aspect is constantly changing owing to the instability of democracy. Hence every day it has to be captivated anew. The representative cannot be sure of the support of the voters, and if they forsake him, he immediately finds himself at a loss, for his position is not by itself high enough to give him visibility among people not in his immediate vicinity. Given the complete independence of the citizenry, moreover, he cannot expect that his friends or the government will find it easy to impose him on an electorate that does not know him. Thus all the seeds of his fortune are sown in the district he represents. This is the corner of the earth from which he must sally forth if he aspires to lead the nation and influence the destinies of the world.

Hence it is natural for the members of political assemblies in democratic countries to think more about their constituents than about their party, whereas in aristocracies they are more concerned with their party than with their constituents.

Now, what has to be said in order to please the voters is not always what would best serve the political opinion they profess.

It is frequently in the general interest of a party that representatives of that party never speak of important matters of which their understanding is poor; that they have little to say about minor matters that might impede progress on more important ones; and, by and large, that they hold their tongues altogether. To remain silent is the most useful service that a mediocre speaker can render to the public good.

That is not how the voters see it, however.

The people of a district elect a citizen to take part in government because they have formed a high opinion of his merit. Since men loom larger to the extent that the things around them are small, it is reasonable to think that the rarer men of talent are among the electorate, the higher the voters' opinion of their elected representative will be. Frequently, therefore, the less voters ought to expect from their representative, the more they will hope to receive. No matter how incapable he may be, moreover, they will not fail to require of him exceptional efforts commensurate with the rank they have bestowed on him.

Voters see their representative not simply as the lawgiver for the state but also as the district's natural protector vis-à-vis the legislature. They see him as almost the proxy of each person who elected him and are pleased to think that he will be no less ardent in promoting their particular interests than in promoting the interests of the country at large.

Voters therefore take it for granted that the representative they choose will be an orator, that he will speak as often as he can, and that, if he must restrain himself, he will at least try in his infrequent speeches to cover all important affairs of state as well as touch on all the minor grievances of his constituents. Thus if he cannot make frequent appearances, he must nevertheless demonstrate what he can do at every opportunity, and rather than always hold forth in a prolix manner, he must on occasion compress all that he has in him into a small volume containing a brilliant and complete résumé of himself and his constituents. In exchange for this, they promise him their votes in the next election.

This drives to despair honest mediocrities who, if only they knew their own limitations, would never step forward voluntarily. Once roused to speech, the representative takes the floor to the great chagrin of his friends and, imprudently ranging himself alongside the most celebrated orators, muddies the discussion and tires his audience.

Thus any law that tends to make the elected official more dependent on the voter alters not only the behavior of lawmakers, as noted earlier, but also their language. Such laws influence both affairs of state and the way in which those affairs are discussed.

There is scarcely a single member of Congress who would willingly return home without having made at least one speech, or who would suffer his oration to be interrupted before he had availed himself of the opportunity to make remarks of every conceivable kind directed to all twenty-four states of the Union and above all to the district he represents. He thus parades before his listeners a series of great general truths, which he himself often fails to perceive clearly and can explain only in a confused manner, along with a host of minute details that he has dug up with some considerable effort and now laboriously sets forth. Hence debates in that great body often become vague and tortuous and seem to drag their feet rather than march straight for their stated goal.

Something analogous to this will, I think, always take place in the public assemblies of democracies.

Under the right circumstances and with good laws it might be possible to attract to the legislature of a democratic nation men far more remarkable than those sent to Congress by the Americans, but it will never be possible to quell the alacrity of mediocre members to make a spectacle of themselves whenever and wherever they can.

This malady is not altogether curable, in my view, because it is a consequence not just of the rules of the assembly but of its constitution, and, indeed, of the constitution of the country itself.

The inhabitants of the United States themselves seem to agree with this way of looking at the matter, and they attest to their long experience of parliamentary life not by abstaining from making bad speeches but by courageously subjecting themselves to listening to them. They resign themselves to this necessity as to an evil that experience has taught them to regard as inevitable.

We have examined the petty side of democratic political debate; now let us discover what is great about it.

What went on inside the Parliament of England over the past hundred and fifty years never caused much of a stir outside. The ideas and sentiments expressed by British orators have never elicited much sympathy even among the nations in closest proximity to the great theater of British liberty. Yet from the time of the Revolution, when the first debates took place in the small colonial assemblies of America, Europe's excitement was palpable.

This was due in part to particular and fortuitous circumstances, but there were also general and durable reasons for it.

Nothing is more admirable or powerful, in my view, than a great orator debating great affairs in a democratic assembly. Since no class is ever represented there by men bound to defend its interests, speakers invariably address the nation as a whole, and it is in the name of the nation as a whole that they speak. This enlarges their ideas and elevates their language.

Because precedents have little force in such assemblies and there are no longer privileges attached to certain forms of property or rights inherent in certain bodies or individuals, the mind is obliged to adduce general truths derived from human nature in dealing with the particular affair at hand. This gives the political debates of even lesser democratic nations a character of generality that often kindles the interest of all mankind. All men are interested in these debates because their subject is man, who is everywhere the same.

In the greatest aristocratic nations, by contrast, the most general questions are almost always dealt with in terms of particular arguments based on the customs of a period or the rights of a class. This is of interest only to the class in question, or at most to the people of which that class forms a part.

This — and not just the greatness of the French nation or the favorable attitude toward France of other nations that follow her political debates — is surely what accounts for the great effect our debates sometimes have in the world.

Our orators often speak to all men even when addressing none but their fellow citizens.

PART II

*Influence of Democracy on
the Sentiments of the Americans*

Chapter 1

WHY DEMOCRATIC PEOPLES SHOW A MORE ARDENT AND ENDURING LOVE OF EQUALITY THAN OF LIBERTY

NEEDLESS to say, the first and most intense of the passions to which equality gives rise is love of equality itself. It should come as no surprise, therefore, that I discuss this passion before all others.

As anyone can see for himself, this passion for equality has lately gained an increasing hold on the human heart, especially in France. It has been said a hundred times that our contemporaries love equality far more ardently and tenaciously than they love liberty, but I do not believe that anyone has yet delved deeply enough into the reasons why this is so. I shall now attempt to do so.

One can imagine an extreme point at which liberty and equality touch and become one.

Suppose that all citizens take part in government and that each has an equal right to do so.

Since no man will then be different from his fellow men, no one will be able to exercise a tyrannical power. Men will be perfectly free, because they will all be entirely equal, and they will all be perfectly equal because they will be entirely free. This is the ideal toward which democratic peoples tend.

This is the most complete form that equality can take on earth, but there are a thousand other forms, which, though not as perfect, democratic peoples nevertheless hold nearly as dear.

Equality can establish itself in civil society yet not prevail in the world of politics. People may enjoy the right to indulge in the same pleasures, to enter the same professions, and to meet in the same places — in short, to live in the same way and pursue wealth by the same means — without all taking the same part in government.

A sort of equality can even be established in the political world even though political liberty does not exist. Each person is the equal of all his fellows save one, who is master of all without distinction and who chooses the agents of his power equally among all.

It is easy to imagine other hypothetical situations in which a significant degree of equality would be comfortably combined with more or less free institutions or even with institutions that were not free at all.

Although men cannot become absolutely equal without being entirely free, so that equality, in its most extreme form, is the same as liberty, a basis therefore exists for distinguishing between the two.

The taste that men have for liberty and the one they feel for equality are in fact two distinct things, and I do not shrink from adding that in democratic nations they are two unequal things.

It is clear to anyone who pays attention that in every century there is one singular, dominant fact to which all other facts are related. This fact almost always gives rise to a fundamental thought or principal passion that ultimately attracts all other feelings and ideas to itself and carries them along, as a great river seems to absorb its tributaries.

Liberty has manifested itself to men in various times and forms. It is not associated exclusively with any social state, and one does not find it only in democracies. Hence it cannot constitute the distinctive characteristic of democratic centuries.

The particular and dominant fact that makes such centuries unique is the equality of conditions; the principal passion that stirs men in such times is love of that equality.

Do not ask what singular charm men in democratic ages see in living as equals, or what particular reasons they may have for clinging so stubbornly to equality rather than to the other goods society has to offer. Equality constitutes the distinctive characteristic of the era in which they live. That alone is enough to explain why they prefer it to all the rest.

Quite apart from that reason, however, there are several others that will usually incline men of any era to prefer equality to liberty.

If it were possible for a people, by itself, ever to destroy or even diminish the equality prevailing within it, it would require long and arduous effort. It would have to modify its social state, abolish its laws, renew its ideas, change its habits, and alter its mores. To lose political liberty, however, is easy: fail to hold on to it, and it slips away.

Hence men do not hold on to equality solely because it is dear to them; they also cling to it because they believe that it must always endure.

Political liberty, if carried to excess, can endanger the tranquillity, property, and lives of private individuals, and no one is so blind or frivolous as to be unaware of this. By contrast, it is only the attentive and clear-sighted who perceive the perils with which equality threatens us, and they usually avoid pointing them out. They know that the miseries they fear are remote and are pleased to think that they will afflict only future generations, for which the present generation evinces little concern. The ills that liberty sometimes brings on are immediate. They are visible to everyone, and to one degree or another everyone feels them. The ills that extreme equality can produce reveal themselves only a little at a time. They gradually work their way into the body of society. Only intermittently do they become visible, and by the time they have become most virulent, habit has already ensured that they will no longer be felt.

The goods that liberty yields reveal themselves only in the long run, and it is always easy to mistake their cause.

The advantages of equality are felt immediately and can be seen daily to flow from their source.

To a certain number of citizens political liberty gives sublime pleasures from time to time.

Equality provides a multitude of lesser pleasures to everyone every day. The charms of equality are constantly apparent and within reach of all. The noblest hearts are not insensible to them, and the most vulgar souls delight in them. The passion to which equality gives rise is therefore both powerful and general.

Men cannot enjoy political liberty without making sacrifices to obtain it, and it has never been won without great effort. But equality offers up its pleasures for the asking. They seem to arise out of the most insignificant episodes of private life, and to savor them one has only to live.

Democratic peoples love equality in all ages, but there are times when their passion for it turns to frenzy. This happens when a long-threatened social hierarchy finally destroys itself in one last intestine struggle and the barriers that once separated citizens are finally knocked down. At such times men swoop down upon equality as upon conquered spoils and cling to it as to a precious good that someone would snatch from their grasp. The passion for equality then inundates the human heart and fills it entirely. No use telling people that such blind surrender to an exclusive passion jeopardizes their most cherished interests: they are deaf. No use pointing out to them that liberty slips through their fingers while their attention is focused elsewhere: they are blind, or, rather, in all the world they see only one good worth coveting.

The foregoing applies to all democratic nations. What follows pertains to us alone.

In most modern nations, and, in particular, among the peoples of the European continent, the taste for and idea of liberty began to take shape and develop only when conditions began to equalize and as a consequence of that very equality. It was the absolute kings who did most to level ranks among their subjects. Among these peoples, equality preceded liberty; equality was therefore an old fact when liberty was still a new thing. The one had already created opinions, customs, and laws of its own before the other emerged alone, and for the first time, into the light of day. Thus the latter still existed only in ideas and tastes, while the former had already insinuated itself into habits, taken hold of mores, and imparted its own peculiar twist to even the least significant of life's actions. Is it any surprise that men nowadays prefer one to the other?

I think that democratic peoples have a natural taste for liberty. Left to themselves, they seek it out, love it, and suffer if deprived of it. For equality, however, they feel an ardent, insatiable, eternal, invincible passion. They want equality in liberty, and if they cannot have it, they want it still in slavery. They will suffer poverty, servitude, and barbarity, but they will not suffer aristocracy.

This is true in all ages, and especially in our own. All men and all governments that seek to combat this irresistible power will be overthrown and destroyed by it. Nowadays, liberty cannot be instituted without its support, and even despotism cannot reign without it.

Chapter 2

ON INDIVIDUALISM IN
DEMOCRATIC COUNTRIES

I HAVE shown how, in centuries of equality, each man seeks his beliefs within himself. I want to show how, in the same centuries, he concentrates all his sentiments on himself.

Individualism is a recent expression arising out of a new idea. Our fathers knew only the word *egoism*.

Egoism is a passionate and exaggerated love of self that impels man to relate everything solely to himself and to prefer himself to everything else.

Individualism is a reflective and tranquil sentiment that disposes each citizen to cut himself off from the mass of his fellow men and withdraw into the circle of family and friends, so that, having created a little society for his own use, he gladly leaves the larger society to take care of itself.

Egoism is born of blind instinct; individualism proceeds from erroneous judgment rather than depraved sentiment. Its source lies as much in defects of the mind as in vices of the heart.

Egoism shrivels the seed of all the virtues; individualism at first dries up only the source of the public virtues, but in the long run it attacks and destroys all the others and in the end will be subsumed in egoism.

Egoism is a vice as old as the world. It is not to any great extent more characteristic of one form of society than of another.

Individualism is democratic in origin, and it threatens to develop as conditions equalize.

Among aristocratic peoples, families maintain the same station for centuries, and often in the same place. All generations are therefore in a sense contemporaneous. A man almost always knows and respects his forebears. In his mind's eye he can already see his great-grandsons, and he loves them. He willingly takes upon himself duties to both ancestors and progeny, and will frequently sacrifice his personal pleasures for others who either no longer exist or have yet to be born.

Yet another effect of aristocratic institutions is to create close bonds between each man and a number of his fellow citizens.

Since classes in an aristocratic nation are highly differentiated and immobile, each becomes for its members a sort of homeland within a homeland, more visible and more cherished than the country at large.

Since all citizens in aristocratic societies occupy fixed positions, some higher than others, it is also true that each sees above him another man whose protection he needs and below him still another whose cooperation he may require.

So men who live in aristocratic centuries are almost always closely tied to something outside themselves and are often disposed to forget about themselves. It is true that in the same centuries the general notion of "one's fellow man" is obscure, and little thought is given to devoting oneself to one's fellow man for the sake of humanity; but people often sacrifice themselves for certain men.

By contrast, in democratic centuries, when the duties of each individual toward the species are far more clear, devotion to one man becomes rarer: the bond of human affection stretches and slackens.

In democratic nations, new families are constantly springing from nothing, while others fall, and those who remain change their appearance. The fabric of time is forever being ripped, and vestiges of the generations disappear. People easily forget those who went before them and have no idea of those who will come after. The only people in whom anyone is interested are those closest to himself.

As each class draws closer to the others and begins to mix with them, its members become indifferent to one another and treat one another as strangers. Aristocracy linked all citizens together in a long chain from peasant to king. Democracy breaks the chain and severs the links.

As conditions equalize, one finds more and more individuals no longer rich enough or powerful enough to have much influence on the fate of their fellow men who have nevertheless acquired or retained enough enlightenment and wealth to take care of themselves. These people owe nothing to anyone, and in a sense they expect nothing from anyone. They become accustomed to thinking of themselves always in isolation and are pleased to think that their fate lies entirely in their own hands.

Thus, not only does democracy cause each man to forget his forebears, but it makes it difficult for him to see his offspring and cuts him off from his contemporaries. Again and again it leads him back to himself and threatens ultimately to imprison him altogether in the loneliness of his own heart.

Chapter 3

HOW INDIVIDUALISM IS MORE PRONOUNCED AT THE END OF A DEMOCRATIC REVOLUTION THAN AT ANY OTHER TIME

M AN'S isolation from other men and the egoism that results from this become especially striking right after a democratic society has taken shape on the ruins of an aristocracy.

The number of independent citizens in such a society is large, and their ranks are daily replenished by men who, having achieved independence only yesterday, are drunk with newfound power. Such people have a presumptuous confidence in their own strength, and, oblivious of the fact that they may some day need to call on their fellow men for assistance, make no bones about showing that they think only of themselves.

An aristocracy usually succumbs only after prolonged struggle, which kindles implacable hatred among the various classes. These passions survive the victory, and their trail can be followed through the ensuing democratic confusion.

Those citizens who were among the most prominent members of the ruined hierarchy cannot suddenly forget their former grandeur. They continue to think of themselves as strangers in the new society for quite some time. They see the many equals whom society imposes on them as oppressors, whose fate cannot arouse their sympathy. Having lost sight of their former equals, they no longer feel bound to their lot by common interest. Each of them, in his separate retreat, therefore thinks he has been reduced to where his only concern is himself. By contrast, those who formerly stood at the bottom of the social ladder and now find themselves abruptly raised up by revolution to the common level feel a sort of hidden anxiety about enjoying their newly acquired independence. If they happen to find themselves among their former superiors, they eye them with a mixture of triumph and fear and keep their distance.

Usually, therefore, it is when democratic societies first come into being that citizens are most likely to isolate themselves.

Democracy tends to make men unwilling to approach their fellows, but democratic revolutions encourage them to shun one another and perpetuate in the midst of equality hatreds originating in inequality.

The great advantage of the Americans is to have come to democracy without having to endure democratic revolution and to have been born equal rather than become so.

Chapter 4

HOW AMERICANS COMBAT INDIVIDUALISM WITH FREE INSTITUTIONS

DESPOTISM, which is fearful by nature, looks upon the isolation of men as the surest guarantee of its own duration and ordinarily does all it can to ensure that isolation. No vice of the human heart suits it better than egoism: a despot will be quick to forgive the people he governs for not loving him, provided they do not love one another. He does not ask for their help in conducting the state; it is enough that they do not seek to run it themselves. Minds that aspire to combine their efforts to promote the common prosperity he calls disruptive and restless, and, altering the natural meaning of the words, he calls those who keep strictly to themselves "good citizens."

Thus the vices that despotism fosters are precisely those that equality encourages. The two things complement and assist each other to disastrous effect.

Equality places men side by side without a common bond to hold them together. Despotism raises barriers between them to keep them apart. The former disposes them not to think of their fellow men, and the latter makes a kind of public virtue of indifference.

Despotism, dangerous at all times, is therefore particularly to be feared in democratic centuries.

It is easy to see that at such times men have a particular need of liberty.

When citizens are forced to concern themselves with public affairs, they are inevitably drawn beyond the sphere of their individual interests, and from time to time their attention is diverted from themselves.

As soon as common affairs are dealt with in common, each man sees that he is not as independent of his fellow men as he initially imagined and that, in order to obtain their support, he must often lend them his cooperation.

When the public governs, no one is unaware of the value of the public's good will, and everyone tries to court it by winning the esteem and affection of the people among whom he is obliged to live.

Several of the passions that chill and divide hearts are then obliged to withdraw into the recesses of the soul and hide there. Pride dissimulates; contempt dares not rear its head. Egoism is afraid of itself.

Under a free government, since most public offices are elective, men whose souls are so lofty or whose desires are so restless that private life feels confining to them are daily made aware of the fact that they cannot do without the people around them.

Thus a man may think about his fellow men for reasons of ambition and may often find it in his own interest to forget himself, as it were. Of course one might object at this point that elections give rise to endless intrigues, that candidates often resort to disgraceful tactics, and that their enemies spread slander about them. Elections are occasions for hatred, and the more frequently they are held, the more often such occasions arise.

These are no doubt great evils, but they are temporary, whereas the goods that attend them remain.

The desire to win an election may induce some men to make war on one another for a time, but in the long run the same desire leads all men to lend each other mutual support. Furthermore, while an election may accidentally divide two friends, the electoral system permanently brings together a multitude of citizens who would otherwise remain strangers. Liberty engenders particular hatreds, but despotism gives rise to general indifference.

The Americans have used liberty to combat the individualism born of equality, and they have defeated it.

America's lawgivers did not believe that, in order to heal a disease of the body social so natural in democratic times, and so fatal, it was enough to provide the nation as a whole with a general representation. They also thought it appropriate to foster political life in each portion of the territory so as to create endless opportunities for citizens to act together and remind them daily of their dependence on one another.

In this they acted wisely.

A country's general affairs occupy only its leading citizens. They come together in designated places only at intervals. And since they are often out of touch afterwards, no durable bonds are established among them. When the inhabitants of a district have to deal with that district's particular affairs, however, the same individuals are in constant touch and are in a sense forced to know and accommodate one another.

It is difficult to draw a man out of himself to interest him in the destiny of the entire state, because he has little understanding of what influence the destiny of the state can exert on his lot. Should it become necessary to construct a small road through his property, however, he will see at a glance how this petty public affair relates to his most important private affairs, and he will discover, without having it pointed out to him, the close connection that exists between the particular interest and the general interest.

Hence if the goal is to foster the interest of citizens in the public good and make them see that they need one another constantly in order to produce it, it is far better to give them responsibility for the administration of minor affairs than to put them in charge of major ones.

With one spectacular stroke one can instantly win the favor of a people, but to earn the love and respect of one's neighbors takes a long series of small services and obscure favors, habitual and unremitting kindness, and a well-established reputation for impartiality.

Thus local liberties, in consequence of which large numbers of citizens come to value the affection of their neighbors and relatives, regularly bring men together, despite the instincts that divide them, and force them to help one another.

In the United States, the most opulent citizens take great care not to isolate themselves from the people. On the contrary, they reach out to the people constantly, listen to them voluntarily, and speak with them daily. They know that the rich in democracies always have need of the poor and that in democratic times one wins the loyalty of the poor more through manners than through benefactions. Indeed, the very magnitude of benefactions, which highlights the difference of conditions, secretly irritates those who profit from them. But simple manners have almost irresistible charms: their familiarity is attractive, and even their crudeness is not always disagreeable.

The rich do not at first grasp this truth. They generally resist as long as the democratic revolution lasts, and even after the revolution ends they still do not accept it immediately. They readily consent to do good for the benefit of the people but prefer to keep them scrupulously at a distance. They think this is enough; they are mistaken. They could ruin themselves in this way without kindling any warmth in the hearts of the people around them. What is asked of them is not the sacrifice of their money; it is the sacrifice of their pride.

It sometimes seems that all the imagination that Americans possess goes to inventing ways of increasing the wealth and satisfying the needs of the public. The most enlightened people in every district regularly use their enlightenment to discover new secrets likely to enhance the common prosperity, and when they find such secrets, they hasten to make them available to the multitude.

On close examination, the vices and weakness of the men who govern America often stand out, and we are therefore surprised by the growing prosperity of the people — but we are wrong to be surprised. American democracy prospers not because of its elected officials but because its officials are elected.

It would be unjust to assume that the patriotism of Americans, and the zeal that each of them demonstrates for the well-being of his fellow citizens, had no basis in reality. Even though private interest controls most human actions in the United States as elsewhere, it does not decide everything.

I am bound to say that I have often seen Americans make large and genuine sacrifices to the public good, and I have noted on countless occasions that when necessary they almost never fail to lend one another a helping hand.

The free institutions that Americans possess, and the political rights of which they make such extensive use, are, in a thousand ways, constant reminders to each and every citizen that he lives in society. They keep his mind steadily focused on the idea that it is man's duty as well as his interest to make himself useful to his fellow man. Since he sees no particular reason to hate others, because he is neither their slave nor their master, his heart readily inclines to the side of benevolence. Men concern themselves with the general interest at first out of necessity and later by choice. What was calculation becomes instinct, and by dint of working for the good of one's fellow citizens, one ultimately acquires the habit of serving them, along with a taste for doing so.

Many people in France regard equality of conditions as the first of all evils and political liberty as the second. If obliged to endure one, they do their utmost to escape the other. But I maintain that to combat the evils that equality may engender, there is only one effective remedy: political liberty.

Chapter 5

ON THE USE THAT AMERICANS MAKE OF ASSOCIATION IN CIVIL LIFE

I DO not wish to speak of those political associations by which men seek to defend themselves against the despotic actions of a majority or the encroachments of royal power. I have already dealt with that subject elsewhere. It is clear that, as each citizen individually becomes weaker and consequently less capable of preserving his liberty single-handed, either he must learn the art of joining with his fellow men to defend it, or tyranny must increase with equality.

Here I am concerned only with associations that form in civil life and whose purpose is in no sense political.

Political associations are but a minor detail in the vast canvas comprising all the associations that exist in the United States.

Americans of all ages, all conditions, and all minds are constantly joining together in groups. In addition to commercial and industrial associations in which everyone takes part, there are associations of a thousand other kinds: some religious, some moral, some grave, some trivial, some quite general and others quite particular, some huge and others tiny. Americans associate to give fêtes, to found seminaries, to build inns, to erect churches, to distribute books, and to send missionaries to the antipodes. This is how they create hospitals, prisons, and schools. If, finally, they wish to publicize a truth or foster a sentiment with the help of a great example, they associate. Wherever there is a new undertaking, at the head of which you would expect to see in France the government and in England some great lord, in the United States you are sure to find an association.

In America I came across types of associations which I confess I had no idea existed, and I frequently admired the boundless skill of Americans in setting large numbers of people a common goal and inducing them to strive toward that goal voluntarily.

Since that time I have traveled in England, from which the Americans took some of their laws and many of their customs, and it seemed to me that the English were a long way from making use of associations with anything like the same frequency or skill as the Americans.

It is common for the English to do great things single-handedly, whereas there is scarcely any undertaking so small that Americans do not join together to complete it. The English obviously regard association as a powerful means of action, but the Americans seem to look upon it as the only means available.

Thus the most democratic country on earth is the one whose people have lately perfected the art of pursuing their common desires in common and applied this new science to the largest number of objects. Is this an accident, or might there actually be a necessary relation between associations and equality?

Aristocratic societies always include, along with a multitude of individuals who can do nothing by themselves, a small number of very powerful and very wealthy citizens, each of whom can undertake great ventures on his own.

Men in aristocratic societies do not need to join together in order to act, because they are firmly bound to one another.

Each wealthy and powerful citizen is like the head of a permanent, compulsory association comprising all who are dependent on him and whose cooperation he enjoins in furtherance of his designs.

Among democratic peoples, by contrast, all citizens are independent and weak; they can do almost nothing by themselves, and none of them is capable of obliging his fellow men to assist him. Hence they become helpless if they do not learn to help one another of their own free will.

If men living in democratic countries had neither the right nor the desire to join together for political ends, they would stand in great danger of losing their independence yet be able to retain what they possessed of wealth and enlightenment for some time to come; whereas if they failed to learn ways of associating with one another in ordinary life, civilization itself would stand in peril. Any nation in which individuals lost the ability to do great things single-handedly without acquiring the capacity to produce them in common would soon relapse into barbarism.

Unfortunately, the same social state that makes associations so necessary in democratic nations makes them more difficult to achieve there than anywhere else.

If several members of an aristocracy wish to associate, they can do so easily. Since each of them brings considerable strength to the partnership, the number of partners can be quite small, and when that is the case, it is very easy for the partners to know and understand one another and establish fixed rules.

The same facility is not found in democratic nations, where the number of associates must always be large if the association is to have any power.

I know that for many of my contemporaries, this is not a problem. They maintain that as citizens become weaker and less capable, government must be made more skillful and active so that society can take upon itself what individuals are no longer capable of doing on their own. In saying this, they believe that they have said all there is to be said on the matter, but in my view they are wrong.

A government could take the place of some of the larger American associations, and several individual states of the union have already attempted to do so. But what political power could ever hope to equal the countless multitude of small ventures in which American citizens participate every day through their associations?

It is easy to foresee that a day is coming when man will be less and less capable of producing life's most common necessities by himself. The task of the social power will therefore increase steadily, and its very exertions will make that task still greater with every passing day. The more the social power tries to take the place of associations, the more individuals, losing sight of the idea of associating, will need its help: here, cause and effect engender one another in an endless circle. Will the public administration ultimately control every industrial venture beyond the capabilities of the isolated citizen? And if land is ultimately divided into such infinitesimal parcels that it can no longer be cultivated except by associations of farmers, will it be necessary for the head of the government to forsake the helm of state and take up the plow?

The morals and intelligence of a democratic people would be no less at risk than its business and industry if government were everywhere to take the place of associations.

Feelings and ideas are renewed, the heart expands, and the human spirit develops only through the reciprocal action of human beings on one another.

I have shown that this action is almost nonexistent in democratic countries. Hence it must be created artificially, and only associations can do it.

When the members of an aristocracy adopt a new idea or conceive a new feeling, in a way they place that idea or feeling alongside themselves on the great stage on which they are players and, by thus exhibiting the novelty to the crowd, also introduce it readily into the minds or hearts of everyone around them.

In democratic countries, only the social power is in a natural position to act this way, but it is easy to see that its action is always insufficient and often dangerous.

A government by itself can no more sustain and revitalize the circulation of feelings and ideas in a great nation than it can control all industrial activity there. The moment it tries to leave the sphere of politics to embark on this new path, it begins to exercise an intolerable tyranny, whether it wishes to do so or not. For a government can only dictate precise rules. It imposes the feelings and ideas that it favors, and it is always difficult to distinguish its recommendations from its orders.

It is even worse if the government believes that it has a real interest in putting a lid on all activity. It will then cling to the status quo and voluntarily surrender to lethargic torpor.

Hence it must not act alone.

In democratic nations associations must take the place of the powerful private individuals who have been eliminated by equality of conditions.

When Americans have a feeling or idea they wish to bring to the world's attention, they will immediately seek out others who share that feeling or idea and, if successful in finding them, join forces. From that point on, they cease to be isolated individuals and become a power to be reckoned with, whose actions serve as an example; a power that speaks, and to which people listen.

The first time I heard it said that in the United States a hundred thousand men had taken a public pledge not to consume strong liquor, the idea struck me as more amusing than serious, and at first I failed to see clearly why such temperate citizens were not content to drink water at home.

Ultimately I understood that these hundred thousand Americans, frightened by the inroads that drunkenness was making around them, wished to give their patronage to sobriety. They behaved precisely as a great noble would do in dressing very simply in order to inspire contempt for luxury in ordinary citizens. We may take it for granted that if these hundred thousand men had lived in France, each of them would have petitioned the government individually to keep an eye on taverns throughout the realm.

Nothing, in my view, is more worthy of our attention than America's intellectual and moral associations. The political and industrial associations of the Americans leap to the eye more readily, but these others escape our notice, and if we do recognize them, we misunderstand them because we have almost never seen anything analogous. It is essential, however, to recognize that they are as necessary to the American people as political and industrial associations, and perhaps more so.

In democratic countries, the science of association is the fundamental science. Progress in all the other sciences depends on progress in this one.

Of all the laws that govern human societies, one seems more precise and clear than all the rest. If men are to remain civilized, or to become so, they must develop and perfect the art of associating to the same degree that equality of conditions increases among them.

Chapter 6

ON THE RELATION BETWEEN
ASSOCIATIONS AND NEWSPAPERS

WHEN the bonds among men cease to be solid and permanent, it is impossible to get large numbers of them to act in common without persuading each person whose cooperation is required that self-interest obliges him to join his efforts voluntarily to those of all the others.

The only way to do this regularly and conveniently is through a newspaper. Only a newspaper can deposit the same thought in a thousand minds at once.

A newspaper is an advisor that does not have to be sought out, an advisor that comes every day unbidden to talk to you briefly about public affairs without disrupting your private pursuits.

Hence the more equal men are, and the more individualism is to be feared, the more necessary newspapers become. To believe that their only purpose is to guarantee liberty would be to diminish their importance; they maintain civilization.

I will not deny that newspapers often induce the citizens of democratic countries to engage in some very rash joint enterprises, but without newspapers there would be almost no joint action at all. The ill they cause is therefore far less than the ill they heal.

Newspapers can not only suggest the same plan to large numbers of people but also enable people jointly to carry out plans they may have conceived on their own.

The leading citizens of an aristocratic country can see one another from afar and if they wish to join forces can make straight for one another, sweeping up multitudes in their train.

In democratic countries, by contrast, large numbers of men who feel the desire and need to associate may often find themselves unable to do so, because all are insignificant and none stands out from the crowd, so that they cannot identify one another and have no idea how to meet. But let a newspaper come and give visibility to the feeling or idea that has occurred simultaneously but separately to each of them, and all will immediately rush toward this light. Wandering spirits that had long sought one another in darkness will meet at last and join forces.

The newspaper brings them together, and they continue to need the newspaper in order to stay together.

If an association is to have some power in a democratic nation, it must be numerous. Its members will therefore be dispersed over a wide area, and each will be bound to the place where he lives by the modesty of his fortune and the need to look after it in countless little ways. The members must find ways to converse every day without seeing one another and to proceed in concert without meeting. Thus virtually no democratic association can do without a newspaper.

Hence there is a necessary relation between associations and newspapers: newspapers make associations, and associations make newspapers. If, moreover, it is true, as stated earlier, that associations must proliferate as conditions equalize, it is no less certain that the number of newspapers increases as associations multiply.

Thus of all the countries in the world, America is the one with both the most associations and the most newspapers.

This relation between the number of newspapers and the number of associations leads us to discover another between the state of the periodical press and the form of a country's administration, and teaches us that the number of newspapers in a democratic nation diminishes or increases in inverse proportion to the degree of administrative centralization. This is because democratic nations cannot entrust the exercise of local power to leading citizens, as is done in aristocracies. Either those powers must be abolished, or a very large number of people must be involved in their use. Those people then constitute a genuine association, permanently established by law for the purpose of administering a portion of the territory, and they need a newspaper that will find them daily wherever their petty concerns happen to occupy them and keep them informed about the current state of public affairs. The greater the number of local powers, the greater the number of people called upon by law to exercise them, the more keenly that need will be felt at every moment, and newspapers will therefore proliferate.

It is the extraordinary fragmentation of administrative power, far more than the great political liberty and absolute independence of the press, that is responsible for the strikingly large number of newspapers in the United States. If everyone who lived in the United States were a voter under a system that limited their electoral right to the choice of national law-makers, they would need only a small number of newspapers, because their opportunities to act together would be very important but very rare. Within the great national association, however, the law has established in each state, each city, and, as it were, each village, small associations devoted to the task of local administration. In this way the law forces every American to participate daily in a common task with a number of his fellow citizens, each of whom needs a newspaper to find out what the others are doing.

I think that a democratic people[1] without national representation but with a large number of petty local powers would eventually come to have more newspapers than a people with centralized administration combined with an elected legislature. To my mind, what best explains the prodigious growth of the daily press in the United States is that Americans as I see them enjoy the greatest national liberty together with local liberties of every kind.

In France and England it is generally believed that it is enough to abolish taxes on the press to increase the number of newspapers without limit. To say this is to greatly exaggerate the effects of such a reform. Newspapers proliferate not only as they become cheaper but also as large numbers of people feel a more frequent need to communicate with one another and act in common.

By the same token, I would also attribute the growing power of newspapers to reasons more general than those usually adduced to explain it.

A newspaper cannot survive unless it reproduces a doctrine or sentiment shared by a great many people. A newspaper

---

[1] I say a *democratic people*. Administration can be very decentralized among an aristocratic people without creating a need for newspapers, because local powers are then in the hands of a very small number of men who act in isolation or who know one another and can easily meet and come to an understanding.

therefore always represents an association, the members of which are its regular readers.

That association can be more or less well-defined, more or less restricted, and more or less numerous, but the seed of it, at least, must exist in people's minds, as evidenced by nothing more than the fact that the newspaper does not die.

This brings us to one final reflection, with which this chapter will end.

The more equal conditions become, the less strong men are individually, the more readily they allow themselves to go along with the crowd, and the harder they find it to adhere by themselves to an opinion the crowd has abandoned.

The newspaper represents the association. It speaks to each of its readers on behalf of all the others, and the weaker those readers are individually, the more easily it sweeps them up in its train.

The sway of newspapers should therefore increase as men become more equal.

Chapter 7

RELATIONS BETWEEN CIVIL ASSOCIATIONS AND POLITICAL ASSOCIATIONS

THERE is only one nation on earth where daily use is made of the unlimited freedom to associate for political ends. That same nation is the only one in the world whose citizens have imagined making constant use of the right of association in civil life and have thereby succeeded in procuring for themselves all the goods that civilization has to offer.

In all nations where political association is banned, civil association is rare.

It is hardly likely that this is the result of an accident. One should conclude, rather, that there is a natural and perhaps necessary relation between these two types of association.

Suppose that by chance some men have a common interest in a certain business matter. It might involve the management of a commercial venture or the negotiation of an industrial contract. The men meet and come to an agreement. In this way they gradually become familiar with association.

The more of these small joint affairs there are, the more capable men become — perhaps unwittingly — of pursuing large affairs in common.

Civil associations therefore facilitate political associations, but then again, political association singularly develops and perfects civil association.

In civil life, anyone may in a pinch persuade himself that he is capable of meeting all his own needs. In politics, such a thing is unimaginable. When a nation has a public life, therefore, the idea of association crosses every citizen's mind every day, and everyone wants to associate. Whatever natural reluctance men may feel about acting in common, they will always be prepared to do so in the interest of a party.

Thus politics generalizes the taste for and habit of association. It takes a crowd of men who would otherwise have lived alone and makes them want to unite, and it teaches them the art of doing so.

Politics not only brings large numbers of associations into being, it also creates very large associations.

In civil life it is rare for large numbers of men to be drawn naturally to joint action by a common interest. Considerable artfulness is required to achieve such a result.

In politics, opportunities of this sort arise by themselves constantly. Furthermore, the general value of association becomes apparent only when associations are large. Citizens who are individually weak have no clear idea in advance of the strength they can acquire by joining forces. They have to be shown before they can understand. Hence it is often easier to enlist a multitude in a common cause than to enlist a few. Where a thousand citizens may fail to see how it is in their interest to join forces, ten thousand will see. In politics, men join forces for great ventures, and the advantage they derive from associating in important matters teaches them in a practical way how it serves their interest to help each other in less important ones.

A political association draws a multitude of individuals out of themselves simultaneously. However inherently different they may be by dint of age, intelligence, or fortune, the association brings them together and places them in contact. Having met once, they can find each other again.

Most civil associations require members to risk a portion of their property. Industrial and commercial companies are all like this. Until men become well-versed in the art of association and learn its principal rules, they may be afraid, on joining an association of this kind for the first time, that the experience will cost them dearly. Hence they would rather deprive themselves of a powerful instrument of success than accept the risks that go along with using it. They are less hesitant, however, to take part in political associations, which do not strike them as dangerous because their money is not at risk. They cannot belong to such associations for long, however, without discovering how order is maintained where large numbers of people are involved, and how those large numbers of people can be made to march in step and according to plan toward a common goal. They learn to subject their will to the will of all and to subordinate their individual efforts to the joint venture — all things that are no less necessary to know in civil associations than in political ones.

Political associations can therefore be looked upon as vast free schools to which all citizens come to learn the general theory of associations.

Even if political association did not contribute directly to progress in civil association, to destroy the former would be to injure the latter.

When citizens can associate only in certain instances, they regard association as a rare and unusual undertaking, and it seldom occurs to them to consider it.

When they are allowed to associate freely for any purpose, they ultimately come to see association as a universal and, as it were, incomparable means of achieving the various ends that mankind proposes for itself. Each time a new need arises, the idea of association comes immediately to mind. The art of association then becomes, as I said earlier, the fundamental science; everyone studies it and applies it.

When certain types of association are prohibited and others permitted, it is difficult to tell in advance to which category a particular association belongs. Being in doubt, people avoid associations in general, and public opinion comes in a way to regard any association whatsoever as a rash and almost illicit enterprise.[1]

It is therefore a delusion to believe that the spirit of associ-

---

[1]This is especially true when it is the executive power that arbitrarily decides whether to permit or prohibit a particular association.

When the law limits itself to prohibiting certain associations and leaves it to the courts to punish those who disobey, the evil is much less great: each citizen then has in advance a rough idea of what to expect. In a way, he judges himself before his judges do, avoiding forbidden associations and joining permitted ones. All free peoples have always understood that the right of association could be limited in this way. If, however, the law made one man responsible for determining in advance which associations were dangerous and which useful, and allowed him to nip in the bud any association he chose while allowing others to grow, no one would be able to predict in advance the purposes for which association was allowed and which were to be avoided, with the result that the associative spirit would be completely paralyzed. The first of these two laws strikes only at certain associations, whereas the second is aimed at society itself and does it harm. I can conceive of a government of laws having recourse to the former but grant no government the right to invoke the latter.

ation, if thwarted in one place, will nevertheless continue to develop with the same vigor everywhere else, and that if only men were permitted to engage in certain joint undertakings they would hasten to do so. When citizens have the ability to associate in all matters and are in the habit of doing so, they will associate as readily in minor matters as in major ones. If they can associate only in minor matters, however, the desire and ability to do so will elude them. It does no good to allow them complete freedom to combine in matters of trade: they will make indifferent use of the rights granted to them, and when you have worn yourself out trying to prevent them from forming forbidden associations, you will be surprised to discover that you cannot persuade them to form permitted ones.

I do not claim that there can be no civil associations in a country where political association is prohibited, for men can never live in society without becoming involved in some joint enterprise. In such a country, however, I do contend that civil associations will always be few in number, weak in conception, and lacking in leadership and will either refuse to entertain ambitious projects or fail in executing them.

This naturally leads me to believe that freedom of association in political matters does not pose as great a danger to public tranquillity as some have assumed, and that such freedom may, after threatening for a time to topple the state, actually help to shore it up.

In democratic countries, political associations are in a sense the only private entities that aspire to rule the state. Accordingly, governments nowadays look upon associations of this kind as medieval kings looked upon great vassals of the crown: they feel a sort of instinctive aversion to them and engage them in combat wherever they meet.

By contrast, they feel a natural benevolence toward civil associations, because they can see readily that these, far from encouraging citizens to take an interest in public affairs, serve to distract them, and encourage them instead to become involved in projects that cannot be carried out without public peace, thereby averting revolution. But they fail to see to it that political associations multiply and greatly facilitate the growth of civil associations, and thus by avoiding a dangerous ill they deprive themselves of an effective remedy. When you see Americans associating freely every day for the purpose of promoting a political opinion, elevating a statesman to government, or removing another man from power, it is hard to understand how men of such independence avoid lapsing into license at every turn.

Consider, moreover, the infinite number of joint industrial ventures in the United States, and the number of people all over America working tirelessly to complete some important and difficult plan that could be upset by even the slightest hint of revolution, and it is easy to see why such well-occupied people are not tempted to disrupt the state or ruin a public tranquillity from which they profit.

Is it enough to notice these things separately, or must we uncover the nexus that ties them all together? It is through political associations that Americans of all walks of life, all casts of mind, and all ages daily acquire a general taste for association and familiarize themselves with its use. Large numbers of people thus see and speak to one another, come to a common understanding, and inspire one another in all sorts of joint ventures. Later, they take the lessons they learn this way and carry them over into civil life, where they put them to a thousand uses.

Thus it is through the enjoyment of a dangerous freedom that Americans learn the art of reducing freedom's perils.

Pick a certain moment in the existence of a nation and it is easy to prove that political associations disrupt the state and paralyze industry; but take the life of a people as a whole and it will perhaps be easy to show that freedom of association in political matters favors the prosperity and even the tranquillity of citizens.

In the first part of this book I said, "the freedom to write should not be confused with unlimited freedom to associate. The latter is both less necessary and more dangerous than the former. A nation can set limits to the freedom to associate without ceasing to be its own master. There are times when it should do so in order to continue being its own master." Later I added: "One should not shut one's eyes to the fact that unlimited freedom of association in the political realm is, of all forms of liberty, the last that a people can tolerate. If it does not plunge them into anarchy, it often brings them close to it."

For these reasons, I do not believe that a nation is always sufficiently mistress of itself to grant its citizens the absolute right to associate in political matters, and I doubt, moreover, that there has ever been a country in which it was not wise to limit the freedom of association in certain ways.

People sometimes say that this or that country cannot maintain peace at home, inspire respect for its laws, or establish a durable government without setting narrow limits to the right of association. Goods such as these are certainly precious, and I grant that, in order to acquire or preserve them, a nation may agree to fetter itself severely for a limited period of time. It is nevertheless good for the country to know precisely what the cost of these goods is.

To save a man's life, I can understand why one might want to cut off his arm, but I will not permit anyone to tell me that he will be just as deft with one arm as he was with two.

Chapter 8

HOW AMERICANS COMBAT INDIVIDUALISM WITH THE DOCTRINE OF SELF-INTEREST PROPERLY UNDERSTOOD

WHEN the world was led by a small number of powerful and wealthy individuals, they liked to conceive of man's duties in the sublimest of terms. They were pleased to profess that it is glorious to forget oneself and proper to do good without self-interest, like God himself. Such was the official doctrine of the age in the matter of morality.

I doubt that men were more virtuous in aristocratic centuries than at other times, but it is certain that people then talked constantly of the beauties of virtue. Only secretly did they study the ways in which virtue might be useful. But as the imagination ceased to soar quite so high and people began to concentrate on themselves, moralists became alarmed by the idea of sacrifice and no longer dared hold it up for the human mind to contemplate. They were accordingly reduced to asking whether citizens might not find it to their individual advantage to work for the good of all, and whenever they happened upon one of the points where the particular interest intersects and converges with the general interest, they were quick to call attention to it. Little by little, such observations proliferated. What was once just an isolated remark became a general doctrine, and ultimately it came to seem as if man, in serving his fellow man, served himself, and as if his private interest lay in doing good.

I have already shown in several places in this book how the inhabitants of the United States were almost always able to combine their own well-being with that of their fellow citizens. What I want to examine here is the general theory that helps them succeed in this.

In the United States people rarely say that virtue is beautiful. They maintain that it is useful and give proof of this daily. American moralists do not hold that a man should sacrifice himself for his fellow man because it is a great thing to do; they boldly assert, rather, that such sacrifices are as necessary to the man who makes them as to the man who profits from them.

They have noticed that in their country man is today driven back on himself by an irresistible force, and having lost hope of stopping him, they think only of guiding him.

They do not deny, therefore, that each man may pursue his own self-interest, but they do their utmost to prove that it is in every man's interest to behave honorably.

I do not wish to go into detail here about their reasons, which would take me far afield. Suffice it to say that their fellow citizens found them persuasive.

Long ago Montaigne said, "Should I not follow a strait path for its straightnesse, yet would I do it because experience hath taught me that in the end it is the happiest and most profitable."

Hence the doctrine of self-interest properly understood is not new, but it has been universally accepted by today's Americans. It has become popular. It lies at the root of all action. It crops up in everything Americans say. It is no less common to hear it in the mouth of the poor man than in the mouth of the rich.

In Europe, the doctrine of self-interest is much cruder than it is in America, but it is also less widespread and above all less advertised, and there are those among us who daily feign a readiness for sacrifice they no longer possess.

Americans, by contrast, are pleased to explain nearly all their actions in terms of self-interest properly understood. They will obligingly demonstrate how enlightened love of themselves regularly leads them to help one another out and makes them ready and willing to sacrifice a portion of their time and wealth for the good of the state. On this point I believe that they often fail to do themselves justice, for one sometimes sees citizens of the United States, like citizens of other countries, yielding to the disinterested, spontaneous impulses that are part of man's nature. But Americans seldom admit that they give in to enthusiasms of this kind. They would rather do honor to their philosophy than to themselves.

I could stop here and not try to judge what I have just described. The extreme difficulty of the subject would be my excuse, but I do not wish to offer it. Rather than leave my readers in suspense, I would have them see clearly what I am driving at and then refuse to agree with me.

Self-interest properly understood is not a very lofty doctrine, but it is a clear and reliable one. It does not seek to attain great goals, but it attains the goals it seeks without untoward effort. Since it is within reach of every intelligence, anyone can grasp it easily and retain it without difficulty. Marvelously tolerant of human weakness, it easily obtains great sway, which it has no difficulty maintaining because it turns personal interest against itself and uses the spurs that excite the passions as a means of guiding them.

The doctrine of self-interest properly understood does not inspire self-sacrifice on a grand scale, but it does prompt small sacrifices every day. By itself it is incapable of making a man virtuous, but it does create a multitude of citizens who are disciplined, temperate, moderate, prudent, and self-controlled. And if it does not lead men directly to virtue by way of the will, it gradually draws them to it by way of their habits.

If the doctrine of self-interest properly understood were ever to achieve total domination of the moral world, extraordinary virtues would no doubt become more rare, but crude depravity would, I think, also become less common. The doctrine of self-interest properly understood may prevent a few men from climbing high above the ordinary level of humanity, but a great many others who used to fall below that level will rise to it and remain there. Consider a few individuals and the doctrine brings them down. Think of the species and the doctrine raises it up.

I am not afraid to say that, of all philosophical theories, the doctrine of self-interest properly understood seems to me the most appropriate to the needs of my contemporaries; I see it, moreover, as the most powerful tool they have left to protect them from themselves. It should therefore be the primary focus of today's moralists. Even if they were to deem it an imperfect instrument, one would still be obliged to adopt it as necessary.

All things considered, I do not believe that egoism is a worse problem in Europe than in America. The only difference is that there it is enlightened and here it is not. Each

American is capable of sacrificing certain of his private interests in order to save the rest. We try to keep a grip on everything, and often it all slips through our fingers.

All around me I see people who by word and deed appear to want to teach their contemporaries that what is useful is never dishonorable. Will I never find anyone willing to make other people understand how what is honorable can also be useful?

No power on earth can prevent growing equality of conditions from prompting the human mind to investigate what is useful or from disposing individual citizens to turn inward on themselves.

It is to be expected, therefore, that individual interest will become more than ever the principal if not the sole motive of human action, but it remains to be seen how each person will interpret his individual interest.

If citizens, in becoming equal, were to remain ignorant and crude, it would be hard to predict to what stupid lengths their egoism might carry them, and it would be impossible to say in advance what sort of shameful wretchedness they might become involved in for fear of sacrificing some of their well-being to the prosperity of their fellow men.

I do not believe that the doctrine of self-interest as preached in America is self-evidently true in all respects, but it does contain a great many truths so obvious that men who are enlightened cannot fail to see them. Enlighten them, therefore, regardless of the cost, for the century of blind self-sacrifice and instinctive virtue is fast receding into the past, and what I see approaching is an age in which liberty, public peace, and social order itself will be unable to do without enlightenment.

Chapter 9

HOW AMERICANS APPLY THE DOCTRINE OF SELF-INTEREST PROPERLY UNDERSTOOD IN THE MATTER OF RELIGION

I F the doctrine of self-interest properly understood had only this world in view, it would be far from adequate, for many sacrifices are rewarded only in the next. And no matter how much mental effort is lavished on proving the usefulness of virtue, it will never be easy to make a man live well who does not wish to die.

It is therefore necessary to know whether the doctrine of self-interest properly understood can be easily reconciled with religious beliefs.

Philosophers who teach this doctrine tell men that to be happy in life they must look to their passions and carefully check any excess; that lasting happiness can be had only by eschewing a thousand ephemeral pleasures; and, finally, that one serves oneself best by continually triumphing over one's self.

The founders of nearly every religion have said much the same thing. Without indicating a different way to reach the goal, they merely set it farther off in the distance. Instead of locating the reward for the sacrifices they impose in this world, they place it in the other.

Still, I refuse to believe that all who practice virtue in a religious spirit do so for no other reason than the prospect of a reward.

I have met zealous Christians who regularly forgot themselves so as to work more ardently for the happiness of all, and I have heard them claim that they did so only to be worthy of the blessings of the other world. But I cannot help thinking that they are deluding themselves. I respect them too much to believe them.

To be sure, Christianity tells us that we must prefer others to ourselves to gain entry to heaven, but Christianity also tells us that we must do good unto our fellow men for love of God.

That is a magnificent expression; man, through his intelligence, enters into the mind of God; he sees that God's purpose is order; he freely associates himself with that grand design; and even as he sacrifices his private interests to that admirable order of all things, he expects no other reward than the pleasure of contemplating it.

I do not believe, therefore, that self-interest is the sole motive of religious men, but I do think that self-interest is the principal means whereby religions themselves guide men's conduct, and I have no doubt that it is from this angle that they appeal to the crowd and become popular.

Hence I see no clear reason why the doctrine of self-interest properly understood should turn men away from religious beliefs. On the contrary, I can make out ways in which it might draw them toward religion.

Suppose that a man, seeking to attain the happiness of this world, resists instinct at every turn and coldly calculates all the actions of his life, and suppose, further, that instead of blindly yielding to the ardor of his first desires, he has learned the art of combating them and has become accustomed to easily sacrificing the pleasure of the moment to the permanent interests of his entire life.

If such a man has faith in the religion he professes, it will cost him little to submit to the constraints it imposes on him. Reason itself counsels him to do so, and custom has prepared him in advance to bear this burden.

Even if he harbors certain doubts about the object of his hopes, he will not easily allow himself to dwell on them, and he will deem it wise to risk some of the goods of this world to preserve his rights to the immense inheritance promised him in the other.

"In deceiving oneself by believing the Christian religion to be true," Pascal says, "there is not very much to lose, but what a misfortune to deceive oneself by believing it to be false!"

Americans do not affect a coarse indifference to the other life; they do not make a show of puerile pride by scorning perils they hope to escape.

They practice their religion accordingly, without shame and without weakness, yet even their zeal is usually suffused with something so tranquil, so methodical, and so calculated that what brings them to the foot of the altar would seem to be the head far more than the heart.

Not only do Americans adhere to their religion out of self-interest, but they often locate the kind of self-interest that might cause a person to adhere to religion in this world rather than in the next. In the Middle Ages priests spoke only of the other life; they were not much concerned with proving that a sincere Christian can be a happy man here below.

But American preachers refer to this world constantly and, indeed, can avert their eyes from it only with the greatest of difficulty. Seeking to touch their listeners all the more effectively, they are forever pointing out how religious beliefs foster liberty and public order, and in listening to them it is often difficult to tell whether the chief object of religion is to procure eternal happiness in the other world or well-being in this one.

Chapter 10

ON THE TASTE FOR MATERIAL
WELL-BEING IN AMERICA

In America, the passion for material well-being is not always exclusive, but it is general. While not everyone experiences it in the same way, all feel it. Minds are universally preoccupied with meeting the body's every need and attending to life's little comforts.

Something similar is becoming more and more apparent in Europe.

Among the causes that produce these similar effects in both worlds, several bear on my subject, and I should point these out.

When wealth is settled on certain families by inheritance, we find large numbers of men who enjoy material well-being but not as an exclusive taste.

What grips the heart most powerfully is not the peaceful possession of a precious object but the imperfectly satisfied desire to possess it and the constant fear of losing it.

In aristocratic societies, the rich, never having known any condition different from their own, have no fear of changing it. They can scarcely imagine anything else. For them, therefore, material well-being is not the purpose of life. It is a way of living. They look upon it, in a sense, as synonymous with existence and enjoy it without thinking about it.

Since the natural and instinctive taste for well-being that everyone shares is thus satisfied without difficulty and without fear, the souls of men turn elsewhere and harness themselves to some grander, more difficult undertaking, which animates and engages them.

So it is that even when material gratifications lie ready to hand, the members of an aristocracy often exhibit a haughty contempt for the very pleasures they enjoy and are able to call upon remarkable reserves of strength when obliged in the end to forgo them. Every revolution that has disrupted or destroyed an aristocracy has shown how easily people accustomed to the superfluous can do without the necessary, whereas men who have achieved comfort laboriously can scarcely go on living after they lose it.

If I turn now from the upper ranks to the lower classes, I will find analogous effects produced by different causes.

In nations where the aristocracy dominates society and keeps it immobile, the people eventually become accustomed to poverty as the rich do to opulence. The latter do not concern themselves with material well-being, because they possess it without effort; the former do not think about it because they have no hope of acquiring it and do not know it well enough to desire it.

In those kinds of society, the poor man's imagination is diverted toward the other world. Though gripped by the miseries of real life, it escapes their hold and seeks its satisfactions elsewhere.

By contrast, when ranks lose their distinctions and privileges are destroyed, when patrimonies are divided and enlightenment and liberty spread, the longing to acquire well-being enters the imagination of the poor man, and the fear of losing it enters that of the rich. A host of modest fortunes are amassed. Those who possess such fortunes enjoy sufficient material gratifications to conceive a taste for them and not enough to be content with them. They cannot obtain more without effort and cannot indulge in those they have without trepidation.

Hence they are forever seeking to pursue or hold on to pleasures that are as precious as they are incomplete and fleeting.

In casting about for a passion that might be natural in men spurred on as well as constrained by the obscurity of their origins and the modesty of their fortunes, I find none that suits them better than the taste for well-being. The passion for material well-being is essentially a middle-class passion. It grows and spreads with that class; it becomes preponderant when the class does. From there it reaches up into the upper ranks of society and descends among the people.

In America I found no citizen so poor that he did not gaze with hope and longing upon the pleasures of the rich, or that his imagination did not savor in advance goods that fate obstinately refused to grant him.

On the other hand, I never found among wealthy Americans that proud disdain for material well-being that can sometimes be seen even in the most opulent and dissolute of aristocracies.

Most of those wealthy people had been poor. They had felt the spur of need. They had waged a long battle against hostile fortune, and though victory was now theirs, the passions that had accompanied the struggle survived. They remained as though intoxicated amid the petty pleasures they had pursued for forty years.

Not that one does not find, in the United States as elsewhere, a fairly large number of wealthy people who, having inherited their property, find themselves effortlessly in possession of an opulence they did not acquire. Yet even they seem no less attached to the gratifications of material life. Love of well-being has become the national and dominant taste. The mainstream of the human passions runs in this direction and sweeps everything along with it.

Chapter 11

ON THE PARTICULAR EFFECTS OF THE LOVE OF MATERIAL GRATIFICATIONS IN DEMOCRATIC CENTURIES

THE foregoing might lead one to believe that the love of material gratifications will inevitably introduce disorder into American mores and trouble into American families and ultimately compromise the future of society itself.

This is not the case, however. The passion for material gratifications yields different effects in democracies than in aristocratic nations.

It sometimes happens that weariness with public affairs, excessive wealth, collapse of faith, and decadence of the state will slowly divert the heart of an aristocracy into an exclusive preoccupation with material gratifications. Or it may happen that the power of the prince or the weakness of the people may, without robbing nobles of their wealth, force them to forsake power and cut them off from great ventures, thus abandoning them to the restlessness of their desires. They then collapse of their own weight upon themselves and look to the gratifications of the body to wipe out memory of their former grandeur.

When the members of an aristocratic body turn in this way exclusively toward love of material gratifications, they generally pour all the energy derived from long familiarity with power into this side of existence alone.

For such men the search for well-being is not enough. They require a sumptuous depravity and a splendid corruption. They erect a magnificent shrine to matter and seem to vie with one another to excel in the art of turning themselves into brutes.

The stronger, more glorious, and freer an aristocracy once was, the more depraved it will become, and no matter how splendid its virtues may have been, I dare to predict that its vices will always be more glaring still.

The taste for material gratifications does not lead democratic peoples into similar excesses. With them, the love of well-being reveals itself to be a tenacious, exclusive, universal, but restrained passion. There is no question of building vast palaces, of vanquishing or deceiving nature, or of depleting the universe the better to gratify the passions of one man. The goal is to add a few acres to one's fields, to plant an orchard, to enlarge a home, to make life constantly more comfortable and more convenient, to forestall want and satisfy the slightest need without effort and virtually without cost. Such goals are small, but the soul invests in them: it contemplates them daily at close range. Ultimately they block its view of the rest of the world and sometimes come between the soul and God.

Someone might object that the foregoing applies only to citizens of modest means. The rich will exhibit tastes analogous to those they displayed in centuries of aristocracy. I challenge this assertion.

When it comes to material gratifications, the most opulent citizens of a democracy will not exhibit tastes very different from those of the people, either because, having emerged from the bosom of the people, they really do share those tastes, or because they feel obliged to submit to them. In democratic societies, the sensuality of the public takes on a certain moderate and tranquil style, to which all souls are required to conform. It is as difficult to escape the common rule by way of one's vices as by way of one's virtues.

Wealthy people who live in democratic nations therefore aim to satisfy the least of their desires rather than to experience extraordinary pleasures. They gratify a host of small desires and avoid unruly grand passions. Thus they lapse into limpness rather than debauchery.

The particular taste that men in democratic centuries conceive for material gratifications is not by nature opposed to order. On the contrary, it often needs order if it is to be satisfied. Nor is it hostile to regularity of mores, for good mores are useful to public tranquillity and helpful to industry. Indeed, it often combines with a kind of religious morality. People want to be as well off as possible in this world without renouncing their chances in the next.

The possession of certain material goods is criminal. From these they are careful to abstain. The use of certain others is permitted by religion and morality. To these they unreservedly surrender their hearts, their imaginations, and their lives, and in striving to possess them they lose sight of those more precious goods that constitute the glory and grandeur of the human race.

I reproach equality not for leading men into the pursuit of forbidden pleasures but for absorbing them entirely in the search for permitted ones.

In this way the world might well come to see the establishment of a kind of respectable materialism, which rather than corrupt souls would soften them and in the end silently loosen the tension in all their springs.

Chapter 12

WHY CERTAIN AMERICANS EXHIBIT SUCH IMPASSIONED SPIRITUALISM

Although the desire to acquire the goods of this world is the dominant passion of Americans, there are brief intervals when their souls seem suddenly to cast off all material bonds and fly impetuously toward heaven.

In all the states of the Union, but primarily in the partly settled regions of the West, one occasionally encounters itinerant preachers who travel from place to place hawking the word of God.

Entire families — elders, women and children — cross difficult country and make their way through vast stretches of uninhabited forest to hear them. Once arrived, the faithful neglect their private business and even their most pressing bodily needs while listening to the preaching for days and nights on end.

Scattered throughout American society one finds souls filled with an impassioned, almost wild spiritualism that one seldom encounters in Europe. From time to time there arise bizarre sects that attempt to open up extraordinary pathways to eternal happiness. Various forms of religious madness are quite common in the United States.

This should come as no surprise.

Man did not bestow upon himself the taste for the infinite and the love of what is immortal. These sublime instincts were not born of a caprice of his will. Their fixed foundation lies in man's nature. They exist in spite of his efforts. He can hinder and deform but not destroy them.

The soul has needs that must be satisfied, and no matter what pains one takes to distract it from itself, it soon grows bored, anxious, and agitated among the pleasures of the senses.

If ever the vast majority of the human race were to concentrate its thoughts on the quest for material goods alone, we may expect a powerful reaction to take place in certain souls. These would plunge headlong into the world of the spirits lest they find themselves trammeled unduly by the fetters the body would impose on them.

Hence it is no grounds for astonishment if in a society that would think only of earth, one finds a small number of individuals whose only wish is to gaze upon heaven. I would be surprised if, in a nation preoccupied solely with its well-being, mysticism did not make some progress before long.

Some say that it was the persecutions of the emperors and the tortures of the arena that populated the deserts of the Thebaid. To my way of thinking, it was rather the exquisite pleasures of Rome and the Epicurean philosophy of Greece.

If the social state, circumstances, and laws did not confine the American spirit so narrowly to the search for well-being, there is reason to believe that when the time came to consider immaterial things, it would demonstrate greater reserve and more experience and easily moderate itself. But it feels imprisoned within limits that apparently it cannot transgress. The moment it surpasses those limits, it can no longer find its bearings and often hastens without stopping beyond the limits of common sense.

Chapter 13

WHY AMERICANS SEEM SO RESTLESS IN THE MIDST OF THEIR WELL-BEING

In certain remote corners of the Old World, one still finds tiny populations all but forgotten amid the universal tumult, populations that remained static while everything around them was in flux. The peoples who inhabit these places are for the most part quite ignorant and quite impoverished. They do not meddle in affairs of government, and often their governments oppress them. Yet they often seem serene of countenance and jovial of disposition.

In America I saw the freest, most enlightened men living in the happiest circumstances to be found anywhere in the world, yet it seemed to me that their features were habitually veiled by a sort of cloud. They struck me as grave and almost sad even in their pleasures.

The principal reason for this is that the former do not think about the evils they endure, whereas the latter never stop thinking about the goods they do not possess.

It is strange to witness the fervent ardor that Americans bring to the pursuit of well-being and to see how tormented they always seem by a vague fear of not having chosen the shortest way of getting there.

The inhabitant of the United States clings to the goods of this world as though assured of not dying, yet he is in such haste to grasp the ones that come his way that he seems almost to suffer from perpetual fear of passing away before finding time to enjoy them. He grasps at everything but embraces nothing and soon lets things slip from his grasp so that he may go chasing after new pleasures.

In the United States, a man carefully builds a home to live in when he is old and sells it before the roof is laid. He plants a garden and rents it out just as he is about to savor its fruits. He clears a field and leaves it to others to reap the harvest. He enters a profession and then quits it. He settles in one place only to leave it a short while later to pursue his changing desires elsewhere. Should his private affairs leave him a moment's respite, he will plunge straightaway into the whirlwind of politics. And when, at the end of a year filled with labors, he discovers that a brief period of leisure remains, he turns his restless curiosity to this or that corner of the vast territory of the United States. Thus will he travel five hundred leagues in a few days the better to distract himself from his happiness.

Death comes at last, catching him before he has tired of this futile pursuit of a complete felicity that remains forever out of reach.

On contemplating the remarkable agitation that so many happy men exhibit in the very midst of abundance, one is at first astonished. Yet this is a spectacle as old as the world; what is new is that the cast now comprises an entire people.

The taste for material gratifications must be regarded as the primary source of that secret restlessness revealed by the actions of Americans and the inconstancy they exhibit every day.

The man who has given his heart entirely to the quest for the goods of this world is always in a hurry, for he has but a limited time to find, possess, and enjoy them. The memory of life's brevity constantly spurs him on. Beyond the goods he possesses, he is forever imagining a thousand others that death will prevent him from savoring unless he makes haste. This thought fills him with anxieties, fears, and regrets and keeps his soul in a state of constant trepidation that impels him again and again to change plans and places.

If the taste for material well-being is coupled with a social state where neither law nor custom still keeps anyone in his place, this restlessness of spirit is further exacerbated. We will then find men constantly changing course for fear of missing the shortest road to happiness.

It is easy to see, moreover, that if the men who passionately seek out material gratifications are ardent in their desires, they will also be easily put off. Since the final goal is to enjoy, the means of attaining it must be quick and easy, for otherwise the trouble required to achieve the gratification would exceed the pleasure it afforded. Most souls are therefore both ardent and listless, violent and enervated. Often death is less feared than persistence of effort toward a single goal.

Equality leads by a still more direct path to several of the effects I have just described.

When all the prerogatives of birth and fortune are destroyed, and all the professions are open to everyone and a person can reach the top of any of them on his own, ambitious men may readily conclude that the road to success is wide and smooth and easily imagine illustrious futures for themselves. This is a mistaken belief, however, and one to which experience applies a daily corrective. The same equality that allows each citizen to entertain vast hopes makes all citizens individually weak. It limits their strength in every respect, even as it allows their desires to expand.

Not only are they powerless by themselves, but at every step they encounter huge obstacles they failed at first to notice.

Having destroyed the obstructing privileges enjoyed by some of their fellow men, they run up against universal competition. The form of the obstacle has changed, but the obstacle remains. When men are nearly alike and all follow the same route, it is quite difficult for any of them to move ahead quickly and break through the uniform crowd that surrounds them and presses in upon them.

The constant tension that exists between the instincts to which equality gives rise and the means it provides for their satisfaction torments and tires the soul.

It is possible to imagine men achieving a degree of liberty that satisfies them completely. They will then enjoy their independence without anxiety or ardor. But no equality instituted by men will ever be enough for them.

Try as they might, no people can ever achieve a perfect equality of conditions. Should a nation be unfortunate enough to reach such a state of absolute and complete leveling, it would still be left with inequalities of intelligence, and these, stemming as they do directly from God, will always elude laws.

However democratic the social state and political constitution of a people may be, we may therefore take it for granted that every citizen will be aware of certain dominating presences around him and will focus his attention stubbornly on these. When inequality is the common law of a society, the greatest inequalities do not call attention to themselves. When everything is more or less on a par, the slightest inequality becomes an eyesore. That is why the desire for equality becomes ever more insatiable as the degree of equality increases.

In democratic nations men easily achieve a certain equality but not the equality they desire. That equality recedes a bit further every day, yet it never disappears from view, and as it recedes, it entices them to chase after it. Although they always think they are about to catch up with it, invariably it eludes their grasp. They get close enough to know equality's charms but not close enough to enjoy them, and they die before having fully savored its delights.

To these causes we must attribute the strange melancholy that the inhabitants of democratic countries often exhibit in the midst of plenty, and the disgust with life that sometimes grips them as they go about their comfortable and tranquil existences.

People in France complain that the number of suicides is increasing. In America, suicide is rare, but I have been assured that insanity is more common there than it is elsewhere.

These are different symptoms of the same malady.

Americans do not kill themselves no matter how distressed they may be, because religion forbids them to do so and because, in a way, materialism does not exist for them, even though the passion for material well-being is general.

Their will resists, but frequently their reason gives way.

In democratic times pleasures are more intense than they are in centuries of aristocracy, and, more important still, the number of people who savor them is infinitely greater. On the other hand, however, hopes and desires are more often disappointed, souls are more disturbed and anxious, and worries are more insistent.

Chapter 14

HOW THE TASTE FOR MATERIAL GRATIFICATIONS IS COMBINED IN AMERICA WITH LOVE OF LIBERTY AND CONCERN ABOUT PUBLIC AFFAIRS

WHEN a democratic state turns to absolute monarchy, the activity previously directed to both public and private affairs is suddenly concentrated on the latter, resulting for a time in great material prosperity, but the pace soon slows and growth of production ceases.

I doubt that one can cite a single manufacturing and commercial people from the Tyrians to the Florentines and the English that was not also a free people. Hence there is a close connection and a necessary relation between these two things: liberty and industry.

This is generally true of all nations but especially true of democratic nations.

I pointed out earlier how men who live in centuries of equality feel a continual need of association in order to procure for themselves nearly all the goods they covet. Furthermore, I showed how great political liberty perfects and popularizes the art of association. In such centuries, liberty is therefore particularly useful in the production of wealth. By contrast, we can see that despotism is particularly inimical to it.

The natural form of absolute power in democratic centuries is neither cruel nor savage but caviling and meddlesome. Although a despotism of this kind does not trample humanity underfoot, it is diametrically opposed to the genius of commerce and the instincts of industry.

Thus men in democratic times need to be free in order to procure for themselves more easily the material gratifications for which they constantly yearn.

Sometimes, however, their excessive taste for such gratifications delivers them into the hands of the first man to assert his mastery. The passion for well-being then turns against itself and unwittingly estranges itself from the object of its desires.

Indeed, there is a very dangerous phase in the life of a democratic people.

When the taste for material gratifications develops in such a people more rapidly than enlightenment or than the habits associated with liberty, there comes a time when men are driven wild and lose nearly all sense of themselves at the sight of new goods ripe for the taking. Solely preoccupied with the need to make their fortunes, they cease to be aware of the close connection that exists between the particular fortune of each one of them and the prosperity of all. There is no need to strip such citizens of their rights: they let those rights slip away voluntarily. Exercise of their political duties strikes them as a troublesome inconvenience that distracts them from their private business. Whether it be a question of choosing their representatives, backing up the authorities with force, or joining with others to deal with common affairs, time is short, and they cannot waste their precious moments in pointless activities. Such pastimes of the idle are inappropriate for serious men taken up with life's serious interests. The people who think this way believe that they are adhering to the doctrine of self-interest, but their idea of that doctrine is crude at best, and in order to tend to what they call their affairs, they neglect the chief affair, which is to remain their own masters.

Because the citizens who work do not choose to turn their minds to the public's business, and because the class that might take this chore upon itself to fill its hours of leisure no longer exists, the place of the government is, in a sense, empty.

If, at this critical juncture, a shrewd and ambitious man happens to seize power, he will find nothing standing between him and every imaginable kind of usurpation.

As long as he devotes some time to making sure that material interests prosper, people will be quite ready to overlook everything else. He must uphold good order above all. Men whose passions run to material gratifications will usually be aware of the ways in which the unrest associated with liberty disrupts well-being before they notice how liberty helps to procure it. Let even the slightest rumor of public passions intrude upon the petty pleasures of their private lives and they will become aroused and anxious. For some time thereafter,

fear of anarchy will keep them in constant suspense and prepared to abandon liberty at the first sign of disorder.

I am quite prepared to concede that public peace is a great
good, yet I do not want to forget that every nation that has
ended in tyranny has come to that end by way of good order.
It certainly does not follow from this that peoples should
scorn public peace, but neither should they be satisfied with
that and nothing more. A nation that asks nothing of government but the maintenance of order is already a slave in the
depths of its heart; it is a slave of its well-being, ready for the
man who will put it in chains.

In such a nation the despotism of factions is no less to be
feared than the despotism of one man.

When the mass of citizens is willing to concern itself only
with private affairs, not even the smallest parties need abandon hope of seizing control of public affairs.

At such times it is not uncommon to find a multitude represented on the world's vast stage by a few men, just as in the
theater. Those few alone speak in the name of an absent or
inattentive crowd. They alone act amid universal immobility.
They decide everything to suit themselves, changing laws and
exerting tyrannical control over mores at will, and it is astonishing to see how few, how weak, and how unworthy are the
hands into which a great people can fall.

Americans have thus far had the good fortune to avoid all
the pitfalls I have just indicated, and for that they truly deserve our admiration.

There is perhaps no country on earth where one meets
fewer idle people than in America, or where all who work are
more passionately devoted to the quest for well-being. Though
the American passion for physical gratifications may be violent, at least it is not blind, and reason, though powerless to
moderate it, does guide it.

An American will attend to his private interests as though
he were alone in the world, yet a moment later he will dedicate himself to the public's business as though he had forgotten them. At times he seems animated by the most selfish
greed, and at other times by the most ardent patriotism. The
human heart cannot be divided this way. The inhabitants of

the United States alternately exhibit a passion for well-being and a passion for liberty so strong and so similar that one can only believe that the two passions are conjoined and confounded somewhere in their souls. Indeed, Americans see their liberty as the best instrument and strongest guarantee of their well-being. They love each of the two things through the other. Hence they do not think that public affairs are none of their business. On the contrary, they believe that their chief business is to secure for themselves a government that will allow them to acquire the goods they desire and that will not interfere with the peaceful enjoyment of those they have acquired already.

Chapter 15

HOW RELIGIOUS BELIEFS SOMETIMES DIVERT THE AMERICAN SOUL TOWARD IMMATERIAL GRATIFICATIONS

In the United States, when the seventh day of each week arrives, the commercial and industrial life of the nation seems suspended. All the noise subsides and is replaced by a profound repose, or, rather, a contemplative solemnity. The soul at last reasserts itself and meditates upon its condition.

On this day, the places consecrated to commerce are deserted. Each citizen, accompanied by his children, goes to a temple. There he listens to strange discourses that hardly seem tailored for his ears. He hears of the countless evils caused by pride and lust. He is reminded of the need to control his desires and of the more refined pleasures associated with virtue alone, as well as of the true happiness that attends it.

When he returns home, he does not make straight for his business ledgers. He opens the book of Holy Scripture. There he finds sublime or touching depictions of the greatness and goodness of the Creator, of the infinite splendor of the works of God, of the high destiny reserved for men, of their duties, and of their rights to immortality.

So it is that the American now and then escapes from his own clutches, as it were, and, freeing himself for a moment from the petty passions that agitate his life and the fleeting interests that fill it, enters all at once into an ideal world where all is great, pure, and eternal.

In another part of this work I looked into the causes to which the maintenance of American political institutions must be attributed and came to the conclusion that religion was among the chief of these. Now that I am concerned with individuals, I come back to this cause, and I find that it is no less useful to each citizen than to the state as a whole.

Americans show by their practice that they are fully aware of the need to instill morality into democracy by way of religion.

What they think about themselves in this respect is a truth in which every democratic nation ought to be steeped.

I have no doubt that the social and political constitution of a people fosters certain beliefs and certain tastes, which then easily become second nature to it, while these same causes eliminate certain opinions and certain penchants without any active effort by the people in question and in a sense without their knowledge.

The whole art of the lawmaker lies in clearly discerning these natural inclinations of human societies in advance so as to determine where citizens need help in their efforts and where they need, rather, to be slowed down. Different times make for different obligations. The only thing that remains fixed is the goal toward which the human race ought always to be striving; the means of getting there are constantly changing.

Had I been born in an aristocratic century, into a nation where the hereditary wealth of some and the irremediable poverty of others not only diverted men from the idea of improvement but also kept souls as though numb in contemplation of another world, I would have liked to stimulate in the people an awareness of needs; I would have turned my thoughts to discovering the quickest and easiest way of satisfying the new desires that I created, and, by diverting the principal efforts of the human mind into physical pursuits, I would have tried to encourage the search for well-being.

If a few people became unduly passionate about the pursuit of wealth and demonstrated an excessive love of material gratifications, I would not have been alarmed. These particular features would soon have vanished from the common physiognomy.

Lawmakers in democracies have other concerns.

Give democratic peoples enlightenment and liberty and leave them alone. They will easily manage to extract from this world all the goods it has to offer. They will perfect each of the useful arts and daily make life more convenient, comfortable, and mild. Their social state naturally pushes them in this direction. I have no fear that anything will stop them.

Though man delights in this proper and legitimate search for well-being, there is reason to fear that he may in the end lose the use of his most sublime faculties, and that, while bent on improving everything around him, he may ultimately degrade himself. There, and nowhere else, lies the peril.

Hence lawmakers in democracies and all decent and enlightened men who live in them must apply themselves unstintingly to the task of uplifting souls and keeping them intent on heaven. All who are interested in the future of democratic societies must unite and together make constant efforts to spread a taste for the infinite, a sense of greatness, and a love of immaterial pleasures.

So if you encounter among the opinions of a democratic people any of those wicked theories that intimate that everything perishes with the body, you must regard those who profess such theories as natural enemies of the people.

There are many things about the materialists that offend me. Their doctrines seem to me pernicious, and their pride revolts me. If their system were of any possible use to man, it would seem to be in giving him a modest idea of himself. But the materialists do not make this point clearly. When they have done enough in their estimation to prove that they are mere brutes, they strut about as proudly as if they had proven they were gods.

Materialism in any nation is a dangerous malady of the human spirit, but it is particularly to be feared in a democratic people, because it weds with marvelous ease the defect of the heart most commonly found in democratic peoples.

Democracy encourages the taste for material gratifications. If this taste becomes excessive, it soon leads men to believe that everything is mere matter, and materialism in turn adds to the forces that propel pursuit of those same gratifications with wild ardor. Such is the fatal circle into which democratic nations are driven. It is good for them to see the danger and pull back.

Most religions are merely general, simple, and practical means of teaching men the immortality of the soul. This is the greatest benefit that a democratic people can derive from its beliefs, and it is what makes beliefs more necessary to such a people than to all others.

Therefore, when any religion whatsoever has sunk deep roots in a democracy, beware of disturbing it. Preserve it carefully, rather, as the most precious legacy of aristocratic centuries. Do not attempt to deprive men of their old religious opinions in order to replace them with new ones, lest the soul, in passing from one faith to another and finding itself momentarily devoid of belief, prove so receptive to the love of material gratifications that this love comes to fill the void entirely.

Metempsychosis is surely not more reasonable than materialism, yet if a democracy were absolutely obliged to choose between the two, I would not hesitate: its citizens, to my mind, would be in less danger of reducing themselves to brutes by thinking that the soul of a man might pass into the body of a pig than by believing that it is nothing.

Belief in an immaterial and immortal principle united for a time with matter is so necessary to the grandeur of man that its effects are still striking even when it is not linked to assessment of rewards and punishments and one believes simply that after death, the divine principle contained in man is absorbed in God or goes to animate another creature.

Even those who subscribe to such beliefs consider the body to be the secondary and inferior portion of our nature, and they scorn it even as they experience its influence, while they have a natural esteem and secret admiration for the immaterial part of man, even though they sometimes refuse to submit to its dominion. This is enough to give a certain loftiness to their ideas and tastes and to make them strive in a disinterested way, and as though of their own accord, toward pure sentiments and great thoughts.

There is no certainty that Socrates and his school had any very definite opinions about what was supposed to happen to man in the other life, but the one belief they did adhere to, that the soul has nothing in common with the body and lives on after it, was enough to give Platonic philosophy the sublime spirit that is its distinguishing characteristic.

When one reads Plato, it becomes clear that many writers both before and during his time advocated materialism. The works of those writers either have not survived or have come down to us only in very fragmentary form. The same is true of nearly every century: most of the great literary reputations were linked to spiritualism. The instinct and taste of the human race support this doctrine. They often save it from men themselves and keep the names of those who subscribe to it from sinking into oblivion. Hence one must not believe that the passion for material gratifications and the opinions associated with it can satisfy an entire people at any time, and regardless of what its political state might be. The heart of man is vaster than people imagine. It can entertain both a taste for the goods of this earth and a love of the goods of heaven at the same time. At times it may seem to surrender utterly to one of the two, but it never goes for long without thinking of the other.

If it is easy to see that it is particularly important to make sure that spiritualist opinions prevail in democratic times, it is not easy to say what those who govern democratic peoples should do to bring this about.

I do not believe that official philosophies can either prosper or endure, and as for state religions, I have always thought that while in certain instances they may temporarily serve the interests of the political powers, sooner or later they inevitably prove fatal to the church.

Nor am I among those who hold that in order to exalt religion in the eyes of the people and do honor to the spiritualism that it preaches, it is wise by some indirect means to grant the ministers of religion a political influence that the law denies them.

I am so thoroughly aware of the almost inevitable dangers that beliefs face when their interpreters become involved in public affairs, and I am so convinced that Christianity must be maintained at all cost in the new democracies, that I would rather chain priests inside their sanctuaries than allow them to venture out.

What means remain to authority, then, to bring men back to spiritualist opinions or to keep them within the religion that prompts such opinions?

What I am about to say will do me no good in the eyes of politicians. I believe that the only effective way for governments to honor the dogma of the immortality of the soul is to act every day as though they believed in it themselves. And I believe that it is only by conforming scrupulously to religious morality in great affairs that they can boast of teaching citizens to know it, love it, and respect it in small ones.

Chapter 16

HOW EXCESSIVE LOVE OF
WELL-BEING CAN IMPAIR IT

THERE is more of a connection than people think between perfection of the soul and improvement of the goods of the body. Man can leave these two things distinct and contemplate each of them alternately, but he cannot separate them entirely without ultimately losing sight of both.

The animals have the same senses as we do and nearly the same appetites: there are no material passions that we do not share with them, and whose seed cannot be found in a dog as well as in ourselves.

Why is it, then, that animals know how to provide only for their primary and crudest needs, while we vary our pleasures endlessly and add to them constantly?

What makes us superior in this respect to the beasts is that we use our souls to find material goods to which they are led by instinct alone. In man, the angel teaches the brute the art of achieving satisfaction. It is because man is capable of rising above the goods of the body and scorning even life itself, something of which the beasts have no idea whatsoever, that he can multiply those same goods to a degree they cannot even begin to imagine.

Anything that elevates, enlarges, and expands the soul makes it more capable of succeeding even in those of its undertakings where it is not at issue.

By contrast, anything that enervates or debases the soul weakens it for every purpose, the most important as well as the least important, and threatens to make it as impotent for the former as for the latter. Thus, the soul must remain great and strong, if only to be in a position on occasion to lend its strength and grandeur to the service of the body.

Should men ever manage to content themselves with material goods, there is reason to believe that they would gradually lose the art of producing them and end up enjoying them indiscriminately and without progress, like brutes.

Chapter 17

HOW, IN TIMES OF EQUALITY AND DOUBT, IT IS IMPORTANT TO SET DISTANT GOALS FOR HUMAN ACTIONS

In centuries of faith, people locate the ultimate purpose of life after life.

Hence the men who live in such times naturally and in a sense involuntarily become accustomed to contemplating, for years on end, a fixed objective toward which they advance steadily, and by imperceptible degrees they learn to repress a thousand fleeting desires the better to gratify the one great and permanent desire that torments them. When these same men turn their attention to earthly matters, the same habits reassert themselves. Such men will easily ascribe a definite and general purpose to their actions here below, a purpose toward which all their efforts can be directed. They do not launch new ventures every day but have fixed designs, which they do not tire of pursuing.

This explains why the accomplishments of religious peoples have often proved durable. Their concern with the other world, it seems, reveals to them the great secret of success in this one.

Religions inculcate the general habit of acting with an eye to the future. In so doing, they contribute as much to the happiness of this world as to the felicity of the other. This is one of their most salient political characteristics.

As the light of faith dims, however, man's vision becomes more constricted, and with each passing day the objectives of human action come to seem nearer.

Once men stop worrying about what is to come when their lives are over, they lapse easily into that state of complete and brutish indifference to the future that is only too consistent with certain instincts of the human species. As soon as they lose the habit of situating their principal hopes in the long run, their natural inclination is to seek to satisfy their slightest desires without delay. The moment they despair of living for an eternity, they are inclined, it seems, to act as though they had but a single day's existence allotted to them.

In centuries of disbelief, therefore, there is always reason to fear that men will perpetually give in to whatever desires chance to arise each day and, giving up entirely on obtaining those things that can only be obtained by dint of long effort, will found nothing great or peaceful or durable.

If, in a people so disposed, the social state should chance to become democratic, the danger I am warning of increases.

When everyone is constantly seeking to change places, and all are free to enter a vast competitive arena, and riches are accumulated and dissipated in the blink of an eye under the tumultuous conditions of democracy, the mind becomes acquainted with the idea of sudden and easy fortune and of great wealth easily won and lost, as well as with the image of chance in all its forms. The instability of the social state encourages the natural instability of human desires. Amid these perpetual fluctuations of fate, the present looms large; it hides the future, which fades from view, and men no longer wish to think beyond tomorrow.

In countries where, as a result of some misfortune, irreligion is combined with democracy, philosophers and people in government must strive constantly to make men look further into the future in setting goals for their actions. This is their most important business.

The moralist, unable to escape his time and country, must learn to defend himself where he stands. He must strive constantly to show his contemporaries that despite the perpetual flux of everything around them, it is easier than they imagine to conceive and execute long-range projects. He must show them that even though the face of humanity has changed, the methods that men can use to achieve prosperity in this world remain the same, and that in democratic nations it is the same as elsewhere: only by resisting the myriad petty and particular passions of everyday life can man satisfy the general passion for happiness that torments him.

The task of those who govern is no less clearly marked out.

In every age it is important for those who rule nations to act with an eye to the future, but this is even more important in democratic and unbelieving centuries. By acting this way, the leaders of democracies not only see to it that public affairs prosper but also set an example that teaches private citizens the art of dealing with private affairs.

Those who govern must do all they can to banish chance from the world of politics.

In an aristocratic country, the sudden and undeserved promotion of a courtier has only a fleeting impact, because the whole range of institutions and beliefs normally forces men to proceed slowly along paths from which they may never depart.

Nothing is more pernicious, however, than to hold out similar examples to a democratic people, for they encourage it to follow a penchant that everything else encourages as well. Hence it is primarily in times of skepticism and equality that one must take care to ensure that the favor of the people or the prince, which chance may confer or withhold, does not take the place of knowledge or service. It is desirable that every advancement should be seen as the fruit of some effort, so that greatness is not too easily acquired and ambition is obliged to set its sights on a goal for a long time before achieving it.

Governments must strive to restore men's taste for the future, which is no longer inspired by religion and the social state, and without saying so they must teach citizens the daily practical lesson that wealth, fame, and power are the rewards for work; that great success comes to those who sustain the desire for it over a long period of time; and that nothing durable is acquired without effort.

When men are used to predicting long in advance what will happen to them here below and to thriving on their hopes for the future, it becomes difficult for them always to confine their thoughts within life's exact boundaries, and they are quite prepared to transcend those limits and cast an eye on what lies beyond.

I have no doubt that instilling in citizens the habit of thinking about the future in this world gradually moves them, without their knowledge, closer to religious belief.

Thus the means that allow men, up to a point, to do without religion are perhaps in the end the only means left of bringing the human race back to faith, roundabout and long though the path may be.

Chapter 18

WHY ALL RESPECTABLE
OCCUPATIONS ARE REPUTED
HONORABLE AMONG AMERICANS

AMONG democratic peoples, where there is no hereditary wealth, everyone works in order to live, or has worked, or was born to people who worked. The idea of work as a necessary, natural, and respectable condition of humanity is therefore evident wherever one looks.

Not only is work not regarded by democratic peoples as dishonorable, it is in fact seen as honorable. Prejudice is not against it but for it. In the United States a rich man feels that he owes it to public opinion to devote his leisure time to some productive or commercial venture or public duty. He would expect his reputation to suffer if he spent his life doing nothing but living. The reason why so many wealthy Americans come to Europe is to avoid this obligation to work. In Europe they find the rubble of aristocratic societies in which idleness is still honored.

Equality not only rehabilitates the idea of work, it exalts the idea of work for money.

In aristocracies, what is held in contempt is not precisely work but work for profit. Work is glorious when inspired by ambition or pure virtue. Under aristocracy, however, it is a frequent occurrence that the man who works for honor is not insensible to the lure of gain. But these two desires are joined only in the uttermost depths of his soul. He takes great pains to hide from all eyes the place where the two are wed. He is apt to hide it from himself. In aristocratic countries, there are few public officials who do not insist that their service to the state is disinterested. Their compensation is a minor matter to which they give little thought and pretend to give none at all.

Thus the idea of gain remains distinct from that of work. Though they be joined in the act, the past separates them.

In democratic societies, by contrast, these two ideas are always visibly wedded. Since the desire for well-being is universal, fortunes are modest and temporary, and everyone needs to add to his resources or prepare to pass resources on to his children, everyone is well aware that gain is, if not the whole reason why they work, then at least part of the reason. Even those who act primarily in the hope of glory inevitably come around to the idea that this is not their only motivation, and they discover, however they may feel about it, that the desire to live coexists in them with the desire to lead an illustrious life.

When, on the one hand, work seems to all citizens an honorable necessity of the human condition and, on the other hand, it is clear that work is always done, at least in part, in exchange for compensation, the huge gap that formerly separated the various occupations in aristocratic societies disappears. Although occupations are not all similar, they have at least one trait in common.

There is no occupation in which people do not work for money. The compensation that all occupations share creates a certain family resemblance among them.

This explains the opinions that Americans have of the various professions.

American servants do not feel degraded because they work, for everybody around them is working. They do not feel degraded by the idea of receiving a wage, for the president of the United States also works for a wage. He is paid to command, just as they are paid to serve.

In the United States, some occupations are more arduous or more lucrative than others, but they are never either high or low. Every respectable occupation is honorable.

Chapter 19

WHY NEARLY ALL AMERICANS ARE INCLINED TO ENTER INDUSTRIAL OCCUPATIONS

O F all the useful arts, agriculture is perhaps the slowest to be perfected in democratic nations. It often seems to be standing still, because any number of other useful arts seem to be moving ahead so rapidly.

By contrast, nearly all the tastes and habits born of equality are naturally conducive to commerce and industry.

Take a man who is active, enlightened, free, well-off, and full of desires. He is too poor to live in idleness but wealthy enough to feel in no immediate fear of need, and he is thinking about improving his lot. This man has developed a taste for material gratifications. Countless others are indulging this taste before his eyes, and he himself has begun to yield to it and is burning to increase his means of satisfying it still more. But life is passing, and time is short. What is he to do?

Cultivation of the soil promises results that are almost certain, but slow. Wealth is amassed only gradually and by dint of much effort. Agriculture suits only the rich, who already have much more than they need, or the poor, who ask only to live. Our man's mind is made up: he will sell his field, leave his home, and take up some risky but lucrative occupation.

Now, people of this sort abound in democratic societies, and as equality of conditions becomes greater, their number increases.

Thus democracy not only multiplies the number of workers, it leads men into one line of work rather than another. It takes away their taste for agriculture and orients them toward commerce and industry.[1]

This spirit can be seen in even the wealthiest citizens.

[1]It has often been remarked that industrials and merchants have an immoderate taste for material pleasures, and for this commerce and industry have been blamed. Here, I believe, the effect has been mistaken for the cause.

It is not commerce and industry that prompt in men a taste for material pleasures but rather the taste for material pleasures that leads men into in-

In democratic countries, no matter how opulent we suppose a man to be, he will almost always be dissatisfied with his fortune, because he is less wealthy than his father and fears that his sons will be less wealthy than himself. Hence most wealthy people in democracies dream constantly of ways to acquire wealth, and they naturally look to commerce and industry, which strike them as the quickest and most powerful means of doing so. In this respect they share the instincts of the poor man without having his needs, or, rather, they are driven by the most imperious of all needs: not to come down in the world.

In aristocracies, the wealthy also govern. The constant attention they devote to great public affairs distracts them from the petty cares associated with commerce and industry. If, despite this, one of them should by chance wish to go into trade, the corporate will of the aristocracy as a whole will immediately stand in his way. For, try as one might to rebel against the law of numbers, one can never completely escape its force, and even within those aristocratic bodies that most stubbornly refuse to recognize the rights of the national majority, there arises a particular majority, which governs.*

In democratic countries, where money, rather than bringing those who have it to power, often excludes them from it, the rich do not know what to do with their leisure. The restlessness and scope of their desires, the extent of their resources, the taste for the extraordinary, which those who rise above the crowd in any way whatsoever almost always feel, press them to act. The only avenue open to them is that of commerce. In democracies, nothing is greater or more splendid than commerce. It is commerce that draws the attention

---

dustrial and commercial careers, where they hope to satisfy themselves more completely and rapidly.

If commerce and industry increase the desire for well-being, that is because any passion is fortified as one becomes more preoccupied with it and is increased by all the efforts that one devotes to assuaging it. Anything that causes love of worldly goods to predominate in the human heart develops industry and commerce. Equality is one such cause. It encourages commerce, not directly by giving men a taste for trade but indirectly by fortifying and generalizing the love of well-being in their souls.

*See Note XIX, page 359.

of the public and fires the imagination of the crowd. All energetic passions are directed toward it. Nothing can prevent the rich from engaging in it, neither their own prejudices nor those of others. In democracies, the rich never constitute a corporation with its own mores and discipline. The particular ideas of their class do not hold them back, and the general ideas of their country propel them forward. Since, moreover, the great fortunes that one finds in a democratic country are almost always commercial in origin, it takes several generations for the possessors of those fortunes to shed the habits of trade entirely.

Confined within the narrow space left them by politics, the rich in democracies therefore throw themselves into commercial ventures of every description. There they can extend themselves and put their natural advantages to use. The very boldness and magnitude of their industrial ventures should in a sense be used to gauge how little store they would have set by industry had they been born into an aristocracy.

A similar remark applies, moreover, to all men in democracies, be they poor or rich.

Those who live amid democratic instability have the image of chance constantly before their eyes, and eventually they come to love all undertakings in which chance plays a role.

Hence they are all propelled toward commerce, not only for the promise of gain it affords but also for love of the emotions it occasions.

It is only half a century since the United States of America emerged from the colonial dependence in which it was kept by England. The number of large fortunes in the country is quite small, and capital is still scarce. Yet no people on earth has made more rapid progress in commerce and industry than the Americans. They are today the second leading maritime nation in the world, and although their manufacturing has to contend with almost insurmountable natural obstacles, it continues to make new advances daily.

In the United States, the greatest industrial ventures are completed without difficulty because the entire population is involved in industry, and the poorest citizen willingly joins forces with the most opulent to ensure its success. It is a source of constant surprise to see what vast projects are carried out easily by a nation that in a sense has no rich people. Only yesterday did the Americans arrive on the soil they now inhabit, and already they have stood the whole natural order on its head for their own profit. They have linked the Hudson to the Mississippi and connected the Atlantic Ocean to the Gulf of Mexico across the more than five hundred leagues of continent that separate the two bodies of water. The longest railroad lines that have been built to this day are in America.

What strikes me most in the United States, however, is not the extraordinary size of some industrial enterprises but the countless number of small firms.

Nearly all farmers in the United States combine some form of commerce with agriculture. Most of them have turned agriculture into a form of commerce.

It is unusual for an American grower to settle permanently on the land he occupies. In the new provinces of the West especially, a man will clear a field in order to resell it and not to harvest a crop from it. He will build a farm in the expectation that the nature of the region will soon change as its population increases, so that he will be able to obtain a good price for it.

Every year, people from the North swarm into the South and settle in regions where cotton and sugar cane are grown. These people cultivate the earth for the purpose of making it produce enough in a few years to make them rich, and they already look forward to the day when they will be able to return to the place of their birth to enjoy the nest egg thus acquired. Americans therefore carry the spirit of trade over into agriculture, and their industrial passions reveal themselves there as they do elsewhere.

Americans are making immense progress in industry because they all engage in it at once, and for the same reason they are subject to very unexpected and formidable industrial crises.

Since they are all engaged in commerce, their commerce is susceptible to influences so numerous and so complex that it is impossible to foresee the troubles they can cause. Since each of them is involved to one degree or another in industry, all private fortunes are set reeling at once by the slightest economic tremor, and the state totters.

Recurrent industrial crises are, I believe, an endemic malady of democratic nations today. This malady can be made less dangerous, but it cannot be cured, because it is due not to an accident but to the very temperament of the peoples in question.

Chapter 20

HOW INDUSTRY COULD GIVE RISE
TO AN ARISTOCRACY

I HAVE shown how democracy encourages the development of industry and increases the number of industrial workers without limit. We shall now look at the roundabout way in which industry might well in turn lead men back to aristocracy.

It has been found that when a worker spends every day working on the same detail of a product, the finished article is produced more easily, more quickly, and more economically.

It has also been found that the larger the scale of an industrial enterprise, with abundant capital and abundant credit, the cheaper its products.

These truths have been dimly recognized for a long time, but in recent years they have been conclusively proven. They are already being applied to several very important industries, and less important industries are taking them up in their turn.

I see nothing in the world of politics that ought to concern lawmakers more than these two new axioms of industrial science.

When an artisan devotes himself constantly and exclusively to the fabrication of a single article, he eventually develops a remarkable dexterity in doing that job. But at the same time he loses the general faculty of applying his mind to the direction of the work. Every day he becomes more skillful and less industrious, and we may say of him that the man is degraded as the workman is perfected.

What should we expect of a man who has spent twenty years of his life making pinheads? And to what can he henceforth apply that powerful human intellect that has often stirred the world, other than the search for the best way of making pinheads?

When a worker has spent a considerable portion of his life this way, his thought invariably revolves around the daily object of his labors. His body acquires certain fixed habits that it cannot shed. In a word, he belongs not to himself any longer but to the occupation he has chosen. It does not matter how much laws and mores have done to break down the barriers surrounding this man and to open up a thousand varied roads to fortune. An industrial theory more powerful than mores and laws has tied him to a trade and in many cases a location he cannot quit. It has assigned him a certain place in society, from which he cannot exit. In the midst of universal change, it has immobilized him.

As the principle of division of labor is more thoroughly applied, the worker becomes weaker, more limited, and more dependent. The art progresses, the artisan regresses. Furthermore, as the scale of manufacturing and capital investment increases, products improve and become cheaper, and as people begin to realize this, very wealthy and very enlightened men move in to exploit industries that had previously been left to ignorant or hard-pressed artisans. These men are attracted by the magnitude of the effort required and the immensity of the results to be obtained.

Thus as industrial science steadily debases the class of workers, it raises the class of masters.

While the worker increasingly concentrates his intellect on the study of single details, the master daily surveys a much vaster range of things, and his mind expands as the worker's contracts. Before long, the worker has no need of anything but physical strength without intelligence; the master needs science, and almost genius, in order to succeed. One comes more and more to resemble the administrator of a vast empire, and the other to resemble a brute.

In this respect, therefore, master and worker are not alike at all, and with each passing day they become increasingly different. They are joined only in the sense of being the two extreme links of a long chain. Each one occupies a place that is made for him, which he does not leave. One is in a state of constant, strict, and necessary dependence on the other and seems born to obey, as the other seems born to command.

What is this, if not aristocracy?

As conditions in the body of the nation move toward greater and greater equality, the need for manufactured objects spreads and increases in intensity, and the low cost that brings such objects within reach of modest fortunes becomes an increasingly important ingredient of success.

Every day, therefore, increasingly opulent and enlightened men devote their wealth and knowledge to industry and seek, by opening large plants with a strict division of labor, to satisfy the new desires that crop up on every side.

Thus, as the mass of the nation turns to democracy, the particular class that is concerned with industry becomes more aristocratic. Men appear to be increasingly similar in the one arena and increasingly different in the other, and the increase of inequality in the smaller society is proportionate to the decrease of inequality in the larger one.

So when one goes back to the source, what one finds is that aristocracy seems to emerge from the very midst of democracy as the result of a natural effort.

But this aristocracy does not resemble any of the ones that preceded it.

Note, first of all, that because it devotes itself solely to industry and to certain industrial occupations, it is an exception, a monster, in relation to the social state as a whole.

The small aristocratic societies that certain industries constitute within the vast democracies of today resemble the great aristocratic societies of old in that they comprise a small number of very opulent men and a very wretched multitude.

The poor have few ways of escaping their condition and becoming rich, but the rich are always becoming poor or quitting business with the profits they have amassed. Thus the elements of the poor class are almost fixed, but the elements of the rich class are not. To tell the truth, although there are rich people, the rich do not exist as a class, because rich people have no common spirit or objectives or traditions or hopes. Hence there are members but no body.

Not only are the rich not solidly united among themselves, but there is no genuine bond between the poor man and the rich man.

They are not fixed in place, side by side, in perpetuity. At any given moment, interest may bring them together or drive them apart. The workman is dependent on masters in general but not on any master in particular. The two men see each other at the factory but have nothing to do with each other anywhere else, and while they come into contact at one point, in all other respects they remain distant. The manufacturer asks nothing of the worker but his labor, and the worker expects nothing from the manufacturer but his wages. The former makes no promise to protect, the latter no promise to defend, and neither habit nor duty creates a permanent bond between them.

The aristocracy that is based on trade almost never settles amidst the industrial population that it directs. Its goal is not to govern that population but to use it.

An aristocracy so constituted cannot have much of a hold on the people it employs. Should it chance to gain such a hold for a moment, the people will soon escape its grasp. It does not know how to exert its will and cannot act.

The territorial aristocracy of centuries past was obliged by law, or believed itself to be obliged by mores, to aid its servants and assuage their miseries. But today's manufacturing aristocracy, having impoverished and brutalized the men it uses, abandons them in times of crisis and turns them over to public assistance to be fed. This is a natural consequence of what has been said thus far. Between the worker and the master, relations are frequent, but no true association exists.

All things considered, I believe that the manufacturing aristocracy that we see rising before our eyes is one of the harshest that has ever existed on earth. But it is also one of the most limited and least dangerous.

Nevertheless, friends of democracy must keep an anxious eye peeled in this direction at all times. For if permanent inequality of conditions and aristocracy are ever to appear in the world anew, it is safe to predict that this is the gate by which they will enter.

PART III

*Influence of Democracy on
Mores Properly So-Called*

Chapter 1

HOW MORES BECOME MILDER AS CONDITIONS BECOME MORE EQUAL

WE have seen that conditions have been tending toward equality for several centuries, and we have also found that mores are becoming milder. Are these two things merely contemporaneous, or is there some hidden connection between them, so that progress in one inevitably spurs progress in the other?

Any number of causes may conspire to make the mores of a people less coarse, but the most powerful of those causes, to my mind, is equality of conditions. Equality of conditions and increasing mildness of mores are therefore not simply contemporary events in my eyes, they are also correlated facts.

When fabulists want us to take an interest in the actions of animals, they give those animals human ideas and passions. Poets do the same when they speak of spirits and angels. There is no misery so deep or felicity so pure that it can seize the mind or grip the heart unless what we are shown in alien guise is a representation of ourselves.

This is directly applicable to the subject that concerns us now.

When all men are irrevocably ranked by profession, property, and birth in an aristocratic society, the members of each class see themselves as children of the same family and therefore feel a constant and active sympathy for one another that can never exist to the same degree among the citizens of a democracy.

This is not the case, however, when it comes to the feelings of the classes toward one another.

In an aristocratic people, each caste has its opinions, its feelings, its rights, its mores, and its own separate existence. Thus, the men who belong to a particular caste do not resemble everyone else. They do not share the same way of thinking or feeling, and they scarcely even think of themselves as belonging to the same humanity.

Hence they cannot fully understand what others feel or judge them on the basis of their own experience.

At times we do find them keen to help one another out, but that is not inconsistent with what has been said thus far.

The same aristocratic institutions that had made creatures of the same species so different nevertheless bound them together with a very tight political bond.

Although the serf had no natural interest in the fate of nobles, he nonetheless felt obliged to dedicate himself to the service of the one noble who happened to be his lord. And although the noble believed himself to be of a different nature from the serfs, he nevertheless felt compelled by duty and honor to risk his life defending those who lived on his estates.

It is clear that these mutual obligations were born not of natural right but of political right, and that society was able to exact a greater commitment than humanity alone could have done. It was not the man as such that one felt obliged to support; it was the vassal or lord. Feudal institutions created acute sensitivities to the woes of certain men but not to the miseries of the human species. They endowed mores with generosity rather than kindness, and although they prompted great acts of devotion, they did not inspire genuine sympathies. For real sympathies exist only between similar people, and in aristocratic centuries people saw only members of their own caste as their fellows.

When the chroniclers of the Middle Ages, who all belonged by either birth or habit to the aristocracy, recount the tragic end of a noble, there is no end to their sorrow, whereas they can relate the massacre and torture of men of the people in a single breath without batting an eye.

The point is not that these writers harbored inveterate hatred or systematic contempt of the people. War between the various classes of the state had yet to be declared. They obeyed an instinct rather than a passion. Since they did not formulate a clear idea of the poor man's sufferings, they took little interest in his fate.

The same can be said about men of the people once the feudal bond was broken. The same centuries that saw so many heroic acts of devotion by vassals to their lords were also witness on occasion to extraordinary cruelties visited by the lower classes upon the upper.

Do not assume that this mutual insensitivity stemmed solely from want of order and enlightenment, for traces of it can be found in subsequent centuries, which, though orderly and enlightened, remained aristocratic.

In the year 1675, the lower classes of Brittany rose up against a new tax. These tumultuous protests were put down with unprecedented atrocity. This is how Mme de Sévigné, who witnessed these horrors, recounted them to her daughter:

> Les Rochers, 3 October 1675
> My God, daughter, how amusing your letter from Aix is! Re-read your letters, at least, before you send them. Allow yourself to be surprised by their delectable qualities, and with that pleasure console yourself for the trouble of writing so many of them. So you've kissed all Provence? It's not as satisfying to kiss all Brittany unless you like the smell of wine. Do you want news of Rennes? A tax of a hundred thousand *écus* has been imposed, and if such a sum is not found within twenty-four hours, it will be doubled and subject to collection by soldiers. The people from an entire main street were driven out and banished, and it was forbidden on pain of death to take in the inhabitants. So one saw all those wretched people — pregnant women, old men, children — milling about in tears outside the city gates with no idea where to go and nothing to eat and nowhere to sleep. The day before yesterday the fiddler who had begun the dance and instigated the theft of stamped paper was put to the wheel; he was quartered, and the four pieces of his body were displayed in four corners of the city. Sixty townspeople were arrested, and tomorrow the hangings begin. This province is a fine example for the rest, and it teaches them above all to respect governors and their wives and not to throw stones into their gardens.[1]
> Mme de Tarente took advantage of yesterday's magnificent weather to visit her woodlands. A room and a meal were not even considered. She passed through the customs gate and returned the same way.

In another letter, she adds:

> You are most amusing on the subject of our miseries. We're no longer being put to the wheel quite so much as before: one a week

---

[1]To appreciate the point of this final quip, one has to recall that Mme de Grignan was the wife of the governor of Provence.

to uphold justice. It's true that I now see hanging as a diversion. I have quite a different idea of justice since I've been in this part of the country. Your galley slaves strike me as a society of respectable people who have withdrawn from the world to lead quiet lives.

It would be a mistake to assume that Mme de Sévigné, the writer of these lines, was a selfish, barbarous creature. She loved her children dearly and was quite sensitive to the sufferings of her friends. It is clear from reading what she wrote that she treated her vassals and servants with kindness and indulgence. But Mme de Sévigné had no clear notion of what it meant to suffer when one was not a nobleman.

Nowadays, even the hardest of men, writing to the most insensitive of correspondents, would never dare to indulge in banter as heartless and cruel as that quoted above, and even if his private mores allowed him to do so, the general mores of the nation would prohibit it.

Why is that? Are we more sensitive than our fathers? I do not know, but of one thing I am certain: our sensibility extends to a wider range of objects.

When ranks in a nation are roughly equal and everyone thinks and feels in almost the same way, then each person can judge everyone else's sensations in an instant: all he has to do is cast a quick glance at himself. Hence there is no misery that he cannot readily conceive, or whose extent is not revealed to him by a secret instinct. No matter if strangers or enemies are involved: his imagination instantly puts him in their place. His pity is thereby tinged with something personal, causing him to suffer when the body of his fellow man is torn to pieces.

In democratic centuries, men rarely sacrifice themselves for one another, but they do exhibit a general compassion for all members of the human species. They do not inflict useless ills, and when they can relieve another person's pain without much harm to themselves, they take pleasure in doing so. They are not disinterested, but they are mild.

Even though Americans have in a sense reduced egoism to a social and philosophical theory, they are nevertheless highly susceptible to pity.

In no country is criminal justice more benignly administered than in the United States. While the English seem bound and determined to preserve bloody traces of the Middle Ages in their penal legislation, the Americans have virtually eliminated the death penalty from their codes.

North America is, I believe, the only region on earth where not a single citizen has been deprived of his life for a political offense for the past fifty years.

What clinches the proof that the singular mildness of Americans is primarily due to their social state is the way in which they treat their slaves.

All things considered, there is perhaps no European colony in the New World where the physical condition of Blacks is less harsh than in the United States. Yet slaves there still endure dreadful miseries and are repeatedly subjected to very cruel punishments.

It is easy to discover that the fate of these unfortunate wretches inspires little pity in their masters, who see slavery not only as a fact from which they profit but also as an evil that barely touches them. Thus, the same man who is full of humanity toward his fellow men when they are also his equals becomes insensitive to their sufferings once equality ceases.

This man's mildness must therefore be attributed to equality more than to civilization or enlightenment.

What I have just said about individuals also applies, up to a point, to peoples.

When each nation has its own distinct opinions, beliefs, laws, and customs, it sees itself as encompassing all of humanity and is impervious to any suffering but its own. If war breaks out between two peoples so disposed, it is sure to be waged barbarically.

In the most enlightened phase of Roman civilization, the Romans slit the throats of enemy generals after dragging them in triumph behind their chariots and threw prisoners to the beasts to entertain the people. Cicero, who moaned so loudly at the idea of a citizen's crucifixion, had not a harsh word to say about such atrocious abuses of victory. In his eyes, clearly, a foreigner did not belong to the same human species as a Roman.

By contrast, as peoples become increasingly similar to one another, they become more compassionate toward one another's miseries, and the law of nations becomes milder.

Chapter 2

HOW DEMOCRACY SIMPLIFIES AND EASES HABITUAL RELATIONS AMONG AMERICANS

DEMOCRACY does not create tight bonds among men, but it does make their habitual relations easier.

Two Englishmen meet by chance at the antipodes. They are surrounded by foreigners, whose language and mores are all but unknown to them.

At first these two men study each other with strange looks and a sort of secret anxiety. Then they will turn away or, should they approach each other, take care to talk about unimportant subjects in a stiff and distant manner.

Yet there is no hostility between them. They have never seen each other before and regard each other as perfectly respectable gentlemen. Why, then, are they so careful to avoid each other?

To understand this we must go back to England.

When men are classed by birth alone, independent of wealth, everyone knows precisely where he stands in the social hierarchy. He does not seek to climb and has no fear of falling. In a society organized in this way, men of different castes have little communication with one another, but when chance brings them together, they approach one another willingly, without hope or fear of being confounded. Their relations are not based on equality, but they are not stiff.

When the aristocracy of birth is supplanted by the aristocracy of money, things change.

Some people still enjoy quite considerable privileges, but the possibility of acquiring such privileges is open to all, from which it follows that those who possess them are constantly preoccupied with the fear of losing them or having to share them, and those who do not yet have them want to possess them at all cost, or, failing that, to appear to possess them, which is not impossible. Since a man's social value is no longer fixed in a visible and permanent way by blood and varies infinitely with wealth, ranks still exist, but it has become impossible to see clearly at first glance who occupies them.

The immediate result of this is that all citizens are secretly at war with one another. Some resort to a thousand artifices to infiltrate the rank above them, whether in reality or in appearance only. Others wage constant battle to repel those who would usurp their rights. Or, rather, the same man fights on both fronts, and, even as he tries to insinuate himself into the sphere above him, maintains his relentless opposition to the effort from below.

Such is the state of England today, and I believe that this state is primarily responsible for the situation I set forth in the foregoing paragraphs.

Because aristocratic pride is still very great among the English, while the boundaries of the aristocracy have become ambiguous, everyone lives in constant fear of presumptions upon his intimacy. Since it is impossible to judge at first glance the social situation of the people one meets, it is prudent to avoid contact with them. People are afraid that by rendering some minor service they will unwittingly enter into an unsuitable association. They are afraid of doing favors and will avoid a stranger's indiscreet greeting as scrupulously as they would deflect his hatred.

Many people adduce purely physical causes to explain the strikingly unsociable character of the English and their reserved and taciturn nature. I am willing to grant that blood counts for something, but I believe that the social state is far more important, as the American example proves.

In America, where privileges of birth never existed, and where wealth confers no particular rights on those who possess it, people who do not know one another easily frequent the same places and see neither advantage nor peril in communicating their thoughts freely. Should they meet by chance, they do not try to avoid one another. Their approach is therefore natural, frank, and open. They clearly have almost nothing to hope or fear from one another, and they are no more keen to show what place they occupy than they are to hide it. If their aspect is often cold and serious, it is never haughty or stiff, and when they do not speak to one another, it is because they are not in a mood to speak and not because they believe it to be in their interest to keep quiet.

In a foreign country, two Americans are friends at once simply because they are Americans. No prejudice keeps them apart, and their shared homeland draws them together. Identity of blood is not enough for two Englishmen; they need identity of rank to draw them together.

Americans are as fully aware as we are of the unsociable attitude of the English toward other Englishmen, and no less astonished by it. Yet the Americans are tied to the English by origin, religion, and language, and in part by mores. The only difference is their social state. Hence it seems fair to say that the reserve of the English stems far more from the country's constitution than from that of its citizens.

Chapter 3

WHY AMERICANS ARE SO SLOW TO TAKE OFFENSE IN THEIR COUNTRY AND SO QUICK TO TAKE OFFENSE IN OURS

LIKE all serious and reflective peoples, Americans have a vindictive temperament. They almost never forget an offense, but it is not easy to offend them, and their resentment is as slow to kindle as it is to subside.

In aristocratic societies, where a small number of individuals are in charge of everything, outward relations among men are subject to mostly stable conventions. So everyone thinks he knows precisely what signs are appropriate to indicate respect or good will, and etiquette is a science of which no one is supposed to be ignorant.

The customs of the leading class then serve as a model for all the others, in addition to which each of the other classes establishes its own separate code, to which all members of that class are required to conform.

Thus the rules of politeness are a complex piece of legislation, which it is difficult to master completely yet from which it is dangerous to deviate, so that every day there is a likelihood that people will repeatedly inflict or receive unintentionally cruel wounds.

But as distinctions of rank vanish and men of diverse education and birth mix and come together in the same places, agreement about the rules of proper behavior is almost impossible. Since the law is uncertain, disobeying it is no crime even in the eyes of those who know what it is. People therefore attach more importance to the substance of actions than to the form, and they are at once less civil and less quarrelsome.

There are countless minor marks of consideration to which an American attaches no importance. Either he does not see them as his due, or he assumes that other people are unaware of their being so. Hence he does not notice that he is being slighted or forgives the person who is slighting him. His manners become less refined and his mores simpler and more manly.

The reciprocal indulgence that Americans exhibit toward one another and the virile confidence they demonstrate also stem from a cause that is more general and more profound. I pointed to this same cause earlier, in the previous chapter.

In the United States, ranks differ only slightly in civil society and not at all in the political world. Hence an American does not feel obliged to treat any of his fellow men with particular care, nor would he dream of demanding special treatment for himself. Since he does not see that his interest lies in ardently seeking out the company of some of his fellow citizens, he finds it hard to imagine that anyone would reject his own company. Since he does not scorn others because of their condition, he cannot imagine that anyone would scorn him on such grounds, and unless he perceives a clear insult, he will not believe that anyone would wish to offend him.

The social state naturally disposes Americans not to take offense readily over minor matters. More than that, the democratic liberty they enjoy extends this forbearance to the national mores.

The political institutions of the United States bring citizens of all classes into constant contact and force them to pursue important ventures in common. People thus occupied scarcely have time to consider the details of etiquette and have too much of an interest in living together in harmony to dwell on them. Hence they easily become accustomed to considering the feelings and ideas rather than the manners of the people they meet and do not allow themselves to become incensed over trifles.

I have often noticed in the United States that it is not easy to make a man understand that his presence is unwelcome. Roundabout ways of accomplishing this are not always enough.

If I contradict an American at every turn in order to let him know that his expostulations bore me, I will only spur him on to further efforts of persuasion. If I maintain a stubborn silence, he will imagine that I am reflecting deeply on the truths he has laid before me. And if, at length, I abruptly take my leave, he will assume that some urgent business calls me elsewhere. Such a man will never understand that he exasperates me unless I tell him so, and there is no way for me to escape him except to become his mortal enemy.

What is surprising at first sight is that this same man, transported to Europe, immediately becomes so sensitive and difficult that I often find it as hard not to offend him as I previously found it to displease him. These two very different effects are produced by the same cause.

Democratic institutions generally give men a vast idea of their fatherland and of themselves.

The American leaves his country with a heart swollen with pride. He arrives in Europe and immediately notices that people there are not as preoccupied as he imagined with the United States and the great people that inhabits it. He begins to feel annoyed.

He has heard that conditions in our hemisphere are not equal. He notices that in fact traces of rank have not been altogether expunged from the nations of Europe, and that wealth and birth retain uncertain privileges that are as difficult for him to ignore as to define. This spectacle surprises and worries him, because it is entirely new to him. Nothing he has seen in his own country helps him to understand it. He is therefore profoundly unsure what place he should properly occupy in this half-destroyed hierarchy, among classes distinct enough to hate and despise one another yet similar enough that he is always on the point of confusing them. He is afraid of setting himself too high and even more of being ranked too low: these twin dangers plague his mind constantly and weigh upon everything he does and says.

Tradition has taught him that in Europe ceremonial ritual once varied infinitely with condition. This shadow cast by the past troubles him, and he is afraid of not receiving the respect he is due, all the more so in that he is not precisely sure what that might be. Thus he proceeds at all times as though beset by traps. For him, society is not relaxation but serious work. He weighs your every move, questions your gaze, and carefully analyzes your words lest they hide some insulting allusion. I am not sure that there has ever been a provincial nobleman as prickly about proper behavior as this American. He strives to conform to the most trivial rules of etiquette and will not permit any of those rules to be neglected as regards himself. He is both exceedingly scrupulous and exceedingly demanding. He would like to do enough but is afraid of doing too much, and since he is unfamiliar with the boundaries in both directions he maintains a perplexed and haughty reserve.

Nor is that all. Here is yet another complication of the human heart.

An American will talk all day long about the admirable equality that prevails in the United States. He will vociferously proclaim his pride in that equality on behalf of his country, but insofar as it pertains to himself he finds it privately distressing, and he aspires to demonstrate that he, for one, is an exception to the general order that he otherwise champions.

One seldom meets an American who is not keen to trace his ancestry back to the original founders of the colonies, and all America seemed to me blanketed with scions of the great families of England.

When an opulent American lands in Europe, his first concern is to surround himself with all the luxury that wealth can afford. He is so afraid that you will take him for an ordinary citizen of a democracy that he will daily bend himself every which way in order to offer you a new image of his wealth. He will usually stay in the most ostentatious part of town and surround himself at all times with numerous servants.

I once heard an American complain that the company to be met in the leading salons of Paris was invariably mixed. The prevailing taste struck him as not sufficiently pure, and he adroitly let slip his opinion that Parisian manners lacked refinement. He could not get used to seeing wit cloaked in such vulgar forms.

Such contrasts should come as no surprise.

If every last trace of the old aristocratic distinctions had not been so completely obliterated in America, Americans would be less simple and less tolerant in their own country and less demanding and affected in ours.

Chapter 4

CONSEQUENCES OF THE THREE PREVIOUS CHAPTERS

WHEN men feel a natural pity for one another's woes, and when easy and frequent relations bring them together every day and no susceptibility divides them, it is easy to see that they will help one another out when the need arises. When an American calls upon the cooperation of his fellow Americans, they seldom refuse, and I have often seen them offer their assistance spontaneously and enthusiastically.

When there is an accident on a public way, people will rush to the victim's aid from every direction. If a great and sudden misfortune should befall a family, a thousand strangers will generously open their purses. Modest but numerous gifts will pour in to alleviate the family's misery.

In the most civilized nations of the globe it is common for an unfortunate individual to find himself as lonely amid the crowd as the savage in his woods. This almost never happens in the United States. Americans, whose manners are always chilly and often coarse, almost never appear to be insensitive, and while they are not quick to offer their services, they do not refuse to render them.

None of this contradicts what I said earlier about individualism. Indeed, far from seeing these things as antagonistic, I see them as complementary.

Equality of conditions makes men aware of their independence but at the same time points up their weakness. They are free but vulnerable to a thousand accidents, and experience is not slow to teach them that although they do not usually need the help of others, there will almost inevitably come a time when they cannot do without it.

In Europe we see men who share the same profession voluntarily helping one another every day. All are exposed to the same ills. That is enough reason for them to seek mutual protection from those ills, no matter how hardened or selfish they may be in other respects. Thus, when one of them is in danger and others can save him by means of a small, temporary sacrifice or a sudden burst of energy, they do not fail to make the attempt. Not that they are profoundly interested in his fate, for if by chance their efforts to assist him should prove fruitless, they will immediately forget him and turn inward once again. But there exists a sort of tacit and almost involuntary agreement among these men, under the terms of which each one owes the others temporary support and may in turn claim the same for himself.

Extend to an entire people what I have just said about a single class and you will understand my thought.

Among the citizens of a democracy there does in fact exist a compact analogous to the one I have just described. Everyone feels subject to the same weakness and the same dangers, and interest as well as sympathy requires them to lend one another mutual assistance.

The more similar conditions become, the more men will show this reciprocal readiness to obligate themselves.

In democracies, where great boons are seldom granted, small favors are done constantly. Few men are prepared to sacrifice themselves, but all are willing to lend a helping hand.

Chapter 5

HOW DEMOCRACY MODIFIES RELATIONS BETWEEN SERVANT AND MASTER

An American who had traveled extensively in Europe once said to me:

The English treat their servants in a haughty and peremptory manner that we find shocking, yet the French are sometimes familiar or considerate toward their servants in ways that we find inconceivable. It almost seems that they are afraid to give orders. They are not good at keeping up the attitudes of superior and inferior.

This remark is accurate, and I have often made similar observations myself.

Of all the countries in the world today, I have always regarded England as the one where the bond of domestic service is tightest and France as the one where it is loosest. Nowhere else does the master stand as high or as low, it seems to me, as in these two countries.

Americans are situated between these two extremes.

This is the superficial and obvious fact. One has to delve deep into the past to discover its causes.

The world has yet to see a society in which conditions were so equal that there were neither rich nor poor and hence neither masters nor servants.

Democracy does not preclude the existence of these two classes of men, but it changes their spirit and modifies their relations.

In aristocratic nations, servants constitute a distinct class, which is as invariable as the class of masters. A fixed order is not slow to arise. In both classes, a hierarchy soon emerges, along with numerous classifications, conspicuous ranks, and generation after generation with no change in relative positions. They are two superimposed societies, always distinct from each other but subject to analogous principles.

The influence of this aristocratic constitution on the ideas and mores of the servants is scarcely less than on the ideas and mores of the masters, and although the effects are different, it is easy to see that the cause is the same.

Servants and masters are like small nations within the larger one. Out of their midst come ultimately certain enduring notions of justice and injustice. Different aspects of human behavior come to be seen in a particular light, which does not change. Within the society of servants, as in the society of masters, men exert substantial influence on one another. They acknowledge fixed rules, and in the absence of law are guided by what they encounter as public opinion. Orderly habits and a kind of discipline prevail.

These men, whose destiny is to obey, certainly do not understand glory, virtue, respectability, and honor in the same way as the masters. But they have formulated for themselves servants' notions of glory, virtue, and respectability and have developed an idea, if I may put it this way, of servile honor.[1]

One must not believe that because a class is low, all of its members are base at heart. This would be a great mistake. No matter how inferior the class may be, the man who is first in that class and never thinks of leaving it occupies an aristocratic position, which inspires in him lofty sentiments, haughty pride, and a self-respect that makes him fit to exemplify great virtues and perform extraordinary deeds.

Among aristocratic peoples it was not uncommon to find in the service of great lords noble and vigorous souls who bore servitude without feeling it and who submitted to the will of their masters without fear of their wrath.

This was almost never the case, however, in the lower ranks of the domestic class. One imagines that the lowest of the low in a hierarchy of valets is very low indeed.

The French coined a word expressly for the lowest of the aristocracy's servants. They called him *lackey*.

The word *lackey* was an extreme term to be used where no

---

[1] If one were to examine closely and in detail the chief opinions that guide the behavior of servants in an aristocracy, the analogy would seem even more striking. It is astonishing to find that these servants, like the proudest members of a feudal hierarchy, are characterized by pride of birth, respect for ancestors and descendants, contempt for those beneath them, fear of contact, and a taste for etiquette, tradition, and Antiquity.

other word would do to represent the lowest form of human baseness. Under the old monarchy, if one wished to portray a vile and degraded creature with a quick stroke, one said that he had "the soul of a lackey." That alone was enough to make the point fully and comprehensibly.

Permanent inequality of conditions not only results in servants' having certain particular virtues and vices but places them in a particular position relative to masters.

Among aristocratic peoples, the poor man is trained from infancy with the idea of being subject to command. Wherever he turns, he is immediately confronted with an image of hierarchy and an aspect of obedience.

In countries where permanent inequality of conditions prevails, the master therefore finds it easy to obtain the prompt, complete, respectful, and compliant obedience of his servants because those servants revere in him not only the master but the class of masters. He weighs upon their will with all the weight of the aristocracy.

He commands their actions; up to a point he also directs their thoughts. In aristocracies, the master, whether he knows it or not, often exerts a prodigious sway over the opinions, habits, and mores of those who obey him, and his influence extends much farther even than his authority.

In aristocratic societies, there are hereditary families of valets, just as there are hereditary families of masters. But in addition to that, the same families of valets will remain for generations with the same families of masters (they are like parallel lines, which never come together and never part). This profoundly alters mutual relations between the two orders of individuals.

Thus under aristocracy, even though master and servant have no natural resemblance — indeed, even though fortune, upbringing, opinions, and rights create an immense distance between them on the chain of being — time ultimately forges a bond between them. Shared memories going back over many years unite them, and no matter how different they may be, they become similar. Whereas in democracies, where they are by nature almost identical, they remain forever alien.

Among aristocratic peoples, the master therefore comes to look upon his servants as an inferior and secondary part of himself, and he often takes an interest in their lot as an ultimate extension of his own selfishness.

Servants, for their part, are not far from seeing themselves in the same light, and they will sometimes identify with the master in such a way that they eventually become his accessory in their own eyes as they are in his.

In aristocracies, the servant occupies a subordinate position, which he cannot leave. Next to him stands another man, who holds a superior rank that he cannot lose. On one side, obscurity, poverty, and obedience in perpetuity; on the other, glory, riches, and command in perpetuity. These conditions are always distinct and always close, and the bond that unites them is as durable as they are themselves.

In this extremity, the servant eventually loses interest in himself. He becomes detached; in a sense he deserts himself, or, rather, he invests himself entirely in his master. There he forges an imaginary personality. He likes to deck himself out in the riches of those from whom he takes orders. He glories in their glory, exults in their nobility, and feasts incessantly on borrowed grandeur, which he often values more than those who are truly and fully in possession of it.

In such a strange confusion of two existences there is something that is at once touching and ridiculous.

When the passions of masters are transported into the souls of valets, they assume the natural dimensions of the place they occupy; they shrink and stoop low. What was pride in the former becomes puerile vanity and miserable pretension in the latter. The servants of a great lord are usually quite exacting when it comes to the respect he is due and set more store by the least of his privileges than the lord himself does.

One still sometimes runs into these old servants of the aristocracy, the last of their breed.

In the United States I did not see anyone like this. Not only are Americans unfamiliar with men of this type, but it takes considerable effort to make them understand why such men exist. It is hardly less difficult for them to imagine such individuals than it is for us to imagine a Roman slave or a medieval serf. All these types of men are to one degree or another products of the same cause. They recede further from our view with each passing day and sink into the obscurity of the past, along with the social state that brought them into being.

Equality of conditions makes new beings of both the servant and the master and establishes new relations between them.

When conditions are almost equal, men change places constantly. A class of valets still exists, as does a class of masters, but neither is composed of an unvarying group of individuals, much less of families, and there is no more perpetuity in command than in obedience.

Since servants do not constitute a separate people, they have no customs, prejudices, or mores of their own. Among them one does not find a distinctive cast of mind or peculiar manner of feeling. They have no vices or virtues peculiar to their estate but share the enlightenment, ideas, sentiments, virtues, and vices of their contemporaries. And they may be either honest men or rogues, just as masters are.

Conditions are no less equal among servants than among masters.

Since we do not find obvious ranks or a permanent hierarchy in the servant class, we should not expect to encounter the extremes of degradation and grandeur that exist in the aristocracy of valets as they do in all aristocracies.

I never saw anything in the United States that called to mind the idea of the elite servant — an idea that lives on in European memory. But neither did I encounter the idea of the lackey. No trace of either remained.

In democracies servants are not only equal among themselves but also, in a sense, equal to their masters.

To understand this fully, explanation is required.

A servant may at any moment become a master, and he aspires to do so. Hence the servant is not a different man from the master.

Why, then, does one have the right to command, and what is it that compels the other to obey? A momentary and free accord of their two wills. Neither one is inferior to the other by nature; inferiority is simply a temporary effect of a contract. Within the limits of that contract, one is the servant and the other the master. Outside those limits, they are two citizens, two men.

What I beg the reader to consider well is that this is not simply a notion that servants conceive of their own estate. Masters see domestic service in the same light, and the precise limits of command and obedience are as firmly fixed in the mind of one as in the mind of the other.

When most citizens have enjoyed roughly similar conditions for a considerable period of time and equality is a long-standing and accepted fact, public understanding, which is never influenced by exceptions, generally ascribes certain limits to a man's value, and it is hard for any man to rise above or fall below those limits for any length of time.

To be sure, wealth and poverty, command and obedience, may accidentally put a great distance between one man and another, but no matter: public opinion, which is based on the ordinary order of things, pulls them back toward the common level and creates a sort of imaginary equality between them despite the actual inequality of their conditions.

Ultimately, this omnipotent opinion pervades the souls even of those whose interest might inspire them to resist it. It alters their judgment even as it subjugates their will.

In the depths of their souls, master and servant no longer see any profound dissimilarity between them, and they harbor neither hope nor fear of encountering any. Hence they are free of both contempt and anger and can look at one another without humility or pride.

The master deems the contract to be the sole source of his power, and the servant sees it as the only reason for his obedience. They do not dispute their relative positions. Each clearly recognizes what place he occupies and sticks to it.

Soldiers in our armies are recruited from more or less the same classes as officers and end up in the same posts. Outside the ranks the soldier sees himself as entirely equal to his commanders, and indeed he is, yet under the colors he has no objection to obeying orders, and his obedience, though voluntary and defined, is nonetheless prompt, precise, and unproblematic.

This will give some idea of what happens between servants and masters in a democracy.

It would be foolish to believe that, between a servant and a master in a democratic society, affection could ever arise as ardent and profound as that which is sometimes kindled in the breasts of servants under aristocracy, or that democracy should offer striking instances of self-sacrifice.

In aristocracies, servant and master see each other only occasionally and often speak only through intermediaries. Yet they are usually firmly devoted to each other.

In democratic nations, servant and master are quite close. They are in constant physical contact, yet their souls do not mix. They have common occupations but seldom have common interests.

Among these democratic peoples, the servant always sees himself as a temporary visitor in the home of his masters. He did not know their ancestors and will not see their descendants. He has no lasting expectations of them. Why would he confound his existence with theirs? What might prompt him to abandon himself in so singular a fashion? His relative position has changed; relations must change with it.

I would like to draw on the American example in support of what I have just said, but in order to do so I must make careful distinctions in regard to persons and places.

In the South of the Union, slavery exists. What I have just said is therefore inapplicable there.

In the North, most servants are freed slaves or children of freed slaves. These people occupy a contested position in the public's esteem: the law draws them toward the level of their masters; mores persistently push them away. They cannot clearly make out their own place and are almost always either insolent or cringing.

But in the same northern states, particularly in New England, one finds a substantial number of Whites who are willing, in return for wages, to submit temporarily to the will of people like themselves. I am told that these servants are usually meticulous and intelligent in fulfilling the duties of their estate and that even though they do not believe themselves to be naturally inferior to the person who gives them orders, they submit to those orders without difficulty.

To my way of thinking, those servants carried over into servitude some of the virile habits born of independence and equality. Having chosen a harsh condition, they did not try to escape it in some roundabout way, and they had enough self-respect not to refuse to obey masters to whom they had freely promised obedience.

Masters, for their part, insist only that their servants faithfully and scrupulously respect the terms of their contracts. They do not ask for respect. They do not require their servants' love or devotion. It is enough if they are scrupulous and honest.

Hence it is not correct to say that relations between servants and masters under democracy are disorderly. They exhibit order of another kind. The rule is different, but there is a rule.

I do not need to consider here whether the new estate that I have just described is inferior to the one that preceded it or simply different. It is enough for my purposes that it is regular and fixed. For what is most important to find among men is not order of a particular kind, but order as such.

What shall I say, though, about those sad and turbulent times when equality sets itself up amid the tumult of revolution, while democracy, having established itself in the social state, remains locked in strenuous struggle with prejudices and mores?

Already, law and to some extent opinion proclaim that no natural and permanent inferiority exists between servant and master. But this new faith has yet to penetrate to the innermost recesses of the master's mind, or, rather, his heart rejects it. In the privacy of his soul, the master still deems himself part of a distinct and superior species, but he dares not say it, and he allows himself to be drawn, quaking, toward the common level. His manner of command becomes at once timid and harsh. Toward his servants he no longer feels the protective and benevolent sentiments that always grow out of a long period of uncontested power, and he is surprised that, being changed himself, his servant changes. Even though the servant is only passing through domestic service, as it were, the master wants him to acquire regular and permanent habits. He wants the servant to seem satisfied and proud of his servile position, which sooner or later he must leave. He wants him to sacrifice himself for a man who can neither protect nor destroy him. And finally, he wants him to feel bound by an eternal bond to beings who resemble him and who have no greater claim on longevity than he does.

In aristocratic nations, domestic service is commonly an estate that does not debase the soul of those who submit to it, because they neither know nor imagine any other, and the extraordinary inequality they observe between themselves and the master strikes them as a necessary and inevitable consequence of some hidden law of Providence.

Under democracy, there is nothing degrading about the estate of domestic service because it is freely chosen and temporarily adopted and because it is not stigmatized by public opinion and creates no permanent inequality between servant and master.

During the transition from one social condition to another, however, there is almost always a moment of hesitation between the aristocratic notion of subjection and the democratic notion of obedience.

Obedience then loses its moral standing in the eyes of the person who obeys. He no longer sees it as an obligation that is in some sense divine, and he does not yet see it under its purely human aspect. In his eyes it is neither holy nor just, and he submits to it as a degrading utilitarian reality.

In that moment, servants glimpse a confused and incomplete image of equality in their mind's eye. At first they cannot make out whether the equality to which they are entitled lies within the estate of domestic service or outside it, and deep in their hearts they rebel against an inferiority to which they have subjected themselves and from which they profit. They agree to serve and are ashamed to obey. They like the advantages of servitude but not the master, or, rather, they are not certain that the master's role does not belong to them and are inclined to look upon the person who assumes command over them as an unjust usurper of their rights.

We then see in each citizen's home something analogous to the sad spectacle we behold in political society. Unremitting intestine warfare pits two suspicious rival powers against each other in smoldering conflict. The master is malevolent and mild, the servant malevolent and intractable. One is forever seeking by ignoble subterfuge to evade his obligation to protect and remunerate, while the other shirks his duty to obey. Each tries to seize the reins of domestic administration, which lie dangling loose somewhere between them. The lines that divide authority from tyranny, liberty from license, and right from fact strike them as jumbled and confused, and no one knows precisely what he is or what he can do or what he should do.

Such a state is not democratic, but revolutionary.

Chapter 6

HOW DEMOCRATIC INSTITUTIONS AND MORES TEND TO RAISE PRICES AND SHORTEN THE TERMS OF LEASES

WHAT I said about servants and masters applies to some extent to landowners and tenant farmers. Nevertheless, the subject deserves to be treated in its own right.

In America, there are no tenant farmers as such. Every man owns the field he cultivates.

It is important to note that democratic laws have a powerful tendency to increase the number of landowners and decrease the number of tenant farmers. Yet what is happening in the United States must be attributed not so much to the country's institutions as to the country itself. In America, land costs little, and anyone can easily become a land owner. It also yields little, so that it would be difficult to divide the product between landlord and farmer.

America is therefore unique in this as in other respects, and it would be a mistake to take it as an example.

As I see it, land owners and farmers are found in democratic countries as well as in aristocracies, but the bond between them is not the same.

In aristocracies, rents are paid not only in money but also in respect, affection, and services. In democratic countries, they are paid only in cash. When patrimonies are divided and change hands, and the permanent relation that existed between families and the land disappears, contact between landlord and tenant becomes a matter of chance. They come together briefly to discuss the terms of their contract and then lose sight of each other. They are two strangers brought together by self-interest, who engage in a rigorous discussion about a business deal in which the sole subject is money.

As properties are divided and wealth is dispersed across the country, the state fills with people whose former opulence is in decline and with the newly rich, whose needs grow more rapidly than their resources. For all of these people, the smallest profit is a matter of consequence, and none of them feels inclined to let any advantage slip through his fingers or to forgo any portion of his income.

As ranks become indistinguishable and very great as well as very small fortunes become increasingly rare, the distance between the social condition of the landlord and that of the tenant farmer decreases daily. There is no natural and uncontested superiority of one over the other. Now, between two men who are equal and neither of whom is well off, what could the basis of a rental contract be if not money?

A man whose property comprises an entire district and who owns a hundred tenant farms understands that his goal must be to win the hearts of several thousand men simultaneously. This strikes him as a goal worthy of effort, and to attain such an important objective he is ready to make sacrifices.

The man who owns a hundred acres is not encumbered by such worries. It is of little importance to him whether he has the private good will of his tenant or not.

An aristocracy does not die as a man does, in one day. Its principle decays slowly in the depths of the soul before being attacked by laws. Thus long before war breaks out against it, we witness a gradual loosening of the bond that had previously united the upper classes with the lower. Indifference and contempt betray themselves on one side, jealousy and hatred on the other. Relations between the poor man and the rich become more infrequent and less temperate; the price of a lease rises. This is not yet a result of democratic revolution, but it is a sure harbinger of one. For an aristocracy that allows the heart of the people to slip through its fingers for good is like a tree whose roots have died, and the taller it is, the easier for the wind to topple it.

Over the past fifty years, farm rents have risen dramatically, not only in France but throughout much of Europe. The striking advances made by agriculture and industry during the same period are not enough, in my view, to explain this phenomenon. Some other cause, more powerful but more hidden, must be responsible. I believe that that cause should be sought in the democratic institutions that several European nations have adopted and in the democratic passions that have to one extent or another agitated all the others.

In recent years I have often heard great English landlords announce with pride that their estates yield much more money now than they did in their fathers' day.

They may be right to rejoice, but they certainly do not know what it is they are rejoicing about. They think they are making a clear profit, but in fact they are only making an exchange. They are surrendering their influence in return for hard cash, and what they gain in money, they will soon forfeit in power.

There is also another sign by which one can easily recognize that a great democratic revolution is under way or about to begin.

In the Middle Ages, nearly all land was leased in perpetuity or at any rate for a very long term. When one studies the domestic economy of those times, it is clear that ninety-nine-year leases were more common then than twelve-year leases are now.

People in those days believed in the immortality of families. Conditions seemed fixed forever, and the whole society seemed so static that no one imagined that anything could ever stir within it.

In centuries of equality the human mind takes on a different cast. It is easy to imagine that nothing stays put. The mind is possessed by the idea of instability.

Given this attitude, both landlord and tenant feel a kind of instinctive horror for long-term obligations. They are afraid that the contract that is profitable today may some day prove limiting. They vaguely expect some sudden and unforeseen change in their condition. They frighten themselves, dreading the idea that if their taste should change, they might not be able to get free of things they had once coveted, and they are right to feel such dread, for in democratic centuries, when everything is in flux, the most mobile thing of all is the human heart.

Chapter 7

INFLUENCE OF DEMOCRACY
ON WAGES

MOST of what I said above about servants and masters can be applied to masters and workers as well.

As respect for the rules of social hierarchy diminishes, while the stature of the great falls and that of the humble rises and poverty as well as wealth cease to be hereditary, the distance that once separated the worker from the master in fact and opinion visibly decreases with each passing day.

The worker conceives a loftier idea of his rights, his future, and himself. A new ambition and new desires well up in him, and he is besieged by new needs. He is forever gazing upon his employer's profits with covetous eyes. In the hope of sharing them, he seeks to set a higher price upon his labor, and usually he succeeds.

In democratic countries, as elsewhere, most industries are frugally managed by men not much above the common level of those they employ with respect to wealth and enlightenment. These industrial entrepreneurs are quite numerous; their interests vary; hence they cannot easily agree among themselves and combine their efforts.

Meanwhile, nearly all workers have some secure resources that allow them to withhold their services when others are unwilling to grant them what they consider a just reward for their labor.

In the constant struggle between these two classes over wages, forces are thus divided, and success alternates.

There is even reason to believe that in the long run, the interests of workers will predominate, because the high wages they have already obtained are making them daily less dependent on their masters, and as they become more independent, it becomes easier for them to obtain higher wages.

As an example I will take the livelihood that is still the most common in France today, as it is in nearly every other country in the world as well: cultivation of the soil.

In France, most people who hire out their services in agriculture own a few parcels of land of their own, and in a pinch these enable them to survive without working for others. If they offer their brawn to a great landlord or neighboring farmer and are denied a certain wage, they retire to their small plots and wait for other opportunities to arise.

All things considered, I think that it is fair to say that one of the general laws governing democratic societies is that wages will slowly and gradually increase. As conditions become more equal, wages rise, and as wages go higher, conditions become more equal.

In recent years, however, a significant and unfortunate exception to this rule has arisen.

In a previous chapter I showed how the aristocracy, driven out of political society, retreated to certain parts of the industrial world, which it ruled in a new way.

This has had a powerful influence on wage levels.

Since a person must already be very wealthy to launch a venture in one of the major industries I have in mind, the number who do so is quite small. Being few in number, they can easily conspire to set whatever price for labor they choose.

By contrast, the number of workers they employ is very large and increases constantly. Now and then there are periods of extraordinary prosperity during which wages rise inordinately, luring surrounding populations into manufacturing. Once a man has embarked on such a career, it is unlikely, as we have seen, that he will be able to leave it, because he will soon acquire habits of body and mind that render him unfit for any other kind of labor. Such a man will generally have little in the way of enlightenment, ambition, or resources, hence he is virtually at the mercy of his master. When competition or other fortuitous circumstances cause the master's profits to fall, he can cut his workers' wages virtually at will and easily recover from them what fortune has taken from him.

Suppose that by common accord the workers refuse to work: the master, who is a wealthy man, can easily wait without driving himself into bankruptcy until necessity brings them back to him, while they must work every day or die, for they have virtually no property other than their brawn. Oppression has long since reduced them to poverty, and the poorer they become, the easier it is to oppress them. This is a vicious circle from which they cannot escape.

It should come as no surprise, therefore, if wages in manufacturing, having risen at times quite suddenly, fall from here on out, while in other walks of life the price of labor, which generally increases only little by little, begins to climb steadily.

The state of dependence and misery in which a segment of the industrial population has found itself in recent years is exceptional and at odds with everything going on around it. For that very reason, however, there is no issue more serious or more deserving of special attention from lawmakers than this. For when the entire society is on the move, it is difficult to keep one class fixed in its place, and when most people are opening up new avenues to fortune, it is hard to force some others to bear the burden of their needs and desires in peace.

Chapter 8

INFLUENCE OF DEMOCRACY
ON THE FAMILY

I HAVE just examined how, among democratic peoples in general and Americans in particular, equality of conditions modifies relations among citizens.

I now want to go one step further and look into the family itself. My goal is not to seek new truths but to show how facts already known relate to my subject.

Everyone has noticed that relations among family members have changed in recent years, that the distance that once separated a father from his sons has decreased and that paternal authority has been if not destroyed then at least impaired.

Something analogous but even more striking can be seen in the United States.

In America, the family — taking the word in its Roman and aristocratic sense — does not exist. What few vestiges remain exist only during the first few years following the birth of children. During that time the father enjoys the unchallenged domestic dictatorship that the weakness of his sons requires and their interest, together with their father's incontestable superiority, justifies.

As the young American approaches manhood, however, the bonds of filial obedience grow looser with each passing day. He first becomes master of his thoughts and soon thereafter of his conduct. In America, to tell the truth, there is no such thing as adolescence. When boyhood ends, the man stands forth and begins to set his own course.

It would be wrong to think that this comes about as the result of an intestine struggle in which the son, exercising a kind of moral violence, takes what his father has refused to grant him. The same habits and principles that impel the former to reach for independence dispose the latter to look upon its exercise as an incontestable right.

We therefore find in the son none of the hateful and unruly passions that continue to stir the hearts of men long after they have wrested themselves free of an established power. The father feels none of the regrets suffused with bitterness and wrath that usually follow a fall from power: well before reaching the limits of his authority, he has divined their approach, and when, in the fullness of time, he does at last reach them, he abdicates easily. The son knows beforehand the precise hour when his will is to become his rule, and he takes up his freedom without haste or effort, as that which is his due and of which no one seeks to deprive him.[1]

It may be worth taking the time to show how closely the changes that are taking place in the family are related to the social and political revolution that is culminating before our eyes.

There are certain great social principles that a people either embraces in every aspect of its existence or roots out entirely.

In countries that are organized aristocratically and hierarchically, power never addresses the totality of the governed directly. Since one man is tied to another, the ruler may confine himself to controlling those at the top of the hierarchy. The rest will follow. This rule applies to the family as it does to any association that has a leader. Among aristocratic peoples, society in fact knows only the father. Only through the hands of the father does it exert a hold on the sons. It governs him, and he governs them. Hence the father enjoys more

---

[1]Still, the Americans have yet to conceive, as we have done in France, of depriving fathers of one of the principal elements of their power by denying them the freedom to dispose of their property after their death. In the United States, there are no limits on what a man may do with his will.

In this as in most other respects, it is easy to see that although American political legislation is far more democratic than ours, our civil legislation is infinitely more democratic than theirs. This is easy to understand.

The author of our civil legislation was a man who believed it to be in his interest to satisfy the democratic passions of his contemporaries in every way that did not pose a direct and immediate threat to his power. He was therefore quite willing to allow a few popular principles to regulate property and govern families, provided that no one sought to introduce similar principles when it came to running the state. While allowing the democratic torrent to inundate the civil laws, he hoped to find ready refuge for himself behind the shelter of political laws. His vision was at once shrewd and self-serving, but such a compromise could not last. For in the long run, political society cannot fail to become the expression and image of civil society, and it is in this sense that one may say that there is nothing more political about a people than its civil legislation.

than just a natural right. He is given a political right to command. He is the author and support of the family; he is also its magistrate.

In democracies, where the arm of government searches each man out individually in the crowd in order to make him bow, isolated from all the rest, to the common laws, no such intermediary is necessary. In the eyes of the law, the father is merely a citizen older and wealthier than his sons.

When conditions are for the most part highly unequal, and inequality of conditions is permanent, the idea of the superior is magnified in man's imagination. Even if the law granted him no prerogatives, custom and opinion would award him a certain number. By contrast, when men differ little from one another and do not remain permanently dissimilar, the general notion of superior becomes weaker and less clear. In vain does the will of the legislator strive to place the man who obeys far below the one who commands; mores will bring the two men closer together and draw them toward the same level.

Thus if I do not see special privileges accorded to heads of families in the legislation of an aristocratic people, I may nevertheless rest assured that their power will be highly respected and more extensive than it would be in a democracy, because I know that, regardless of the laws, the superior will always seem higher and the inferior lower in an aristocracy than in a democratic people.

When remembrance of what was rather than preoccupation with what is dominates the lives of men, and they worry about what their ancestors thought far more than they try to think for themselves, the father is the natural and necessary bond between the past and the present, the link wherein these two chains meet and join. In aristocracies, the father is therefore not only the political head of the family; he is the organ of tradition, the interpreter of custom, the arbiter of mores. He is listened to with deference and approached only with respect, and the love that one bears for him is always tempered with fear.

When the social state becomes democratic and men adopt as a general principle that it is good and legitimate to judge all things in relation to oneself, taking old beliefs as information and not as rule, the power of opinion that a father exerts over his sons diminishes, as does his legal power.

The division of patrimonies, which is a consequence of democracy, contributes more than anything else, perhaps, to changing the relationship between a father and his children.

When a father has little in the way of property, he and his sons live in the same place constantly and work side by side. Habit and need bring them together and force them to communicate with one another regularly. Inevitably, a sort of familiar intimacy develops among them, which makes the father's authority less absolute and which is difficult to reconcile with external signs of respect.

Now, among democratic peoples, the class that possesses these small fortunes is precisely the class that gives power to ideas and shapes mores. It causes its opinions and its will to predominate everywhere, and even those who are most likely to resist its orders eventually allow themselves to be overwhelmed by its example. I have seen fiery enemies of democracies allow their children to address them in the most familiar of terms.

So as power slips away from the aristocracy, we see all that was austere, conventional, and legal vanishing from paternal power as well, and a kind of equality establishing itself around the domestic hearth.

I do not know whether, all things considered, society loses as a result of this change, but I am inclined to believe that the individual gains. I believe that as mores and laws become more democratic, relations between father and sons become more intimate and tender. Rule and authority are less frequently encountered. Confidence and affection are often greater, and the natural bond seems to grow tighter as the social bond is relaxed.

In the democratic family, the father exercises little power other than that which others are pleased to grant to tenderness and to the experience of an old man. His orders may be ignored, but his advice is usually powerful. While he may not be surrounded by official marks of respect, his sons at least approach him with confidence. There is no recognized formula for addressing him, but he is spoken to constantly and freely consulted every day. The master and magistrate have vanished; the father remains.

In order to judge the difference between the two social states in this respect, it suffices to look through the domestic correspondence that has come down to us from aristocracies. The style is always correct, formal, rigid, and so cold that the heart's natural warmth can barely be felt through the words.

Among democratic peoples, by contrast, every word that a son addresses to his father bears the stamp of something that is at once free, familiar, and tender, which reveals immediately that a new kind of relationship has been established at the very heart of the family.

An analogous revolution modifies the mutual relations among children.

In an aristocratic family, as in aristocratic society generally, every place is marked. Not only does the father occupy a distinct rank and enjoy immense privileges, but children are not equal to one another. Age and sex irrevocably fix the rank and determine the prerogatives of each child. Democracy overturns or lowers most of these barriers.

In an aristocratic family, the eldest son inherits most of the property and almost all of the rights and thus becomes the head of the family and, up to a point, master of his brothers. Grandeur and power go to him, mediocrity and dependence to them. Yet it would be a mistake to believe that among aristocratic peoples the privileges of the eldest are advantageous to him alone and excite only envy and hatred around him.

The eldest son usually seeks to procure wealth and power for his brothers, because the general brilliance of the house redounds to the credit of the man who represents it; and the younger sons seek to facilitate the undertakings of the eldest, because the grandeur and strength of the head of the family put him in a better and better position to improve the lot of all the offspring.

The various members of an aristocratic family are therefore closely tied to one another. Their interests mesh, their minds are in harmony, but rarely do their hearts coincide.

Democracy also attaches brothers to one another, but it goes about it in a different way.

Under democratic laws, children are perfectly equal, hence independent. Nothing necessarily draws them together, but neither does anything drive them apart. And since they have a common background, grow up under the same roof, receive the same care, and are neither distinguished nor set apart by particular prerogatives of any kind, a gentle, childlike intimacy develops easily among them in their early years. Few occasions arise that might lead to the breaking of the bond thus formed at the beginning of life, because fraternity daily draws them together without inhibiting them.

Hence it is not through interests but through shared memories and free sympathy of opinion and taste that democracy attaches brothers to one another. It divides their inheritance but allows their souls to come together.

Democratic mores are so mild that even partisans of aristocracy find them attractive, and after savoring them for a time they are not tempted to revert to the chilly and respectful formalities of the aristocratic family. They would willingly preserve the domestic habits of democracy if only they could reject its social state and laws. But these things go together, and it is impossible to enjoy the one without enduring the others.

What I have just said about filial love and fraternal tenderness should be understood as applying to all passions that spring spontaneously from nature itself.

When a certain way of thinking or feeling is the product of a particular state of humanity, and that state happens to change, nothing remains. For instance, the law may create a very close bond between two citizens. If the law is abolished, they separate. Nothing was closer than the bond linking vassal to lord in the feudal world. Now the two men no longer recognize each other. The fear, gratitude, and love that bound them together have vanished. Not a trace remains.

This is not the case, however, with sentiments natural to the human species. Rarely does the law, in striving to shape those sentiments in a certain way, fail to sap their vigor; in seeking to add to them, it rarely fails to subtract some of them away. Left to themselves, they are always stronger.

Democracy, which destroys or obscures nearly all the old social conventions and prevents men from easily settling on new ones, completely eliminates most of the sentiments born of those conventions. But it merely modifies the others and often imparts to them an energy and gentleness they did not previously possess.

It is not impossible, I think, to sum up the entire meaning of this chapter and several of those that precede it in a single sentence. Democracy relaxes social bonds but tightens natural bonds. It brings kin closer together while at the same time driving citizens further apart.

Chapter 9

RAISING GIRLS IN
THE UNITED STATES

THERE has never been a free society without mores, and as I said in the first part of this work, it is woman who makes mores. To my way of thinking, therefore, anything that influences the condition of women, their habits, and their opinions is of great political interest.

In nearly all Protestant nations, girls are far more mistresses of their actions than is the case among Catholic peoples.

They are still more independent in Protestant countries like England, which have preserved or acquired the right to govern themselves. Liberty then works its way into the family through political habits and religious beliefs.

In the United States, Protestant doctrine combines with a very liberal constitution and a very democratic social state, and nowhere is a girl more quickly or completely left to herself.

Long before the young American woman reaches marriageable age, she begins little by little to be set free from her mother's tutelage. Before her childhood has quite ended, she is already thinking for herself, speaking freely, and acting on her own. The great spectacle of the world is set constantly before her. Rather than being hidden from her view, more and more of it is revealed to her as time goes by, and she is taught to consider it with a steady and tranquil eye. Thus the vices and perils that society presents soon become apparent to her. She sees them clearly, judges them without illusion, and confronts them without fear. For she is full of confidence in her own strength, and her confidence seems to be shared by everyone around her.

Hence one should almost never expect to find in an American girl the virginal innocence amid nascent desires or the naïve and ingenuous graces that generally accompany the European girl's passage from childhood to youth. It is rare for an American girl of any age to exhibit childish timidity or ignorance. Like the European girl, she wants to please, but she knows precisely how much she is willing to give up in order to do so. If she does not surrender to evil, at least she knows what it is. She has pure mores rather than a chaste mind.

I have often been surprised and almost frightened by the singular skill and pleasing audacity with which young American girls marshal thoughts and words while deftly negotiating the shoals of a sprightly conversation. A philosopher might well stumble a hundred times along the narrow path these girls travel without incident or difficulty.

Indeed, it is easy to see that even in the independence of early youth, the American girl never entirely relinquishes her self-control. She enjoys all allowed pleasures without giving herself up to any of them, and her reason never lets go of the reins, though at times its grip on them may seem rather loose.

In France, where our opinions and tastes are still a strange mix combining vestiges of all the ages of the past, we often give women a timid, sheltered, almost cloistered upbringing, and then we suddenly abandon them, without guidance or assistance, to the disorders that are inseparable from democratic society.

Americans are more consistent.

They realized the inevitability in a democracy of a high degree of individual independence, of youthful impatience, ill-controlled desires, changing customs, frequently uncertain or impotent public opinion, weak paternal authority, and challenges to marital domination.

Given this state of affairs, they judged that there was little likelihood of preventing a woman from experiencing the most tyrannical passions of the human heart and that a safer course would be to teach her the art of combating those passions herself. Since they could not ensure that a woman's virtue would not be frequently imperiled, they wanted her to be able to defend that virtue and for that relied more on the free effort of her will than on shaky or ruined safeguards. Rather than encourage her to distrust herself, they therefore sought constantly to increase her confidence in her own strength. Being both unable and unwilling to keep a girl in a state of complete and perpetual ignorance, they hastened to equip her with precocious knowledge in all areas. Far from hiding the world's corruptions from her, they wanted her to see them from the first and practice fleeing them on her own, and they chose to protect her decency rather than respect her innocence all too thoroughly.

Although the Americans are a highly religious people, they did not rely on religion alone to defend a woman's virtue; they sought to arm her reason. They adopted the same method in this as in many other circumstances. First they made incredible efforts to ensure that individual independence would regulate itself, and only after reaching the ultimate limit of human strength did they at last invoke the aid of religion.

I am aware that such an upbringing is not without danger. I am also aware that it tends to develop judgment at the expense of imagination, and to make women respectable and cold rather than tender wives and amiable companions of men. Although society is more tranquil and better regulated as a result, private life often has fewer charms. But these are secondary ills, which ought to be braved for the sake of a greater interest. At this point no choice remains: a democratic upbringing is necessary to protect women from the perils with which the institutions and mores of democracy surround them.

Chapter 10

HOW THE TRAITS OF THE GIRL
CAN BE DIVINED IN THE WIFE

In America, a woman forfeits her independence forever when she embraces the bonds of matrimony. Although girls in America are less restricted than they are anywhere else, wives submit to stricter obligations. A girl turns her father's house into a place of freedom and pleasure, whereas a wife lives in her husband's home as in a cloister.

These two very different conditions may not be as contrary as one assumes, and it is natural for Americans to pass through one to reach the other.

Religious peoples and industrial nations have a particularly serious idea of marriage. The former take the view that the regularity of a woman's life is the best guarantee and surest sign of the purity of her morals. The latter see it as the certain warrant of the order and prosperity of the household.

Americans constitute both a puritanical nation and a commercial people. Hence both their religious beliefs and their industrial habits lead them to require of women a degree of self-denial and constant sacrifice of pleasure to business that are rarely asked of women in Europe. Thus, in the United States, an inexorable public opinion reigns, carefully confining women within the restricted circle of domestic interests and duties and prohibiting them from venturing outside.

On entering the world, the young American woman finds these notions already firmly established. She recognizes the rules that derive from them. It does not take her long to convince herself that she cannot for a moment escape the usages of her contemporaries without immediately jeopardizing her tranquillity, her honor, and even her social existence, and in the steadfastness of her reason and the virile habits acquired from her upbringing she finds the energy to submit to them.

It is fair to say that it is through the use of independence that she develops the courage to endure the sacrifice of that independence without a struggle or a murmur when the time comes.

Moreover, the American woman never falls into the bonds of matrimony as into a trap set to ensnare her simplicity and ignorance. She has been taught in advance what is expected of her, and she accepts the yoke freely and of her own accord. She bears her new condition bravely because she has chosen it.

Since paternal discipline in America is quite lax and the marital bond is quite strict, girls are cautious and fearful about entering into it. Early marriage is rare there. Thus American women marry only when their reason is practiced and mature, whereas most women elsewhere begin to acquire maturity in the exercise of their reason only after they marry.

I am a long way from thinking, moreover, that the great change that takes place in all of a woman's habits in the United States the moment she marries is entirely attributable to the constraints imposed by public opinion. In many cases women impose this change on themselves by sheer force of will.

When the time comes to choose a husband, this cold and austere reason, enlightened and bolstered by the freedom to view the world, indicates to the American woman that a frivolous and independent mind in the bonds of matrimony is a subject of eternal trouble, not pleasure; that the things that amused the girl cannot be allowed to divert the wife; and that for a woman the sources of happiness are to be found in the conjugal home. Seeing in advance, and with clear eyes, the only path that can lead to domestic happiness, she enters it with her first steps and follows it to the end without attempting to turn back.

The same strength of will that young wives exhibit in America by bowing immediately and uncomplainingly to the austere duties of their new estate can be seen as well in all the other great trials of their lives.

There is no country in the world in which private fortunes are more unstable than in the United States. It is not rare for a man in the course of his lifetime to work his way all the way up the ladder from poverty to opulence and then tumble back down again.

The women of America bear these revolutions with quiet, indomitable energy. Their desires seem to contract with their fortunes as readily as they expand.

Most of the adventurers who go each year to populate the solitudes of the West belong, as I remarked in my first book, to the old Anglo-American race of the North. Many who hastened so boldly after wealth were already well off in the places from which they set out. They took their wives with them and made them share the perils and miseries that invariably attend the early stages of such undertakings. At the uttermost edge of the wilderness I frequently met young women raised amid the many refinements of life in the big cities of New England who had gone virtually without transition from the wealthy homes of their parents to drafty cabins in the woods. Fever, loneliness, and boredom had failed to sap the springs of their courage. Their faces seemed drawn and pale, but their gaze was steady. They seemed both sad and resolute.

I have no doubt that it was the early upbringing of these young American women that gave them the inner strength on which they later drew.

So in the United States we can still divine the young girl in the features of the wife. Her role has changed, her habits are different, but her spirit is the same.*

---

*See Note XX, page 360.

Chapter 11

HOW EQUALITY OF CONDITIONS HELPS TO MAINTAIN GOOD MORALS IN AMERICA

SOME philosophers and historians have stated or implied that the severity of women's morals varies directly with the distance they live from the equator. To say this is to take the easy way out of answering the question, and if we were to accept this view, a globe and a compass would suffice to resolve in an instant one of the most difficult problems with which humanity confronts us.

The facts, in my view, do not support this materialist doctrine.

The same nations have been chaste in one period of their history, dissolute in another. Hence the moral regularity or disorder of these nations depended on changing causes and not simply on the nature of the country, which did not change.

I will not deny that in certain climates the passions that are born of the mutual attraction of the sexes are particularly ardent. I believe, however, that this natural ardor can always be stimulated or restrained by the social state and political institutions.*

Although travelers who have visited North America differ about many things, all agree that mores are infinitely more severe there than anywhere else.

In this respect, the Americans are clearly quite superior to their forefathers, the English. To see this, a superficial glance at the two nations is enough.

In England, as in all the other countries of Europe, the frailties of women come in for constant public scorn. One often hears philosophers and statesmen complaining that mores are not sufficiently regular, and literature daily suggests that this is the case.

In America, all books, including novels, assume that women are chaste, and none tell of amorous adventures.

*See Note XXI, page 362.

This great regularity of American mores is doubtless due in part to the country, to race, and to religion. But all these causes are found elsewhere and together do not suffice to explain it. Some specific reason is needed.

As I see it, that reason is equality and the institutions that derive from it.

Equality of conditions does not by itself produce regularity of mores, but there can be no doubt that it does foster and augment such regularity.

Among aristocratic peoples, birth and fortune often make such different creatures of men and women that a successful union becomes impossible. The passions bring them together, but the social state and the ideas it prompts prevent them from forming a permanent and public bond. Because of this, large numbers of fleeting and clandestine attachments are inevitable. Nature secretly exacts compensation for the constraints that laws impose on her.

When equality of conditions has swept away all the barriers, real or imaginary, that formerly separated man from woman, things are no longer the same. No girl who is the object of a man's attention thinks that she cannot become his wife, and moral impropriety prior to marriage therefore becomes quite difficult, for no matter how credulous passion may be, there is scarcely any way for a woman to persuade herself that a man loves her if that man is perfectly free to marry her and does not do so.

The same cause operates in marriage, though in a more indirect manner.

Nothing does more to legitimate illegitimate love in the eyes of those who experience it, or of the multitude who contemplate it, than forced marriages or marriages made by chance.[1]

[1] Study of the various European literatures bears out the truth of this observation.

When a European wishes to retrace in fiction some of the great catastrophes that so commonly befall our marriages, he is careful first to arouse the reader's pity by showing him two people who are either ill-matched or married under duress. Although tolerance has long since relaxed our morals, he would find it difficult to interest us in the misfortunes of his characters if he did not first supply us with reasons to forgive their transgression. This

In a country where the woman always freely exercises her choice, and where her upbringing has put her in a position to choose well, public opinion is inexorable in regard to her faults.

The strictness of the Americans is partly a consequence of this. They see marriage as a contract which, though often onerous, must be rigorously respected, because the parties had the opportunity to study all of its provisions in advance and were entirely free to refrain from entering into any agreement at all.

That which makes fidelity more obligatory makes it easier.

In aristocratic countries the goal of marriage is to unite properties rather than persons, hence the husband is sometimes taken from school and the wife from the bosom of her nurse. It is not surprising that the conjugal bond that joins the fortunes of the two spouses leaves their hearts free to rove at will. This is a natural consequence of the spirit of the contract.

By contrast, when each person chooses his or her own companion without external hindrance or compulsion, what brings the man and woman together is usually nothing but similarity of tastes and ideas, and that same similarity keeps them together and steadily at each other's side.

Our fathers had a peculiar opinion of marriage.

Having observed that what few marriages of inclination were made in their time almost always ended badly, they resolutely concluded that it was very dangerous to consult one's own heart in such matters. Chance struck them as more clairvoyant than choice.

Yet it is not very difficult to see that the examples they had before their eyes proved nothing.

Begin by noting that if democratic peoples grant women the right to choose their husbands freely, they are careful first to furnish their minds with the enlightenment and their wills

---

device seldom fails. The spectacle to which we are daily witness prepares us in advance to be indulgent.

American writers cannot make such excuses seem plausible to their readers. Their usages and laws resist this, and since they despair of making irregularity likable, they do not depict it at all. This is part of the reason why so few novels are published in the United States.

with the strength that may be necessary for such a choice, whereas among aristocratic peoples the girls who furtively escape from paternal authority and fling themselves into the arms of a man whom they have not been granted either time to get to know or capacity to judge are without any such guarantees. It is hardly surprising that at their first opportunity to exercise freedom of choice, they misuse it so badly, or that they succumb to such cruel errors when they attempt in marrying to adhere to the customs of democracy without having received a democratic upbringing.

But that is not all.

When a man and a woman seek to meet despite the inequalities of the aristocratic social state, they have immense obstacles to overcome. After stretching or breaking the bonds of filial obedience, they must make one final effort to escape the dominion of custom and the tyranny of opinion, and when at length they come to the end of this arduous undertaking, they find themselves as strangers among their natural friends and close relatives: the prejudice they have braved separates them. This situation soon breaks their courage and embitters their hearts.

So if a couple joined in this manner succumbs first to unhappiness and later to culpable behavior, we must not place the blame on their having freely chosen each other but rather on their living in a society that does not accept such choice.

We must not forget, moreover, that the same energy that impels a man to rebel in a violent way against a common error almost always carries him beyond the bounds of reason; that in order for a man to declare war — even legitimate war — on the ideas of his time and country, he must have a certain violent and adventurous cast of mind, and men of this character, no matter what direction they take, rarely arrive at happiness and virtue. And in passing let it be said that this also explains why even in the most necessary and holy of revolutions, one encounters so few moderate and honest revolutionaries.

No one should be surprised, therefore, that if a man in an aristocratic century makes so bold as to rely solely on his own private opinion and taste when choosing a mate, moral disorder and misery may soon overtake his household. But when this same course of conduct is part of the natural and ordinary order of things; and the social state facilitates it; and paternal authority consents to it and public opinion approves; there can be no doubt that the inner peace of families increases as a result, and conjugal faith is better kept.

Almost all men in democracies pursue a political career or some other occupation, whereas the modesty of fortunes forces women to stay home every day in order to supervise the minutest details of domestic administration.

All these distinct and obligatory occupations are like so many natural barriers between the sexes, making the solicitations of the one less frequent and less ardent and the resistance of the other easier.

Although equality of conditions can never make man chaste, it can make the irregularity of his morals less dangerous. Since no one then has the leisure or opportunity to attack those virtues that wish to defend themselves, one sees both a large number of courtesans and a multitude of respectable women.

Such a state of affairs leads to deplorable individual miseries, but it does not prevent the social body from being fit and strong. It does not destroy family ties or sap national mores. What puts society in danger is not great corruption in some but laxity in all. In the eyes of the lawmaker, prostitution is much less to be dreaded than amorous adventures.

The tumultuous life of constant worry that equality brings to men not only discourages love by depriving them of the leisure to indulge in it but also leads them off in another direction by a more hidden but more certain path.

All men who live in democratic times acquire to one degree or another the intellectual habits of the industrial and commercial classes. Their minds take on a serious, calculating, and positive cast. They gladly turn away from the ideal and aim for some visible nearby goal, which stands out as the natural and necessary object of their desires. Equality does not destroy the imagination in this way, but it does limit it, forcing it to hew close to the earth as it flies.

No one is less given to reverie than the citizens of a democracy, and few are keen to abandon themselves to the kinds of idle and solitary contemplation that usually precede and provoke major agitations of the heart.

They do, to be sure, attach great value to obtaining the kind of deep, regular, and quiet affection that lends life its charm and makes it secure, but they do not voluntarily court the violent and capricious emotions that disturb and shorten it.

I am well aware that the foregoing is applicable in its entirety only to America and cannot at present be extended in a general way to Europe.

In the half century during which laws and habits have been driving a number of European peoples toward democracy with unparalleled energy, there is no sign that relations between men and women in these nations have become more regular or more chaste. In some places the opposite appears to be the case. Some classes are more disciplined; general morality seems more lax. I do not shrink from saying so, because I am no more disposed to flatter my contemporaries than to slander them.

This spectacle ought to be a source of distress but should come as no surprise.

The beneficial influence that a democratic social state can have on regularity of habits is one of those facts that emerges only in the long run. If equality of conditions encourages good morals, the social travail that makes conditions equal is very damaging to morality.

In the fifty years during which France has been transforming herself, we have seldom had liberty but always had disorder. In the midst of this universal confusion of ideas and general upheaval of opinions, this incoherent mix of justice and injustice, truth and falsehood, right and fact, public virtue has become uncertain and private morality unsteady.

But all revolutions, no matter what their purposes or agents, initially produced similar effects. Even those that ended up tightening the bonds of morality began by loosening them.

The disorders to which we are often witnesses therefore do not seem to me to be a durable fact. Already there are certain curious signs that point in this direction.

Nothing is more miserably corrupt than an aristocracy that conserves its wealth while losing its power and that, though reduced to vulgar pleasures, still possesses a vast amount of time for leisure. The energetic passions and great thoughts that once animated it then disappear, and little remains but a multitude of petty, gnawing vices that cling to it as worms to a corpse.

No one denies that the French aristocracy of the last century was very dissolute, while long-standing habits and old beliefs still maintained respect for morals in other classes.

Nor would anyone disagree that, today, a certain severity of principles has begun to emerge from the debris of that same aristocracy, whereas moral disorder appears to have spread in the middle and lower ranks of society. Thus the same families that were the most dissolute fifty years ago are today the most exemplary, and democracy seems to have chastened only the aristocratic classes.

The Revolution, by dividing noble fortunes, forcing nobles to devote themselves assiduously to their affairs and their families, compelling them to live under the same roof as their children, and making them think in a more reasonable and serious way, led them without their noticing to a respect for religious beliefs and a love of order, tranquil pleasures, domestic joys, and well-being, whereas the rest of the nation, which naturally had these same tastes, was swept into disorder by the very effort required to overthrow political laws and customs.

The old French aristocracy suffered the consequences of the Revolution but did not experience revolutionary passions or share the often anarchic enthusiasm that produced it. It is easy to see why it would have experienced the salutary moral influence of the Revolution even before the people who made it.

Surprising though it may seem at first sight, we may therefore state that, today, it is the most anti-democratic classes of the nation that allow us to see most clearly the kind of morality that it is reasonable to expect from democracy.

I can only conclude that when the full effects of the democratic revolution have emerged and the tumult to which it has given rise has ended, what is today true of a few will little by little become true of all.

Chapter 12

HOW THE AMERICANS UNDERSTAND THE EQUALITY OF MAN AND WOMAN

I HAVE shown how democracy destroys or modifies the various inequalities to which society gives rise. But is that the end of it? Or is it not finally beginning to affect the great inequality between man and woman, which has seemed until now to be based upon eternal foundations in nature?

I think that the social movement that is bringing son and father, servant and master, and, in general, inferior and superior closer to the same level is raising woman and will make her more and more the equal of man.

On this point, however, more than any other, I feel the need to make myself clear, for there is no subject about which the present century's crude and undisciplined imagination has allowed itself freer rein.

There are people in Europe who, confounding the various attributes of the sexes, claim to make man and woman into creatures not only equal but alike. They ascribe the same functions to both, assign them the same duties, and grant them the same rights. They mix them in all things: work, pleasure, affairs. It is easy to see how trying in this way to make one sex equal to the other degrades them both and how the only thing that can ever come of such a crude mixture of nature's works is weak men and disreputable women.

This was not how Americans understood the kind of democratic equality that can be established between woman and man. They believed that because nature had made man and woman so different in physical and moral constitution, its clear purpose was to assign different uses to the diverse faculties of each. They judged, moreover, that progress lay not in making dissimilar beings do virtually identical things but in seeing to it that each acquitted itself of its task in the best possible way. Americans applied to the two sexes the great principle of political economy that dominates today's industry. They carefully divided the functions of man and woman in order to carry out the great work of society more effectively.

229

No country in the world has been more persistent than America in tracing clearly separated lines of action for the two sexes or in wanting both to proceed at an equal pace but along two permanently different paths. You do not see American women managing the family's outside affairs, conducting a business, or entering the sphere of politics, but neither do you find American women forced to do hard labor or engage in any of the arduous activities that require the development of physical strength. There are no families so poor as to constitute exceptions to this rule.

If the American woman is not permitted to escape from the quiet circle of domestic occupations, neither is she ever compelled to leave it.

That is why American women, who often display a manly intelligence and an energy that is nothing less than virile, generally maintain a very delicate appearance and always remain women in manners, although they sometimes reveal themselves to be men in mind and heart.

Americans, moreover, never assumed that the consequence of democratic principles would be to topple the husband from power and confuse lines of authority within the family. They believed that every association needs a leader in order to be effective and that the natural leader of the conjugal association was the man. Hence they did not deny him the right to direct his helpmate, and they believed that in the small society consisting of husband and wife, as in the larger political society, the purpose of democracy is to regulate and legitimate necessary powers and not to destroy all power.

This is not an opinion held by one sex and contested by the other.

American women did not, in my view, appear to regard conjugal authority as a felicitous usurpation of their rights, nor did they believe that it was degrading to submit to it. On the contrary, it seemed to me that in a way they prided themselves on the voluntary sacrifice of their will and demonstrated their greatness by freely accepting the yoke rather than seeking to avoid it. That, at any rate, was the sentiment expressed by the most virtuous among them. The others remain silent, and in the United States, one does not hear adulterous wives loudly insisting on the rights of women while trampling the most sacred duties underfoot.

It has often been observed that in Europe the flattery that men lavish on women conceals a certain contempt. Although the European male may frequently allow himself to be enslaved by women, he plainly never thinks of these women in a sincere way as his equals.

In the United States, men seldom praise women but daily give evidence of the esteem in which they hold them.

American men consistently demonstrate full confidence in the reasoning abilities of their helpmates and deep respect for their freedom. They deem a woman's mind as capable of discovering the naked truth as a man's and her heart as stalwart in adhering to it, and they have never sought to protect her virtue any more than his behind a shelter of prejudice, ignorance, and fear.

In Europe, where men so readily submit to the despotic sway of women, they nevertheless seem to deny them some of the principal attributes of humankind and look upon them as seductive but incomplete beings. What is most surprising is that European women ultimately come to see themselves in the same light and are not far from considering it a privilege that they are allowed to seem frivolous, weak, and fearful. American women insist on no such rights.

In regard to morals, moreover, it might seem that we have granted man a peculiar sort of immunity, so that there is one kind of virtue for his use and another for his wife's, and the same act can appear in the public eye as a crime or merely a peccadillo.

Americans are unfamiliar with this iniquitous apportionment of duties and rights. In their eyes the seducer is as dishonored as his victim.

It is true that American men seldom show women the eager attention that is lavished on them in Europe, yet their conduct invariably proves that they assume women are virtuous and delicate, and they have such great respect for the moral freedom of women that in their presence every man minds his speech lest the women be obliged to listen to offensive language. In America, girls take long trips by themselves, without fear.

In the United States, lawmakers who have lessened the severity of nearly all provisions of the penal code punish rape by death, and no crime is more relentlessly pursued by public opinion. There is an explanation for this: since Americans cannot imagine anything more precious than a woman's honor or more deserving of respect than her independence, they deem no punishment too severe for anyone who would deprive her of these things against her will.

In France, where the same crime incurs much milder punishments, it is often difficult to find a jury prepared to convict. Is this because of contempt for chastity or contempt for woman? I cannot help thinking that it is both.

Thus, Americans do not believe that man and woman have the duty or right to do the same things, but they hold both in the same esteem and regard them as beings of equal value but different destinies. Although they do not ascribe the same form or use to a woman's courage as to a man's, they never doubt her courage; and while they hold that a man and his helpmate should not always use their intelligence and their reason in the same way, at least they believe that a woman's reason is as secure as a man's and her intelligence just as clear.

Americans have thus allowed woman's social inferiority to persist but have done all they could to raise her intellectual and moral level to parity with man, and in this respect they seem to me to have shown an admirable grasp of the true notion of democratic progress.

I, for one, do not hesitate to say that although women in the United States seldom venture outside the domestic sphere, where in some respects they remain quite dependent, nowhere has their position seemed to me to be higher. And now that I am nearing the end of this book, in which I have described so many considerable American accomplishments, if someone were to ask me what I think is primarily responsible for the singular prosperity and growing power of this people, I would answer that it is the superiority of their women.

Chapter 13

HOW EQUALITY NATURALLY DIVIDES THE AMERICANS INTO A MULTITUDE OF SMALL PRIVATE SOCIETIES

O NE might be inclined to believe that the ultimate consequence and necessary effect of democratic institutions is
to blur distinctions among citizens in private life as well as
public life and force them all to lead a common existence.

This would be to understand the equality to which democracy gives rise in a very crude and quite tyrannical way.

No social state and no laws can make men so similar that
upbringing, fortune, and tastes do not create some difference
between them, and while different men may at times find it in
their interest to do certain things in common, we must assume
that they will never find pleasure in doing so. Hence no matter
what the lawmaker does, they will always elude his grasp. One
way or another they will escape from the sphere to which he
tries to confine them and establish, alongside the larger political society, small private societies bound together by similarity of conditions, habits, and mores.

In the United States, citizens have no preeminence over
one another. They owe one another no reciprocal obedience
or respect. Together they administer justice and govern the
state, and in general they all meet to deal with affairs that influence the common destiny. Yet I never heard anyone pro-
pose that they should all be encouraged to amuse themselves
in the same way or take their pleasure indiscriminately in the
same places.

Americans, who mix so easily in political assemblies and tribunals, are careful, by contrast, to divide into very distinct
small associations to savor the pleasures of private life apart
from others. Each freely recognizes all his fellow citizens as
his equals, yet he never receives more than a small number as
his friends and guests.

This seems very natural to me. As the ambit of public society expands, one should expect the sphere of private relations
to shrink. Far from believing that citizens of the new societies

will eventually live their lives in common, I am fearful that they will ultimately confine themselves to very small coteries.

In aristocratic nations, the various classes are like vast enclosures that no one may either exit or enter. The classes do not communicate with one another, but within each of them men are bound to live in close daily contact. Even though they might not be naturally suited to one another, general conformity to a shared condition draws them together.

But when neither law nor custom takes it upon itself to establish frequent and habitual relations between certain men, accidental similarity of opinions and predilections decide the outcome, giving rise to an endless variety of private societies.

In democracies, where there is never much difference between one citizen and another and citizens are by nature so close that they may at any moment find themselves confounded in a common mass, a host of artificial and arbitrary classifications arise, and individuals use these to set themselves apart lest they be dragged against their will into the crowd.

This will always be the case, because human institutions can be changed, but man cannot. No matter what general effort a society expends to make citizens equal and alike, pride will always impel individuals to escape the common level and somewhere establish an inequality that is to their own advantage.

In aristocracies, men are separated from one another by high fixed barriers. In democracies, they are divided by a multitude of small, almost invisible threads, which are constantly being broken and moved about from place to place.

Thus in democratic nations, no matter what progress is made toward equality, large numbers of small private associations will always be springing up in the midst of the larger political society. So far as manners are concerned, however, none of these will resemble the upper class that rules in aristocracies.

Chapter 14

SOME REFLECTIONS ON
AMERICAN MANNERS

THERE is nothing, at first sight, that seems less important than the outward form of human actions and nothing to which men attach greater value. They can get used to anything except living in a society that does not share their manners. Hence the influence of the social and political state on manners is worthy of serious examination.

Manners generally emerge from the very depths of mores. In addition, they are sometimes the result of an arbitrary convention among certain men. They are at once natural and acquired.

When men become aware of enjoying unchallenged primacy without expenditure of effort, when they spend their days attending to great purposes while leaving the details to others, and when they live amid wealth they did not acquire and do not fear to lose, one sees how they might feel a sort of proud disdain for life's petty interests and material cares and exhibit a natural grandeur of thought in their words and manners.

In democratic countries, grand manners are rare because private life is usually quite petty. Manners are often vulgar, because thought seldom has occasion to rise above a preoccupation with domestic interests.

Genuine dignity of manners consists in always appearing to be in one's place, neither higher nor lower. The peasant can manage this as well as the prince. In democracies, everyone's place is in doubt. Hence manners there are often haughty but seldom dignified. What is more, they are never well disciplined or instructed.

Men who live in democracies are too mobile to allow some group of them to establish and enforce a code of etiquette. Each individual therefore behaves more or less as he pleases, and manners are always to some extent incoherent because they are shaped by each individual's feelings and ideas rather than conforming to an ideal model held up in advance for everyone to imitate.

Still, this is much more evident immediately after the fall of the aristocracy than it is later on.

New political institutions and new mores then cause men whose upbringing and habits are still remarkably dissimilar to come together in the same places and often force them to live their lives in common. Great disparities are thus constantly brought to light. People still remember that a precise code of etiquette once existed, but they no longer know what its content was or where it could be found. Men have lost the common law of manners but have yet to make up their minds to do without it. Each person nevertheless strives to assemble the remains of old customs into some sort of arbitrary and changing rule. As a result, manners have neither the regularity nor grandeur that one sometimes sees in aristocratic peoples nor the simplicity and freedom that one sometimes detects in democracy. They are at once stiff and uninhibited.

This is not the normal state of things.

When equality is complete and long-standing, men having roughly the same ideas and doing roughly the same things do not need to agree with or copy one another in order to act and speak in the same way. You constantly see a host of minor variations in their manners but no major differences. They are never perfectly alike, because they do not share the same model; they are never highly dissimilar, because they do share the same condition. At first glance the manners of all Americans look exactly alike. Only on much closer inspection do you begin to see the peculiarities that make them all different.

The English have made a good deal of fun of American manners, but what is peculiar is that the people who have drawn us this highly amusing portrait of the Americans belong mostly to the English middle classes, whom that portrait resembles quite nicely. These pitiless detractors thus generally exemplify the very shortcomings they criticize in the United States. They do not see that they are mocking themselves, much to the delight of their own country's aristocracy.

Nothing does more harm to democracy than the outward form of its mores. Many who could readily tolerate its vices cannot put up with its manners.

Nevertheless, I will not concede that there is nothing to praise in the manners of democratic peoples.

In aristocratic nations, all who stand close to the leading class will usually seek to resemble it, and this gives rise to some quite ridiculous and insipid imitations. While democratic peoples may lack any model of grand manners, they are at least spared the obligation of staring daily at vile copies.

In democracies, manners are never as refined as they are among aristocratic peoples, but neither are they ever as crude. You hear neither the swearing of the rabble nor the noble and choice expressions of the high nobility. There is often vulgarity in mores but not brutality or baseness.

I said earlier that no well-defined code of social graces can take shape in a democracy. This has its drawbacks as well as its advantages. In aristocracies, the rules of polite society impose a uniformity of appearance; these rules make all members of the same class alike, despite their particular predilections. They adorn and hide what is natural. Among democratic peoples, manners are neither as instructed nor as regular, but they are often more sincere. They constitute something like a thin and poorly woven veil, through which each person's true feelings and individual ideas can easily be seen. Hence the form and substance of human action are often intimately related there, and if the grand tableau of humankind is less ornate, it is also more true. In one sense, therefore, it is fair to say that the effect of democracy is not precisely to give men certain manners but to prevent their being mannered.

In a democracy one can on occasion find some of the sentiments, passions, virtues, and vices of aristocracy but not the manners. These are lost and vanish forever when the democratic revolution is complete.

Nothing is more durable, it seems, than the manners of an aristocratic class, for it holds on to these for some time after it loses its property and its power. Nor is anything so fragile, for no sooner have its manners disappeared than it becomes impossible to find any trace of them, and once they are gone, it is difficult to say what they were. A change in the social state works this miracle; a few generations suffice to carry it through.

The principal traits of aristocracy remain graven in history after aristocracy is destroyed, but the slight and delicate forms of its mores disappear from human memory almost immediately after its fall. No one can imagine what those forms were like once they have vanished from sight. They slip away without anyone's noticing or sensing what is happening, because in order to experience the refined pleasure that comes from distinction and choice in manners, one's heart must be prepared by habit and upbringing, and without the practice one easily loses the taste.

Thus not only is it impossible for democratic peoples to have the manners of aristocracy, it is also impossible for them to conceive of or desire such manners. They cannot imagine aristocratic manners. For them, it is as though such manners had never existed.

One should not attach too much importance to this loss, but one may regret it.

I know that it is by no means rare for the same man to have very distinguished manners and very vulgar sentiments. Anyone who knows court life from the inside is well aware that the grandest of exteriors can often conceal the basest of hearts. Yet though the manners of aristocracy did not create virtue, they sometimes adorned it. A numerous and powerful class in which all of life's outward acts seemed to reveal a natural elevation of sentiment and thought, a disciplined delicacy of taste, and an urbanity of manners was no ordinary sight.

The manners of the aristocracy draped human nature in beautiful illusions, and though the portrait was often deceptive, there was noble pleasure in looking at it.

Chapter 15

ON THE GRAVITY OF AMERICANS AND WHY IT DOES NOT PREVENT THEM FROM ACTING RASHLY

MEN who live in democratic countries do not prize the naïve, boisterous, coarse entertainments to which the popular classes in aristocracies are addicted: they find them puerile or insipid. Nor do they exhibit much greater taste for the refined intellectual diversions of the aristocratic classes. They require something productive and substantial in their pleasures and want their joy alloyed with satisfaction.

In aristocratic societies, the people are wont to outbursts of tumultuous, raucous gaiety, which abruptly wrest them from contemplation of their woes. People who live in democracies do not like such violent intrusions upon their privacy and always regret any loss of self-possession. Instead of such frivolous transports, they prefer grave and silent relaxations that look more like business and do not require them to put their affairs altogether out of their minds.

An American, instead of dancing joyously in the public square in his hours of leisure as many people of similar occupation still do throughout much of Europe, may retire to his private sanctum to drink alone. Such a man will savor two pleasures at once: while thinking about business he can become decently inebriated in familial seclusion.

I used to think that the English were the most serious-minded people on earth, but now that I have seen the Americans, I have changed my mind.

I do not mean to deny that temperament counts for a great deal in the character of inhabitants of the United States, but I think that political institutions contribute still more.

I think that the gravity of Americans stems in part from their pride. In democratic countries, even a poor man has a high idea of his personal worth. He is indulgent toward himself and is easily persuaded that he enjoys the regard of others. Because he has this attitude, he is careful about what he says and does, and he does not expose himself lest he reveal his shortcomings. In order to look dignified he imagines that he has no choice but to remain grave.

But I see another more intimate and powerful cause which instinctively gives rise to the astonishing gravity of Americans.

Under despotism, peoples will occasionally give way to wild outbursts of joy, but in general they are gloomy and reserved because they are afraid.

In absolute monarchies tempered by custom and mores, the people are often even-tempered and cheerful, because they enjoy some liberty and fairly substantial security and are therefore diverted from life's most important concerns. But all free peoples are grave, because their minds are habitually absorbed in the contemplation of some dangerous or difficult project.

This is especially true in free peoples constituted as democracies. In all classes one then finds countless people who are constantly preoccupied with serious affairs of government, and those who do not dream of directing the public fortune are left entirely to increasing their private fortunes. In such a people, gravity is no longer peculiar to certain men; it becomes a national habit.

People talk about the small democracies of Antiquity, whose citizens went into public places garlanded with roses and spent nearly all their time dancing or watching theatrical performances. I do not believe in this kind of republic any more than in Plato's kind, but even if things there were indeed as we have been told, I would nevertheless not hesitate to point out that those so-called democracies consisted of elements very different from ours, with which they have nothing in common but the name.

Do not suppose, moreover, that people who live in democracies, absorbed in their toils, think of themselves as objects of pity. Quite the contrary: no men cling to their condition more than these. They would find life without savor if delivered from the concerns that vex them so, and they seem more attached to their cares than aristocratic peoples to their pleasures.

Why, I wonder, do the same democratic peoples who are so grave sometimes behave so rashly?

Americans, who are almost always sober in their bearing and chilly in their appearance, nevertheless frequently allow themselves to be propelled well beyond the limits of reason by a sudden passion or ill-considered opinion, and at times they will in all seriousness behave in the most strikingly thoughtless ways.

This contrast should come as no surprise.

There is a kind of ignorance that stems from extreme publicity. In despotic states men do not know how to act, because they are told nothing; in democratic nations, they often act erratically, because nothing is supposed to be left unspoken. The former know nothing; the latter forget, as the main features of any scene are swallowed up by a host of details.

One is astonished by the number of imprudent statements that a public man in a free state, and especially a democratic state, will at times allow himself to make without fear that he will compromise himself by doing so, whereas in an absolute monarchy, a few words that chance to escape his lips suffice to unmask him forever and ruin him beyond all remedy.

The foregoing explains all this. When a man speaks in the middle of a large crowd, much of what he says is either not heard or soon forgotten, but in the silence of a mute and motionless multitude, the slightest whisper strikes the ear.

In democracies, men never stand still. For countless incidental reasons they are constantly on the move, and there is always something unexpected and in a sense improvised about their lives. Hence they are often forced to do things they have barely learned, to speak of things they scarcely understand, and to engage in labors for which no long apprenticeship has prepared them.

In aristocracies, each person has but a single goal, which he pursues constantly. Among democratic peoples, however, man's existence is more complicated. It is rare for a mind not to embrace several objects at once, and often these objects are quite unrelated to one another. Since he cannot know all of them well, he settles easily for imperfect notions.

For the man who lives in a democracy, when needs are not pressing, desires at least are, for no ambient good seems entirely beyond his reach. Hence he always acts in haste, makes do with approximations, and never stops for more than a moment to consider each of his actions.

His curiosity is at once insatiable and relatively easily satisfied, for he is intent on knowing a lot quickly rather than knowing some things well.

He scarcely has time to delve into things deeply and soon loses any taste he might have for doing so.

Hence democratic peoples are grave because their social and political state constantly compels them to deal with serious matters, and they act rashly because they give but little time and attention to each.

Habitual inattention must be regarded as the greatest defect of the democratic mind.

Chapter 16

WHY THE NATIONAL VANITY OF
THE AMERICANS IS MORE RESTLESS
AND ARGUMENTATIVE THAN
THAT OF THE ENGLISH

ALL free peoples boast of their glories, but national pride does not manifest itself in all of them in the same way.*

Americans, in their relations with foreigners, seem impatient of the slightest censure and insatiable in their appetite for praise. They are pleased by the merest of commendations and seldom satisfied by the fullest. They pester you constantly for your praise, and if you hold out against their importuning, they will laud themselves. Doubtful perhaps of their own merit, they wish to have its portrait constantly before their eyes. Their vanity is not only greedy but also restless and envious. It gives nothing yet is always asking to receive. It is simultaneously grasping and argumentative.

I say to an American that he lives in a beautiful country. He replies, "Yes, indeed, there is none other like it in the world!" I admire the liberty that its inhabitants enjoy, and he responds, "Liberty is a precious gift, but very few peoples are worthy of it." I remark on the purity of morals prevailing in the United States: "I can imagine," he says, "that a foreigner struck by the corruption that is so glaringly apparent in all other nations might be surprised by such a sight." Ultimately I leave him to contemplate himself, but he returns to my side and refuses to leave until he has made me repeat what I have just told him. A patriotism more trying or loquacious is impossible to imagine. It wearies even those who honor it.

The English are different. The Englishman quietly enjoys whatever real or imagined advantages he believes his country to possess. Although he grants nothing to other nations, neither does he ask anything for his own. Criticism from foreigners does not upset him, nor is he much flattered by their praise. Toward the rest of the world he adopts a reserved

*See Note XXII, page 363.

stance rife with disdain and ignorance. His pride needs no
nourishment; it feeds on itself.

That two peoples recently sprung from the same stock
should feel and talk in such contrasting ways is remarkable.

In aristocratic countries the great possess immense privileges, which form the basis of their pride, without seeking to
avail themselves of the lesser advantages that go along with
their position. Since these privileges come to them through
inheritance, they consider them in a way as a part of themselves, or at least as a natural right inherent in their person.
Hence they enjoy a tranquil sense of superiority. It never
occurs to them to boast of prerogatives that everyone can see
and no one would deny. They are too little surprised by these
to bother mentioning them. They stand still in solitary grandeur, certain of being seen by all without making any effort
to show themselves and sure that no one will attempt to force
them out.

When an aristocracy conducts public affairs, its national
pride naturally takes this reserved, insouciant, and haughty
form, and all the other classes of the nation imitate it.

By contrast, when there is little difference in conditions, the
slightest advantages are important. Since each person is surrounded by a million others who possess quite similar or analogous advantages, pride becomes exigent and jealous; it
fastens on trifles and defends them stubbornly.

Since conditions in democracies are highly mobile, it is
almost always the case that whatever advantages men possess
were recently acquired, so that they take tremendous pleasure
in showing them off in order to demonstrate to others and
attest to themselves that they actually do enjoy them. Furthermore, since those advantages can slip away at any moment,
those who possess them are in a constant state of alarm and
seek to let others know that they still have them. Men who
live in democracies love their country in the same way that
they love themselves, and they carry the habits of their private
vanity over into their national vanity.

The restless and insatiable vanity of democratic peoples is
a product of equality and fragility of conditions; so much so
that members of the proudest nobility will exhibit absolutely
the same passion in those limited segments of their lives

where some element of instability and contentiousness is to be found.

An aristocratic class is always profoundly different from the other classes of a nation owing to the extent of its prerogatives and their perpetual nature. It is sometimes the case, however, that certain members of this aristocratic class differ from one another only by virtue of small, fleeting advantages that can be gained or lost from one day to the next.

One knows of cases in which the members of a powerful aristocracy, gathered together in a capital or court, have fought tooth and nail over frivolous privileges that depend on the caprices of fashion or the will of the master. In these situations they exhibited the same puerile jealousies of one another as men in democracies, the same ardor to grab the slightest advantage over the equals with whom they were obliged to contend, and the same need to make a show of whatever advantages they enjoyed.

If it ever occurred to courtiers to demonstrate national pride, I have no doubt that it would be quite like the pride exhibited by democratic peoples.

Chapter 17

HOW SOCIETY IN THE UNITED STATES SEEMS BOTH AGITATED AND MONOTONOUS

THE United States, it seems, is unmatched when it comes to arousing and sustaining our curiosity. Fortunes, ideas, and laws are in constant flux there. Even immutable nature sometimes seems mutable, so great are the transformations she daily endures at the hand of man.

In the long run, however, this very agitated society can seem monotonous, and the spectator, having contemplated this very fluid scene for some time, succumbs to boredom.

Among aristocratic peoples, each man is all but fixed in his sphere, but men are extraordinarily dissimilar. Their passions, ideas, habits, and tastes vary in essential ways. Nothing budges, but difference abounds.

By contrast, in democracies, all men are similar and do roughly similar things. They are, to be sure, subject to great and continual vicissitudes. But since the same successes and the same reverses recur constantly and only the names of the actors change, the play remains the same. The appearance of American society is agitated, because men and things are constantly changing; and it is monotonous, because all the changes are the same.

Men who live in democratic times have many passions, but most of their passions either culminate or originate in the love of wealth. This is not because their souls are pettier but because money in such circumstances really is more important.

When citizens are all independent and indifferent, the only way to obtain their cooperation is by paying for it. Hence the uses of wealth are multiplied *ad infinitum*, and its value is increased.

Now that the prestige that once attached to ancient things has vanished, men are no longer distinguished by birth, estate, or occupation, or barely are. Money is virtually the only thing that still creates very visible differences among them and sets some apart from their peers. The distinction that is born of wealth is enhanced by the disappearance and diminution of all the others.

Among aristocratic peoples, money leads to only a few points on the vast circumference of desires; in democracies it seems to lead everywhere.

Hence one ordinarily finds love of wealth as the principal or subsidiary cause underlying the actions of Americans, which lends a family resemblance to all their passions and soon makes their image tiresome to behold.

This perpetual return of the same passion is monotonous, as are the particular methods that this passion employs to satisfy itself.

In a constituted and peaceful democracy such as that of the United States, where no one can enrich himself through war, public employment, or political confiscations, love of wealth steers men primarily toward industry. Now, industry, though it often brings vast disorders and major disasters in its wake, cannot prosper without the aid of very regular habits and a long series of highly uniform small actions. The more energetic the passion, the more regular the habits and the more uniform the actions. It is fair to say that what makes Americans so methodical is the very vehemence of their passions. This troubles their souls but organizes their lives.

What I say about America applies, moreover, to nearly all men of the present day. Variety is vanishing from the human species. In all corners of the world we find the same ways of acting, thinking, and feeling. This is not only because all peoples have more to do with one another and copy each other more faithfully than in the past but also because men in each country, deviating more and more from the ideas and sentiments peculiar to a caste, occupation, or family, are simultaneously converging on something more nearly derived from the constitution of man, which is everywhere the same. Thus without imitating one another they are becoming more alike. They are like travelers scattered throughout a vast forest in which all trails lead to the same spot. If they all recognize this central point and head toward it, they will imperceptibly come together without intending to and without noticing or being aware of one another, and in the end they will be surprised to find themselves gathered at the same place. All peoples that take not a particular man but man as such as the object of their study and imitation will ultimately find themselves coming together in a common set of mores like these travelers meeting at the forest crossroads.

Chapter 18

ON HONOR IN THE UNITED STATES AND IN DEMOCRATIC SOCIETIES[1]

MEN seem to employ two quite distinct methods in making public judgments of the actions of their fellow men: sometimes they rely on simple notions of the just and unjust that exist everywhere; at other times they use very particular notions associated with one country or period. These two rules often differ. In some cases they are at odds, but they never entirely coincide with or negate each other.

Honor, when its power is greatest, governs will more than belief, and even when men submit to its dictates without hesitation or murmur, they still feel, through an obscure but powerful instinct, that there exists a law more general, more ancient, and more holy, which they sometimes disobey without ceasing to recognize. There are actions that have been deemed both virtuous and dishonorable. The refusal to fight a duel often falls into this category.

I think that such phenomena can be explained other than by invoking the caprices of certain individuals or peoples, as has been done up to now.

The human race experiences certain permanent and general needs, and these have given rise to moral laws. All men, in all times and places, have associated failure to observe these laws with the ideas of blame and shame. They refer to evading these laws as *doing wrong* and to obeying them as *doing right*.

Within the vast human association, moreover, more limited associations known as peoples have come into being, and, within these, still smaller associations referred to as classes or castes.

---

[1]The word *honor* is not always used in the same sense in French.

(1) It signifies first the esteem, glory, and consideration that a man obtains from his fellow men: it is in this sense that one says *to win honor*.

(2) Honor also refers to the set of rules that aid in obtaining such glory, esteem, and consideration. Thus we say that *a man has always conformed strictly to the laws of honor* or that *he has forfeited his honor*. In writing the present chapter, I have always used the word *honor* in this second sense.

Each of these associations forms something like a particular species within the human race, and even though it does not differ essentially from the mass of men, it stands somewhat apart and experiences needs of its own. These are special needs, which in some respects and in certain countries modify the way in which human actions are envisaged and judged.

It is a general and permanent interest of the human race that men not kill one another, but in some cases it may be in the particular and temporary interest of a people or class to excuse or even honor homicide.

Honor is nothing other than a particular rule based on a particular state that a people or class uses to assign blame or praise.

Nothing is more unproductive for the human mind than an abstract idea. I therefore hasten to get down to facts. An example will make my thinking clear.

I shall choose the most extraordinary kind of honor the world has ever known, and the one that is most familiar to us: the aristocratic honor that arose in feudal society. I will use what I have just said to explain this and vice versa.

There is no need here to inquire when and how the aristocracy of the Middle Ages came into being, why it was so profoundly separate from the rest of the nation, or what undergirded and buttressed its power. Instead, I shall take it as I find it, already standing on its own two feet, and try to understand why it judged most human actions in so peculiar a light.

What strikes me first of all is the fact that in the feudal world actions were not always praised or blamed in accordance with their intrinsic value but judged in certain cases solely in relation to the person who was their author or object — a procedure repugnant to the general conscience of the human race. Thus certain acts that were dishonorable if committed by a noble were considered neither good nor bad if committed by a commoner. Others changed character depending on whether the person who suffered from them belonged to the aristocracy or lived outside it.

At the time when these different opinions originated, the nobility formed a separate body amid the people, which it dominated from the inaccessible heights to which it had repaired. In order to maintain this distinctive position, from which it derived its strength, it not only needed political privileges but also required virtues and vices tailored to its own use.

That a particular virtue or vice belonged to the nobility or the common sort, or that a particular action was neither right nor wrong when its object was a humble villager but condemnable when it concerned a noble — these were matters of arbitrary choice. But that honor or shame should attach to a man's actions depending on his condition — this stemmed from the very constitution of an aristocratic society. The same thing can be seen, in fact, in all countries that have had an aristocracy. So long as a single vestige of aristocracy remains, such peculiarities can be found: to debauch a colored girl does little harm to the reputation of an American, but to marry her would dishonor him.

In some cases feudal honor prescribed vengeance and stigmatized pardon for insults. In others it imperiously commanded men to conquer their passions and neglect their own interests. It made no law of either humanity or gentleness. Yet it praised generosity; it prized liberality more than benevolence, and it allowed a man to enrich himself through gambling or war but not through work. It preferred great crimes to small gains. Greed revolted it less than avarice, and violence often met with its approval, while cunning and treachery it deemed always contemptible.

These bizarre notions were not merely caprices of those who conceived them.

A class that has reached the pinnacle and set itself above all others and that strives constantly to maintain itself in that supreme rank must particularly honor those virtues that possess grandeur and luster and can readily be combined with pride and love of power. It does not shrink from disrupting the natural order of conscience to place those virtues above all others. One can even see why it would deliberately place certain bold and brilliant vices above peaceable and modest virtues. It is in a sense constrained to do so by its condition.

Ahead of all other virtues and in place of many of them, the nobles of the Middle Ages put martial courage.

This, too, was an unusual opinion that stemmed directly from the unusual character of the social state.

The feudal aristocracy was born in war and for war. It had found its power in arms and maintained it by arms. Hence nothing was more essential to it than martial courage, and it was natural that it should glorify this above all else. Hence it approved of, and often insisted on, every outward manifestation of this courage, even those that came at the expense of reason and humanity. Individual fancy affected only the details.

That a man should regard a slap on the cheek as a tremendous insult and feel bound to fight a duel to the death with the person who struck him — that was arbitrary. But that a noble could not calmly accept an insult and was dishonored if he allowed himself to be slapped without fighting — that grew out of the very principles and needs of a military aristocracy.

Hence it was true, up to a point, to say that honor was in some respects capricious, but the caprices of honor were always contained within certain necessary limits. The particular rule that our forebears called honor was to my mind so far from an arbitrary law that I would be quite prepared to trace its most incoherent and bizarre prescriptions back to a small number of fixed and invariable needs of feudal society.

If I were to pursue feudal honor into the field of politics, I would find it just as easy to explain its actions there.

The social state and political institutions of the Middle Ages were such that the national power never governed citizens directly. In a sense, no such power existed in their eyes. Each individual knew only one man whom he was obliged to obey. It was through that man that each person was linked, unbeknownst to himself, to everyone else. In feudal societies, all public order therefore hinged on the sentiment of fidelity to the very person of the lord. Once that was destroyed, anarchy followed at once.

Furthermore, fidelity to the political leader was a sentiment whose value all members of the aristocracy perceived daily, since each of them was both lord and vassal and obliged to give orders as well as obey them.

To keep faith with one's lord; to sacrifice oneself for him if necessary; to share his fortune, good or bad; to aid him in his undertakings, whatever they might be — these were the primary requirements of feudal honor in the political realm. Public opinion condemned treachery by a vassal with extraordinary severity. Particular opprobrium attached to the name coined for this crime: it was known as "felony."

By contrast, we find few traces in the Middle Ages of a passion on which ancient societies thrived, namely, patriotism. In our idiom the word "patriotism" is not very old at all.[2]

Feudal institutions obscured the fatherland and made loving it less necessary. They made people forget the nation and invest their passions in a man. Hence loyalty to country was never a strict requirement of feudal honor.

Not that our fathers did not love the fatherland in their hearts. But that love existed only as a feeble and obscure instinct; it grew clearer and stronger as classes were destroyed and power was centralized.

This is clear from the contrary judgments that the peoples of Europe make of the various facts of their history, depending on which generation is doing the judging. What dishonored the Constable of Bourbon above all else in the eyes of his contemporaries was the fact that he bore arms against his king. What dishonors him most in our eyes is the fact that he made war on his country. We are as critical of him as our ancestors were but for different reasons.

I chose to clarify my thinking by discussing feudal honor, because its features are especially stark and clear, but I might have chosen a different example and arrived at the same goal via another route.

Although we know less about the Romans than about our ancestors, we do know that they held particular opinions about glory and dishonor that did not derive from general notions of good and evil. They looked at many human actions in a different light depending on whether they were committed by a citizen or a foreigner, a free man or a slave. They glorified certain vices and honored some virtues above all others.

"Now, in those days," Plutarch wrote in his life of Coriolanus, "prowess was honored and prized in Rome above all other virtues, as attested by the fact that it was called *virtus*, using the very word for virtue and thus attributing the name of the common genus to a particular species, so that to say

---

[2]Even the word *patrie* was not used by French authors before the sixteenth century.

'virtue' in Latin was the same as saying 'valor.' " Who cannot see in this a reflection of the particular need of this singular association, which was formed for the conquest of the world?

Similar observations could be made of any other nation, for as I said earlier, whenever men gather to form a particular society, a characteristic form of honor immediately springs up among them, that is, a distinctive set of opinions regarding what is to be praised or blamed. And these particular rules always have their source in the special habits and special interests of the association.

To a certain extent this applies to democratic societies as it does to others, as we shall soon see in the case of the Americans.[3]

Scattered among the opinions of Americans one still finds certain notions taken from the old European conception of aristocratic honor. These traditional opinions are very few in number, not deeply rooted, and have little power. This conception of honor is a religion, some of whose temples have been left standing but in which no one any longer believes.

Amidst these half-effaced notions of an exotic form of honor we find new opinions, which constitute something that might today be called American honor.

I have shown how the Americans were constantly driven toward commerce and industry. Their origin, social state, political institutions, and even the very land they live in have all propelled them irresistibly in that direction. At present they therefore constitute an almost exclusively industrial and commercial association, which is situated inside a vast new country and whose principal purpose is to exploit it. This is the characteristic feature that most sharply distinguishes the American people from all others today.

All the peaceful virtues that tend to regulate social activities and encourage trade should therefore enjoy special honor among Americans, and neglecting those virtues ought to incur the public's contempt.

By contrast, the turbulent virtues, which often fascinate so-

---

[3]I am speaking here of those Americans who live in regions where slavery does not exist. Only they can give a complete picture of a democratic society.

ciety but still more often bring disruption in their wake, will all be held in lower esteem by public opinion. A person may neglect these virtues without losing the respect of his fellow citizens and might lose their respect by acquiring them.

The American classification of vices is no less arbitrary.

Certain inclinations that are condemnable in the eyes of general reason and the universal conscience of the human race happen to accord with the particular and temporary needs of the American association. These it disapproves weakly at best, and sometimes praises. I will mention in particular the love of wealth and its associated preferences. In order to clear, plant, and transform the vast uninhabited continent that is his domain, the American needs the daily support of an energetic passion. Love of wealth is the only passion that will do. Hence the passion for wealth is not stigmatized in America, and so long as it does not exceed the limits that public order sets for it, it is honored. What our ancestors in the Middle Ages called servile greed, the American calls noble and estimable ambition, just as he ascribes the name "blind and barbaric fury" to the conquering ardor and warlike spirit that drove those warriors into new battles every day.

In the United States, fortunes easily collapse and rise anew. The country is boundless and its resources are inexhaustible. The people have all the needs and appetites of a growing individual, and no matter how hard they try, there is always more wealth in the environment than they can lay hold of. What is to be feared in such a people is not the ruin of a few individuals, which can be repaired quickly, but the inactivity and listlessness of all. The audacity of their industrial undertakings is the primary reason for their rapid progress, their strength, and their grandeur. For Americans, industry is like a vast lottery, in which a small number of men lose daily but the state wins constantly. Such a people should therefore look favorably on boldness in industry and honor it. Now, any bold undertaking risks the fortune of the person who attempts it and of those who place their trust in him. Americans, who make a kind of virtue of commercial recklessness, cannot in any case stigmatize the reckless.

That is why people in the United States are so remarkably indulgent toward businessmen who go bankrupt. An accident of this sort leaves no stain on his honor. In this respect, Americans are different not only from the peoples of Europe but from all other modern trading nations. So, too, are they unlike all other nations with respect to their position and needs.

In America, any vice likely to pollute the purity of morals and destroy the bond of matrimony is treated with a severity unknown anywhere else in the world. At first this makes a strange contrast with the tolerance shown in other respects. It is surprising to find in the same people a morality at once so relaxed and so austere.

These things are not as incoherent as one might assume. Public opinion in the United States is only mildly critical of love of wealth, which serves the industrial grandeur and prosperity of the nation, and it is particularly harsh on bad morals, which would distract the human spirit from the pursuit of well-being and disrupt the internal order of the family, which is so essential to success in business. In order to win the respect of their fellow men, Americans are therefore obliged to acquire regular habits. In this respect we may say that they make chastity a point of honor.

American honor coincides with the old European honor in one respect: it makes courage the paramount virtue and the greatest of moral necessities for man. But it does not look at courage in the same way.

In the United States, martial valor is not particularly prized. The courage that people know best and respect most is that which allows men to brave the ocean's wrath to reach port sooner and to tolerate without complaint the miseries of the wilderness and the even crueler solitude; the courage that makes a man almost immune to the sudden reversal of a laboriously acquired fortune and prompts him to turn his efforts at once to amassing another. This is the sort of courage that is most needed to preserve the American association and ensure its prosperity, and it is particularly honored and glorified. A man cannot exhibit lack of such courage without dishonor.

One last feature will help to bring out the idea of this chapter.

In a democratic society like that of the United States in which fortunes are small and relatively insecure, everyone works, and there is no door that work cannot open. This has turned the point of honor upside down and directed it against idleness.

In America I occasionally met wealthy young men who, though temperamentally opposed to all arduous effort, were nevertheless forced to take up an occupation. Their nature and fortune were such that they might have remained idle; public opinion adamantly forbade this, however, and they had no choice but to obey. In Europe, by contrast, in nations where aristocracy is still struggling against the torrent that is sweeping it away, I have often seen men prodded by an endless succession of needs and desires nevertheless remain idle so as not to forfeit the esteem of their equals, men who accept boredom and impoverishment more easily than they could accept work.

Clearly, these two quite contrary obligations embody two different rules, yet both originate in honor.

What our forefathers saw as the quintessence of honor was in fact only one of its forms. They gave a generic name to what was merely a species. Honor can thus be found in democratic centuries as well as in ages of aristocracy, but it is not difficult to show that in democratic centuries it takes on a different appearance.

Not only are its prescriptions different, but, as we shall see, there are fewer of them, they are not as clear, and people are not as strict in abiding by its laws.

The situation of a caste is always more particular than that of a people. Nothing in the world is more exceptional than a small society always composed of the same families, such as the aristocracy of the Middle Ages, whose purpose was to concentrate and retain, exclusively and hereditarily, enlightenment, wealth, and power in its midst.

Now, the more exceptional the position of a society is, the greater the number of its special needs; and its notions of honor, which correspond to its needs, will proliferate.

Hence there will be fewer prescriptions of honor in a people that is not divided into castes than in a people that is. Should nations arise in which it is difficult even to find classes, honor will be limited to a small number of precepts, and the distance between those precepts and the moral laws adopted by the common run of humanity will diminish.

Accordingly, the prescriptions of honor will be less bizarre and less numerous in a democratic nation than in an aristocracy.

They will also be more obscure; this is a necessary consequence of what has been said thus far.

Because the characteristic features of honor are fewer in number and less peculiar, it will often be difficult to make them out.

There are other reasons as well.

In the aristocratic nations of the Middle Ages, generation followed generation without change. Each family was in a sense immortal, and its position remained perpetually fixed. There was little more variation in ideas than in conditions.

Hence each man gazed always upon the same objects, and always from the same point of view. Little by little his eye probed their smallest details, and in the long run his perception could not fail to become clear and distinct. Thus not only did the men of feudal times base their conception of honor on some quite extraordinary opinions, but each of those opinions inscribed itself in their minds in a clear and precise form.

This can never be the case in a country like America, where all citizens are on the move and society, in the course of modifying itself every day, changes its opinions along with its needs. In such a country, one catches a glimpse of the rules of honor, but seldom does one have the leisure to contemplate them steadily.

Even if society were unchanging, it would still be difficult to fix the meaning to be ascribed to the word "honor."

Because each class in the Middle Ages had its own conception of honor, the number of men who held the same opinion at any one time was never very large and therefore that opinion could be made sharp and precise; and this was all the more true because those who did hold any particular opinion shared exactly the same position, and that position was highly exceptional, so that they had a natural disposition to agree about the prescriptions of a law that was made for themselves alone.

Honor thus became a complete and detailed code in which everything was foreseen and specified in advance, and which laid down a fixed and permanently visible rule for human actions. In a democratic nation like the American people, in which ranks are confounded and all of society constitutes but a single mass, all of whose elements are analogous without being entirely alike, there can never be agreement in advance about what is permitted by honor and what is prohibited.

To be sure, certain national needs do indeed exist among these people, and these give rise to common opinions about honor. But these similar opinions never occur at the same time, in the same way, and with equal force to all citizens. The law of honor exists, but often it lacks people to interpret it.

The confusion is far greater still in a democratic country like ours, in which the various classes that made up the old society, having mixed without yet having been able to blend, daily import diverse and often contrary notions of their honor from one to another; and in which each man, following his whims, renounces some of the opinions of his forebears while holding on to others; so that amid so many arbitrary measures no common rule can ever be established. It is therefore almost impossible to say in advance which actions will be honored and which stigmatized. These are wretched times, but they will not last.

In democratic nations, honor, being ill-defined, is necessarily less powerful, because it is difficult to apply with certitude and firmness a law that is imperfectly understood. Public opinion, which is the natural and sovereign interpreter of the law of honor, cannot see distinctly where blame and praise are to be bestowed and is therefore hesitant in issuing its decree. Sometimes it contradicts itself; often it does nothing and refrains from intervening.

There are several additional reasons for the relative weakness of honor in democracies.

In aristocratic countries, a given idea of honor is never accepted by more than a certain — often quite small — number of men, who are always separate from their fellows. In their minds honor therefore mingles quite easily with, and becomes indistinguishable from, all that sets them apart. To them it seems like the distinctive feature of their physiognomy. They apply its various rules with all the ardor of personal interest and become, if I may say, passionate about obeying them.

This can be seen quite clearly in discussions of judicial duels in medieval customary law. It emerges that nobles were required to settle their disputes with lances or swords, whereas villeins used clubs, "inasmuch," as the texts put it, "*as villeins have no honor*." This did not mean, as we might be tempted to assume today, that such men were contemptible. It merely meant that their actions were not judged according to same rules as those of the aristocracy.

What is at first sight astonishing is that when honor reigns with such omnipotence, its prescriptions are generally quite odd, so that the more it deviates from reason, the better it seems to be obeyed. This has led some to the conclusion that honor was powerful precisely because it was so outlandish.

In fact, both of these things stem from the same source, but they do not flow from each other.

Honor is bizarre to the extent that the needs it represents are more particular and experienced by a smaller number of men; and it is because it represents needs of this kind that it is powerful. Hence honor is not powerful because it is bizarre, but it is bizarre and powerful for the same reason.

I would add a further remark.

Among aristocratic peoples, all ranks are different, but all are also fixed. Each individual occupies, within his own sphere, a place that he cannot quit, and he lives among other men similarly moored all around him. In such nations, no one can either hope or fear that he will not be seen. No man is placed so low as to be deprived of a theater and likely to escape blame or praise by dint of obscurity.

In democratic states, by contrast, where all citizens are indistinguishable members of the same crowd and in a state of constant agitation, public opinion has no hold. Its object is forever disappearing and slipping away. Hence honor in such states will always be less imperious and less oppressive, for honor acts only with the public in view. In this respect it is different from plain virtue, which is its own reward and content to be its own witness.

If the reader has fully grasped the foregoing, he will have understood that there is a close and necessary connection between inequality of conditions and what I have called honor, and unless I am mistaken this connection has never been clearly pointed out before. I should therefore make one last effort to make my point perfectly clear.

A nation sets itself apart from the rest of the human race. Independent of certain general needs inherent in the human species, the nation has particular interests and needs of its own. Certain opinions concerning praise and blame immediately come into being, and these opinions, which are peculiar to this particular nation, its citizens call honor.

Within this same nation, a caste arises, which, on setting itself apart in turn from all other classes, acquires particular needs of its own, and these in turn give rise to special opinions. The honor of this caste, a bizarre composite of notions peculiar to the nation and notions more peculiar still to the particular caste, will grow as remote as one might imagine from the simple and general opinions of humankind. Having attained this extreme, let us now climb back down.

Ranks mingle; privileges are abolished. The men who make up the nation revert to being similar and equal, and their interests and needs become indistinguishable, so that we see all the distinctive notions that each caste called honor vanish one by one. Honor now derives only from the particular needs of the nation itself. It represents its individuality among peoples.

Finally, if there were to come a day when all races coalesced and all the peoples of the world had the same interests and needs and no characteristic feature any longer set them apart, then people would cease to ascribe any conventional value to human actions altogether. Everyone would look at those actions in the same light. The general needs of mankind, revealed by consciousness to every man, would be the common measure. We would then find in this world only simple and general notions of good and evil, which would be associated in a natural and necessary way with the ideas of praise and blame.

So, to sum up all my thinking in a single formula, it is dissimilarities and inequalities among men that created honor; the importance of honor fades as those differences diminish; and it will presumably disappear when they do.

Chapter 19

WHY THERE ARE SO MANY AMBITIOUS MEN AND SO FEW GREAT AMBITIONS IN THE UNITED STATES

THE first striking thing about the United States is the huge number of people bent on escaping their original condition. The second is the small number of great ambitions that stand out amid this universal outpouring of ambition. The desire to rise apparently gnaws at every American, yet almost no one seems to nurse vast hopes or to aim very high. All are persistent in their desire to acquire property, reputation, and power; few take a grand view of such things. At first sight this is surprising, since there is nothing obvious in American mores or laws that would set limits to desire or clip its wings.

Equality of conditions hardly seems a sufficient explanation for this unusual situation. When this same equality first established itself in France, it immediately unleashed ambitions that were virtually without limit. Nevertheless, I think that the cause of the foregoing is to be sought primarily in the Americans' social state and democratic mores.

Every revolution enlarges men's ambitions. This is especially true of a revolution that overthrows an aristocracy.

When ancient barriers that have kept the crowd away from renown and power suddenly fall, there is an impetuous and universal upward movement toward grandeur long-envied and now at last within reach. In the first exaltation of victory, nothing seems impossible to anyone. Not only is there no limit to desire, but the power to satisfy desire seems virtually unlimited. Amid the general and unexpected recasting of customs and laws, with all men and all rules thrust into confusion on a vast scale, citizens rise and fall with unprecedented speed, and power passes so quickly from one hand to another that no one need despair of eventually grabbing some for himself.

Bear in mind, moreover, that the people who destroy an

aristocracy have lived under its laws. They have seen its splen-
dors and unwittingly absorbed feelings and ideas that it
conceived. Hence when an aristocracy dissolves, its spirit continues to hover over the masses, and its instincts are preserved
long after it has been defeated.

Thus very great ambitions remain in evidence as long as the
democratic revolution lasts. This continues to be the case for
some time after it is over.

The extraordinary events that men witness do not vanish
from memory in a day. Passions prompted by revolution do
not disappear when the revolution ends. The feeling of instability lingers amidst order. The idea of easy success outlives
the strange vicissitudes from which it sprang. Vast desires
remain, while the means of satisfying them diminish daily.
The taste for great fortunes persists, even though great fortunes themselves become rare, and everywhere overweening
and frustrated ambitions secretly consume the hearts that
harbor them, to no avail.

Little by little, however, the last traces of conflict fade from
view. The vestiges of aristocracy eventually disappear. The
great events that attended its downfall are forgotten. Calm
takes the place of war, and regularity reasserts itself in a new
world. Desires proportion themselves to means. Needs, ideas,
and sentiments follow from one another. Leveling is complete: democratic society has finally found its footing.

If we consider a democratic people that has achieved this
permanent and normal state, it will look very different from
the scene we have just been contemplating, and we will easily
come to the conclusion that if ambition becomes great while
conditions are tending toward equality, it loses that character
when equality becomes a fact.

As great fortunes are divided up and knowledge spreads, no
one is left absolutely devoid of enlightenment or property. Because the privileges and disqualifications of class have been
abolished and men have forever cast off the bonds that kept
them in their place, the idea of progress is on everyone's mind.
All hearts long to rise, and every man wishes to leave his place.
Ambition is the universal feeling.

But if equality of conditions gives all citizens some resources,
it prevents anyone from amassing very extensive amounts of

them, and this necessarily imposes fairly strict limits on desire. Among democratic peoples, ambition is therefore ardent and constant, but it cannot habitually aim very high, and people usually spend their lives ardently coveting the petty things they see as being within their reach.

What most discourages people in democracies from conceiving great ambitions is not the pettiness of their fortunes but the violence of their daily efforts to increase them. They coerce their souls into spending all their strength on mediocre things, which before long cannot help but constrict their vision and circumscribe their power. They could be much poorer and remain greater.

The few opulent citizens that a democracy may include are no exception to this rule. A man who slowly climbs to wealth and power acquires, in the course of his lengthy labors, habits of prudence and restraint that he cannot then shed. A man cannot expand his soul gradually, as he can his house.

A similar remark applies to the sons of such a man. While it is true that they are born into a high position, it is also true that their parents were humble people. They grow up surrounded by feelings and ideas from which it is hard to free themselves later on, and in all likelihood they inherited their father's instincts along with his property.

By contrast, the poorest scion of a powerful aristocracy may display vast ambition, because the traditional opinions of his race and the general spirit of his caste will for a time lift him up above his fortune.

Another thing that makes it hard for men in democratic ages to commit themselves to ambitious undertakings is the amount of time they expect to have to devote to preparation. Pascal said that "the great advantage of being well-born is that it sets a man on his way by the age of eighteen or twenty, while another man may have to wait until he is fifty to get that far, thus yielding a gain of thirty years without effort." Those thirty years are what ambitious men in democracies ordinarily must do without. Equality allows anyone to go anywhere but prevents people from quickly achieving great stature.

In a democratic society, as elsewhere, the number of large fortunes to be made is limited, and since careers leading to such success are open to every citizen without distinction, progress toward that goal must be slower for all of them. Since the candidates seem almost alike and it is difficult to choose among them without violating the principle of equality, which is the supreme law in democratic societies, the first idea that comes to mind is to make everyone proceed at the same pace and subject them all to the same trials.

Thus as men become more alike, and as the principle of equality penetrates more peacefully and deeply into institutions and mores, the rules of advancement become more rigid, and advancement slows. The difficulty of quickly achieving a certain stature increases.

Hatred of privilege and the difficulty of selection thus create a situation in which all men, regardless of stature, are forced to follow the same course and are indiscriminately subjected to a host of trivial preliminary exercises, in which they squander their youth and see their imagination stifled, so that they despair of ever being able to enjoy fully the goods they are offered. And by the time they finally reach the point where they are able to do extraordinary things, they have lost the taste for them.

In China, where equality of conditions is very great and very old, a man cannot move from one public office to another without submitting to an examination. He has to face this ordeal at every stage of his career, and the idea has become such an accepted part of Chinese mores that I recall reading one Chinese novel in which the hero, after a series of ups and downs, at last succeeds in moving the heart of his mistress by passing an important examination. Great ambitions breathe uneasily in such an atmosphere.

What I say about politics extends to everything else. Equality produces the same effects everywhere. Wherever the law does not take it upon itself to regulate and slow the movement of men, competition suffices to do so.

In a well-established democratic society, great and rapid promotions are therefore rare. They are exceptions to the common rule. The fact that they are so special makes people forget how seldom they occur.

Eventually men in democracies develop some awareness of all this. In the long run they come to realize that although lawmakers have created a boundless field in which all men can easily take a few steps forward, no one can presume to get ahead quickly. Between them and the ultimate object of their desires they see a host of small obstacles that will take time to overcome. This prospect nips their ambition in the bud and disheartens them. They therefore set aside their remote and uncertain expectations and look close to home for pleasures less exalted and more facile. The law does not limit their horizons; they do so themselves.

I said that great ambitions were rarer in democratic centuries than in aristocratic times. I will add that when they come into being despite the natural obstacles I have mentioned, they have a different look about them.

In aristocracies, ambition frequently enjoys a wide arena, but its limits are fixed. In democratic countries, its field is usually narrow, but should it overstep its bounds, nothing seems capable of stopping it. Since men are weak, isolated, and mobile, and since precedents have little influence and laws are short-lived, resistance to innovation is soft, and society as a body seems somehow to lack a firm backbone and a solid footing. So once ambitious men have power in their hands, they believe they can venture anything. And when it slips through their fingers, their thoughts turn immediately to overthrowing the state in order to regain it.

That gives great political ambition a violent and revolutionary character, which one rarely finds to the same degree in aristocratic societies.

A host of quite reasonable if petty ambitions out of which will spring from time to time a few grand if ill-disciplined desires: such is the picture we ordinarily see in democratic nations. A proportionate ambition, moderate yet vast, is seldom encountered.

I showed earlier the secret force by which equality causes the passion for material pleasures and the exclusive love of the present to predominate in the human heart. These various instincts mingle with the sentiment of ambition and tint it, as it were, with their colors.

I think that ambitious men in democracies are less concerned than all others with the interests and judgments of the future: the present moment alone occupies and absorbs them. They complete a large number of projects rapidly rather than erect a few long-lasting monuments. They like success far more than glory. What they ask of men is obedience above all. What they want first and foremost is influence. Their mores almost invariably fail to keep pace with their condition, so they often bring very vulgar tastes with them into extraordinarily fortunate situations, and they seem to have raised themselves to sovereign power only to gratify trivial and coarse appetites more easily.

I think that it is quite necessary nowadays to purify the sentiment of ambition, regulate it, and keep it in proportion, but it would be very dangerous to try to impoverish it or constrict it unduly. We must try to set limits to it in advance — limits that it must never be allowed to exceed. Within those limits, however, we should take care not to hinder its expression.

I confess that for democratic societies I am far less afraid of audacity of desire than of mediocrity. What is most to be feared, it seems to me, is that the spark and grandeur of ambition might be swallowed up by the ceaseless petty occupations of private life, and that the human passions might subside and diminish at the same time, leaving society looking more tranquil but also less impressive as time goes by.

I therefore think that the leaders of these new societies would be wrong to try to lull citizens into a state of unnecessarily undisturbed and peaceful prosperity, and that it is good for leaders to set difficult and dangerous challenges for their citizens from time to time so as to inspire ambition and create a theater for its expression.

Moralists complain constantly that pride is the favorite vice of our age.

In a certain sense this is true: indeed, there is no one who does not think himself better than his neighbor and no one willing to obey a superior. But in another sense it is quite false, for the same man who cannot tolerate either subordination or equality has such contempt for himself that he thinks the only pleasures he is made to savor are vulgar ones. He voluntarily limits himself to mediocre desires and never dares to reach for anything high: he can scarcely imagine a lofty undertaking.

Hence far from thinking that we should recommend humility to our contemporaries, I think we should try to give them a more ample idea of themselves and their species. Humility is not healthy for them. What they lack most, in my opinion, is pride. I would readily give up any number of our petty virtues for this one vice.

Chapter 20

ON PLACE-HUNTING IN CERTAIN DEMOCRATIC NATIONS

IN the United States, the moment a citizen acquires some education and resources he will try to enrich himself in commerce or industry, or else he will buy a field covered with forest and transform himself into a pioneer. All he asks of the state is not to interfere with his labors and to protect the fruits thereof.

In most European nations, when a man begins to feel his strength and extend his desires, the first idea that occurs to him is to obtain a public position. Such different effects stemming from the same cause are worth pausing a moment to consider.

When public offices are few in number, badly paid, and precarious, while careers in industry are numerous and productive, the new and impatient desires that are daily born of equality will naturally direct themselves toward industry rather than public administration.

But if, as ranks are being equalized, enlightenment remains incomplete, or minds remain timid, or commerce and industry, hindered in their development, offer at best a slow and difficult route to fortune, citizens will despair of improving their lot by themselves and besiege the head of state clamoring for assistance. To achieve comfort for themselves at the expense of the public treasury seems, if not the only course open to them, then at least the easiest and best way to escape a condition that no longer seems adequate: place-hunting thus attracts more job-seekers than any other line of work.

This is inevitable, especially in large centralized monarchies, where the number of paid posts is enormous and officials enjoy fairly secure existences, so that one need not despair of obtaining a post and enjoying it in peace like any other form of heritable property.

It goes without saying that this universal and immoderate desire for public office is a great social ill; that it destroys the spirit of independence in each citizen and injects a venal and servile humor into the nation's bloodstream; and that it suffocates virile virtues. Nor will I point out that this kind of traffic in jobs is an unproductive activity that unsettles the country without yielding any benefit. All that is obvious.

But I do want to remark that the government that encourages such a tendency puts its tranquillity at risk and its very existence in great danger.

In a time like ours, which has witnessed the gradual extinction of the love and respect that used to attach to power, I know that rulers may think it necessary to bind each man more tightly in chains of self-interest and may find it convenient to use men's own passions to impose order and silence on them. But things cannot go on that way for long, and what may seem for a time a source of strength will surely prove to be a great cause of trouble and weakness in the long run.

In all nations, including democratic ones, the number of public posts ultimately turns out to be limited, but the number of ambitious men is not. It grows steadily in a gradual and irresistible process as conditions become more equal. It reaches its limits only when the country runs out of men.

Hence when the public administration is the only outlet for ambition, the government inevitably encounters a permanent opposition, because its task is to satisfy with limited means desires that proliferate without limit. There is no escaping the conclusion that of all the nations in the world, the most difficult to control and rule are those where everyone is petitioning for something. Whatever the leaders do, the people are never satisfied, and there is always reason to fear that they will ultimately overthrow the constitution and change the face of the state solely to create vacancies in government.

Therefore, if I am right, today's sovereigns, who strive to make themselves the focal point of all the new desires aroused by equality and then to satisfy those desires, will eventually repent of having embarked on such a course. Some day they will find out that they put their power at risk by making it so indispensable, and that it would have been both safer and more honest to have taught their subjects the art of providing for themselves.

Chapter 21

WHY GREAT REVOLUTIONS
WILL BECOME RARE

A PEOPLE that has lived for centuries under the regime of castes and classes can achieve a democratic social state only by way of a long series of more or less painful transformations abetted by violent outbursts and involving numerous episodes in which property, opinions, and power are all subject to rapid change.

Even after such a great revolution ends, the revolutionary habits it creates live on for quite some time, and deep turmoil follows in its wake.

Since all this takes place as conditions are tending toward equality, people conclude that there is a hidden relation and secret bond between equality itself and revolution, such that the former cannot exist without giving rise to the latter.

On this point reason seems to accord with experience.

In a nation where ranks are almost equal, no obvious bond brings men together and holds them firmly in their place. No one has the permanent right or power to command, and no one is of a condition such that he must obey. Since each individual can lay claim to some degree of enlightenment and some resources, he can choose his own course and proceed separately from his fellow men.

The same causes that make citizens independent of one another daily give rise to novel and restless desires and continually urge them on.

It therefore seems only natural to believe that in a democratic society, ideas, things, and men must perpetually change forms and places and that democratic centuries will be times of rapid and constant transformation.

Is this in fact true? Does equality of conditions habitually and permanently incline men to revolution? Does it contain some perturbing principle that prevents society from establishing itself on a firm footing and leads citizens constantly to recast their laws, doctrines, and mores? I think not. The subject is important; I beg the reader to follow me closely.

Almost all the revolutions that have changed the face of nations were made to consecrate or destroy equality. Eliminate the secondary causes that have given rise to great social turmoil and you are almost always left with inequality. Either the poor sought to plunder the rich, or the rich tried to clap the poor in irons. Thus if you can establish a state of society in which everyone has something to hold on to and little to take, you will have done a great deal for the peace of the world.

I am of course aware that in any great democratic people there will always be some citizens who are very poor and others who are very rich. But the poor, instead of constituting the vast majority of the nation as is invariably the case in aristocratic societies, are few in number, and the law does not hold them fast in bonds of irreparable and hereditary misery.

The rich, for their part, are scattered and impotent. They have no privileges that draw attention to themselves. Even their wealth, no longer incorporated into the earth and represented by it, is intangible and almost invisible. Just as there are no longer races of paupers, so, too, are there no longer races of the rich. The wealthy emerge from the crowd daily and time and again lapse back into it. Hence they do not constitute a separate class easy to define and despoil. Besides, a thousand hidden threads connect them to the mass of their fellow citizens, so that the people can hardly strike at them without injuring themselves. Between these two extremes of democratic society stand a vast multitude of men who are almost alike and who, while not exactly rich or poor, own enough property to want order but not enough to arouse envy.

These men are of course enemies of violent movements. Their immobility keeps things quiet above and below them and ensures that society rests on a firm footing.

Not that they are satisfied with their present fortune or that they shrink with natural horror from a revolution whose spoils they would share without experiencing its woes. On the contrary, they want to get rich, with unparalleled ardor, but the difficulty is to know whose wealth they can lay hold of. The same social state that incessantly spurs their desires circumscribes those desires within necessary limits. It gives men more freedom to change and less of an interest in seeing change occur.

Men in democracies not only have no natural desire for revolutions, they also fear them.

Every revolution poses, to one degree or another, a threat to property. Most people who live in democratic countries own property. And not only do they own it, they live in the condition in which property is most prized.

If we attentively consider each of the classes that make up society, it is easy to see that there are none in which the passions to which property gives rise are keener or more tenacious than they are among the middle classes.

Often the poor are not much concerned about what they own because their suffering on account of what they lack far exceeds their enjoyment of what little they have. The rich have many passions to satisfy other than the passion for riches, besides which long and arduous intimacy with a great fortune sometimes ends up dulling their sensitivity to its charms.

But men who live in comfort equally distant from opulence and misery set great store by their property. Since poverty still exists in their vicinity, they see its rigors up close, and are frightened by them. All that stands between it and them is a small patrimony to which they immediately pin their hopes and fears. Their interest in this patrimony increases regularly owing to the constant care they must devote to it, and the daily effort to add to it also rivets their attention. They regard as intolerable the idea of giving up the least bit of it and look upon losing the whole thing as the worst of misfortunes. Now, what equality of conditions does is to increase the number of these ardent and restless owners of small property constantly.

Thus in democratic societies, the majority of citizens do not see clearly what they might gain by a revolution, yet in a thousand ways they are constantly aware of what they might lose.

Elsewhere in this book I showed how equality of conditions naturally steers men toward careers in industry and commerce and how it increases and diversifies landed property. Finally, I showed how it inspires in each individual an ardent and unwavering desire to enhance his well-being. Nothing is more inimical to revolutionary passions than these things.

In some cases the end result of a revolution may prove beneficial to industry and commerce, but the initial effect is almost always to plunge industrialists and merchants into ruin, because at first it cannot fail to alter the general state of consumption and temporarily upset the existing proportion between production and needs.

Furthermore, I know of nothing more opposed to revolutionary mores than commercial mores. Commerce is naturally the enemy of all violent passions. It likes moderation, delights in compromise, and is careful to avoid anger. It is patient, supple, and insinuating, and resorts to extreme measures only when obliged to do so by the most absolute necessity. Commerce makes men independent of one another. It gives them an exalted idea of their individual worth. It leads them to want to manage their own affairs and teaches them to do so successfully. It therefore disposes them to liberty but steers them away from revolutions.

In a revolution, the owners of movable property have more to fear than everyone else, because on the one hand their property is often easy to seize and on the other it can vanish completely at any moment. Landowners have less to fear on this score, for while they may lose the income from their land, they can at least hope to hold on to the land itself whatever course events may take. Thus we find the former far more frightened at the sight of revolutionary movements than the latter.

Thus the more abundant and diversified a nation's movable property is, and the larger the number of people who own such property, the less disposed that nation's people will be to revolution.

All men share one common trait, moreover, regardless of what occupation they embrace and what sort of property they enjoy.

Nobody is ever fully satisfied with his present lot in life, and everybody is always trying to improve that lot in a thousand different ways. Take any person at any stage of existence and you will find him preoccupied with new plans intended to ease his situation. Do not speak to him of the interests and rights of the human race. That little private venture of his absorbs all his thoughts for the time being and makes him want to put off public troublemaking for another day.

Not only are people thus prevented from making revolutions, they are distracted from wanting to do so. Violent political passions have little hold on men who have devoted their souls wholly to the pursuit of well-being. The ardor they invest in petty affairs calms them when it comes to great ones.

It is true that enterprising and ambitious citizens arise from time to time in democratic societies, citizens whose boundless desires cannot be satisfied by following the beaten track. Such people love revolutions and hope that they will come to pass, but they have great difficulty making them happen unless extraordinary events come to their aid.

There is no advantage to any man in struggling against the spirit of his age and country, and it is hard for anyone, however powerful we suppose him to be, to persuade his contemporaries to share feelings and ideas that run counter to their desires and feelings generally. Hence it is a mistake to assume that once equality of conditions has become a long-standing and uncontested fact and impressed its character on mores, men will rush headlong to embrace risk at the urging of some rash leader or bold innovator.

I do not mean to suggest that they will resist such a leader openly with clever stratagems or even a premeditated plan. They will not combat him energetically; they may even applaud him from time to time; but they will not follow him. They will quietly oppose his impetuousness with their inertia, his revolutionary instincts with their conservative interests, his adventurous passions with their homely tastes, the aberrations of his genius with their common sense, and his poetry with their prose. He may lift them up for a time by dint of tremendous effort, but soon they will slip from his grasp and fall back to earth as if dragged down by their own weight. He will wear himself out with his desire to breathe life into this indifferent and distracted multitude and in the end find himself reduced to impotence not because he has been defeated but because he is alone.

I am not arguing that men who live in democratic societies are naturally immobile. On the contrary, I believe that perpetual motion is ubiquitous in such societies and rest unknown, but that agitation is confined within certain limits that are seldom exceeded. Men in democracies change, alter, and replace things of secondary importance every day but are extremely careful not to tamper with things of primary importance. They like change but dread revolutions.

Although Americans are constantly amending or abrogating certain of their laws, they are a long way from exhibiting revolutionary passions. It is easy to see from the promptness with which they stop and calm themselves just when public agitation starts to turn menacing and passions seem to be running highest that they dread revolution as the greatest of misfortunes, and that each of them is internally resolved to make great sacrifices to avoid one. There is no country in the world in which the feeling for property is keener or more anxious than in the United States, and where the majority exhibits less of a penchant for doctrines that threaten to alter the constitution of property in any way whatsoever.

I have often observed that theories that are revolutionary by nature in the sense that they cannot be put into practice without a complete and perhaps sudden change in the status of property and individuals are infinitely less in favor in the United States than in the great monarchies of Europe. Although some people profess such theories, the masses reject them with a sort of instinctive horror.

Without hesitation I say that most of the maxims that are usually called democratic in France would be proscribed by the democracy of the United States. It is easy to see why. In America people have democratic ideas and passions; in Europe we still have revolutionary ideas and passions.

If America ever experiences great revolutions, they will be brought on by the presence of Blacks on the soil of the United States: in other words, they will result not from equality of conditions but, on the contrary, from inequality.

When conditions are equal, each individual is likely to withdraw into himself and forget about the public. If the lawmakers of democratic nations did not try to correct this unfortunate tendency, or encouraged it in the hope that it would steer citizens away from democratic passions and thus from revolution, they might well end up provoking the ill they hoped to avoid, and there might come a time when the unruly passions of a few individuals, abetted by the unintelligent selfishness and cowardice of the majority, would compel society to follow a peculiar course.

In democratic societies it is generally only small minorities that desire revolutions, but a minority is sometimes enough to bring a revolution about.

So I am not saying that democratic nations are safe from revolution but only that the social state of such nations inclines them not in that direction but rather away from it. Democratic peoples, left to themselves, do not readily embark on great adventures. Only unwittingly are they dragged into revolutions; they may at times be subjected to revolutions but do not make them. When, moreover, they are allowed to acquire enlightenment and experience, they do not allow revolutions to occur.

I am well aware that in this connection public institutions themselves can do a great deal: they can either foster or restrain instincts stemming from the social state. Hence, to repeat myself, I am not arguing that a nation is safe from revolution simply because conditions among its people are equal. But I do believe that, whatever institutions such a people may adopt, great revolutions will always be infinitely less violent and far more rare than is generally assumed, and I can easily imagine a political state which, when combined with equality, would make society more stationary than it has ever been in our West.

What I have just said about facts applies in part to ideas.

Two things are astonishing about the United States: the great mobility of most human actions and the singular fixity of certain principles. Men are constantly on the move, while the human mind seems almost immobile.

Once an opinion has spread across the land and taken root in American soil, it almost seems that no power on earth is strong enough to uproot it. In the United States, general doctrines concerning religion, philosophy, morality, and even politics do not vary, or at any rate are modified only at the conclusion of a hidden and often imperceptible process. Even the grossest prejudices are inconceivably slow to vanish despite the constant contact of men and things.

I hear it said that it is in the nature and habits of democracies to change feelings and thoughts constantly. That may have been true of small democratic nations, like those of Antiquity, where the entire population could gather in a public place and be swayed by an orator. I saw nothing of the kind in the great democratic nation that occupies the opposite shore of our Atlantic Ocean. What struck me in the United States was the difficulty of disabusing the majority of an idea it has taken into its head or of detaching it from a man it has decided to adopt. Neither the written nor the spoken word is adequate to the task. Only experience can do it, and sometimes that experience needs to be repeated.

This is surprising at first sight, but a more attentive examination explains it.

I do not think that it is as easy as people imagine to eradicate the prejudices of a democratic people; to change its beliefs; to substitute new religious, philosophical, political, and moral principles for established ones; in short, to bring about great and frequent intellectual revolutions. Not that the human mind is idle in democracies. It is constantly active, but it exerts itself in endlessly varying the consequences of known principles, or discovering new consequences, rather than in looking for new principles. It dances agilely in place rather than spring forward in a quick and direct motion. With small, constant, jerky movements it expands its sphere little by little; it does not suddenly leap to a new place.

Men equal in rights, education, and fortune — men of like condition, in short — necessarily have needs, habits, and tastes that are not very dissimilar. Since they see things from the same angle, their minds are naturally inclined toward analogous ideas, and while each of them may diverge from his contemporaries and form beliefs of his own, all end up unwittingly and unintentionally sharing a certain number of opinions in common.

The more closely I consider the effects of equality on the mind, the more I am persuaded that the intellectual anarchy we see all around us is not, as many people assume, the natural state of democratic peoples. In my view it should be looked upon rather as an accidental consequence of their youth, and it manifests itself only in this era of transition, in which men have already broken the ancient bonds that once held them together yet still differ prodigiously in origin, education, and mores. Having preserved highly diverse ideas, instincts, and tastes, they thus find that nothing now prevents them from giving expression to this diversity. The principal opinions that men hold become similar insofar as their conditions are alike. This, to my mind, is the permanent and general fact; the rest is fortuitous and temporary.

Rarely, I believe, will a man living in democratic society suddenly conceive a system of ideas far removed from what his contemporaries have already accepted. Were such an innovator to appear, moreover, I suspect that he would at first have great difficulty getting people to listen to him and even greater difficulty getting them to believe him.

When conditions are almost alike, it is not easy for one man to persuade another. Since everyone can see everyone else at close range, and all have learned the same things together and lead the same life, they are not naturally inclined to accept one of their number as a guide and follow him blindly. It is unlikely that one man will take on faith what he hears from another man just like himself or his equal.

It is not just that confidence in the enlightenment of certain individuals declines in democratic nations. As I said earlier, the general idea that one man can acquire intellectual superiority over all others soon falls into obscurity.

As men come to resemble one another more and more, the dogma of equality of intellect gradually insinuates itself among their beliefs, and it becomes more difficult for an innovator of any kind to acquire and exercise great power over the mind of a people. In such societies, sudden intellectual revolutions are therefore rare, for if one looks at the history of the world, it is clear that great and rapid mutations in human opinions result not so much from the force of an argument as from the authority of a name.

Note, moreover, that since nothing binds the men who live in democratic societies to one another, they have to be persuaded one by one, whereas in aristocratic societies it suffices to influence the minds of a relatively small number of people and all the others will follow. If Luther had lived in a century of equality and had not had lords and princes among his audience, he might have found it more difficult to change the face of Europe.

The point is not that men in democracies are by nature completely convinced of the validity of their opinions and very firm in their beliefs. They often have doubts that, as they see it, no one can resolve. In such times the human mind might willingly change its position, but since nothing urges or guides it forward, it simply wavers and goes nowhere.[1]

Even when one has gained the confidence of a democratic people, it is still no small matter to gain its attention. It is very difficult to get men who live in democracies to listen to you unless you are talking to them about themselves. They do not listen to what people say to them because they are always deeply preoccupied with what they are doing.

Indeed, one seldom encounters idle people in democratic nations. Life there unfolds amid commotion and noise, and men are so involved with action that they have little time left to think. What I am most keen to point out is that not only are they busy, but their occupations engage their passions. They are perpetually in action, and they invest their souls in everything they do. The ardor they put into their activities prevents them from becoming passionate about ideas.

It is not at all easy, I think, to arouse the enthusiasm of a democratic people for any theory that has no visible, direct, and immediate relation to their daily practice. Hence such a people will not readily abandon its long-standing beliefs, for

[1]If I ask what state of society is most conducive to major intellectual revolutions, I find that the answer lies somewhere between complete equality for all citizens and absolute separation of classes.

Under a caste regime, generation follows generation without any change in the relative position of individuals. Some have nothing more to desire, while others are without hope of improvement. The imagination slumbers in such conditions of universal silence and immobility, and the very idea of change vanishes from the human mind.

When classes have been abolished and conditions have become almost equal, all men are in constant turmoil, but each of them is isolated, independent, and weak. This latter state differs markedly from the former but is analogous to it in one respect. Great revolutions of the human spirit are very rare here as well.

Between these two extremes in the history of nations, however, lies an intermediate age, a glorious and troubled epoch, in which conditions are not stable enough to put the intellect to sleep and are still unequal enough for men to exert a very great power over one another's minds, so that a few can modify the beliefs of all. It is in such times that powerful reformers arise and new ideas suddenly change the face of the world.

it is enthusiasm that drives the human mind off the beaten track and brings about great intellectual as well as great political revolutions.

Thus democratic peoples have neither the leisure nor the desire to seek out new opinions. Even when they come to doubt the opinions they have, they hold on to them nevertheless because it would take too much time and require too much study to change them. They hold on to them not as certain but as established.

There are also other, more powerful reasons that tend to prevent any great change in the doctrines of a democratic people from coming about easily. I pointed these out at the beginning of this book.

If the influence of individuals on such a people is weak and almost non-existent, the power exerted by the mass on the mind of each individual is very great. I have explained the reasons for this elsewhere. What I want to say now is that it would be wrong to believe that this was solely a consequence of the form of government and that the majority must inevitably lose its intellectual sway along with its political power.

In aristocracies, men often possess a grandeur and strength that is all their own. When they find themselves at odds with a majority of their fellow men, they withdraw into themselves and there find support and consolation. This is not the case in democratic nations. There, public favor seems as necessary as the air one breathes, and to be out of tune with the masses is in a sense to be deprived of life. The masses do not need to use laws to force those who think differently into submission. All they need to do is register their disapproval. Those who meet with such disapproval are immediately overwhelmed by feelings of isolation and impotence and plunged into despair.

Whenever conditions are equal, the general opinion weighs very heavily indeed on the mind of each individual. It envelops, directs, and oppresses each man's thinking. This has far more to do with the constitution of society itself than with its political laws. As men come to resemble each other more, each individual feels weaker and weaker vis-à-vis all the others. Not seeing anything that lifts him far above the rest and sets him apart, he loses confidence in himself when they combat him. Not only does he doubt his strength, but he begins to doubt his rectitude and comes very close to admitting that he is wrong when most people say he is. The majority has no need to force him; it convinces him.

Hence no matter how the powers of a democratic society are organized, and no matter what weight is assigned to each of them, it will always be very difficult to believe what the masses reject and to profess what they condemn.

This does wonders for stability of belief.

When an opinion takes hold in a democratic nation and establishes itself in a majority of minds, it becomes self-sustaining and can perpetuate itself without effort, because nobody will attack it. Those who initially rejected it as false end up accepting it as general, and those who continue to oppose it in the depths of their hearts do not show it. They take great pains to avoid dangerous and futile struggle.

It is true that when the majority of a democratic people does change its opinion, it can arbitrarily instigate peculiar and sudden revolutions in the world of the intellect. But it is very difficult for the majority to change its opinion and almost as difficult to determine that it has changed.

Time, events, or individual effort by solitary minds can in some cases ultimately undermine or gradually destroy a belief without giving any external sign that this is happening. No one combats the doomed belief openly. No forces gather to make war on it. Its proponents quietly abandon it one by one, until only a minority still clings to it.

In this situation, its reign persists.

Since its enemies continue to hold their peace or to communicate their thoughts only in secret, it is a long time before they can be sure that a great revolution has taken place, and, being in doubt, they make no move. They watch and keep silent. The majority no longer believes, but it still appears to believe, and this hollow ghost of public opinion is enough to chill the blood of would-be innovators and reduce them to respectful silence.

We are living in a time that has witnessed extraordinarily rapid changes in men's minds. Soon, however, the chief opinions of mankind may well be more stable than in any previous

century of our history. That time has not yet come, but it may
be drawing near.

The more closely I examine the natural needs and instincts
of democratic peoples, the more I am convinced that if equality is ever established in the world in a general and permanent
way, great intellectual and political revolutions will become
quite difficult, and rarer than people imagine.

Because men in democracies always seem excited, uncertain,
impatient, and ready to change both what they want and
where they stand, it is easy to imagine that they are on the
verge of suddenly abolishing their laws, adopting new beliefs,
and taking on new mores. No one notices that if equality
prompts men to change, it also stimulates interests and tastes
that require stability in order to be satisfied. It drives men forward and at the same time holds them back, spurs them on
yet keeps them tethered to the earth. It inflames their desires
and limits their strengths.

This is not immediately apparent: the passions that drive
citizens in a democracy apart are self-evident, but the hidden
force that restrains them and holds them together is not obvious at first sight.

Standing as I do in the midst of ruins, dare I say that what
I fear most for generations to come is not revolutions?

If citizens continue to confine themselves ever more narrowly within the sphere of petty domestic interests and there
engage in ceaseless activity, there is reason to be apprehen-
sive that they may end up becoming all but invulnerable to
those great and powerful public emotions that roil nations but
also develop and renew them. When I see property becoming
so mobile, and love of property so restless and ardent, I cannot
overcome my fear that men may come to the point of looking upon every new theory as a danger, every innovation as a
vexing disturbance, and every sign of social progress as a first
step toward revolution, and that they may refuse to change
altogether lest they be induced to change more than they
wish. I tremble, I confess, that they might eventually allow
themselves to become so entranced by a contemptible love of
present pleasures that their interest in their own future and
the future of their offspring might disappear, and that they

might choose to acquiesce in their fate without offering any resistance rather than make a sudden and energetic effort to set it right.

People think that the new societies will constantly be changing their identity, while I am afraid they will end up all too invariably attached to the same institutions, the same prejudices, and the same mores, so that the human race will stop progressing and narrow its horizons. I fear that the mind will forever subdivide itself into smaller and smaller compartments without producing new ideas, that man will exhaust his energies in petty, solitary, and sterile changes, and that humanity, though constantly on the move, will cease to advance.

Chapter 22

WHY DEMOCRATIC PEOPLES NATURALLY DESIRE PEACE AND DEMOCRATIC ARMIES NATURALLY DESIRE WAR

THE same interests, the same fears, the same passions that keep democratic peoples away from revolution estrange them from war. The military spirit and the revolutionary spirit grow weaker at the same time and for the same reasons.

The steadily increasing number of property owners friendly to peace; the growth of movable wealth, which war so rapidly devours; the mildness of mores, softness of heart, and disposition to pity that equality inspires; the coldness of reason, which makes people relatively insensitive to the poetic and violent emotions to which combat gives rise — all these causes conspire to extinguish the military spirit.

I think it is fair to say that as a general and constant rule, the martial passions will become rarer and less intense among civilized peoples as conditions become more equal.

Yet war is a hazard to which all peoples are subject, democratic peoples along with all the rest. Whatever taste these nations may have for peace, they must stand ready to repel war; in other words, they must have an army.

Fortune, which has so especially favored the inhabitants of the United States, has placed them in the midst of a wilderness where in a sense they have no neighbors. A few thousand soldiers are all they need, but this is a fact about America, not about democracy.

Neither equality of conditions nor the mores and institutions that derive from such equality exempt a democratic people from the obligation to maintain armed forces, and their armed forces will always exert a very substantial influence over their fate. Hence it is singularly important to ask what the natural instincts of the men who serve in those armed forces are.

Among aristocratic peoples, especially those in which birth alone governs rank, inequality exists in the army as it does in the nation; officers are nobles, ordinary soldiers are serfs. One is invariably called upon to command, the other to obey. In aristocratic armies, the soldier's ambition is therefore confined within very strict limits.

Nor is the officer's ambition unlimited.

An aristocratic body is not just part of a hierarchy; it always contains a hierarchy within itself. Its members are ranked in a certain way that does not vary. One man is naturally called by birth to command a regiment, another to command a company. Once these ultimate hopes are achieved, both will voluntarily stop and declare themselves satisfied with their lot.

In aristocracies, moreover, there is a powerful cause that tends to cool the officer's desire for advancement.

Among aristocratic peoples, the officer, quite apart from his rank in the army, also occupies a high rank in society. In his eyes the former rank is almost invariably a mere accessory to the latter. When a noble embraces a military career, he is obeying not so much the dictates of ambition as a kind of duty imposed on him by his birth. He joins the army as an honorable pastime with which to occupy the idle years of his youth and as a source of honorable recollections of military life to bring home and share with his peers. His principal object is not to acquire property, respect, or power, for these advantages are his already, and he can enjoy them without leaving home.

In a democratic army, any soldier can become an officer, so that the desire for advancement is general and military ambition almost boundless.

The officer, for his part, sees no natural or necessary reason for stopping at one rank rather than another, and each promotion seems immensely valuable to him because his rank in society almost always depends on his rank in the army.

Among democratic peoples it is common for an officer to have no property other than his pay and to command no respect other than that owed him for his military honors. Hence whenever he changes posts, his fortune also changes, and he becomes in a sense another man. What was an accessory of existence in the aristocratic army has thus become the central fact, the whole — existence itself.

Under the old French monarchy, officers were addressed only by their noble titles. Today they are addressed only by their military titles. This small change in linguistic forms is enough to show that a great revolution has taken place in the constitution of both the society and the army.

In democratic armies the desire for promotion is almost universal. It is ardent, tenacious, and continuous. It feeds upon all the other desires and ends only with life itself. Now, it is easy to see that, of all the armies in the world, the ones in which advancement in peacetime must be slowest are the democratic armies. Since the number of posts is of course limited, and the number of people competing for those posts is virtually boundless, and the inflexible law of inequality weighs on everyone, no one can progress rapidly and many cannot move at all. Thus the need for promotion is greater in such armies, while the ease of promotion is less than it is elsewhere.

Hence all the ambitious men in a democratic army vehemently desire war, because war creates vacancies and ultimately makes it possible to violate the right of seniority, which is the only natural privilege in a democracy.

This brings us to a striking conclusion: of all armies the ones that desire war most ardently are the democratic ones, while the most peace-loving of peoples are also the democratic ones. And what makes this even more extraordinary is that equality is responsible for both of these effects, contradictory though they are.

Citizens, being equal, daily conceive the desire and discover the possibility of changing their condition and improving their well-being. This disposes them to love peace, which causes industry to prosper and allows each individual to carry his small undertakings through to completion. On the other hand, this same equality, by enhancing the value of military honors in the eyes of those who pursue careers in arms and by making those honors accessible to all, sets soldiers to dreaming of battlefields. In both instances the restlessness of heart is the same, the taste for pleasure is just as insatiable, and the ambition is equal; only the means of satisfying it is different.

These opposing dispositions of nation and army pose great dangers to democratic societies.

When the military spirit forsakes a people, military careers cease to be honored, and men of war fall to the lowest rank among public functionaries. They are held in low esteem and are no longer understood. What happens then is the opposite of what one sees in aristocratic centuries. It is no longer the leading citizens who join the army but the lowliest ones. A man will pursue a military ambition only when no other course is open to him. This creates a vicious circle from which it is difficult to escape. The nation's elite avoids the military career because it is not honored, and it is not honored because the nation's elite no longer embraces it.

Therefore it should come as no surprise that democratic armies are often restless, low in morale, and ill-satisfied with their lot, even though physical conditions are usually much milder and discipline less rigid than in other armies. The soldier feels himself to be in an inferior position, and his wounded pride completes the job of giving him a taste for war, which will make him necessary, or a liking for revolutions, during which he can hope by force of arms to win the political influence and individual respect he is otherwise denied.

Because of the composition of democratic armies this last peril is greatly to be feared.

In a democratic society, almost all citizens have some property to preserve, but democratic armies are generally led by proletarians. Most of them have little to lose in civil disturbances. The nation's masses are naturally much more afraid of revolution than in aristocratic centuries, but the army's leaders are much less fearful.

Moreover, as I said earlier, since the wealthiest, best educated, most capable citizens of democratic nations are unlikely to pursue careers in the military, the army comes to be a nation within a nation in which intelligence is less widespread and habits are coarser than in the nation as a whole. But this uncivilized smaller nation within the larger one possesses arms, and it alone knows how to use them.

Indeed, what makes the danger that the army's turbulent and bellicose spirit poses to democratic peoples even greater is the pacific temper of the citizens. Nothing is as dangerous as an army in a nation that is not warlike. The citizens' excessive love of tranquillity leaves the constitution always at the mercy of the military.

In general, therefore, one can say that if democratic peoples are naturally inclined toward peace by their interests and instincts, they are constantly drawn toward war and revolutions by their armies.

Military revolutions, which are almost never to be feared in aristocracies, are always to be dreaded in democratic nations. These must be counted among the most terrifying perils that such nations will have to face in the future. Statesmen will have to apply themselves unremittingly to the search for a remedy.

When a nation feels itself roiled within by the restless ambition of its army, the first thought that comes to mind is to find an outlet for this inconvenient ambition in the form of war.

I do not wish to speak ill of war. War almost always enlarges the thought and ennobles the heart of a people. There are cases in which war alone can halt the excessive development of certain penchants to which equality naturally gives rise, and in which it must be considered a necessary corrective to certain deep-seated afflictions of democratic societies.

War has great advantages, but we must not delude ourselves into thinking that it diminishes the peril signaled above. It only postpones the danger, which returns in more terrifying form when the conflict is over, because armies are far more impatient with peace after they have had a taste of war. War would be a remedy only for a people with an unquenchable thirst for glory.

I predict that any warrior prince who may arise in a great democratic nation will find that it is easier to lead the army to conquest than to make it live in peace after a victory. There are two things that will always be very difficult for a democratic people to do: to start a war and to finish it.

Furthermore, while war has particular advantages for democratic peoples, it also exposes them to certain dangers that aristocracies need not fear to the same degree. I shall cite only two.

If war satisfies the army, it hampers and in many cases sows despair among the innumerable host of citizens whose petty passions need peace every day if they are to be satisfied. It therefore threatens to produce the disorder it is supposed to prevent, but in a different form.

In a democratic country a long war inevitably poses a great danger to liberty. What is to be feared, however, is not that victorious generals will seize sovereign power by force after every victory in the manner of Sulla and Caesar. The danger is of another kind. War does not always deliver democratic peoples into the hands of military government, but it cannot fail to bring about a vast increase in the prerogatives of civilian government. It almost inevitably leads to centralization in the latter of control over men and things. If it does not lead immediately to despotism by way of violence, it gently pulls in that direction by way of habit.

All who seek to destroy liberty in a democratic nation should know that war offers them the surest and shortest route to success. This is the first axiom of science.

A seemingly obvious remedy when there is reason to fear the ambition of officers and soldiers is to increase the number of posts on offer by expanding the size of the army. This alleviates the present ill but compounds the future danger.

Enlarging the army can have a lasting effect in an aristocratic society because military ambition is limited to a single kind of man and remains within certain bounds for each individual, so that it is possible to satisfy nearly everyone who feels it.

In a democratic nation, however, there is nothing to be gained by increasing the size of the army, because the number of ambitious men always increases by exactly the same proportion as the army itself. Those whose wishes you fulfill by creating new posts are immediately replaced by a host of new men whom you cannot satisfy, and even those you have satisfied will soon begin to complain anew, for the same agitation of mind that prevails among the citizens of a democracy manifests itself in the army too. What soldiers want is not to achieve a certain rank but to keep on being promoted. While their desires are not immense, they are continually renewed. A democratic nation that enlarges its army thus quells the ambitions of its men of war only for a moment. Soon those ambitions become more fearsome than ever, because more people experience them.

For my part, I believe that a restless and turbulent spirit is an evil inherent in the very constitution of a democratic army, and one should therefore give up trying to cure it. Democratic lawmakers must not expect to find a form of military organization capable by itself of calming and restraining men of war; to attempt to do so would be an exhausting waste of effort.

The remedy for the army's vices can be found not in the army but in the country.

Democratic peoples are naturally afraid of turmoil and despotism. It is merely a matter of turning these instincts into reflective, intelligent, and stable tastes. When citizens finally learn to make peaceful and beneficial use of liberty and experience its benefits, and when they acquire a virile love of order and voluntarily submit to rules, they will unwittingly and, as it were, in spite of themselves carry those habits and mores with them when they join the military. The general spirit of the nation, permeating the particular spirit of the army, will either temper the opinions and desires to which the military estate gives rise or else repress those opinions and desires through the all-powerful force of public opinion. If you have enlightened, orderly, steadfast, and free citizens, you will have disciplined and obedient soldiers.

Any law attempting to dampen the army's turbulent spirit that tended to diminish the spirit of civil liberty and obscure the nation's idea of law and rights would therefore defeat its own purpose. It would do more to encourage than to impede the establishment of military tyranny.

In the end, no matter what one does, a great army in the midst of a democratic nation will always be a great peril, and the most effective means of reducing that peril is to reduce the size of the army. It is not within the power of every nation to apply this remedy, however.

Chapter 23

WHICH CLASS IN DEMOCRATIC ARMIES IS THE MOST WARLIKE AND REVOLUTIONARY

IT IS of the essence of a democratic army to be very numerous relative to the people from which it draws its manpower. I shall discuss the reasons for this in a moment.

Yet men living in democratic times seldom choose military careers.

Hence democratic peoples are soon forced to give up on voluntary recruitment and rely on compulsory conscription. It is a necessity of their condition that compels them to take this step, and it is safe to predict that all will eventually do so.

Since military service is compulsory, the burden is equally and indiscriminately shared by all citizens. This is also a necessary consequence of the condition of democratic peoples and of their ideas. Government in a democratic society can do almost anything it wants provided that it addresses itself to all the people at once. What leads to resistance is unequal sharing of the burden and not the burden itself.

Now, since military service is common to all citizens, it obviously follows that each of them spends only a few years in uniform.

Thus it is in the nature of things that the soldier is only a visitor to the army, whereas in most aristocratic nations, the military estate is a profession that the soldier takes up, or is forced to take up, for life.

This has major consequences. Some of the soldiers who make up a democratic army will form an attachment to military life, but most, forced to join up against their will and ready to return home at a moment's notice, do not see themselves as seriously committed to military careers and think only of being mustered out. These latter soldiers do not acquire the needs, and never more than partially share the passions, that grow out of a career in the military. Though they bow to their military duties, their souls remain tethered to the interests and desires that occupied them in civilian life. Hence they do not acquire the army spirit but bring the spirit of society with them into the army, where they cling to it. In democratic nations, it is the private soldiers who remain most fully citizens. The habits of the nation retain the most influence over them, and public opinion retains the most power. Soldiers such as these can above all be counted on to bring into a democratic army whatever love of liberty and respect for rights it has been possible to inspire in the people themselves. The opposite is true in aristocratic nations, where soldiers end up having nothing in common with their fellow citizens, living among them as aliens and often as enemies.

In aristocratic armies, the conservative element is the officer, because only the officer maintains close ties to civil society, in which he has every intention of one day resuming his place. In democratic armies the conservative element is the soldier, for exactly the same reason.

By contrast, it is often the case in democratic armies that officers acquire tastes and desires entirely distinct from those of the nation. This is understandable.

In democratic nations, a man who becomes an officer breaks all his ties to civilian life. He leaves it for good and has no interest in returning. His true homeland is the army, because without the rank he occupies he is nothing. His fortunes therefore coincide with those of the army, and because he now rises and falls with the military, he now invests his hopes in it alone. Since the officer's needs are quite distinct from those of the country, it is possible for him ardently to desire war or to work toward a revolution while the nation aspires above all to stability and peace.

There are, however, factors that temper his warlike and restless humor. Although ambition in democratic nations is universal and constant, we have seen that it is rarely great. A man who has risen from the nation's secondary classes through the lower ranks of the army to the grade of officer has already taken an immense step. He has gained a foothold in a higher sphere than he occupied in civil society, and there he has acquired rights that most democratic nations will always regard as inalienable.[1] Having made such a great effort, he is glad to stop and dreams of enjoying his conquest. The fear of compromising what he has begins to dampen his desire to acquire what he has not. Having overcome the first and greatest obstacle to his advancement, he is less impatient about resigning himself to the slowness of further progress. His ambition cools even more as he rises still higher in rank and discovers that he has more to lose in the risks that remain ahead. If I am not mistaken, the least bellicose and least revolutionary part of a democratic army will always be its leadership.

What I have just said about officers and soldiers is not applicable to the large intermediate class that is found in all armies, namely, the class of noncommissioned officers.

This class of noncommissioned officers, which has left no mark in history until the present century, is, I believe, henceforth destined to play a role.

Like the officer, the noncommissioned officer has in his own mind severed all his ties to civil society. Like the officer, he has made the military his career, and even more than the officer perhaps, he has turned all his desires in this one direction. But unlike the officer, he has not yet achieved a high and solid position where he might reasonably stop and breathe more easily while awaiting further advancement.

By the very nature of his functions, which cannot change, the noncommissioned officer is condemned to lead an obscure, narrow, uncomfortable, and precarious existence. He still sees only the dangers of the military estate. He knows only the privations and the obedience, which are even harder to bear than the dangers. It is all the more difficult for him to endure his present miseries because he knows that the constitution of society and of the army offer him a way out: he can in fact become an officer from one day to the next. He will then be in command and enjoy honors, independence, rights, and pleasures. Hence he sees the object of all his hopes as immense, yet until he lays hold of it he can never be sure that it is his. There is nothing permanent about his rank. He is daily

---

[1]The officer's position is in fact far more assured in democratic nations than elsewhere. The less importance the officer has in himself, the greater the relative value of his rank, and the more just and necessary it seems to lawmakers to ensure his enjoyment of it.

subject to the whims of his leaders; the imperious needs of discipline demand that it be so. A slight fault, a caprice, can in a moment cost him the fruit of several years of work and effort. Until he achieves the coveted rank, he has therefore accomplished nothing. Only then, it seems, does his career begin. In a man thus constantly goaded by his youth, needs, and passions, by the spirit of his time, by his hopes and fears, a desperate ambition cannot fail to be kindled.

The noncommissioned officer therefore wants war; he wants it always and no matter what the cost, and if war is denied him, he will desire revolutions, which suspend the authority of rules and give him hope that, abetted by confusion and political passions, he may drive out his officer and take his place. It is not out of the question, moreover, that he will have the revolutions he wants, because he exerts a great influence over the soldiers, whose origins and habits he shares, even though he differs considerably from them in regard to passions and desires.

It would be a mistake to believe that these various dispositions of the officer, the noncommissioned officer, and the soldier are peculiar to any one time or country. They will manifest themselves in all periods and all democratic nations.

In any democratic army, the noncommissioned officer will always be the least representative, and the private soldier the most representative, of the country's peaceable and law-abiding spirit. The soldier will bring the strengths and weaknesses of the nation's mores into the military, where he will present a faithful image of the nation. If the nation is ignorant and weak, he will allow himself to be drawn into chaos by his leaders, either unwittingly or in spite of himself. If the nation is enlightened and energetic, he will personally impose respect for order on his superiors.

Chapter 24

WHAT MAKES DEMOCRATIC ARMIES WEAKER THAN OTHER ARMIES AT THE START OF A CAMPAIGN BUT MORE FORMIDABLE IN PROTRACTED WARFARE

ANY army that takes to the field after a lengthy peace risks defeat; any army that has waged war for a long time stands a good chance of victory. This truth applies particularly to democratic armies.

In aristocracies, the military estate, being a privileged career, is honored even in peacetime. Men of great talent, great enlightenment, and great ambition embrace it. The army is in all respects at the level of the nation; often it even surpasses that level.

By contrast, we have seen how the elite in democratic nations gradually turned away from military careers to seek respect, power, and above all wealth by other routes. After a lengthy peace — and in democratic times peace is long-lasting — the army is always inferior to the country itself. This is the state in which war finds it, and until war changes it, there is danger for the country and the army.

I have shown that in democratic armies in peacetime, the right of seniority is the supreme and inflexible law of promotion. This is not solely, as I stated, a consequence of the constitution of these armies but also of the constitution of the nation itself, and will always be so.

Furthermore, since the officer in a democratic nation is of no account in the country at large except by virtue of his position in the military, from which he derives whatever respect and comfort he enjoys, he will not retire from the army or be mustered out until he reaches the end of his life.

For these two reasons, when a democratic people does at last take up arms after a long respite, all the leaders of the army will be elderly men. I am not speaking only of the generals but also of the lower-ranking officers, most of whom will have advanced only slowly if at all. If one looks at a democratic army after a lengthy peace, one is surprised to discover that all the soldiers are close to being children and all the commanders are men whose powers are waning, so that the former lack experience and the latter, vigor.

This is one great cause of misfortune, because the first condition of successful leadership in war is youth. I would not dare to say this had it not already been said by the greatest military commander of modern times.

These two factors do not have the same effect on aristocratic armies.

Since promotion in aristocratic armies is based on rights of birth much more than on rights of seniority, these armies always contain, at every rank, a certain number of young men who bring to war all the primary energies of body and soul.

Furthermore, since the men who seek military honors in an aristocratic nation hold assured positions in civil society, they seldom linger in the army until old age overtakes them. After devoting the most vigorous years of youth to careers in arms, they retire voluntarily in order to spend the remainder of their mature years at home.

A lengthy peace not only fills the ranks of democratic armies with elderly officers but also fosters in all officers habits of body and mind that ill equip them for the rigors of war. Anyone who has lived for long in the peaceful and tepid moral climate of democracy finds it difficult at first to adjust to the harsh labors and austere duties imposed by war. If he does not lose his taste for arms altogether, he nevertheless adopts a way of life that prevents him from winning.

Among aristocratic peoples, the softness of civilian life exerts less influence on military mores because in these nations it is the aristocracy that leads the army, and an aristocracy, no matter how immersed in pleasures it may be, always has a number of passions other than well-being and will readily sacrifice its well-being temporarily to satisfy those passions more fully.

I have shown that in democratic armies in peacetime, promotion comes extremely slowly. At first the officers are impatient with this state of affairs. They become restless, anxious, and desperate. In the long run, however, most of them resign themselves to it. Those who have the greatest ambition and the most resources leave the army. The rest, adjusting their tastes and desires to the mediocrity of their lot, eventually come to regard the military estate with a civilian eye. What they value most about it is the comfort and stability it brings. Relying on this small good fortune, they form an image of their future and ask only to be allowed to enjoy it in peace.

Thus a lengthy peace not only fills the ranks of democratic armies with elderly officers but in many cases fosters the instincts of old men even in those who are still of vigorous age.

I have also shown that in democratic nations in peacetime, little honor comes of a military career, and few people pursue it.

This public disfavor is a very heavy burden, which weighs on the spirit of the army. The souls of the troops are bowed down by it, so to speak, and when war finally comes, they cannot immediately regain their elasticity and vigor.

No such cause undermines the morale of aristocratic armies. The officers of these armies are never debased in their own eyes or those of their fellow men, because they are great in themselves, quite apart from their military greatness.

Even if both armies experienced the effects of peace in the same way, the results would still be different.

When officers in an aristocratic army lose the martial spirit and the desire to improve their position by arms, they still retain a certain respect for the honor of their order and old habits of being first and setting an example. But when the officers of a democratic army no longer love war or experience military ambition, they are left with nothing.

I therefore think that a democratic nation that enters into war after a lengthy peace runs a far greater risk of defeat than any other kind of nation, but it should not allow itself to be easily discouraged by reverses, because its army's chances will improve as the war lingers on.

When war, becoming protracted, finally wrests all citizens from their peaceful labors and ruins their petty enterprises, the same passions that caused them to value peace so highly turn toward arms. War, having destroyed all industry, itself becomes the great and sole industry, and all the ardent and ambitious desires born of equality are now focused exclusively on it from every quarter. That is why the same democratic nations that are so difficult to entice onto the battlefield sometimes perform prodigious feats when at last someone succeeds in putting arms in their hands.

As war increasingly becomes the focus of everyone's attention and is seen to produce great reputations and great fortunes in a short period of time, the nation's elite begin to pursue military careers. Everyone of naturally enterprising, proud, and martial spirit, not just from the aristocracy but from the country as a whole, is drawn in this direction.

Because the number of people competing for military honors is immense and war brusquely separates the wheat from the chaff, great generals invariably turn up. A long war has the same effect on a democratic army that a revolution has on the people themselves. It breaks the rules and brings all the extraordinary men to the fore. Those officers who have grown old in body and soul during peacetime are weeded out, retire, or die. Hastening to fill their place is a host of young men already hardened by war, and whose desires war has magnified and inflamed. These men want to achieve greatness at all cost, and they never stop wanting it. After them come others with the same passions and desires, and after them still others, with no limit but the size of the army itself. Equality allows everyone to be ambitious, and death affords plenty of opportunity for all their ambitions. Death continually creates openings in the ranks, makes vacancies, ends some careers and begins others.

There is, moreover, a hidden relation between military mores and democratic mores that war uncovers.

Men in democracies naturally feel a passionate desire to acquire quickly and enjoy easily the goods they desire. Most adore risk and fear death far less than toil. It is in this spirit that they pursue commerce and industry; and this same spirit, when they carry it to the battlefield, makes them willing to risk their lives in order to assure themselves in an instant of the spoils of victory. No form of grandeur satisfies the imagination of a democratic people more fully than military grandeur, which is spectacular and sudden and obtained without effort, merely by risking one's life.

Thus while interest and taste make the citizens of a democracy averse to war, the habits of their souls prepare them to wage it well. They readily become good soldiers once they can be wrested away from their affairs and from concern with their well-being.

If peace is particularly hard on democratic armies, war thus assures them of advantages that other armies never possess. And while those advantages are not easy to see at first, they cannot fail to bring victory in the long run.

An aristocratic people that does not succeed in destroying a democratic nation in the first campaigns of a conflict is always at great risk of being defeated by it.[*]

[*]See Note XXIII, page 364.

Chapter 25

ON DISCIPLINE IN
DEMOCRATIC ARMIES

I T IS a very widely held opinion, especially in aristocracies, that the great equality that prevails in democracies ultimately makes soldiers independent of officers and thus destroys the bond of discipline.

This is an error. There are in fact two kinds of discipline, which must not be confused.

When the officer is a noble and the soldier a serf; one rich, the other poor; one enlightened and strong, the other ignorant and weak; it is easy to establish the strictest bond of obedience between them. The soldier, in a manner of speaking, bows to military discipline before joining the army, or, to put it another way, military discipline is merely a perfection of social servitude. In aristocratic armies, the soldier is fairly readily reduced to a state of being almost impervious to everything but the orders of his commanders. He acts without thinking, triumphs without ardor, and dies without complaint. In this condition he is no longer a man, but he is still a very fearsome animal trained for war.

Democratic peoples must abandon hope of ever obtaining the kind of blind, punctilious, resigned, and always equable obedience that aristocratic peoples impose without difficulty on their soldiers. The state of society does not prepare for this: democratic societies would risk losing their natural advantages if they sought to acquire these other advantages by artificial means. Among democratic peoples, military discipline should not attempt to destroy the free expression of men's souls. It can aspire only to guide it. The obedience that results from this is less precise but more enthusiastic and intelligent. It is rooted in the will of the person who obeys. It does not rely solely on his instinct but also on his reason, so it will frequently tighten up by itself as the danger calls for it. The discipline of an aristocratic army is likely to be relaxed in war, because this discipline is based on habits, which war disrupts. By contrast, the discipline of a democratic army becomes stronger in the face of the enemy, because each soldier then sees quite clearly that silence and obedience are necessary for victory.

The nations that have achieved the most remarkable things by means of war have known no other form of discipline than the one I have described. The Ancients allowed only free men and citizens to fight in their armies, and these men differed little from one another and were accustomed to treating each other as equals. In this respect, it is fair to say that the armies of Antiquity were democratic, even though they were drawn from the ranks of the aristocracy. Hence a sort of fraternal familiarity prevailed between officers and soldiers. To read Plutarch's lives of the great captains is to convince oneself of this. In this text soldiers speak to their generals constantly and quite freely, and generals eagerly listen to what their soldiers have to say and respond to them. They lead by word and example far more than by coercion and punishment. They seem to have been companions as much as commanders.

I do not know whether Greek and Roman soldiers ever achieved the same degree of perfection in the small details of military discipline as the Russians have done, but that did not prevent Alexander from conquering Asia or Rome from conquering the world.

Chapter 26

SOME REMARKS ON WAR IN DEMOCRATIC SOCIETIES

WHEN the principle of equality develops not just in one nation but at the same time in a number of neighboring peoples, as can be seen today in Europe, the men who inhabit these various countries, despite the disparity in languages, customs, and laws, nevertheless resemble one another in that they equally dread war and conceive an identical love of peace.[1] In vain will ambition or wrath arm princes, for a sort of apathy and universal benevolence calms them in spite of themselves and causes the swords to fall from their hands: wars become increasingly rare.

As equality, developing at once in several countries, simultaneously drives the men who live in them into industry and commerce, not only do their tastes converge but their interests mingle and become entangled in such a way that no nation can inflict harm on the others without repercussions to itself, and in the end all come to see war as a calamity almost as great for the victor as for the vanquished.

So on the one hand it is very difficult in democratic centuries to induce nations to fight, while on the other hand it is almost impossible for two of them to make war in isolation. The interests of all are so intertwined, and their opinions and needs are so similar, that none can remain quiet when the others are in turmoil. Wars therefore become rarer, but when they break out, they have a wider scope.

Some neighboring democratic peoples come to resemble each other not merely in certain respects, as I have just indicated, but ultimately in nearly all respects.[2]

[1]The fear of war displayed by the peoples of Europe is not due solely to the progress that equality has made among them, as I think I hardly need point out to the reader. Apart from this permanent cause, any number of accidental causes are quite powerful. I would cite above all the extreme state of lassitude that the wars of the Revolution and Empire have left behind.

[2]This is not only because these peoples have the same social state but also

Now, this similarity between nations has very important consequences when it comes to war.

When I ask myself why the Swiss Confederation of the fifteenth century made the greatest and most powerful nations of Europe tremble, whereas today its power is exactly proportional to its population, I find that the Swiss have become like everyone around them and vice versa. Since numbers now make all the difference, victory necessarily belongs to the biggest battalions. One result of the democratic revolution that is taking place in Europe is therefore to make sure that numerical strength will prevail on every battlefield and to compel all small nations to merge with larger ones or at any rate to acquiesce in their policies.

Since victory is decided by numbers, every nation must devote all its effort to putting as many men in the field as possible.

When it was possible to enlist troops of a type superior to

---

because that social state naturally leads men to imitate and become indistinguishable from one another.

When citizens are divided into castes and classes, not only are they different from one another, but they have neither the taste nor the desire to look alike. On the contrary, each person seeks more and more to maintain intact his own opinions and habits and to remain himself. The spirit of individuality is very tenacious.

When a nation has a democratic social state, which is to say when it no longer contains either castes or classes and all of its citizens are nearly equal in enlightenment and property, the human spirit proceeds in the opposite direction. Men resemble one another, and what is more, they suffer in a sense from not resembling one another. Far from wanting to preserve whatever may still make each of them singular, they ask only to lose this singularity in order to blend into the common mass, which alone in their eyes represents both right and might. The spirit of individuality is almost destroyed.

In aristocratic times, even those who are naturally alike aspire to create imaginary differences between themselves. In democratic times, those who do not naturally resemble one another ask only to become identical and to copy one another, so strongly is each person's mind inevitably swayed by the general tendency of humanity.

Something similar can also be seen between nations. Two peoples might have the same aristocratic social state yet remain perfectly distinct and very different, because the spirit of aristocracy is to individualize. But two neighboring peoples cannot have the same democratic social state without immediately adopting similar opinions and mores, because the spirit of democracy makes men tend to assimilate to one another.

all others, such as the Swiss infantry or French cavalry of the sixteenth century, people felt no need to raise very large armies, but this ceases to be true when one soldier is as good as another.

The same cause that gives rise to this new need also provides the means to satisfy it. For as I have said, when all men are alike, all are weak. Social power is naturally much stronger among democratic peoples than it is elsewhere. Thus when these peoples feel the desire to call their entire male population to arms, they also have the ability to do so. In centuries of equality, armies therefore seem to grow as the military spirit dwindles.

In these same centuries, methods of warfare change for the same reasons.

Machiavelli says in his book *The Prince* "that it is far more difficult to subjugate a people headed by a prince and barons than a nation led by a prince with slaves." To avoid offending anyone, let us substitute "public functionaries" for "slaves." We will then have a great truth, which can be applied to our subject quite readily.

It is very difficult for a great aristocratic people to conquer its neighbors or to be conquered by them. It can never conquer them, because it can never assemble all its forces and hold them together for a lengthy period; and it cannot be conquered, because the enemy meets everywhere with small pockets of resistance that halt his progress. I would compare war in an aristocratic country with war in a mountainous land: the vanquished are always able to find new positions in which to rally and make a stand.

Precisely the opposite can be seen in democratic nations.

A democratic nation can easily put all its available forces into the field, and if it is rich and populous, it can readily become a conqueror. Once defeated and invaded, however, it is left with few resources, and if its capital is seized, the nation is lost. This is easy to explain: since each citizen is individually quite isolated and weak, no one can either defend himself or serve as a rallying point for others. Nothing is strong in a democratic country except the state. Once the state's military force has been eliminated by destruction of its army, and its civil power has been paralyzed by the capture of its capital, all that remains is a multitude without discipline or strength, which cannot counter the organized power that is attacking it. I know that the danger can be reduced by creating provincial liberties and, as a result, provincial bodies, but this remedy will always prove inadequate.

Not only will the population then be unable to carry on the war, but there is reason to fear that it will not even wish to make the attempt.

According to the international law adopted by the civilized nations, the purpose of war is not to appropriate the property of individuals but only to seize political power. Private property is destroyed only incidentally in order to achieve the latter objective.

When an aristocratic nation is invaded after its army has been defeated, nobles, even though they are also rich, will continue to defend themselves individually rather than submit, because if the victor were to remain master of the country, he would strip them of their political power, to which they are even more attached than they are to their property. They therefore prefer combat to conquest, which for them is the greatest of misfortunes, and they easily carry the people along with them, because the people have long since become accustomed to following and obeying them and in any case have virtually nothing to lose in war.

By contrast, in a nation where equality of conditions prevails, each citizen has only a small share of political power and in many cases no share at all. Furthermore, everyone is independent and has property to lose. People therefore fear conquest far less and war far more than they would in an aristocratic nation. It will always be quite difficult to persuade a democratic population to take up arms when war comes to their territory. That is why it is necessary to give democratic peoples rights and a political spirit that suggests to each citizen some of the interests that cause nobles to act in aristocracies.

Princes and other leaders of democratic nations must remember that only the passion and habit of liberty can struggle successfully against the habit and passion of well-being. I can imagine nothing better prepared for conquest in case of defeat than a democratic people without free institutions.

People used to go into battle with a small number of soldiers. They fought small skirmishes and made lengthy sieges.
Now they engage in great battles, and as soon as the road
ahead is clear, they march straight on the capital in order to
end the war with a single blow.

Napoleon supposedly invented this new system, but no
man, no matter who he might be, has the power to create anything of the sort. The way in which Napoleon waged war was
suggested to him by the state of society in his time, and it was
successful because it was marvelously well suited to that state
and because he was the first to put it to use. Napoleon was
the first man to tour all the capitals at the head of an army,
but it was the destruction of feudal society that allowed him
to pursue this course. It is fair to say that if this extraordinary
man had been born three hundred years earlier, he would not
have reaped the same fruits from his method, or, rather, he
would have chosen a different method.

I shall add only a few words about civil wars lest I try the
reader's patience.

Most of the things I said about foreign wars apply even
more to civil wars. Men who live in democratic countries do
not have a military spirit by nature. They sometimes acquire
one when compelled in spite of themselves to take to the battlefield. But to rise up en masse of their own free will and
deliberately expose themselves to the rigors that war, and
especially civil war, entails, is not a course that men in democracies will follow. Only the most adventurous citizens would
consent to run such risks. The bulk of the population would
take no action.

Even if the population wanted to act, it would not find it
easy to do so, for it would not find within its ranks men of
long-standing and well-established influence to whom it
would be willing to submit or known leaders already capable
of rallying, disciplining, and leading malcontents. Nor would
it find political authorities below the national government capable of lending effective support to the resistance against it.

In democratic countries, the moral power of the majority
is immense, and the material forces at its disposal are disproportionate to those that can initially be mustered against it.
The party that sits in the seat of the majority, speaks in its

name, and wields its power therefore triumphs instantly and effortlessly over all particular resistances. It does not even allow them time to be born; it stamps out the seed.

People in these countries who want to launch an armed revolution therefore have no recourse but to seize the ready-made machinery of government without warning, and this is more easily accomplished by a coup than by war, for as soon as there is a regular war, the party representing the state is almost always sure to win.

Civil war can occur only if the army divides, with one faction raising the standard of revolt and the other remaining loyal. An army constitutes a small, tightly bound, and very robust society capable of standing on its own for a period of time. The war may be bloody, but it will not be long, for either the rebel army will draw the government to its side merely by demonstrating its strength or winning its first victory, thus ending the conflict, or battle will be joined, and the portion of the army not backed by the organized power of the state will soon either disband of its own accord or be destroyed.

It can therefore be accepted as a general truth that in centuries of equality civil wars will become much rarer and much shorter.[3]

---

[3]Of course I am speaking here only of *single* democratic nations and not confederated ones. In confederations — fiction notwithstanding — the preponderance of power always resides in the state governments and not the federal government, so that civil wars are only foreign wars in disguise.

PART IV

*On the Influence That Democratic Ideas and
Sentiments Exert on Political Society*

I would not do justice to the purpose of this book if, having explored ideas and sentiments prompted by equality, I did not conclude by showing what general influence these same sentiments and ideas can exert on the government of human societies.

In order to do this successfully, I shall often be obliged to retrace my steps. I nevertheless hope that the reader will not refuse to follow me when familiar paths promise to lead to some new truth.

Chapter 1

EQUALITY NATURALLY GIVES MEN
A TASTE FOR FREE INSTITUTIONS

EQUALITY, which makes men independent of one another, fosters the habit of and taste for governing their course in private actions solely by their own will. This complete independence, which they enjoy constantly vis-à-vis their equals and in the ordinary course of private life, disposes them to take a dim view of all authority and soon suggests to them the idea and love of political liberty. Men who live in such times therefore proceed with a natural bias toward free institutions. Choose any one of them at random and if possible delve down to his basic instincts: you will find that, of all the possible forms of government, the one that he thinks of first and prizes above all others is the one whose head he has elected and whose actions he controls.

Of all the political effects produced by equality of conditions, this love of independence is the one that is most striking and most frightening to timid spirits, and it cannot be said that they are absolutely wrong to be frightened, because anarchy has a more terrifying aspect in democratic countries than elsewhere. Since citizens do not act directly on one another, it would seem that if the national power that keeps them all in their place should fail, disorder must immediately rise to a fever pitch, and with each citizen going his own way, the social fabric will instantly be reduced to dust.

I am nevertheless convinced that anarchy is not the principal evil that democratic centuries must dread, but rather the least of those evils.

Equality in fact produces two tendencies: one leads men directly to independence and can drive them all the way to anarchy in an instant, while the other leads by a longer, more hidden, but also more certain path to servitude.

Peoples are quick to recognize the first of these tendencies and resist it. They allow themselves to be carried away by the latter without seeing it. Hence it is particularly important to point it out.

Rather than reproach equality for inspiring intractability, I for one see that as the primary reason for praising it. I admire equality when I see it deposit an obscure notion of, and instinctive penchant for, political independence in every man's heart and mind, thereby preparing the remedy for the ill that it provokes. It is this aspect of equality that I hold dear.

Chapter 2

WHY THE IDEAS OF DEMOCRATIC PEOPLES ABOUT GOVERNMENT NATURALLY FAVOR THE CONCENTRATION OF POWER

THE idea of subsidiary powers placed between sovereign and subjects occurred naturally to aristocratic peoples because those powers comprised individuals and families marked out by birth, enlightenment, and wealth as exceptional and destined to command. For opposite reasons, the same idea is naturally absent from the minds of men in centuries of equality. It can be introduced only artificially and retained only with difficulty, whereas the idea of an unrivaled central power that leads all citizens by itself is one that they conceive as it were without thinking.

In politics, moreover, as in philosophy and religion, the intelligence of democratic peoples delights in simple and general ideas. It finds complicated systems repellent and likes to imagine a great nation whose citizens all conform to a single model and are directed by a single power.

After the idea of an unrivaled central power, the idea that occurs most spontaneously to men in centuries of equality is that of uniform legislation. Since each man sees himself as not very different from his neighbors, he finds it difficult to understand why a rule that applies to one man should not apply equally to all the others. The merest of privileges are therefore repugnant to his reason. The slightest dissimilarities in the political institutions of the nation offend him, and legislative uniformity strikes him as the primary prerequisite of good government.

By contrast, I find that this same notion of a uniform rule imposed equally on all members of the society is in a sense alien to the human mind in aristocratic centuries. Either the mind cannot take in the idea, or it rejects it.

In both cases, these opposing penchants of the intellect ultimately become instincts so blind and habits so invincible that they continue to direct action without regard to particular facts. Despite the immense variety of the Middle Ages, individuals did at times appear who were perfectly alike, yet this did not prevent lawmakers from assigning distinct duties and different rights to each. Nowadays, by contrast, governments do their utmost to impose the same usages and laws on populations that still bear no resemblance to one another.

As conditions in a nation become more equal, individuals appear smaller and society seems greater, or, rather, each citizen, having become just like all the others, is lost in the crowd, until nothing can be seen any more but the vast and magnificent image of the people itself.

This naturally gives men in democratic times a very high opinion of the privileges of society and a most humble idea of the rights of the individual. They readily concede that the interest of the former is everything and that of the latter, nothing. They are willing enough to grant that the power that represents society possesses far more enlightenment and wisdom than any of the men who compose it and that its duty as well as its right is to take each citizen by the hand and guide him.

If we look closely at our contemporaries and dig down to the roots of their political opinions, we find some of the ideas that I have just described, and we may be surprised to discover so much agreement among people who are so frequently at war.

Americans believe that the social power in each state should emanate directly from the people, but once that power is constituted, they do not, as it were, imagine it as having limits. They are prepared to grant that it has the right to do anything.

As for particular privileges granted to cities, families, and individuals, they have forgotten the very idea of such things. It has never occurred to them that one might not apply the same law uniformly to all parts of the same state and all the men who inhabit it.

These same opinions are increasingly widespread in Europe. They have even made their way into the hearts of the nations that have most violently rejected the dogma of popular sovereignty. These nations disagree with the Americans as to the source of power but see power in the same light. In all of them, the notion of intermediate power grows dim and disappears. The idea of a right inherent in certain individuals is rapidly vanishing from the minds of men; the idea of society's all-powerful and in a sense unrivaled right is taking its place. These ideas take root and grow as conditions become more equal and men more alike. They are born of equality and in turn hasten the progress of equality.

In France, where the revolution I am speaking of is more advanced than in any other nation of Europe, these same opinions have completely captivated people's minds. If you listen attentively to the voices of our various parties, you will see that there is not a single one that has not adopted them. Most believe that the government acts badly, but all think that the government must act continually and take a hand in everything. Even those who attack one another most harshly agree about that. The unity, ubiquity, and omnipotence of the social power and the uniformity of its rules constitute the most salient features of all the political systems born in recent years. We find these things underlying even the most bizarre utopias. The human mind still pursues these images in its dreams.

If such ideas occur spontaneously to individual minds, they are even more likely to grip the imagination of princes.

While the old social state of Europe is deteriorating and dissolving, sovereigns are forging new beliefs about their capabilities and duties. They understand for the first time that the central power which they represent can and should administer by itself, and on a uniform plane, all affairs and all men. This opinion, which I dare say no king of Europe ever conceived before our time, has sunk into the deepest recesses of these monarchs' minds, where it holds its own against all the other views that swirl around it.

Men today are therefore far less divided than some imagine. They fight constantly about who should wield sovereignty, but they agree readily as to the duties and rights of that sovereignty. All conceive of government in terms of an unrivaled, simple, providential, and creative power.

All subsidiary ideas about politics are changeable, but this one remains fixed, unalterable, and always the same. Legal scholars and statesmen adopt it, and the crowd eagerly latches onto it. The governed agree to pursue it with the same ardor as their governors: it comes first; it seems innate.

It is therefore no whim of the human mind but a natural condition of man's present state.[*]

Chapter 3

HOW THE SENTIMENTS OF DEMOCRATIC PEOPLES ACCORD WITH THEIR IDEAS TO BRING ABOUT A CONCENTRATION OF POWER

IF MEN in centuries of equality readily perceive the idea of a great central power, there can be no doubt that their habits and sentiments also predispose them to recognize such a power and lend it a hand. The proof of this can be given in short order, most of the reasons having already been provided elsewhere.

Since men who live in democratic countries have neither superiors nor inferiors nor habitual and necessary associates, they are apt to fall back on themselves and consider themselves in isolation. I discussed this at considerable length in dealing with individualism.

Hence it always takes effort for such men to tear themselves away from their private affairs in order to take up common ones. Their natural inclination is to leave common affairs in the charge of the sole visible and permanent representative of collective interests, which is the state.

Not only is a taste for the public's business not in their nature, but often they lack the time for it as well. Private life in democratic times is so active, so agitated, so filled with desires and labors that individuals have virtually no energy or leisure left for political life.

Such penchants are not invincible: I would be the last man to deny this, since my chief purpose in writing this book has been to combat them. I merely claim that an occult force has been developing these penchants in the human heart steadily of late, and they will fill it if left unchecked.

I have also had occasion to show how the growing love of well-being and the mobile nature of property caused democratic peoples to dread material disorder. The love of public tranquillity is often the only political passion that these peoples retain, and in them it becomes more active and more

powerful as all the others dwindle and die. This naturally inclines citizens to grant or surrender new rights to the central
power, which alone seems to have the interest and the means
to defend them against anarchy in the course of defending
itself.

Since no one in centuries of equality is obliged to lend his
strength to his fellow man, and no one has the right to expect
substantial support from his fellow man, each individual is
at once independent and weak. These two states, which must
neither be viewed separately nor confounded, give the citizen
of a democracy quite contrary instincts. His independence fills
him with confidence and pride among his equals, and his de-
bility causes him on occasion to feel the need of outside help,
which he cannot expect to receive from any of them because
they are all powerless and cold-hearted. In this extreme, he
naturally turns his attention to the one immense being that
alone stands out amid the universal abasement. It is to that
being that he is constantly drawn by his needs and above all
his desires, and in the end he comes to see it as the sole and
necessary support of individual weakness.[1]

[1]In democratic societies, only the central power enjoys some stability in its
foundations and some permanence in its undertakings. All the citizens are
constantly on the move and in a permanent state of transformation. Now, it
is in the nature of every government to seek to expand its sphere continually.
Hence in the long run it is unlikely that it will not succeed in doing so, since
it acts with a fixed thought and constant will on men whose position, ideas,
and desires vary from day to day.

It is common for citizens to work on its behalf without intending to.

Democratic centuries are times of trial, innovation, and adventure. There
are always a host of men engaged in difficult or novel enterprises which they
pursue independently, unencumbered by their fellow men. These people
accept the general principle that the public authorities should not intervene
in private affairs, but each of them seeks, as an exception to this rule, help in
the affair that is of special concern to him and tries to interest the government in acting in that area while continuing to ask that its action in other
areas be restricted.

Because so many men take this particular view of so many different objectives at the same time, the sphere of the central power imperceptibly expands in every direction, even though each one of them wishes to restrict it.
A democratic government therefore increases its prerogatives simply by enduring. Time works in its favor. Every accident redounds to its benefit.
Individual passions aid it unwittingly, and we can say that the older a democratic society is, the more centralized its government becomes.

This sums up what often happens in democratic nations, where men who find it very difficult to put up with superiors will patiently endure a master, proving themselves to be both proud and servile at the same time.

The hatred that men bear toward privilege increases as privileges become rarer and less substantial, so that democratic passions seem to burn hottest precisely when they are most starved for fuel. I have already given the reason for this phenomenon. When all conditions are unequal, no inequality is great enough to be offensive, whereas the slightest dissimilarity seems shocking in the midst of general uniformity. The more complete the uniformity, the more unbearable the sight of inequality. Hence it is natural for love of equality to grow steadily with equality itself; by satisfying it, one fosters its growth.

This hatred, immortal and increasingly inflamed, which animates democratic peoples against the most insignificant privileges, powerfully encourages the gradual concentration of all political rights in the hands of the sole representative of the state. The sovereign, being of necessity and incontestably above all citizens, arouses no envy in any of them, and each one believes that any prerogative he concedes to the sovereign is one that he has taken from his equals.

A man in democratic times is extremely reluctant to obey his neighbor, who is his equal. He refuses to recognize in his neighbor enlightenment superior to his own. He is wary of his neighbor's justice and jealous of his power. He fears and despises him. He likes to make his neighbor constantly aware of the fact that both are dependent on the same master.

Any central power that follows these natural instincts loves equality and encourages it, because equality markedly facilitates, extends, and secures the action of such a power.

It is also fair to say that every central government adores uniformity. Uniformity eliminates the need to examine an endless host of details with which it would have to concern itself were it necessary to make rules for men instead of subjecting all men indiscriminately to the same rule. Thus the government loves what the citizens love, and it naturally hates what they hate. This community of feeling, which in democratic nations constantly unites each individual with the sovereign in an identical frame of mind, establishes a secret and permanent sympathy between them. The government's faults are forgiven for the sake of its tastes; despite its excesses and errors, public confidence abandons it only under duress and revives when summoned. Democratic peoples often hate the repositories of central power, but they always love the power itself.

Thus I have reached the same conclusion by two different routes. I showed earlier how equality suggested the idea of a single, uniform, and powerful government. I have just shown that it also inspires a taste for such a government. Hence nations are today tending toward a government of this kind. The natural inclination of their minds and hearts leads them toward that end, and to arrive there it suffices that they not hold themselves back.

In the democratic centuries that are about to begin, I think that individual independence and local liberties will always be a product of art. Centralization will be the natural form of government.*

*See Note XXV, page 365.

Chapter 4

CONCERNING CERTAIN PARTICULAR AND ACCIDENTAL CAUSES THAT EITHER LEAD A DEMOCRATIC PEOPLE TO CENTRALIZE POWER OR DIVERT THEM FROM IT

If ALL democratic peoples are instinctively drawn to centralization of powers, they move toward such centralization unequally. Particular circumstances may either enhance or limit the natural effects of the social state. The number of such circumstances is very large; I shall mention only a few.

Among men who have lived free for a long time before becoming equals, the instincts bred by liberty to some extent combat the penchants prompted by equality, and while the privileges of the central power increase, individuals never entirely lose their independence.

But when equality develops in a nation that has never known liberty or has long since forgotten it, as is happening across the continent of Europe, old national habits combine suddenly, through a sort of natural attraction, with new habits and doctrines stemming from the social state, so that all powers seem to hasten toward the center of their own accord. There they accumulate with surprising rapidity, and the state abruptly reaches the utmost limits of its strength, while individuals allow themselves to sink in an instant to the ultimate degree of weakness.

The English who came three centuries ago to found a democratic society in the wilderness of the New World had all become used to taking part in public affairs while still living in the motherland. They were familiar with the jury system. They had freedom of speech and of the press, individual liberty, the idea of law, and the habit of relying on it in practice. They carried these free institutions and virile mores with them to America, and these sustained them against encroachments by the state.

With the Americans, therefore, it is liberty that is old; equality is comparatively new. The contrary is true in Europe, where equality, introduced by absolute power and under the eye of kings, had already penetrated the habits of peoples long before liberty figured among their ideas.

I said earlier that among democratic peoples the human mind naturally conceives of government exclusively in the form of an unrivaled central power and is unfamiliar with the notion of intermediate powers. This statement applies in particular to those democratic nations that have seen the principle of equality triumph with the help of a violent revolution. Because the classes that managed local affairs suddenly vanished in the revolutionary tempest, and because the confused mass that remained still lacked the organization and habits that would have allowed it to take administration of those affairs in hand, only the state itself seemed capable of dealing with all the details of government. Centralization in a sense became a necessary fact.

Napoleon should neither be praised nor blamed for concentrating nearly all administrative powers in his hands alone, for after the sudden demise of the nobility and haute bourgeoisie, those powers fell to him by default. It would have been almost as difficult for him to refuse them as to take them up. No such necessity ever forced itself upon the Americans, who, because they had no revolution and governed themselves from the outset, were never obliged to make the state their temporary guardian.

Thus centralization in a democratic nation develops in accordance not only with the progress of equality but also with the way in which equality is established.

At the beginning of a great democratic revolution, when the war between the different classes has only just begun, the people strive to centralize the administration in the hands of the government in order to wrest control of local affairs from the aristocracy. By contrast, toward the end of the revolution, it is usually the vanquished aristocracy that tries to surrender control of all affairs to the state because it fears the petty tyranny of the people, who have become its equal and in many cases its master.

Thus it is not always the same class of citizens that endeavors to increase the prerogatives of power. As long as the democratic revolution lasts, however, there is always one class in the nation, powerful by virtue of either numbers or wealth, that is moved by special passions and particular interests to centralize public administration, independent of the hatred of government by one's neighbor that is a general and permanent sentiment among democratic peoples. Note that today it is the lower classes in England that are working with all their might to destroy local independence and transfer administration from all points on the periphery to the center, while the upper classes are attempting to confine the administration within its traditional limits. I dare to predict that we will some day see the exact opposite come to pass.

The foregoing makes it quite clear why the social power must always be stronger and the individual weaker in a democratic people that has gone through lengthy and arduous social travail in order to achieve equality than in a democratic society where citizens have always been equals from the beginning. This is what the American example is proving conclusively.

The men who inhabit the United States were never separated by privilege of any kind. They never knew the reciprocal relation of inferior and master, and since they neither fear nor hate one another, they never felt the need to call upon the sovereign to manage the details of their affairs. The destiny of the Americans is singular: they took from the aristocracy of England the idea of individual rights and the taste for local liberties, and they were able to preserve both because they had no aristocracy to fight.

If enlightenment has helped men to defend their independence in every age, this has been especially true in democratic ages. When all men are alike, it is easy to establish a government that is unrivaled and all-powerful; instincts suffice. But men must possess considerable intelligence, science, and art to organize and maintain secondary powers in these same circumstances, and to create, in a situation characterized by the independence and weakness of individual citizens, free associations that are in a position to struggle against tyranny without destroying order.

The concentration of powers and individual servitude will therefore increase in democratic nations not only in proportion to equality but also in proportion to ignorance.

It is true that in relatively unenlightened centuries, governments often lack the enlightenment needed to perfect despotism, just as citizens lack the enlightenment needed to avoid it. But the effect is not equal on both sides.

However coarse a democratic people may be, the central power that rules it is never completely devoid of enlightenment, because it has no difficulty drawing to itself what little enlightenment exists in the country and if necessary can search for it outside. Hence in a nation that is ignorant as well as democratic, a prodigious difference between the intellectual capacity of the sovereign and that of each of his subjects will inevitably manifest itself before long. In the end this will easily concentrate all powers in the sovereign's hands. The administrative power of the state grows steadily, because it alone possesses sufficient skill in administration.

We never see this sort of spectacle in aristocratic nations, however unenlightened we suppose them to be, because in them enlightenment is sufficiently equally distributed among the prince and the leading citizens.

The pasha who rules Egypt today found a population of very ignorant and very equal individuals, and he appropriated the science and intelligence of Europe to govern them. With the particular enlightenment of the sovereign combined in this way with the ignorance and democratic weakness of his subjects, the utmost degree of centralization was easily achieved, and the prince was able to turn the country into his factory and its inhabitants into his workers.

I believe that extreme centralization of political power ultimately enervates society and thus in the long run weakens government itself. But I will not deny that a centralized social force is in a position to carry out great undertakings easily at a given time and place. This is especially true in war, where success depends a good deal more on the ability to bring all one's resources to bear at a certain place than on the extent of those resources. Hence it is chiefly in war that nations feel the desire and often the need to increase the prerogatives of the central power. All military geniuses love centralization, which increases their strength, and all centralizing geniuses love war, which obliges nations to concentrate all powers in the hands of the state. Thus the democratic tendency that leads men constantly to multiply the privileges of the state and to restrict the rights of individuals works with far greater speed and continuity in democratic nations that by virtue of their location are subject to frequent major wars and whose existence can often be imperiled than is the case elsewhere.

I have shown how fear of disorder and love of well-being imperceptibly led democratic peoples to increase the prerogatives of the central government, the only power that seems to them sufficiently strong, sufficiently intelligent, and sufficiently stable to protect them from anarchy. I hardly need add that any particular circumstances that tend to make the state of a democratic society more troubled and precarious will exacerbate this general instinct and make individuals more and more likely to sacrifice their rights to their tranquillity.

Hence a people is never so disposed to increase the prerogatives of the central power as at the end of a long and bloody revolution, which, after wresting property from the hands of its former possessors, shakes all beliefs and fills the nation with furious hatreds, opposing interests, and contrary factions. The public's taste for tranquillity then becomes a blind passion, and citizens are likely to succumb to a very disorderly love of order.

I have just examined a number of accidents that together contribute to the centralization of power, but I have yet to mention the principal one.

The most important of all the accidental causes that can draw direction of all affairs in democratic nations into the hands of the sovereign is the very origin of that sovereign and of its penchants.

Men who live in centuries of equality naturally love the central power and willingly enlarge its privileges. But if that power should happen to represent their interests faithfully and reproduce their instincts precisely, their confidence in it will be virtually without limit, and they will believe that whatever they grant to the central power is something they accord to themselves.

The attraction of administrative powers toward the center will always be less easy and less rapid with kings, who are still associated in some way with the old aristocratic order, than with the new princes, children of their works, who seem inextricably tied to equality by virtue of their birth, prejudices, instincts, and habits. I do not mean to say that princes of aristocratic origin who live in centuries of democracy do not seek to centralize. I think they work at it as diligently as everyone else. For them, the only advantages of equality lie in this direction. But their capabilities are comparatively limited, because citizens, rather than naturally anticipating their desires, are often reluctant to go along with them. In democratic societies, the less aristocratic the sovereign, the greater the centralization: that is the rule.

When an old race of kings rules an aristocracy, the natural prejudices of the sovereign are in perfect accord with the natural prejudices of the nobles, so that the vices inherent in aristocratic societies will develop freely, and no remedy for them will emerge. The opposite happens when the scion of a feudal line becomes the head of a democratic people. By virtue of his upbringing, habits, and memories, the prince daily inclines toward feelings prompted by the inequality of conditions, while the people, by virtue of their social state, tend constantly toward mores born of equality. Citizens will then often seek to restrain the central power, not so much because it is tyrannical as because it is aristocratic, and they will steadfastly maintain their independence, not only because they want to be free but above all because they intend to remain equal.

A revolution that overthrows an ancient family of kings in order to place new men at the head of a democratic people may momentarily weaken the central power. Yet no matter how anarchical it may seem initially, one should not hesitate to predict that its final and necessary result will be to extend and secure the prerogatives of that same power.

The most important, and in a sense the only necessary, condition for centralizing public power in a democratic society is to love equality or to make a show of loving it. Thus the science of despotism, once so complicated, is made simpler: it can be reduced, as it were, to a single principle.

Chapter 5

HOW SOVEREIGN POWER IN TODAY'S EUROPEAN NATIONS IS INCREASING, ALTHOUGH SOVEREIGNS ARE LESS STABLE

WHEN one reflects on what has just been said, it is surprising and frightening to see how everything in Europe seems to be conspiring to increase the prerogatives of the central power indefinitely and to make individual existence daily more tenuous, more subordinate, and more precarious.

The democratic nations of Europe exhibit all the general and permanent tendencies that are leading Americans toward centralization of powers, besides which they are also subject to a multitude of secondary and accidental causes that Americans do not have to contend with. It seems as though every step they take toward equality brings them closer to despotism.

To be convinced of this we need only cast our eyes about us and upon ourselves.

During the aristocratic centuries that preceded our own, the sovereigns of Europe were either deprived of or relinquished several of the rights inherent in their power. We do not have to go back even a hundred years to find, in most European nations, individuals or almost independent corporate bodies that administered justice, levied and maintained troops, collected taxes, and in many cases even made or explained the law. Everywhere the state has reclaimed these natural attributes of sovereign power for itself alone. In everything pertaining to government, the state suffers no intermediary to come between it and its citizens, and it rules them directly in matters of general concern. Far be it from me to criticize this concentration of powers; I am merely pointing it out.

In the same period, there existed in Europe a large number of secondary powers, which represented local interests and administered local affairs. Most of these local authorities have already disappeared. All are rapidly either on their way out or moving toward more complete dependence. From one end of Europe to the other, the privileges of lords, the liberties of towns, and provincial administrations have either been destroyed or soon will be.

For half a century Europe has experienced many revolutions and counterrevolutions, which have moved it in opposite directions. But all the changes are similar in one respect: they all shook or destroyed secondary powers. Local privileges that the French nation did not abolish in the countries it conquered eventually succumbed to the efforts of the princes who defeated it. Those princes rejected all the novelties that the revolution created in their countries except for centralization: that was the only gift they were willing to accept from it.

What I want to point out is that all the diverse rights that have been wrested in recent years from classes, corporations, and individuals were not used to establish new secondary powers on a more democratic basis but were concentrated instead in the hands of the sovereign. States everywhere are increasingly likely to rule directly over the humblest of citizens and to manage the least of his affairs without assistance.[1]

Nearly all the charitable institutions of old Europe were in the hands of private individuals or corporations. All have fallen more or less under the sway of the sovereign, and in a number of countries the sovereign controls them. It is the state that has undertaken virtually alone to give bread to the hungry, aid and shelter to the sick, and work to the idle, the state that has made itself virtually the sole healer of all miseries.

Not only charity but also education has become a national

---

[1] This gradual weakening of the individual vis-à-vis society manifests itself in a thousand ways. I shall cite an example having to do with wills.

In aristocratic countries, one ordinarily professes profound respect for a man's last will. Among the ancient peoples of Europe this sometimes reached the point of superstition: far from standing in the way of a dying man's whims, the social power lent its strength to the least of them; it assured him of a perpetual power.

When all living individuals are weak, less respect is shown to the will of the dead. A very narrow circle is drawn around it, and if it transgresses those limits, the sovereign nullifies or controls it. In the Middle Ages, the testamentary power was in a sense unlimited. In France today, it is impossible to distribute one's property to one's children without having the state intervene. Having asserted its domination over the individual during his lifetime, the state wants to regulate his final act as well.

affair in most countries today. The state receives, and often takes, the child from its mother's arms in order to turn it over to state agents. It is the state that assumes responsibility for inspiring each generation with feelings and supplying it with ideas. Uniformity reigns in studies as in everything else; diversity, like liberty, is vanishing day by day.

Furthermore, I do not hesitate to say that in nearly all Christian nations today, Catholic as well as Protestant, religion is in danger of falling into the hands of the government. Not that sovereigns are terribly keen to establish dogma themselves, but they are increasingly usurping the will of those who explain dogma: they are depriving the clergy of its property and putting clergymen on salary, and they are using the priest's influence and turning it to their own exclusive profit. They are turning clergymen into functionaries and, often, servants, and they are using the clergy to reach the deepest recesses of the individual soul.[2]

But this is still only one side of the picture.

Not only has the power of the sovereign expanded, as we have just seen, throughout the entire sphere of his former powers, which is no longer sufficient to contain it; it exceeds those limits in every direction and will soon encroach upon the domain hitherto reserved for individual independence. A host of actions that formerly escaped society's control entirely have recently been subjected to it, and their number is growing steadily.

Among aristocratic peoples, the social power was ordinarily limited to the direction and supervision of citizens in all matters having a direct and obvious relation to the national interest. In all other matters they were left free to choose for themselves. Among these peoples, the government often seemed to forget that there comes a point when the mistakes

---

[2]As the prerogatives of the central power grow, the number of functionaries representing it increases as well. They form a nation within each nation, and since they share in the stability of the government, they are more and more taking the place of the aristocracy.

Almost everywhere in Europe, the sovereign rules in two ways: some citizens follow him because they fear his agents, while others do so because they hope some day to become his agents.

and miseries of individuals compromise the well-being of all, and that to prevent the ruin of a single individual must sometimes be a matter of public concern.

The democratic nations of our time lean toward the opposite excess.

It is obvious that most of our princes want more than just to rule an entire nation. Apparently they deem themselves responsible for the actions and fates of each of their subjects individually and have undertaken to lead and enlighten each and every one of them in everything they do and, if need be, to make them happy in spite of themselves.

Private individuals, for their part, increasingly view the social power in the same light. They call upon its assistance for all their needs and look to it constantly as a teacher or guide.

I maintain that there is no country in Europe in which public administration has failed to become not only more centralized but also more inquisitive and exacting. Everywhere it delves more deeply than in the past into private affairs. It applies its own rules to more types of action, and to more minute actions, than ever before, and with each passing day we find it more firmly established alongside, around, and above each individual in order to assist, counsel, and coerce.

In the past, the sovereign lived on the revenue from his land or the proceeds from taxes. This is no longer the case now that his needs have increased along with his power. In the same circumstances in which a prince would formerly have established a new tax, he will today resort to a loan. Little by little the state has thus become a debtor to most of the rich, and it has centralized the largest sources of capital in its hands.

It attracts lesser sources of capital in a different way.

As men mingle and conditions become more equal, the poor man comes to have more resources, enlightenment, and desires. He conceives the idea of improving his lot, and he seeks to accomplish this through saving. Saving thus daily gives rise to an immense number of new repositories of small capital, the slowly and patiently accumulated fruit of the labor of many people. These sums increase steadily, but most would remain unproductive if they continued to be dispersed. This has given rise to a philanthropic institution that unless I miss my guess will soon become one of our greatest political institutions. Charitable men have come up with the idea of collecting the savings of the poor and putting them to productive use. In some countries, these benevolent associations have remained entirely separate from the state, but almost everywhere there is a clear tendency for them to merge with it, and there are even some places where the government has replaced these associations and taken upon itself the immense task of creating a central repository for the daily savings of several million workers and finding profitable ways to invest the resulting sums.

Through borrowing the state thus attracts the money of the rich, and through savings institutions it gains the ability to do as it wishes with the pennies of the poor. The wealth of the country is thus constantly flowing into its hands. The greater the equality of conditions becomes, the more wealth the state accumulates, for in a democratic nation only the state inspires confidence in private individuals because nothing else seems to possess both power and permanence.[3]

Thus the sovereign does not limit himself to controlling public wealth. He also insinuates himself into private wealth. To each citizen he is the leader and often the master, and he makes himself the steward and banker as well.

Not only does the central power alone fill, extend, and transcend the entire sphere of the former powers, but within that sphere it moves with greater agility, strength, and independence than ever before.

In recent years, all the governments of Europe have perfected administrative science to a remarkable degree. They do more things than ever before, and each thing is done with more discipline and dispatch and at lower cost. Governments always seem to be reaping the benefit of all the enlightenment they have taken from private individuals. With each passing day, the princes of Europe assert stricter authority over their representatives and invent new methods for managing them more minutely and supervising them more readily. It is not

---

[3]On the one hand, the taste for well-being increases steadily, and on the other hand, the state increasingly controls all the sources of well-being.

Men are therefore moving toward servitude along two paths. The taste for well-being diverts them from participating in government, and the love of well-being makes them increasingly dependent on those who govern.

enough for them to manage all affairs through their agents; they seek to direct their agents' conduct in matters of every sort, so that the public administration not only depends on one source of authority but is increasingly confined to one place and concentrated in fewer hands. The government centralizes its action even as it increases its prerogatives: two sources of strength.

Two things stand out when one looks into how the judicial power used to be constituted in most European nations, namely, the independence of that power and the extent of its prerogatives.

Not only did courts of justice once decide nearly all disputes between private individuals, but in a great many cases they also served as arbiters between individuals and the state.

At this point I want to discuss not the political and administrative prerogatives that the courts usurped in some countries but rather the judicial prerogatives that they possessed everywhere. In all the nations of Europe there were and still are many individual rights, mostly connected with the general right of property, which were placed under the safeguard of judges and which the state could not violate without a judge's permission.

It was primarily this semi-political power that distinguished European tribunals from all others, for all nations have had judges, but they have not all granted them the same privileges.

If we now look at what happens in the democratic nations of Europe that are called free as well as the others, we find that everywhere special, less independent tribunals have been set up alongside the existing courts for the specific purpose of deciding such contentious issues as may arise between the public administration and citizens. The old judicial power is allowed to retain its independence, but its jurisdiction is limited, and there is a growing tendency to use it exclusively as an arbiter of private interests.

The number of these special tribunals is increasing steadily, and their prerogatives are expanding. Hence governments are daily less constrained by the obligation to have their wishes and rights sanctioned by another power. Unable to do without judges, they want at the very least to choose their judges themselves and to hold them perpetually in check. In other words, what governments are placing between themselves and individuals is still an image of justice rather than justice itself.

Thus it is not enough for the state to become the pole toward which affairs of all kinds gravitate; increasingly it is moving toward deciding all these cases by itself, without oversight or possibility of appeal.[+]

In modern European nations there is one major cause, which, independently of all that I have mentioned thus far, constantly contributes to expanding the action of the sovereign and increasing his prerogatives. Not enough attention has been paid to it. That cause is the development of industry, which the progress of equality encourages.

Industry usually groups a multitude of men in the same place and establishes new and complex relations among them. It exposes them to great and sudden alternations of abundance and misery, during which public tranquillity is threatened. Industrial labor can also compromise the health and even the life of those who profit from or engage in it. Thus the industrial class needs to be regulated, supervised, and restrained more than other classes, and it is natural for the prerogatives of government to grow along with it.

This truth has general applicability, but it also pertains in a more particular way to the nations of Europe.

In the centuries prior to the one we live in, the aristocracy owned the land and was in a position to defend it. Landed property was therefore hedged about with guarantees, and its owners enjoyed considerable independence. This gave rise to laws and habits that have been perpetuated despite the division of estates and the ruin of the nobility, and landowners and farmers can today evade control by the social power more readily than all other citizens.

In those same aristocratic centuries, where all the wellsprings of our history are found, movable property was of little importance, and its owners were despised and weak.

[+]In France, the sophistry on this subject is striking. When a case pits the administration against a private individual, it cannot be heard by an ordinary judge, allegedly in order to keep administrative power distinct from judicial power — as if such a rule did not amount to mixing the two powers, and mixing them in the most dangerous and tyrannical way, by investing the government with the right both to judge and to administer.

The industrial class constituted an exception in the midst of the aristocratic world. Its members had no assured patronage, so they were not protected and often could not protect themselves.

It therefore became habitual to regard industrial property as a good of a particular nature, which did not deserve the same respect and ought not to be granted the same guarantees as property in general, and to regard the industrial class as a class apart in the social order, whose independence was of little value and which was rightly left to the regulatory passions of princes. Indeed, when one looks at medieval codes, it is astonishing to discover how industry in those centuries of individual independence was constantly regulated by kings down to the smallest detail. In this respect, centralization was as active and detailed as could be.

Since that time, a great revolution has taken place in the world. Industrial property, which was only an embryo, has developed; it covers Europe. The industrial class has expanded; it has enriched itself with the debris of all other classes. It has increased in number and importance and wealth. It is growing steadily. Nearly all who do not belong to it are connected with it in one way or another. Having been the exceptional class, it is now threatening to become the principal class and, in a manner of speaking, the only class. Yet the political ideas and habits to which it gave rise in an earlier time still remain. Those ideas and habits have not changed, because they are old and also because they happen to be in perfect harmony with the new ideas and general habits of men today.

Hence the rights of industrial property have not increased as rapidly as its importance. The industrial class has not become less dependent as it has become more numerous. On the contrary, it seems to carry despotism within itself, and despotism naturally spreads as the industrial class develops.[5]

As a nation becomes more industrial, it feels a proportionately greater need for roads, canals, ports, and other works of

[5]In support of this contention I shall cite a number of facts. Mines are natural sources of industrial wealth. As industry has developed in Europe and the output of mines has become a matter of more general interest, while at the same time it has become more difficult to exploit them owing to the division of property that equality brings, most sovereigns have claimed own-

a semi-public nature, which facilitate the acquisition of wealth. And to the extent that it becomes more democratic, private individuals experience proportionately greater difficulty in completing such works, while the state finds it easier to do so. I do not hesitate to say that the obvious tendency for all sovereigns nowadays is to assume sole responsibility for undertakings of this kind, thereby constricting the independence of the populations they rule more and more each day.

Furthermore, as the power of the state grows and its needs increase, it consumes a steadily growing quantity of industrial products itself — products that it usually manufactures in its own arsenals and factories. Thus in every kingdom the sovereign becomes the greatest of industrialists. A prodigious number of engineers, architects, mechanics, and artisans are attracted and retained by the services of the state.

Not only is the sovereign the leading industrialist; he tends increasingly to become the chief, or rather the master, of all the others.

Since citizens have become weaker while becoming more equal, they can do nothing in industry without forming associations. The public authorities naturally wish to assert control over these associations.

There is no denying that the collective entities known as associations are stronger and more formidable than any mere individual could possibly be, and that they are less accountable

---

ership of the contents of mines along with the right to oversee mining activities — claims not made with respect to other types of property.

Mines, which used to be individual properties subject to the same obligations and covered by the same guarantees as other real property, thus became part of the public domain. The state either operated them or granted concessions to operate them. The owners were transformed into users. They received their rights from the state, and, what is more, the state claimed the power to direct them almost everywhere. It laid down rules, dictated methods, and subjected them to continuous oversight, and if they resisted, an administrative tribunal stripped them of ownership, and the public administration transferred their privileges to others. Hence the government not only owned the mines but held all the miners in the palm of its hand.

As industry develops, however, exploitation of the old mines is increasing. New mines are being opened. The population of the mines is expanding and growing. Sovereigns are daily extending their domain beneath our feet and populating it with their servants.

for their actions, and therefore it seems reasonable that the social power allow them less independence than it might grant to an individual.

Sovereigns are all the more inclined to act this way since it suits their taste. In democratic nations, citizen resistance to the central power can arise only through association. The central power accordingly takes a dim view of associations not under its control. Particularly worthy of note is the fact that among these democratic peoples, citizens often look upon such badly needed associations with secret feelings of fear and jealousy, which prevent their defending them. The power and longevity of these small private societies amid weakness and general instability astonishes and worries them, and they come close to seeing the free use that associations make of their natural faculties as a dangerous kind of privilege.

Moreover, all the associations that are coming into being today are moral persons of a new type, whose rights have not been hallowed by time; they come into the world at a time when the idea of private rights is weak and social power is without limits. It is not surprising that they are losing their liberty at their inception.

In all the nations of Europe, certain associations are not allowed to organize until the state has examined their statutes and authorized their existence. In a number of countries, efforts are being made to extend this rule to all associations. It is easy to see where the success of such an undertaking might lead.

If the sovereign were ever to obtain the general right to establish conditions that associations of all kinds must meet in order to be authorized, he would soon claim the further right to supervise and control those associations in order to ensure that they could not deviate from the rules he laid down. In this way, the state, after imposing its authority on everyone who wished to associate, would impose its authority on everyone who had associated, that is, on virtually everyone alive today.

Sovereigns thus increasingly appropriate the greater part of the new force that industry is creating in the world today and put it to their own use. Industry leads us, and they lead it.

I attach so much importance to everything I have just said that I am tormented by the fear that, in trying to make my thinking as clear as possible, I may have done it harm.

Therefore, if the reader finds the examples cited in support of my words insufficient or ill-chosen; or if he thinks that I have exaggerated the progress of social power in some places or that I have unduly constricted the sphere in which individual independence still survives; I beg him to put down this book for a moment to consider for himself the things that I have tried to show him. Let him examine attentively what is happening every day both here and elsewhere. Let him question his neighbors, and, finally, let him contemplate himself. Unless I am badly mistaken, he will arrive unguided, by some other route, at the same point to which I have sought to lead him.

He will see that, during the half century that has just elapsed, centralization has grown everywhere in a thousand different ways. Wars, revolutions, and conquests have contributed to its development. All men have toiled to increase it. During this same period, throughout which men have succeeded one another in leadership roles at a prodigious pace, their ideas, interests, and passions have varied endlessly, yet all sought in one way or another to centralize. The instinct for centralization has been virtually the one fixed point in the striking mobility of their lives and thought.

And when the reader, after reviewing human affairs in this detail, comes to consider the whole vast tableau as one, he will not cease to be astonished.

On the one hand, the most stalwart dynasties have been shaken or destroyed. Peoples everywhere are violently escaping from the strictures of their laws. They are destroying or limiting the authority of their lords and princes. Even nations not in revolution seem at best anxious and trembling. An identical spirit of rebellion animates them. On the other hand, in this very same age of anarchy and among these very same recalcitrant peoples, the social power is steadily increasing its prerogatives. It is becoming more centralized, more enterprising, more absolute, and more extensive. Citizens are constantly succumbing to the control of the public administration.

They are insensibly and seemingly unwittingly being induced to sacrifice some new portion of their individual independence to it every day, and the same men who at one time or another in the past toppled a throne and rode roughshod over kings are increasingly likely to bend without resistance to the merest whims of a clerk.

Today, therefore, two revolutions seem to be working in opposite directions: one is continually weakening power, and the other constantly reinforcing it. In no other era of our history has power seemed either so weak or so strong.

In the end, however, when we come to take a closer look at the state of the world, we find that these two revolutions are intimately related, that both proceed from the same source, and that, after following different courses, both ultimately lead men to the same place.

Once again I do not hesitate to repeat one last time what I have already said or indicated at more than one place in this book: one must be careful not to confuse the fact of equality with the revolution that is responsible for introducing it into the social state and laws. Therein lies the reason for nearly all the phenomena that we find surprising.

All the old political powers of Europe, from the greatest to the least, were founded in centuries of aristocracy, and to one degree or another they represented or defended the principle of inequality and privilege. In order for the new needs and interests prompted by growing equality to prevail in government, the men of our time therefore had to overthrow or coerce the old powers. This led them to make revolutions and inspired in many of them the unbridled taste for disorder and independence to which all revolutions, regardless of their purpose, give rise.

I do not think that there is a single country in Europe in which the development of equality was not preceded or followed by certain violent changes in the status of property and persons, and nearly all these changes were accompanied by considerable anarchy and license because they were carried out by the least disciplined portion of the nation against the most disciplined.

From this emerged the two contrary tendencies that I pointed out above. In the heat of democratic revolution, the men who set about destroying the old aristocratic powers that opposed the revolution proved themselves to be animated by a great spirit of independence, but as the victory of equality moved toward completion, they little by little gave themselves up to the natural instincts engendered by that very same equality, and they reinforced and centralized social power. They had wanted to be free in order to be equal, and as equality increasingly established itself with the aid of liberty, it made liberty more difficult for them.

These two states did not always occur in succession. Our fathers showed how a people could organize an immense tyranny within even as they freed themselves from the authority of nobles and braved the power of all kings, thus teaching the world how to win independence and lose it at the same time.

Men today are witnessing the collapse of the old powers everywhere. They see all the old influences dying, all the old barriers falling. This clouds the judgment of even the cleverest among them. They see only the prodigious revolution that is taking place before their eyes, and they think that the human race is about to succumb to anarchy forever. If they thought about the ultimate consequences of this revolution, they might conceive different fears.

As for me, I confess that I have no confidence in the spirit of liberty that seems to animate my contemporaries. I see clearly that nations today are turbulent, but I have no clear evidence that they are liberal, and I fear that when the agitations that are rocking every throne in the world are over, sovereigns may find themselves more powerful than ever.

Chapter 6

WHAT KIND OF DESPOTISM DEMOCRATIC NATIONS HAVE TO FEAR

D URING my stay in the United States I had observed that a democratic social state similar to that of the Americans might make it unusually easy to establish despotism, and on my return to Europe I saw how many of our princes had already made use of ideas, sentiments, and needs engendered by that same social state in order to enlarge their sphere of power.

This led me to the thought that Christian nations might ultimately fall victim to oppression similar to that which once weighed on a number of peoples of Antiquity.

A more detailed examination of the subject and five years of new meditations have not diminished my fears but have changed their focus.

In centuries past, no sovereign was ever so absolute and so powerful as to undertake to administer by himself, and without the assistance of secondary powers, all the parts of a great empire. No ruler ever attempted to subject all his people indiscriminately to the minute details of a uniform code, or descended to their level to dictate and manage the lives of each and every one of them. The idea of such an undertaking never occurred to the mind of man, and had anyone conceived of such a thing, the want of enlightenment, the imperfection of administrative procedures, and above all the natural obstacles created by the inequality of conditions would soon have halted the execution of such a vast design.

When the power of the Caesars was at its height, the various peoples that inhabited the Roman world preserved their diverse customs and mores: though subject to the same monarch, most of the provinces were separately administered. Powerful and active municipalities were everywhere, and even though all the government of the empire was concentrated in the hands of the emperor alone, and he remained, when necessary, the arbiter of all things, the details of social life and of individual existence ordinarily escaped his control.

To be sure, the emperors wielded vast power without any counterweight, which enabled them to freely indulge their most bizarre penchants and to use the entire force of the state to gratify them. Often they abused this power to deprive a citizen arbitrarily of his property or his life. Their tyranny weighed mightily on a few, but it did not extend to a large number. It fastened on certain great objectives as primary and neglected the rest; it was violent and limited.

If despotism were to establish itself in today's democratic nations, it would probably have a different character. It would be more extensive and more mild, and it would degrade men without tormenting them.*

I have no doubt that in centuries of enlightenment and equality like our own, it will be easier for sovereigns to gather all public powers into their hands alone and to penetrate the sphere of private interests more deeply and regularly than any sovereign of Antiquity was ever able to do. But the same equality that facilitates despotism also tempers it. As men become increasingly similar and more and more equal, we have seen how public mores become milder and more humane. When no citizen has great power or wealth, tyranny in a sense lacks both opportunity and a stage. Since all fortunes are modest, passions are naturally contained, the imagination is limited, and pleasures are simple. This universal moderation moderates the sovereign himself and confines the erratic impulses of his desire within certain limits.

Quite apart from these reasons, which derive from the very nature of the social state, I could add many others, but to do so would take me far afield, and I prefer to remain within the limit that I have set for myself.

Democratic governments may become violent and even cruel in certain moments of great effervescence and great peril, but such crises will be rare and temporary.

When I think of the petty passions of men today, of the softness of their mores, the extent of their enlightenment, the purity of their religion, and the mildness of their morality, of their laborious and orderly habits, and of the restraint that nearly all of them maintain in vice as well as in virtue, what I

*See Note XXVI, page 365.

fear is not that they will find tyrants among their leaders but rather that they will find protectors.

I therefore believe that the kind of oppression that threatens democratic peoples is unlike any the world has seen before. Our contemporaries will find no image of it in their memories. I search in vain for an expression that exactly reproduces my idea of it and captures it fully. The old words "despotism" and "tyranny" will not do. The thing is new, hence I must try to define it, since I cannot give it a name.

I am trying to imagine what new features despotism might have in today's world: I see an innumerable host of men, all alike and equal, endlessly hastening after petty and vulgar pleasures with which they fill their souls. Each of them, withdrawn into himself, is virtually a stranger to the fate of all the others. For him, his children and personal friends comprise the entire human race. As for the remainder of his fellow citizens, he lives alongside them but does not see them. He touches them but does not feel them. He exists only in himself and for himself, and if he still has a family, he no longer has a country.

Over these men stands an immense tutelary power, which assumes sole responsibility for securing their pleasure and watching over their fate. It is absolute, meticulous, regular, provident, and mild. It would resemble paternal authority if only its purpose were the same, namely, to prepare men for manhood. But on the contrary, it seeks only to keep them in childhood irrevocably. It likes citizens to rejoice, provided they think only of rejoicing. It works willingly for their happiness but wants to be the sole agent and only arbiter of that happiness. It provides for their security, foresees and takes care of their needs, facilitates their pleasures, manages their most important affairs, directs their industry, regulates their successions, and divides their inheritances. Why not relieve them entirely of the trouble of thinking and the difficulty of living?

Every day it thus makes man's use of his free will rarer and more futile. It circumscribes the action of the will more narrowly, and little by little robs each citizen of the use of his own faculties. Equality paved the way for all these things by preparing men to put up with them and even to look upon them as a boon.

The sovereign, after taking individuals one by one in his powerful hands and kneading them to his liking, reaches out to embrace society as a whole. Over it he spreads a fine mesh of uniform, minute, and complex rules, through which not even the most original minds and most vigorous souls can poke their heads above the crowd. He does not break men's wills but softens, bends, and guides them. He seldom forces anyone to act but consistently opposes action. He does not destroy things but prevents them from coming into being. Rather than tyrannize, he inhibits, represses, saps, stifles, and stultifies, and in the end he reduces each nation to nothing but a flock of timid and industrious animals, with the government as its shepherd.

I have always believed that this kind of servitude — the regulated, mild, peaceful servitude that I have just described — could be combined more easily than one might imagine with some of the external forms of liberty, and that it would not be impossible for it to establish itself in the shadow of popular sovereignty itself.

Our contemporaries are constantly wracked by two warring passions: they feel the need to be led and the desire to remain free. Unable to destroy either of these contrary instincts, they seek to satisfy both at once. They imagine a single, omnipotent, tutelary power, but one that is elected by the citizens. They combine centralization with popular sovereignty. This gives them some respite. They console themselves for being treated as wards by imagining that they have chosen their own protectors. Each individual allows himself to be clapped in chains because he sees that the other end of the chain is held not by a man or a class but by the people themselves.

In this system citizens emerge from dependence for a moment to indicate their master and then return to it.

There are many people nowadays who adjust quite easily to a compromise of this kind between administrative despotism and popular sovereignty and who believe that they have done enough to guarantee the liberty of individuals when in fact they have surrendered that liberty to the national government. That is not enough for me. The nature of the master matters far less to me than the fact of obedience.

I will not deny, however, that a constitution of this kind is infinitely preferable to one that concentrates all powers and then deposits them in the hands of an irresponsible man or body. Of all the various forms that democratic despotism might take, that would surely be the worst.

When the sovereign is elected or closely supervised by a truly elective and independent legislature, he may in some cases subject individuals to greater oppression, but that oppression is always less degrading because each citizen, hobbled and reduced to impotence though he may be, can still imagine that in obeying he is only submitting to himself, and that it is to one of his wills that he is sacrificing all the others.

I also understand that when the sovereign represents the nation and is dependent on it, the forces and rights that are taken from each citizen not only serve the head of state but profit the state itself, and that private individuals derive some fruit from the sacrifice of their independence to the public.

To create a national representation in a highly centralized country is therefore to diminish but not to destroy the harm that extreme centralization may do.

Clearly, individual intervention in the most important matters can be preserved in this way, but it is no less ruthlessly expunged in smaller and private matters. What people forget is that it is above all in matters of detail that the subjugation of men becomes dangerous. I, for one, should be inclined to believe that liberty is less necessary in great things than in lesser ones if I thought that one could ever be assured of one without possessing the other.

Subjection in lesser affairs manifests itself daily and is felt by all citizens indiscriminately. It does not make them desperate, but it does constantly thwart their will and lead them to give up on expressing it. In this way it gradually smothers their spirit and saps their soul, whereas obedience, which is required only in a limited number of very serious but very rare circumstances, only occasionally points up the existence of servitude, whose weight only certain men must bear. In vain will you ask the same citizens whom you have made so dependent on the central government to choose the representatives of that government from time to time. This use of their freedom to choose — so important yet so brief and so rare —

will not prevent them from slowly losing the ability to think, feel, and act on their own and thus from sinking gradually beneath the level of humanity.

Furthermore, they will soon become incapable of exercising the one great privilege they have left. The democratic peoples that have introduced liberty in the political sphere while increasing despotism in the administrative sphere have been led into some very peculiar kinds of behavior. When it is necessary to deal with minor affairs in which simple common sense would suffice, they deem their citizens incapable of it, but when it is a matter of governing the entire state, they grant those same citizens vast prerogatives. They treat them alternately as playthings of the sovereign and as his masters, as more than kings yet less than men. After trying out all the various systems of election without finding one that suits them, they are surprised and keep on looking, as if the ills they see did not have far more to do with the constitution of the country than with that of the electoral body.

It is indeed difficult to imagine how men who have entirely renounced the habit of managing their own affairs could be successful in choosing those who ought to lead them. It is impossible to believe that a liberal, energetic, and wise government can ever emerge from the ballots of a nation of servants.

The possibility of a constitution's being republican in its head and ultramonarchical in all of its other parts has always struck me as an ephemeral monster. The vices of those who govern and the imbecility of the governed would quickly bring about its ruin, and the people, tired of their representatives and of themselves, would either create freer institutions or soon return to prostrating themselves at the feet of a single master.*

---

*See Note XXVII, page 366.

Chapter 7

CONTINUATION OF THE PRECEDING CHAPTERS

I BELIEVE that it is easier to establish an absolute and despotic government in a nation where conditions are equal than in any other, and I believe that if such a government were established in such a nation, it would not only oppress men in general but in the long run would rob each one of them of several of the principal attributes of humanity.

Despotism therefore seems to me particularly to be feared in democratic ages.

I would have loved liberty in all times, I think, but at the present time I am inclined to worship it.

I am convinced, moreover, that anyone who attempts to base liberty on privilege and aristocracy in the age we are now embarking on will fail. Anyone who attempts to amass and hold authority within a single class will fail. No sovereign today is clever enough or strong enough to establish despotism by restoring permanent distinctions among his subjects. Nor is any lawmaker wise or powerful enough to maintain free institutions if he does not take equality for his first principle and creed. Those of our contemporaries who seek to create or secure the independence and dignity of their fellow men must therefore show themselves to be friends of equality, and the only honest way to show themselves so is to be so: the success of their sacred enterprise depends on it.

Thus the goal is not to reconstruct an aristocratic society but to bring forth liberty from the midst of the democratic society in which God has decreed we must live.

These two fundamental truths are to my mind simple, clear, and fruitful, and they naturally lead me to consider what kind of free government can be established in a nation in which conditions are equal.

From the very constitution of democratic nations and their needs it follows that the power of the sovereign in such nations must be more uniform, more centralized, more extensive, more invasive, and more forceful than it is elsewhere. Society is naturally more dynamic and powerful, the individual more subordinate and weak: the one does more, the other less. This is inescapable.

Hence there is no reason to expect that the sphere of individual independence will ever be as large in democratic countries as in aristocratic ones. But that is not something to wish for, because in aristocratic nations society is often sacrificed to the individual and the prosperity of the majority to the grandeur of a few.

It is both necessary and desirable for the central power that guides a democratic people to be dynamic and forceful. The point is not to make it weak or indolent but only to prevent it from abusing its agility and strength.

What contributed most to securing the independence of private individuals in aristocratic centuries was the fact that the sovereign did not assume sole responsibility for governing and administering the citizens. He was obliged to leave portions of this charge to members of the aristocracy. The social power was therefore always divided and never brought its full weight to bear on each individual in exactly the same way.

Not only did the sovereign not do everything himself, but most of the officials who acted in his stead derived their power from their birth rather than from him and were therefore not under his thumb at all times. He could not create and destroy them at will, according to his whim, and force all to bow as one to his every wish. This further guaranteed the independence of private individuals.

I am well aware that today these methods will not do, but I see democratic procedures replacing them.

Rather than transfer all administrative powers from corporations and nobles to the sovereign alone, some of those powers can be entrusted to secondary bodies temporarily constituted of ordinary citizens. In this way, the liberty of private individuals can be made more secure without diminishing their equality.

Americans, who do not set as much store by words as we do, have retained the name "county" for the largest of their administrative districts, but to some extent they have replaced counties with provincial assemblies.

I am perfectly willing to concede that in an era of equality such as our own, it would be unjust and unreasonable to make the positions of government officials hereditary, but there is no reason why they cannot be replaced to some extent by elected officials. Election is a democratic expedient which ensures that officials will be at least as independent of the central power as heredity would make them in an aristocratic nation.

Aristocratic countries are full of wealthy and influential private individuals who are capable of looking after their own interests and who cannot be easily or secretly oppressed. They oblige the government to maintain general habits of moderation and restraint.

I am well aware that such individuals are not naturally found in democratic countries, but one can artificially create something analogous.

I am firmly convinced that aristocracy cannot be reestablished in the world. But ordinary citizens, by associating, can constitute very opulent, very influential, and very powerful entities — in a word, they can play the role of aristocrats.

In this way one could obtain several of the most important political advantages of aristocracy without its injustices or dangers. A political, industrial, commercial, or even scientific or literary association is an enlightened and powerful citizen that cannot be made to bow down at will or subjected to oppression in the shadows, and by defending its rights against the exigencies of power it saves common liberties.

In aristocratic times each man is always very closely tied to a number of his fellow citizens, so that it is impossible to attack anyone without others rushing to his defense. In centuries of equality, each individual is naturally isolated. He has no hereditary friends whose cooperation he can insist on, no class of whose sympathy he is assured. He is easily shoved aside or trampled underfoot. A citizen who is oppressed today therefore has only one way of defending himself. That is to address himself to the nation as a whole or, if it is deaf to his pleas, to the human race. He has only one way of doing this: the press. Thus freedom of the press is far more precious in democratic nations than in all the rest. It is the only cure for most of the ills that equality can produce. Equality isolates and weakens men, but the press places a very powerful weapon within each man's reach, a weapon that can be used by the weakest and most isolated. Equality deprives each individual of the support of his neighbors, but the press enables him to call all of his fellow citizens and fellow men to his aid. The printing press has hastened the progress of equality and is one of its best correctives.

I think that men who live in aristocracies can if need be do without freedom of the press, but those who live in democratic countries cannot. To guarantee their personal independence, I do not rely upon great political assemblies or parliamentary prerogatives or the proclamation of popular sovereignty.

To a degree all of these things can be reconciled with individual servitude. But that servitude cannot be complete if the press is free. The press is, par excellence, the democratic instrument of liberty.

I shall say something analogous about judicial power.

It is of the essence of judicial power to be concerned with particular interests and to direct its attention deliberately to the petty objects that are placed before it. It is also of the essence of this power not to come to the aid of the oppressed on its own initiative but rather to be ready at all times to assist the humblest among them. No matter how weak that humble litigant may be, he can always force the judge to hear his complaint and respond to it: this is implicit in the very constitution of the judicial power.

Such a power is therefore especially pertinent to the needs of liberty at a time when the sovereign's eye and hand are perennially involved in the smallest details of human actions, and when private individuals, too weak to protect themselves, are too isolated to be able to count on the aid of their peers. The power of the courts has always been the greatest guarantee of individual independence, but this is especially true in democratic centuries. Private rights and interests are always in peril unless the judicial power grows and expands as conditions become more equal.

Equality suggests to men several penchants that are quite dangerous to liberty, and the lawmaker must always be alert to these dangers. I shall recall only the main ones.

Men who live in democratic centuries do not readily comprehend the utility of forms. They harbor an instinctive disdain for them. I have explained the reasons for this elsewhere. Forms arouse their contempt and even their hatred. Since they ordinarily aspire only to facile and immediate pleasures, they hasten impetuously after the object of each of their desires. The slightest delay plunges them into despair. This temperament, which they carry over into political life, makes them impatient of forms that continually slow or halt the realization of their designs.

Yet the very inconvenience of forms about which men in democracies complain is what makes them so useful for liberty, their principal merit being to serve as a barrier between the strong and the weak, the governing and the governed, slowing the former while allowing the latter time to take his bearings. The more active and powerful the sovereign is, and the more indolent and debilitated private individuals become, the more necessary forms are. Thus democratic peoples by their very nature have greater need of forms than other peoples, and by their very nature they respect them less. This deserves very serious attention.

There is nothing more wretched than the arrogant disdain of most of our contemporaries for questions of form, for the smallest of such questions have today taken on an importance they never had in the past. Several of mankind's greatest interests are connected with such questions.

I believe that while statesmen who lived in aristocratic centuries could at times safely exhibit contempt for forms and often rise above them, today's leaders must show respect for the least of them and can neglect them only when imperious necessity requires it. In aristocracies, people were superstitious about forms; what we need is to worship them in an enlightened and thoughtful way.

Another very natural — and very dangerous — instinct in democratic peoples is the one that impels them to scorn individual rights and pay them little heed.

Men generally adhere to a right and show respect for it either because it is important or because they have made use of it over a long period of time. Individual rights in democratic nations are usually not very important, of quite recent date, and highly unstable. Hence they are often sacrificed without difficulty and almost always violated without remorse.

Now, in nations and times where men conceive a natural contempt for individual rights, the rights of society may naturally be extended and consolidated. In other words, men become less attached to particular rights at the very moment when it is perhaps most necessary to hold on to and defend the few such rights that still exist.

Hence it is above all in the present democratic age that the true friends of liberty and human grandeur must remain constantly vigilant and ready to prevent the social power from lightly sacrificing the particular rights of a few individuals to the general execution of its designs. In such times there is no citizen so obscure that it is not very dangerous to allow him to be oppressed, and there are no individual rights so unimportant that they can be sacrificed to arbitrariness with impunity. The reason for this is simple: when the particular right of an individual is violated in an age when the human mind is steeped in the idea that rights of this kind are important and sacred, harm is done only to the person who is deprived of his right; but to violate a similar right today is to deeply corrupt the national mores and to place the entire society in jeopardy, because there is among us a tendency for the very idea of rights of this kind to deteriorate and be lost.

Certain habits, certain ideas, and certain vices are inherent in a state of revolution, and a lengthy revolution, regardless of its character, purpose, or theater, cannot fail to bring these to the fore and make them commonplace.

When any nation changes leaders, opinions, and laws several times within a short period, the men who compose it end up acquiring a taste for change and becoming accustomed to the idea that all change occurs rapidly with the help of force. They then naturally conceive a contempt for forms, whose lack of power they witness daily, and they become impatient with the dominion of rules, which they have so often seen flouted before their very eyes.

Since ordinary notions of equity and morality are not enough to explain or justify all the novelties to which the revolution daily gives rise, people subscribe to the principle of social utility; they create the dogma of political necessity; and they easily get used to sacrificing particular interests without scruple and to trampling on individual rights so as to achieve more quickly the general goal they have set for themselves.

These habits and ideas, which I call revolutionary because all revolutions produce them, can be seen in aristocracies as well as in democratic nations. But in aristocracies they are often less powerful and always less durable, because there they encounter habits, ideas, faults, and shortcomings that contradict them. Hence they vanish of their own accord as soon as the revolution ends, and the nation returns to its old political ways. This is not necessarily the case in democratic countries, where there is always reason to fear that revolutionary instincts, rather than being snuffed out, will grow milder and more regular and gradually transform themselves into governmental mores and administrative habits.

Thus I know of no countries in which revolutions are more dangerous than in democracies, because in addition to the accidental and temporary ills that revolutions inevitably produce, there is always a risk that they will create permanent and, as it were, eternal ones.

I believe that there are honest forms of resistance and legitimate rebellions. Hence I do not say in any absolute way that men in democratic times should never make revolutions. But I think that they have reason to hesitate longer than anyone else before taking such a step, and that it is better for them to suffer many discomforts in their present state than to have recourse to so perilous a remedy.

I shall end with a general idea that contains not only all the particular ideas that have been set forth in this chapter but most of those which it has been the purpose of this book to explore.

In the centuries of aristocracy that preceded our own, there were very powerful private individuals and a highly debilitated social authority. The very image of society was obscure and was constantly getting lost among all the various powers that ruled over citizens. Man's chief effort in those days had to be directed toward expanding and fortifying the social power and increasing and securing its prerogatives while at the same time confining individual independence within strict limits and subordinating the particular interest to the general interest.

Other perils and other cares await the men of today.

In most modern nations, the sovereign, whatever its origin, constitution, and name, has become almost omnipotent, and private individuals are increasingly falling to the lowest degree of weakness and dependence.

Everything was different in earlier societies. Unity and uniformity were nowhere to be found. Nowadays, everything is threatening to become so much alike that the peculiar features of each individual will soon be altogether lost in the common physiognomy. Our forefathers were always ready to abuse the notion that particular rights are worthy of respect, whereas we are naturally inclined to exaggerate the different notion that the interest of one individual should always give way to the interest of several individuals.

The political world changes. We must now seek new remedies for new ills.

To set broad but visible and immovable limits on social power; to grant certain rights to private individuals and guarantee their uncontested enjoyment of those rights; to preserve what little independence, strength, and originality is left to the individual; to raise him up alongside and support him vis-à-vis society: these seem to me the primary goals of lawmakers in the age upon which we are just now embarking.

It may seem as though sovereigns nowadays are interested in men only to make great things with them. I would rather they gave a little more thought to making great men. Better that they should attach less value to the work and more to the worker, and that they always bear it in mind that a nation cannot remain strong for long when each individual in it is weak, and that no one has yet found social forms or political stratagems that can turn soft and faint-hearted citizens into an energetic people.

Among our contemporaries I see two ideas which, though contradictory, are equally disastrous.

Some see in equality only the anarchic tendencies to which it gives rise. They are terrified of their free will; they are afraid of themselves.

Others, fewer in number but more enlightened, take a different view. Alongside the road that leads from equality to anarchy, they have at last discovered the path that seems to lead men ineluctably into servitude. They adapt their souls in advance to this inescapable servitude and in despair of remaining free already worship from the bottom of their hearts the master who is waiting in the wings.

The former abandon liberty because they deem it to be dangerous, the latter because they judge it to be impossible.

If I held the latter belief, I would not have written this book. I would have confined myself to bewailing the fate of my fellow men in private.

I chose to speak out publicly about the dangers that equality poses to human independence because I firmly believe that those perils are the most formidable that the future holds, as well as the least anticipated. But I do not believe that they are insurmountable.

Men living in the democratic centuries upon which we are now embarking have a natural taste for independence. They are naturally impatient of rules: the permanence of the very state they prefer tires them. They like power, but they are inclined to scorn and hate the man who exercises it, and their very minuteness and mobility makes it easy for them to evade his grasp.

These instincts will always be found because they stem from the depths of the social state, which will not change. For some time to come they will prevent the establishment of any form of despotism, and they will provide new arms to any future generation that is willing to fight for man's liberty.

Let us therefore face the future with the salutary fear that keeps us vigilant and ready for battle, and not with the spineless and idle terror that afflicts and saps the heart.

Chapter 8

GENERAL VIEW OF THE SUBJECT

BEFORE bringing this journey to its ultimate conclusion, I would like to take in all the various features of the new world with one final glance and at last offer a judgment of the general influence that equality is likely to have on man's fate. The difficulty of such an undertaking gives me pause, however. Faced with such a huge subject, my vision grows cloudy and my reason falters.

The new society that I have sought to describe and want to judge has only just come into being. Time has not yet fixed its form. The great revolution that created it is still under way, and in what is happening today it is almost impossible to make out what will likely pass away with the revolution itself and what will remain after it has gone.

The world that is on the rise remains half buried beneath the debris of the world that is in collapse, and in the vast confusion of human affairs no one can say what will remain of old institutions and ancient mores and what will ultimately disappear.

Although the ongoing revolution in man's social state, laws, ideas, and sentiments is still far from over, it is already clear that its works cannot be compared with anything the world has ever seen before. Looking back century by century to remotest Antiquity, I see nothing that resembles what I see before me. When the past is no longer capable of shedding light on the future, the mind can only proceed in darkness.

Yet in this very vast, very novel, and very confusing tableau, I can already make out some of the main new features that are just now taking shape, and I shall point them out.

I find that goods and evils are fairly equally distributed throughout the world. Great riches are disappearing. The number of small fortunes is increasing. Desires and pleasures are proliferating. Extraordinary prosperity no longer exists, nor does irremediable misery. Ambition is a universal sentiment, but vast ambitions are rare. Each individual is isolated and weak. Society is agile, far-sighted, and strong. Private individuals do small things, while the state's undertakings are immense.

Souls are not energetic, but mores are mild and legislation is humane. Although heroic devotion and other very lofty, spectacular, and pure virtues are seldom encountered, habits are orderly, violence is rare, and cruelty is almost unknown. Men are beginning to live longer, and their property is more secure. Life is not very stylish, but it is quite comfortable and peaceful. There are few very exquisite pleasures and few very crude ones, and there is little politeness in manners and little brutality in taste. One meets scarcely any men who are very learned or populations that are very ignorant. Genius is becoming rarer and enlightenment more commonplace. The human mind is developing as a result of the combined small efforts of all rather than the powerful impetus of a few. The works of man are less perfect but more plentiful. All bonds of race, class, and country are becoming looser; the great bond of humanity is growing tighter.

If I search these various traits for the one that seems to me most general and most striking, I find that what is happening to fortunes is also reproducing itself in a thousand other forms. Nearly all extremes are being softened and blunted. Almost anything that stands out is being wiped out and replaced by something average — neither as high nor as low, neither as brilliant nor as obscure as what the world once knew.

I cast my eyes upon this innumerable host of similar beings, among whom no one stands out or stoops down. The sight of such universal uniformity saddens and chills me, and I am tempted to mourn for the society that is no more.

When the world was full of men both very great and very small, very rich and very poor, very learned and very ignorant, I used to avert my gaze from the latter to focus solely on the former, and they gladdened my eyes, but I know that my pleasure was a consequence of my weakness: it is because I cannot take in everything around me at a single glance that I am allowed to choose in this way among so many objects those that it pleases me to contemplate. This is not true of the Almighty Eternal Being, whose eye necessarily encompasses all things and sees the entire human race and each man distinctly yet simultaneously.

It is natural to believe that what is most satisfying to the eye of man's creator and keeper is not the singular prosperity of a few but the greater well-being of all: what seems decadence to me is therefore progress in his eyes; what pains me pleases him. Equality is less lofty, perhaps, but more just, and its justice is the source of its grandeur and beauty.

I am doing my best to enter into this point of view, which is that of the Lord, and trying to consider and judge human affairs from this perspective.

No one on earth can yet state in an absolute and general way that the new state of societies is superior to the old one, but it is already easy to see that it is different.

Certain vices and virtues that were once associated with the constitution of aristocratic nations are so contrary to the genius of the new nations that they could not possibly be introduced into them. There are good penchants and bad instincts that were foreign to the former and are natural to the latter. Some ideas occur spontaneously to the imagination of the one yet are rejected by the mind of the other. These are like two distinct humanities, each of which has its peculiar advantages and drawbacks, its inherent goods and evils.

Hence we must be careful not to judge nascent societies by ideas drawn from societies that are no more. To do so would be unjust, for these societies are so extraordinarily different as to be incomparable.

It would scarcely be more reasonable to expect men today to exhibit the particular virtues that derived from the social state of their ancestors, since that social state has collapsed and in its fall has swept away pell-mell all the goods and evils it bore within it.

At present, however, these things are still dimly understood.

I see many of my contemporaries trying to choose among institutions, opinions, and ideas that grew out of the aristocratic constitution of the old society. They are prepared to give up some of these but would like to hold on to others and carry them over into the new world.

I think that these people are wasting their time and effort in honest but unproductive labor.

The task is no longer to hold on to the particular advantages that inequality of conditions procured for mankind but to secure the new goods that equality can provide. We must not try to make ourselves like our fathers but do our best to achieve the kind of grandeur and happiness that is appropriate to us.

As for me, having reached the end of my journey, I can now see, all at once but from afar, the various objects that I contemplated separately along the way, and I am full of fears and hopes. I see great dangers that can be warded off and great evils that can be avoided or held in check, and I feel ever more assured in my belief that in order to be virtuous and prosperous, democratic nations have only to want to be so.

I am well aware that any number of my contemporaries believe that nations are never their own masters here below and are necessarily obedient to I know not what insurmountable and unthinking force born of previous events or race or soil or climate.

These are false and cowardly doctrines, which can only produce weak men and pusillanimous nations: Providence did not create mankind entirely independent or altogether enslaved. Around each man it traced, to be sure, a fatal circle beyond which he may not venture, but within the ample limits thus defined man is powerful and free, and so are peoples.

It is beyond the ability of nations today to prevent conditions within them from becoming equal, but it is within their power to decide whether equality will lead them into servitude or liberty, enlightenment or barbarism, prosperity or misery.

NOTES

XIX, PAGE 169

There are, however, aristocracies that have engaged ardently in commerce and successfully cultivated industry. The history of the world offers several striking examples. In general, though, one has to say that aristocracy is not favorable to the development of industry and commerce. The only exceptions to this rule are the aristocracies of money.

In these there is virtually no desire that does not require riches to be satisfied. Love of wealth becomes, as it were, the highway of the human passions. All other roads either lead to it or intersect it.

The taste for money and the thirst for consideration and power then blend so completely in the same souls that it becomes difficult to make out whether it is ambition that makes men greedy or greed that makes them ambitious. This is what is happening in England, where people want to be wealthy in order to acquire honors and desire honors as a manifestation of wealth. The human spirit is then caught up every which way and dragged into commerce and industry, which are the shortest routes to opulence.

This, however, strikes me as an exceptional and transitory condition. When wealth becomes the only sign of aristocracy, it is very difficult for the wealthy to maintain themselves alone in power and exclude everyone else.

Aristocracy of birth and pure democracy are the two extremes of the social and political state of nations. Aristocracy of money falls in between. It resembles aristocracy of birth in that it confers great privileges on a small number of citizens. It is akin to democracy in that these privileges can be acquired by all in their turn. It often serves as a natural transition between the two, and it is impossible to say whether it ends the reign of aristocratic institutions or is already ushering in the new era of democracy.

VOLUME TWO, PART III

XX, PAGE 221

In my travel diary, I find the following passage, which is useful for what it reveals of the ordeals to which American women who agree to accompany their husbands into the wilderness are often subjected. This description has nothing to recommend it to the reader other than its complete truthfulness:

From time to time we come to new clearings. All of these settlements resemble one another. I shall describe the one at which we have stopped tonight. It will leave me with an image of all the others.

The existence of the clearing is heralded from a long way off by the little bells that the pioneers hang around the necks of their animals so that they can find them in the woods. Soon we hear the sound of axes attacking the trees of the forest. As we draw near, traces of destruction announce the presence of civilized man. Cut branches cover the trail; stumps half-burned by fire or mutilated by hatchets remain along our path. We continue on our way and enter a stand of forest in which all the trees seem to have been struck dead in an instant. It is the middle of summer, but already they give an image of the dead of winter. On examining them more closely, we see that deep circles have been cut into their bark, thus halting the flow of sap and quickly causing the trees to die. We learn that this is how the pioneer usually starts out. Since he cannot cut down all the trees growing on his new property in the first year, he sows corn beneath their branches and by killing the trees prevents them from casting a shadow on his crop. Beyond this hint of what will some day be a field — civilization's first step in this wilderness — we suddenly catch sight of the owner's cabin. It is situated in the center of a field more carefully cultivated than the rest, but showing signs that man is still locked in unequal battle with the forest. Here the trees have been cut but not uprooted; their stumps remain, cluttering the land they once shaded. Around these desiccated remains, wheat and seedlings of oak and plants of all kinds and weeds of every variety grow pell-mell on recalcitrant land that remains partially wild. In the middle of this profuse and varied vegetation stands the pioneer's house, or "log house," as it is called in the region. Like the field around it, this rustic dwelling speaks of recent and hasty construction. Its length does not appear to us to exceed thirty feet, its height fifteen. Its walls and roof are fashioned from rough-hewn tree trunks packed with moss and earth to keep out the cold and rain.

As night is approaching, we decide to ask the owner of the log house for shelter.

At the sound of our footsteps, the children, who had been rolling about on the forest floor, spring to their feet and flee toward the house as if frightened by the sight of a man, while two large, half-wild dogs with ears pricked and muzzles outstretched emerge from their house and move toward us, growling to cover the retreat of their young masters. The pioneer himself comes to the door of his dwelling. With a quick and appraising glance he takes us in, signals his dogs to go back inside, and himself leads the way, all without giving any sign that the sight of us has aroused either his curiosity or his anxiety.

We enter the log house. The interior is in no way reminiscent of the peasant cottages of Europe. There is more of the superfluous and less of the necessary.

There is only one window, with a muslin curtain hanging in it. Crackling on the hearth of packed earth is a large fire, which illuminates the whole inside of the house. Above the hearth one can see a beautiful carbine, a deerskin, and some eagle feathers. To the right of the fireplace a map of the United States is displayed, and the wind blowing through chinks in the wall lifts it up and causes it to flap about. Nearby, on a shelf of rough-hewn lumber, sit several volumes, among which I notice a Bible, the first six cantos of Milton, and two plays by Shakespeare. Chests rather than wardrobes line the walls. In the center of the room a crudely made table has feet of green wood with the bark still attached, feet that seem to grow out of the earth they stand on. On this table I see a teapot of English porcelain, silver spoons, some chipped cups, and newspapers.

The master of these premises has the angular features and lank build that mark him out as a New Englander. It is obvious that this man was not born in the solitude in which we have found him. His physical constitution alone is enough to suggest that his early years were spent in an intellectual society and that he belongs to that restless, calculating, and adventurous race of men who coolly undertake to do what only the ardor of the passions can explain and who for a time subject themselves to a savage life, the better to conquer and civilize the wilderness.

When the pioneer sees us cross the threshold of his home, he comes to meet us and reaches out his hand, as custom dictates, but his face remains rigid. He is the first to speak, questioning us about what is happening in the world, and when his curiosity is satisfied, he falls silent. Perhaps the importunate visitors and the noise have tired him. We question him in turn, and he gives us all the information we need. Then, without alacrity but not without diligence, he sets about taking care of our needs. As we watch him perform these acts of kindness, our gratitude runs cold in spite of ourselves. Why? Because in showing his hospitality he seems to be bowing to a painful necessity of his lot: he sees what he is doing as a duty required of a man in his position rather than a pleasure.

At the opposite end of the hearth a woman sits dandling a baby in her lap. She nods to us without interrupting what she is doing. Like the pioneer, this woman is in the prime of life, looks to be superior to her condition, and dresses in a way that speaks of a lingering taste for finery. But her delicate limbs seem frail, her features drawn, and her gaze meek and grave. Her whole face is suffused with an air of religious resignation, a profound peace exempt from passion, and I know not what natural and quiet determination to confront all of life's woes without fear or defiance.

Her children crowd around her, and they are full of health, rambunctiousness, and energy. They are true sons of the wilderness. From time to time their mother glances at them with a look of mingled melancholy and delight. To judge by their strength and her weakness, it might seem that she has been draining herself to give them life, yet she seems to feel no regret about what they have cost her.

The house these immigrants live in has no inside partitions or loft. At night, the entire family seeks refuge in the sole apartment it contains. Their dwelling is like a small world unto itself. It is the ark of civilization, lost in a sea of foliage. A hundred paces beyond, the eternal forest spreads its shade, and solitude resumes.

XXI, PAGE 222

It is not equality of conditions that makes men immoral and irreligious. But when men are immoral and irreligious at the same time they are equal, the effects of immorality and irreligion can easily manifest themselves externally, because men have little influence on one another and there is no class that can take charge of imposing order and discipline on society. Equality of conditions never creates corruption of mores but sometimes allows such corruption to manifest itself.

XXII, PAGE 243

Leaving aside those who do not think and those who do not dare to say what they think, one still finds that the vast majority of Americans appear to be satisfied with the political institutions that govern them, and in fact I think they are satisfied. I regard this state of public opinion as an indicator though not a proof of the absolute goodness of American laws. National pride, satisfaction of certain dominant passions through legislation, fortuitous events, unseen vices, and, most of all, the interest of a majority that shuts the mouths of its opponents can delude a whole people as well as a man for quite some time.

Look at England all during the eighteenth century. No nation ever burned more incense to itself. No people was ever more perfectly self-contented. All was well with its constitution at the time. Indeed, everything about it was beyond reproach, including even its most glaring defects. Today, a host of Englishmen seem to be busy with nothing else but proving that this same constitution was defective in a thousand places. Who was right, the English people of the last century or the English people of today?

The same thing happened in France. Under Louis XIV it is certain that the great mass of the nation was passionately in favor of the form of government that then ruled society. Those who believe that the French character was debased in those days are greatly mistaken. In certain respects servitude could exist in France in that century, but the spirit of servitude certainly did not exist. The writers of the time were in a way genuinely enthusiastic when they extolled the royal power above all others, and not even the obscurest peasant in his cottage failed to take pride in the glory of the sovereign or die for joy shouting "Vive le roi!" These same forms have become odious to us. Who was mistaken, the Frenchmen of Louis XIV's time or the Frenchmen of today?

Hence one's judgment of a people's laws should be based not solely on their attitudes, since these change from one century to the next, but rather on higher grounds and a more general experience.

The love that a people demonstrates for its laws proves only one thing, that one should be in no haste to change them.

XXIII, PAGE 300

In the chapter to which this note refers, I have pointed out one danger. I want to indicate another which is rarer but, should it ever appear, more to be feared.

If the love of material pleasures and taste for well-being that equality naturally suggests to men were to take hold of the spirit of a democratic nation and fill it entirely, the national mores would become so antipathetic to the military spirit that armies themselves might end up loving peace in spite of the particular interest that impels them to desire war. Living amidst such universal softness, soldiers would come to believe that the gradual but comfortable and effortless promotion of peacetime was preferable to paying the price of rapid advancement, namely, the fatigue and misery of camp life. In this spirit, the army would take up arms without ardor and use them without energy. It would allow itself to be led to the enemy rather than marching off on its own.

It should not be assumed that such a pacific disposition on the part of the army would keep it out of revolutions, for revolutions, and especially military revolutions, which are usually quite rapid, often entail great perils but not protracted effort. They satisfy ambition at a lower cost than war. The only thing a man risks in a revolution is his life, and in democracies men are less attached to their lives than to their comforts.

Nothing is more dangerous to the liberty and tranquillity of a people than an army that is afraid of war: no longer seeking grandeur and influence by way of the battlefield, it seeks these things elsewhere. Hence the men who make up a democratic army may lose the interests of the citizen without acquiring the virtues of the soldier, and the army may cease to be martial without ceasing to be a source of turmoil.

I shall repeat here what I said earlier. The remedy to such dangers lies not in the army but in the country. A democratic people that preserves virile mores will always find martial mores in its soldiers when they are needed.

VOLUME TWO, PART IV

XXIV, PAGE 316

Men see the grandeur of the idea of unity in the means, God in the end. That is why the idea of grandeur leads us into a thousand forms of pettiness. To force all men to march in step toward a single goal — that is a human idea. To introduce endless variety into actions but to combine those actions in such a way that all lead via a thousand diverse paths to the accomplishment of a grand design — that is a divine idea.

The human idea of unity is almost always sterile; God's idea is immensely fertile. Men believe that they attest to their grandeur when they simplify the means: it is God's purpose that is simple, while his means vary endlessly.

XXV, PAGE 320

What inclines a democratic people to centralize power is not only its tastes. The passions of all its leaders constantly drive it in the same direction.

It is easy to foresee that nearly all ambitious and capable citizens in a democratic country will work unremittingly to extend the prerogatives of the social power because all hope some day to lead it. It is a waste of time to try to prove to these people that extreme centralization can be harmful to the state because it is for their own benefit that they seek to centralize.

Among public men in democracies, virtually the only ones willing to decentralize power are those who are either very disinterested or very mediocre. The former are rare and the latter powerless.

XXVI, PAGE 341

I have often wondered what would happen if, given the mildness of democratic mores and the restless spirit of the army, a military government were ever established in some of today's nations.

I think that the government itself would not differ much from the portrait I have indicated in the chapter to which this note refers, and that it would not reproduce the fierce characteristics of military oligarchy.

I am convinced that what would happen in this case would be a sort of fusion of the habits of the clerk with those of the soldier. The administration would take on something of the military spirit and the military some of the customs of the civil administration. The result would be a regular, clear, precise, absolute chain of command. The people would reflect an image of the army, and society would be regimented like a barracks.

XXVII, PAGE 345

One cannot say in an absolute and general way whether the greatest danger today is license or tyranny, anarchy or despotism. Both are equally to be feared, and both can arise equally easily out of one and the same cause, which is *general apathy*, the fruit of individualism. Because of this apathy, the executive power is in a position to oppress as soon as it assembles a moderate array of forces, and the day after, if a party can put thirty men in the field, it acquires a similar ability to oppress. Neither one is capable of founding anything that will last, so that what makes for easy success prevents lasting success. They rise because nothing resists them and fall because nothing supports them.

What is important to combat is therefore not so much anarchy or despotism as apathy, which can create either one almost indifferently.

Translator's Note

MORE than most writers, Alexis de Tocqueville was an architect of language. In *Democracy in America* he sought to create a harmonious edifice, a structure in which each part was carefully proportioned and subordinated to a conception of the whole. In a letter to his friend and traveling companion Gustave de Beaumont, he said, "I am more and more convinced that the overall effect is chief among the merits of a book and that one must have the courage to make all the sacrifices necessary to achieve it."[1] Tocqueville was perfectly conscious of the overall effect he wished to achieve. He described it well in characterizing the literary qualities that an aristocratic nation would be likely to value: "Style will seem almost as important as ideas and form almost as important as substance. Tone will be polite, measured, and even. The mind will invariably move at a stately pace, seldom with haste, and writers will devote more effort to perfecting their works than to producing them."[2] At the same time, he recommended avoiding "aristocratic jargon," because jargon excludes: "Any aristocracy that sets itself entirely apart from the people becomes impotent. This is true in literature as well as in politics."

In preparing this translation, these lines of Tocqueville's have been my guide. Fidelity to his ideas is perhaps easier to achieve than fidelity to his style — a style of classical sobriety, "almost anachronistic for the Romantic era."[3] His first tutor, Abbé Lesueur, had also been his father's tutor. As a citizen of the Republic of Letters, Tocqueville was therefore more a man of the 18th century than of the 19th, and he seems to have taken from his tutor something of the 18th century's love of clarity, elegance, and balance in prose. His father's library, filled with translations of ancient authors as well as the French classics of the 17th century and the great *philosophes* of the 18th,

[1] Françoise Mélonio, *Tocqueville et les Français* (Paris: Aubier, 1993), p. 34.
[2] See page 64.31–35 in this volume.
[3] André Jardin, *Alexis de Tocqueville*, (Paris: Hachette, 1984), p. 357.

probably influenced his writing even more than his classes in rhetoric, a subject in which he excelled.[4]

What stands out above all in Tocqueville's style is a remarkable and almost paradoxical combination of solidity and grace. His affirmations buttress one another without ever becoming ponderous or ungainly. Although he is the most quotable of authors, his sentences do not go in for what he disparaged as "facile beauties," nor do they depend on "surprise and novelty" or "intense and rapid emotions" for their effects. The "polite, measured, even tone" and "stately pace" at which he aimed may be prosaic qualities, but heedless translation can undo them all too easily. A writer of Tocqueville's mastery can cast a spell over his translator. The rightness of his French seems so incontestable that one hesitates to tamper with his choices. If an English cognate is available for a word he used in French, there is always a temptation to use it rather than cast about for a more adequate English equivalent. If he ordered his words and clauses in a certain way in order to achieve a balanced period in the original, there is a temptation to acquiesce in his example rather than make the extra effort necessary to achieve a similar equilibrium in English. Yet to succumb to these temptations is at times to betray the author by excess of fidelity. A fine discrimination is required, a tactful judgment as to what sacrifices are necessary and warranted in order to achieve the desired "overall effect." Each such decision may in itself be small and almost negligible, but a translation is the concatenation of thousands of small choices. Like the writer, the translator needs the courage to make sacrifices. At times, that may mean eschewing a misguided literalism in order to preserve some quality of the original that would not otherwise survive. At other times, it may mean translating literally even at the risk of producing a formulation that sounds oddly foreign in English.

In one instance it was necessary to take issue with Tocqueville himself. In Volume One, Part I, Chapter 5, Tocqueville placed the English word "township" in parentheses after the French phrase *la commune de la Nouvelle-Angleterre*. Previous translators have taken this as an indication that Tocqueville

[4]*Ibid.*, pp. 60–63.

intended the French *commune* to be equivalent to the English "township." Hence they have him refer in subsequent passages to "township meetings," "township officers," and the like. But New England was famous for its "town meetings"; Tocqueville took his local nomenclature from a book called *The Town Officer*; and a letter that he wrote to Jared Sparks on December 2, 1831, refers to *communes* as "towns." Sparks, his principal informant on these matters, consistently refers to "towns," not "townships."[5] Hence it seems forced and artificial to perpetuate what I believe to be a slip of Tocqueville's pen by emulating the choice that previous translators have made. I have accordingly broken with tradition on this point.

There are in *Democracy in America* certain words that amount to terms of art, words that acquire a special meaning from the way Tocqueville deploys them in his argument. One such term of particular importance is *mœurs*, which I have rendered into English using the cognate term "mores." Tocqueville uses "mores" to mean something more than "the accepted traditional customs and usages of a particular social group." Although he is usually content to allow special meanings to emerge from his use of a word in a variety of contexts, in this key instance he supplies a definition, but not until the word has been used many times: "By *mores* I mean here what the Ancients meant by the term: I apply it not only to mores in the strict sense, what one might call habits of the heart, but also to the various notions that men possess, to the diverse opinions that are current among them, and to the whole range of ideas that shape habits of mind. Thus I use this word to refer to the whole moral and intellectual state of a people."[6] Here the translation of a French word by a cognate is not misleading, because in both languages the meaning of the term is inflected by Tocqueville's idiosyncratic usage.

Tocqueville often uses the terms "nation" and "people" interchangeably as a stylistic device to avoid repetition. I have therefore allowed myself on occasion to substitute one for the other when necessary to achieve a more euphonious English

[5] I am grateful to Olivier Zunz for directing my attention to the Sparks-Tocqueville correspondence on this point.

[6] See page 331.27–33 in volume one.

sentence. There are places, however, where Tocqueville speaks of a nation composed of more than one people, and there the distinction has been rigorously maintained. In addition, he sometimes refers to the states of the Union as "nations" when he wants to emphasize their sovereign rights. Where a literal translation would have obscured his meaning, I have translated as "state" (and indicated the alteration in the Notes). *La souveraineté du peuple* is often rendered as "popular sovereignty," a phrase common enough in English and frequently conducive to less cumbersome translation than the more literal "sovereignty of the people."

Tocqueville refers to the various branches of the American government as "powers": *le pouvoir judiciaire*, for example. While it might be more natural to translate as "the judicial branch," something would surely be lost, so I have repatriated the Gallicism.

Tocqueville makes frequent use of the verb *se confondre*, whose translation proved problematic. Previous translators have generally rendered this as "intermingled," but this translation implies that the components of a mixture retain their identities, whereas *se confondre* suggests a loss of identity, a condition of indistinguishability, so I have preferred to translate the term in most instances as "blend." The nuance may be of some significance, particularly in the chapter on the "three races that inhabit the United States" (pages 365–476 in this volume), where the frequent occurrence of this verb is worth noting.

In one respect this translation departs significantly from previous translations of *Democracy in America*. Tocqueville translated passages from a substantial number of English texts into French and included them in his book. Some of his translations are quite faithful, while others are so free as to amount to interpretations of the originals. It was therefore decided to provide the reader with translations of Tocqueville's more liberal renderings. These retranslated passages have been incorporated into the body of the text; the original English passages are included in the Notes so as to allow the reader to judge what Tocqueville did in each case.

It is a rare honor for a translator to work on a classic of the magnitude of *Democracy in America*. I hope that I have been able to do it justice. I would like to thank Daniel Gordon, Patrice Higonnet, and Cheryl Welch for comments on portions of the manuscript and above all Jon Elster and Olivier Zunz for their careful reading of the entire text. These vigilant readers have improved the translation substantially. Any flaws that remain are of course entirely my own.

This is not the first translation of *Democracy in America*, nor will it be the last. I hope that it has qualities that will give the reader without French an idea of the stately grace of Tocqueville's style as well as a rigorous and faithful rendering of his ideas. Tocqueville enjoys a unique position in the history of literature and thought: a philosopher also notable as a literary stylist, he is the only Frenchman who can claim to be part of the American canon as well as the French. It is my fervent hope that the pleasure I took in translating his work will prove contagious.

Arthur Goldhammer
Cambridge, Massachusetts, 2003

Chronology

1805　　Alexis Charles-Henri Clérel de Tocqueville is born in Paris on July 29, the third son of Hervé and Louise-Madeleine de Tocqueville. (Hervé Louis François Bonaventure Clérel de Tocqueville was born in 1772. His family owned the château de Tocqueville in Normandy, about 12 miles east of Cherbourg, and was of the *noblesse d'épée*, aristocrats whose nobility derived originally from their military service; one of his Clérel ancestors fought at the battle of Hastings in 1066. Louise-Madeleine Le Peletier de Rosanbo, born in 1771, was from a family predominantly of the *noblesse de robe*, aristocrats who derived nobility from their positions in the judiciary and royal administration. Her father, Louis Le Peletier de Rosanbo, served as a president of the Parlement of Paris, the highest appellate court; her grandfather, Chrétien-Guillaume de Lamoignon de Malesherbes, who had protected the *philosophes* while director of the book trade during the reign of Louis XV, served as a reformist minister early in the reign of Louis XVI, and then came out of retirement in 1792 to help defend the king at his trial before the National Convention. Hervé de Tocqueville and Louise-Madeleine de Rosanbo were married on March 12, 1793. They were arrested by the revolutionary regime in December 1793 along with Malesherbes, Rosanbo, and several other members of the family. Malesherbes; Le Peletier de Rosanbo and his wife, Marguerite; Louise-Madeleine's sister, Aline-Thérèse, and her husband, Jean-Baptiste de Chateaubriand, the older brother of the Romantic writer François-René de Chateaubriand — the great-grandfather, grandfather, grandmother, aunt, and uncle of Alexis de Tocqueville — were all guillotined in Paris in April 1794. While waiting for his execution, Malesherbes had to watch the beheading of his own daughter and granddaughter. Tocqueville's parents remained imprisoned until after the execution of Robespierre on July 28, 1794, or 10 Thermidor. Hervé de Tocqueville's hair turned prematurely white, while Louise-Madeleine suffered from persistent depression and anxiety as a result of her experiences. Hervé regained some of the family's fortune and became guardian of the orphaned Louis and Christian de Chateaubriand. Tocqueville's brother Hippolyte was born in 1797 and his brother Édouard in 1800.)

1805–13   The family resides in the winter in the Faubourg St. Germain in Paris and in the summer in a château at Verneuil-sur-Seine inherited from the Malesherbes family. Despite having fragile health, Tocqueville will remember having a happy childhood at Verneuil, where the family plays parlor games, has literary evenings with play readings and poetry recitations, and annually celebrates Saint Louis on the occasion of Louise-Madeleine's birthday. Chateaubriand occasionally comes to visit his nephews, and once greets Hervé de Tocqueville while disguised as an old woman. Tocqueville is tutored by Abbé Christian Lesueur, a conservative priest with Jansenist leanings who had been Hervé de Tocqueville's tutor. He studies French composition and writings by Blaise Pascal that emphasize strict morality and inward faith. Although two distant older cousins, Louis Honoré Félix Le Peletier d'Aunay and Louis-Mathieu Molé, who would become Tocqueville's political mentors in the July monarchy, rally to the Napoleonic regime, most family members remain "Legitimists" loyal to the deposed Bourbon dynasty.

1814   Tocqueville and his family join in a demonstration in Paris on April 3 calling for the restoration to the throne of Louis XVIII, the brother of Louis XVI. Napoleon abdicates on April 6 and Louis XVIII enters Paris on May 3. Hervé de Tocqueville is appointed prefect (the administrative representative of the central government in a French department) of Maine-et-Loire and moves to Angers. Tocqueville remains with his mother in Paris and continues his education with Abbé Lesueur; he will sometimes visit his father at his various posts. Hippolyte becomes an officer in the army (he will serve until 1830).

1815   Hervé de Tocqueville leaves Angers in March when Napoleon returns from his exile on Elba. After the Second Restoration of the Bourbon monarchy in July, Hervé de Tocqueville is appointed prefect of the Oise and moves to Beauvais.

1816   Hervé de Tocqueville is appointed prefect of the Côte d'Or and moves to Dijon. Édouard enters the army (he will serve until 1822).

1817   Hervé de Tocqueville is appointed prefect of the Moselle and moves to Metz.

1820   Tocqueville joins his father in Metz.

1821   When he is 16, Tocqueville is overcome by religious doubt when reading the works of the 18th-century *philosophes* in his father's library. In 1857 he described the experience in a letter to his friend, the Russian mystic and Parisian society figure Madame Swetchine: "My life up to then had flowed in an interior full of faith which had not even allowed doubt to penetrate my soul. Then doubt entered, or rather rushed in with unheard-of-violence, not merely the doubt of this or that, but universal doubt. I suddenly felt the sensation those who have witnessed an earthquake speak of, when the ground moves under their feet, the walls around them, the ceilings over their head, the furniture in their hands, all nature before their eyes. I was seized with the blackest depression, taken by an extreme disgust for life without having experienced it, and I was as if overwhelmed by trouble and terror at the sight of the road which I had still to travel in the world." He enters the lycée in Metz in November.

1822–23   Tocqueville is a brilliant student at the lycée, where he studies rhetoric and philosophy. At 17 he fathers a child, Louise Charlotte Meyer, with a servant at the prefecture. (Nothing is known of the child's life.) He later falls in love with Rosalie Malye, the daughter of a local civil servant. Perhaps because of a rivalry for the young woman, Tocqueville fights a duel in May 1823 with a classmate in which no one is hurt. Although his distant cousin and childhood friend Louis de Kergorlay dissuades Tocqueville from pursuing a relationship with a woman unsuitable for someone of his aristocratic background, the affair lingers until Malye is married in 1828. At the lycée Tocqueville also begins a lifelong friendship with Charles and Eugène Stöffels, young men of lesser social standing. He graduates with his baccalaureate in the summer of 1823, just as his father becomes prefect of the Somme and

moves to Amiens. In the fall Tocqueville enters the law
school of the University of Paris.

1824–26   Tocqueville studies Roman law, the Napoleonic civil
code, civil and criminal procedure, and criminal law, but
is a less distinguished student than at the lycée. Louis
XVIII dies in 1824 and is succeeded by his brother,
Charles X. Tocqueville receives his degree in 1826 after
writing two short theses, one in French and one in Latin.
In December he travels to Italy and Sicily with his brother
Édouard. During the trip he writes a journal in which he
notes the consequences for aristocratic society of the fragmentation of property ownership.

1827   In January, Hervé de Tocqueville, who has become prefect of Seine-et-Oise and settled in Versailles, writes to the
minister of justice to find a job for his son. As a result, in
April Tocqueville is appointed a *juge auditeur* (apprentice
judge) at the tribunal in Versailles; the position is an
unpaid internship in which he assists the judges and public
prosecutors in hearing and presenting civil and criminal
cases. In November Hervé de Tocqueville is named to the
Chamber of Peers, an institution recreated under the
Bourbon Restoration.

1828   In January Tocqueville moves into an apartment in Versailles with Gustave de Beaumont (born 1802), a lawyer
at the tribunal of Versailles with the rank of *substitut*, one
step above *auditeur*. In a speech he makes to the court on
dueling, Tocqueville explores the conflict between honor
and law. During the year he meets and falls in love with
Mary ("Marie") Mottley, an English woman of middle-
class origin, who lives with her aunt on the same street as
Tocqueville.

1829   Beginning in April, Tocqueville attends, along with Beaumont, the course on the history of French civilization
taught at the Sorbonne by François Guizot, whose lec-
tures he finds "extraordinary." (Guizot was a leader of the
liberal opposition to the Bourbons, as well as one of the
most influential historians of the 19th century. Along with
the political philosopher and famous orator Pierre-Paul
Royer-Collard, he was a major figure in the "Doctri-
naires," a group of political thinkers who had reconciled

the liberal principles of the Revolution of 1789 with the legitimacy of the monarchy.) Tocqueville and Beaumont attend a few sessions of *Aide-toi, le ciel t'aidera* ("Heaven helps those who help themselves"), a liberal political society founded by Guizot in 1827. While traveling with Kergorlay in Switzerland, Tocqueville learns in October that Beaumont is leaving Versailles for a new position in Paris, and that the position of *substitut*, which he had hoped to receive, has been given to his childhood acquaintance Ernest de Chabrol. Although he is initially despondent about both pieces of news, he overcomes his disappointment and becomes a roommate and friend of Chabrol.

1830   Tocqueville closely follows the French expedition against Algiers, in which Kergorlay serves as an artillery officer. Algiers capitulates on July 5, beginning the French conquest of Algeria. Charles X promulgates ordinances on July 25 abolishing freedom of the press, restoring censorship, restricting the electoral franchise, dissolving the Chamber of Deputies, and calling for new elections under new electoral rules. Protests against the July ordinances in Paris lead to three days of street fighting ("les trois glorieuses") from July 27 to 29. Tocqueville helps his parents hide at St. Germain-en-Laye on July 29, then returns to Versailles, where he volunteers to serve in the newly reconstituted National Guard to help prevent violence between royalists and insurgents. Charles X withdraws the ordinances on July 30, then flees from the palace at St. Cloud outside Paris on July 31. Tocqueville watches with contempt as the royal convoy moves through Versailles on its way to Rambouillet. "As for the Bourbons, they have behaved like cowards and do not deserve a thousandth part of the blood that has been spilled over their cause," he writes to Marie Mottley. On July 31 the Marquis de La Fayette presides over the acclamation of the Duc d'Orléans at the Hôtel de Ville in Paris, the first step toward a new constitutional monarchy led by the junior branch of the royal family. Charles X abdicates on August 2 and the Duc d'Orléans becomes King Louis-Philippe on August 9.

Hervé de Tocqueville loses his seat in the upper chamber when the new regime abolishes the peerages created by Charles X. He refuses to serve the constitutional monarchy and goes into retirement. Tocqueville takes the oath of loyalty required of public officials on August 16 and repeats it in October, chilling relations with some members of his pro-Bourbon family, though his father and brother Édouard may have urged him to take the oath. On August 26 he writes to Charles Stöffels: "For a long time now, I have wanted to visit North America. I will see there what a great republic is. All I fear is that, while I am over there, a republic will be established in France." In October he and Beaumont petition the minister of the interior to be sent to the United States to study the American penitentiary system, a subject of great interest in French reform circles. Le Peletier d'Aunay, Tocqueville's cousin and a deputy in the Orleanist chamber, intervenes on their behalf.

1831   Tocqueville and Beaumont receive authorization for their trip from the interior ministry and an 18-month leave of absence from the ministry of justice. On April 2 they sail from Le Havre on an American ship. During the voyage Tocqueville and Beaumont discuss writing a book on American society and government in addition to their official prison report.

On May 9 they land at Newport, Rhode Island, a town that looks to Tocqueville like "an array of houses no bigger than chicken coops," then travel by steamboat to New York City, where they arrive on May 11 and move into a boarding house on Broadway. Their arrival is reported in the New York newspapers (stories about their activities will appear in other newspapers during their trip). Accompanied by the mayor and aldermen, the two commissioners visit the House of Refuge, a reformatory for delinquent minors; Bloomingdale hospital for the insane; an asylum for the deaf and mute; the poor house; and Blackwell's Island prison. They also attend parties given in their honor by local dignitaries in the city and in summer country homes.

Tocqueville and Beaumont interrupt their stay in the city for a visit, May 29–June 7, to Sing Sing, the 900-inmate prison in Ossining on the Hudson River. They watch inmates work in quarries and stonecutting sheds in total silence, under the threat of the whip, and then return to solitary confinement at night. (Inmates in French prisons were thrown together in large rooms, a condition that Tocqueville believed hindered their reformation.) Though

Tocqueville and Beaumont abhor the use of flogging at Sing Sing, they are impressed by the obedience and silence of the prisoners.

After their return to New York City they meet with James Kent, the former chief justice and chancellor of New York State, who gives them a copy of his *Commentaries on American Law*, and with the Swiss-born Albert Gallatin, who had served as secretary of the treasury in the Jefferson and Madison administrations. They also attend the trial of an accused thief in criminal court.

Upstate New York, June 30–July 19:

On June 30 Tocqueville and Beaumont leave New York City and travel by sloop and the steamboat *North America* up the Hudson to Albany, where they march with state officials in the Independence Day parade and inquire about the workings of the state government. They then travel by way of Utica to Syracuse, where on July 7 they interview Elam Lynds, the former warden of Auburn prison who had also overseen the construction of Sing Sing. From Syracuse they go to Oneida Lake and explore Frenchman's Island, which they believe to have been settled some 40 years earlier by a refugee from the French Revolution and his wife. In describing his impressions of the island to his sister-in-law Émilie, Hippolyte's wife, Tocqueville predicts his letter will keep her "daydreaming" for eight days. (Tocqueville later writes a longer account of his visit, *Voyage au Lac Onéida*, which is published posthumously by Beaumont in 1861.)

After visiting the Auburn prison, Tocqueville and Beaumont travel by horseback on July 16 to Canandaigua, where they visit the home of lawyer, state legislator, and former congressman John Canfield Spencer. Tocqueville encourages Spencer to talk about the ways American institutions affect social practices. Spencer shares his detailed knowledge of the workings of the judiciary; he explains that the freedom of the press in America is balanced by the heavy fines to which newspapers are subjected if convicted of printing libelous statements; tells them that religion in America supports liberty and free institutions; and stresses the importance of legislative bicameralism. During their stay at Canandaigua Tocqueville and Beaumont enjoy the company of Spencer's daughters,

Mary and Catherine. "We were more inclined to look at the daughters than at the father's books," Tocqueville writes Émilie. "They have among other charms, four blue eyes (that is, two each)" such as "you have never seen on the other side of the water."

On July 18 Tocqueville and Beaumont ride to Buffalo, where they see Indians waiting to receive government payments owed them for their land rights. Tocqueville, "full of memories of M. de Chateaubriand and of Cooper," had imagined encountering Indians bearing the "marks" of "proud virtues" and "liberty," and is disillusioned by the dependency and widespread drunkenness he sees.

The Great Lakes and Canada, July 19–September 2:

The next day the two friends board the steamboat *Ohio* on Lake Erie and reach Detroit on July 22 after a stop in Cleveland. In Detroit they interview Gabriel Richard, a French-born priest and educator, and John Biddle, the register of the land office, who explains to them the land acquisition and settlement process. His conversation with Biddle prompts Tocqueville to write to Chabrol: "How to imagine a revolution in a country where such a sequence of events can meet the needs and passions of men, and how to compare the political institutions of such a people to that of any other?" Tocqueville and Beaumont go on horseback to Pontiac, then cross the Flint River and travel through dense forest to the village of Saginaw, which is inhabited by about 30 Americans, French Canadians, Indians, and "bois brûlés" (children of French-Canadian men and Indian women). During their return Tocqueville turns 26 on July 29, a day he spends in the forest remembering the revolution in Paris the previous year.

On August 1 Tocqueville and Beaumont leave Detroit along with 200 other passengers on a steamboat excursion to Sault Ste. Marie, Mackinac Island, and Green Bay, Wisconsin. Tocqueville notes that Episcopalian passengers seem content to listen to a sermon by a Presbyterian minister, and writes: "This may be tolerance but may I die if this is faith." At Sault Ste. Marie they travel by canoe to Lake Superior, then go to Mackinac Island, where Tocqueville witnesses sectarian division between Catholics and Presbyterians. During the voyage he writes *Quinze jours dans le désert* ("Two Weeks in the Wilderness"), an account of their trip to Saginaw (it is published posthumously by Beaumont in 1861).

The *Superior* returns to Detroit on August 14, and on August 17 Tocqueville and Beaumont arrive in Buffalo by steamboat. They rent a carriage and spend two days exploring Niagara Falls, then take a steamboat across Lake Ontario and down the Saint Lawrence River to Montreal and Quebec City. "The old France is in Canada, the new one at home," Tocqueville notes. Although Tocqueville and Beaumont appreciate the hospitality shown to them, they do not like the dated French they hear and feel people lack spark. Tocqueville blames the Catholic Church for discouraging individualism and education, which he believes reduces the political effects of a broad electoral base. He also uncovers anachronistic, if limited, remnants of French feudal taxation and landholding practices.

New England, September 2–October 12:

Tocqueville and Beaumont leave Montreal on September 2. Traveling by way of Lake Champlain and Albany, on September 9 they reach Boston, where Tocqueville is overcome by sadness at the news in the mail of the death of his old tutor Abbé Lesueur.

During their stay in Boston Tocqueville and Beaumont visit the state prison at Charlestown three times. They also have numerous political conversations with former Federalists who oppose President Andrew Jackson, many of whom will later become members of the Whig party. At a rally in support of Polish independence they meet Josiah Quincy, the president of Harvard and a former congressman and mayor of Boston, who becomes a helpful source of information and documents. They form a friendship with Francis (Franz) Lieber, a German political exile who had been wounded during the Waterloo campaign while fighting with the Prussian army.

Their most important Boston informant is Jared Sparks, a Unitarian minister and former editor of the *North American Review* and future professor of history at Harvard, who explains to them that the "political dogma of this country is that the majority is always right." (Sparks will later protest that Tocqueville made too much of the idea of "the tyranny of the majority.") They also meet Senator Daniel Webster, but are disappointed by his dismissive attitude toward prison reform. At a dinner at the home of diplomat Alexander Everett on October 1, Tocqueville is seated next to former president John Quincy Adams, who had been defeated by Jackson in 1828; they discuss slavery and the South in French. Adams characterizes white southerners as a "class" with "all the ideas, all the passions, all the prejudices of an aristocracy," finding work "dishonorable" even though there is nothing in the southern climate that should prevent them from working. Before leaving Boston on October 3, Tocqueville and Beaumont discuss religion and democracy with the Unitarian minister William Ellery Channing. (In a letter to his mother, Tocqueville describes him as a leader of those Unitarians who "take from the Bible only what reason can admit.")

On October 5 they visit the Connecticut state prison at Wethersfield, where prisoners are punished by complete isolation in their cells and are rarely whipped. As they travel through Hartford and New York City, Tocqueville reflects on his conversations in New England regarding the jury, and writes that the institution is the "most direct and most powerful application of the dogma of popular sovereignty."

Philadelphia and Baltimore, October 12–November 22:

The two commissioners arrive in Philadelphia on October 12. Tocqueville and Beaumont make eight visits to the Eastern State Penitentiary, where Tocqueville individually interviews each of the inmates. They are deeply impressed by the Quaker-inspired "Philadelphia system" in which prisoners are encouraged to repent by means of uninterrupted solitary confinement and Bible study in cells large enough to provide individual workspaces. While in Philadelphia Tocqueville discusses American institutions, mores, population movements, and race relations with several informants, including Charles J. Ingersoll, a lawyer and former congressman, and Peter S. Duponceau, a French-born lawyer and expert on American Indian languages. He also meets with Quaker philanthropists and attends the theater, where he is struck by the restlessness of the audience.

As news of the cholera epidemic spreading through Europe reaches Philadelphia, Tocqueville sends Chabrol a shipment of cajeput oil, not available in France, with instructions not only to divide it among family members but to set a vial aside for Marie Mottley, the woman he loves "with all my soul." He also writes his mother: "The most valuable documents I am returning with are two small notebooks where I have written down, word for word, the conversations I have had with the most remarkable men of this country. . . . Up to now I have expressed only a few general ideas on America, in the letters I have sent to the family and a few other people in France. I have written them in haste, on steamboats or in some corner where I had to use my knees as a table. Will I ever publish anything on this country? . . . I have a few good ideas but I am not sure about what form to put them in and I am afraid of going public."

On October 28 Tocqueville and Beaumont travel to Baltimore, the center of American Catholicism, where Tocqueville is impressed by his conversations with lawyer John H. B. Latrobe on political parties, universal suffrage, and the American legal profession. They visit with 94-year-old Charles Carroll, the last surviving signer of the Declaration of Independence, before returning to Philadelphia on November 6. During their second stay in Philadelphia they speak with Nicholas Biddle, president of the Bank of the United States, and Joel Poinsett, a former ambassador to Mexico and strong supporter of Andrew Jackson.

The Ohio and the Mississippi, November 22–December 31:

Tocqueville and Beaumont leave Philadelphia on November 22 and travel by stagecoach to Pittsburgh, arriving on November 24 after crossing the Allegheny Mountains during a snowstorm. In Pittsburgh they visit the Western State Penitentiary before taking the steamboat *Fourth of July* down the Ohio. The vessel runs aground near Wheeling, but another steamboat brings its passengers to Cincinnati on December 1. In Cincinnati, Tocqueville discusses universal suffrage at length with the 23-year-old antislavery lawyer Salmon Portland Chase, who will later serve as secretary of the treasury and as chief justice of the U.S. Supreme Court, and also meets with U.S. Supreme Court Justice John McLean. Observing the contrast between Ohio and Kentucky, Tocqueville writes in a notebook that on one side of the Ohio "work is honored and leads to all else, on the other it is despised as the mark of servitude." He attributes the difference to slavery, which "degrades the black population and enervates the white."

Tocqueville and Beaumont leave Cincinnati on December 4, intending to go down the Ohio and the Mississippi, but the next day their steamboat is blocked when the river freezes over in exceptionally cold weather. They go ashore at Westport, Kentucky, and walk 25 miles through snow to Louisville, then travel overland to Nashville by coach. While riding from Nashville to Memphis in a one-horse open coach, Tocqueville falls ill and the two friends have to stop for three days in an isolated log cabin inn. On December 17 they finally reach Memphis and discover that the Mississippi is full of ice. As they wait for navigation to resume, Tocqueville hunts birds in the nearby forests with Chickasaw Indians and reflects on Tennessee politics in his notebook: "When voting rights are universal, it is a strange thing how low the people's choice can descend and how far it can be mistaken. Two years ago the inhabitants of the district of which Memphis is the capital sent to the House of Representatives of Congress an individual called David Crockett, who had received no education, could read only with difficulty, had no property, no fixed dwelling, but spent his time hunting, selling his game for a living, and spending his whole life in the woods. His competitor, who failed, was a fairly rich and able man."

On December 25 Tocqueville and Beaumont leave Memphis for New Orleans on the steamboat *Louisville*, which also carries a group of 50 to 60 Choctaw Indians who are being sent by the federal government to the Indian territory west of Arkansas. This instance of "Indian removal" deeply affects Tocqueville, who predicts in a letter to his mother that American policy will eventually result in the extinction of the Indians. After the Choctaws disembark in Arkansas, Tocqueville and Beaumont discuss at length the situation of the Indians with their fellow passenger, Sam Houston, who had been living among the Cherokees in the Indian territory since resigning as governor of Tennessee in 1829.

1832   Tocqueville and Beaumont arrive in New Orleans on January 1 and stay until January 3, when they begin their return to the northeast without having visited a plantation worked by slave labor. (At some point in their American trip they apparently had received instructions from the French government to return sooner than they had originally intended.) They travel by steamboat to Mobile, then take a series of stagecoaches across Alabama, Georgia, South Carolina, and North Carolina, to Norfolk, Virginia, which they reach on January 16. In South Carolina they are joined by Joel Poinsett, who talks with Tocqueville at length about slavery, tariffs, and the nullification movement. From Norfolk they travel by steamboat to Washington, D.C., where they arrive on January 17.

In Washington they have a brief interview with President Jackson and attend debates in the Senate and the House of Representatives. Secretary of State Edward Livingston, an expert on the Louisiana penal system, helps them collect numerous books and documents. Tocqueville and Beaumont leave Washington on February 3 and return to New York City by way of Philadelphia. They embark in New York for Le Havre on February 20, with their trunks full of documents, sketchbooks, diaries, and records of conversations with over 200 known informants; they had also instructed their friends and families at home to keep all of their letters.

The date of their landing is not known, but by April 4 Tocqueville is in Paris. His return coincides with the arrival of the cholera epidemic, which claims more than 12,000 lives in Paris by the end of April. In May and June, he travels to Toulon, Geneva, and Lausanne to inspect their prisons. While in Toulon he learns that Beaumont has been dismissed from his post as a magistrate for a minor act of insubordination, and immediately resigns in solidarity. During his trip he also visits his friend Kergorlay, who was imprisoned earlier in May for his participation in a Legitimist plot, led by the Duchesse de Berry, to overthrow the July monarchy. After his return to Paris Tocqueville resumes his collaboration with Beaumont on their report on American prisons. Beaumont writes most of the report, while Tocqueville, uncertain about his future, makes comments and writes responses to his friend's queries.

1833   *Du Système pénitentiaire aux États-Unis et de son application en France* appears in January. Tocqueville and Beaumont contrast the Auburn system of collective work during the day, discipline by whipping, and night isolation with the

Philadelphia system of total isolation, without expressing a preference for either system. (An American edition, translated and edited by Francis Lieber, is published in Philadelphia later in the year.) On March 9 Tocqueville appears as co-counsel for the defense at the trial of Kergorlay in Montbrison in the Loire department. In his speech to the jury he defends Kergorlay's character and convictions, not the Legitimist cause. Kergorlay is acquitted. (This will be Tocqueville's only appearance as a defense attorney.) In early August Tocqueville travels to England to witness what he describes as "the last performance of a beautiful play" as English society moves away from aristocratic dominance. He watches debates in the House of Lords, visits Oxford, imagines scenes from Walter Scott's novels in the ruins of Kenilworth and Warwick castles, and becomes friends with Lord Radnor, a social reformer, and Nassau Senior, a political economist who is preparing a report on the British poor laws with a view to making them more restrictive. In September, Tocqueville returns to Paris and moves into an attic room in his parents' house to work on his book on America (he and Beaumont had abandoned their plan to collaborate on another book after the publication of the prison report).

1834   Tocqueville secures the services of two young Americans living in Paris, Theodore Sedgwick III, whom he had met in Stockbridge, Massachusetts, and Francis J. Lippitt, a secretary at the American legation. They provide him with summaries of over 200 books and documents, including *Commentaries on the Constitution of the United States* by Justice Joseph Story, *Notes on the State of Virginia* by Thomas Jefferson, and *The Federalist*, as well as of the many official papers Edward Livingston had helped assemble. Tocqueville also begins carefully to study a lengthy essay on the political history of New England towns that Jared Sparks had written at his request. Occasionally Tocqueville reads drafts of his work to friends and family and submits manuscripts to them for suggestions, which he frequently accepts. In the late summer he submits a complete manuscript to his publisher, Charles Gosselin, and corrects proofs in October.

1835   Volume One of *De la démocratie en Amérique* is published in Paris on January 23 in a printing of 500 copies. Uncertain of its reception, Tocqueville writes to Camille d'Orglandes "the best thing for me would be if no one read my book." Beaumont publishes *Marie ou l'Esclavage aux États-Unis, tableau de mœurs américaines*, a novel about the doomed love affair of a French immigrant and a white American woman with a distant mulatto ancestor; the book contains lengthy documentary appendices on slavery and race relations, religion, and American Indians. Tocqueville writes *Mémoire sur le paupérisme*, an essay published later in the year by the Academic Society of Cherbourg, in which he denounces aid to unwed mothers as "a dowry of infamy" while advocating charity to those incapable of fending for themselves. In March, Tocqueville meets Henry Reeve, a young Englishman who agrees, after some hesitation, to translate *De la démocratie en Amérique*. (*Democracy in America* is published in England later in the year; an American edition of the Reeve translation, edited by John Canfield Spencer, is published in 1838.) Chateaubriand introduces Tocqueville to the literary salon of Madame Récamier, where he meets members of the Parisian literary elite who will help make *De la démocratie en Amérique* a success (seven editions of the book are printed by June 1839).

In late April, Tocqueville and Beaumont travel to London. Tocqueville meets again with Nassau Senior, Lord Radnor, and Henry Reeve; is introduced to the Whig politicians Lord Lansdowne and Lord Brougham; and begins a friendship with John Stuart Mill, who is one year his junior. In late June they leave London and visit Coventry, Birmingham, Manchester, and Liverpool, investigating the growth of industrialization and urban poverty, before traveling to Ireland in early July. Tocqueville remains in Ireland until the middle of August; before returning to France, he writes: "If you wish to know what the spirit of conquest, religious hatred, combined with all the abuses of aristocracy without any of its advantages, can produce, come to Ireland." On October 26 he marries Marie Mottley. His family and friends, including initially Kergorlay and Beaumont, disapprove of the marriage. (As a commoner and a foreigner, and a woman nine years older than her husband, Marie is never fully accepted by the Tocqueville family, although she has formally abjured Protestantism and fervently embraced Catholicism.) In November Tocqueville begins work on the second volume of *De la démocratie en Amérique*.

Minister to France Edward Livingston returns to the United States late in the year with a copy of *De la démocratie en Amérique*, where he is singled out as the person most helpful in assembling the necessary documentation, but without having resolved the indemnity crisis that brought France and America close to war. French-American diplomatic relations are temporarily suspended (until February 1836) as President Jackson demands, and finally obtains, reparations for French seizure of American ships and cargoes during the Napoleonic blockade of the continent.

1836 Louise-Madeleine de Tocqueville dies in January. After his mother's death, Tocqueville is given the château de Tocqueville, uninhabited since the Revolution, and also the title of *Comte*, which he will never use. With the château he also receives land that will provide most of his income. The political philosopher Pierre-Paul Royer-Collard introduces Tocqueville into the fashionable literary salon of the Duchesse de Dino, a niece of Talleyrand. At the request of John Stuart Mill, Tocqueville writes *L'État social et politique de la France avant et après 1789*, his first study of the French Old Regime, in which he presents the French Revolution as a local manifestation of a larger European movement toward equality; the essay is published in translation in the April *London and Westminster Review*. The Tocquevilles spend the summer in Switzerland. During a brief stay in Bern, Tocqueville observes the functioning of the federal diet. In July Beaumont marries Clémentine de La Fayette, a granddaughter of the Marquis de La Fayette. While Marie is resting and taking the waters in Baden, Tocqueville reads Machiavelli's *Florentine History*, which he describes as a "learned lecture on the art of crime in politics," as well as works by the 17th-century Catholic bishop and famous pulpit orator Bossuet, whom he admires; by Voltaire, whom he resents as illiberal and anti-democratic; by Plato; and by the Church fathers. (Later that year, Tocqueville writes to Kergorlay: "there are three men with whom I live a little daily, they are Pascal, Montesquieu and Rousseau.")

1837 Tocqueville works on a second essay on pauperism (left unfinished) in which he considers the ways French industrial workers could gain economic security through savings accounts and the forming of associations. In June he and Marie go to the château de Tocqueville and remain there until November; in future years they will spend winter and spring in Paris and summer and fall in Normandy. Tocqueville publishes two unsigned letters on Algeria in the newspaper *La Presse de Seine-et-Oise*, June 23 and August 22, expressing hope that French colonists will be able to coexist peacefully with the Arabs in Algeria. With support from Marie, Tocqueville prepares to run for office, rejecting Royer-Collard's suggestion that his lack of oratorical ability will prevent him from becoming a politician. ("Do not believe that I have a blind enthusiasm, or indeed any kind of enthusiasm," he writes to Kergorlay, "for the intellectual life.") After considering the 10th *arrondissement* of Paris, Versailles, and Cherbourg, Tocqueville chooses the Norman town of Valognes, about 10 miles southwest of his family estate, as his electoral base. He runs for election to the Chamber of Deputies, but on November 4 loses in the second round of voting, 247–220, to the incumbent, Comte Jules-Polydor Le Marois. (As a self-proclaimed "liberal of a new kind," he had rejected the support of his cousin, prime minister Louis-Mathieu Molé, causing Molé to remark: "Isolation is not independence.") After John Quincy Adams writes to him contesting its accuracy, Tocqueville agrees to delete from the sixth edition of *De la démocratie en Amérique* a sentence stating that, while president, Adams had dismissed many officials from the preceding Monroe administration.

1838   Tocqueville is elected to the Académie des sciences morales et politiques on January 6. Although at first reluctant to sit with some former participants in the Revolutionary Terror, he comes to appreciate the opportunity to meet such historians as Jules Michelet, François Mignet, François Guizot, and the philosopher Victor Cousin. Tocqueville reads and makes notes on a French translation of the Koran. Without consulting Beaumont, he writes a letter to the *Journal de Valognes* endorsing the Philadelphia system of complete solitary confinement of prison inmates.

1839   On March 2 Tocqueville defeats Le Marois, 318–240, in the first round of voting and becomes the deputy for Valognes after an expensive self-financed campaign of banquets for the electors. His good friend Francisque de Corcelle is elected in the Orne, but Beaumont is defeated for the second time in Saint Calais (he is elected in December in another district of the Sarthe). Tocqueville, who insists on sitting on the left of the Chamber to avoid being labeled a Legitimist, supports the pro-monarchial center-left party led by Odilon Barrot; one of his main political aims is to overturn the "September Laws" restricting freedom of speech and of the press that were adopted in 1835 following an assassination attempt on the king.

He gives his first major speech on foreign affairs on July 2, outlining the diverging interests of France, Russia, and Great Britain in the Middle East and advocating French support for Muhammad Ali Pasha, the ruler of Egypt who had conquered Syria and effectively established his independence from the Ottoman Empire. On July 23 he submits a report to the Chamber on slavery in the colonies of Martinique, Guadeloupe, French Guiana, and the Isle of Bourbon (Réunion), calling for the immediate emancipation of all slaves, the payment of an indemnity to the slaveowners, and a state-guaranteed wage for the freedmen during a transition period, but the report is never debated. His involvement in politics makes it difficult for Tocqueville to complete the second volume of *De la démocratie en Amérique*, and he writes to Beaumont: "I must at all costs finish this book. It and I have a duel to the death — I must kill it or it must kill me."

1840 The second volume of *De la démocratie en Amérique* is published by Gosselin on April 20. (A translation by Reeve appears in London simultaneously, and it is published in New York with a preface by Spencer later in the year.) More abstract than the first volume, it is not nearly as successful, and Tocqueville writes to Royer-Collard: "I cannot hide from myself the fact that the book is not much read and not well understood by the great public." In the Chamber Tocqueville advocates adoption of the Philadelphia system in a report on prison reform submitted on June 20, but no action is taken on the proposal.

On July 15 Great Britain, Russia, Austria, Prussia, and the Ottoman Empire sign a treaty in London intended to preserve Ottoman sovereignty over Egypt and to force Muhammad Ali to withdraw from most of Syria. The exclusion of France from the concert of the great powers

causes angry talk of going to war against Britain, and the
Chamber votes extraordinary credits for military preparations. In late October Louis-Philippe refuses to endorse
further belligerent measures and dismisses the ministry led
by Adolphe Thiers. He appoints Guizot as foreign minister and effective head of government (a position Guizot
retains for the remainder of the July monarchy). Unhappy
with what he considers to be the policy of appeasement
adopted by Guizot, Tocqueville proclaims in a speech to
the Chamber on November 30 that "a government that is
unable to make war is a detestable government." His
speech prompts John Stuart Mill to retort in a letter to
Tocqueville: "You know how repugnant to the English
character is anything like bluster, and that instead of in-
timidating them, its effect when they do not treat it with
calm contempt is to raise a dogged determination in them
not to be bullied."

1841   In February the Ottoman sultan makes Muhammad Ali
the hereditary ruler of Egypt under Ottoman sovereignty. Tocqueville travels to Algeria with his brother
Hippolyte and Beaumont, arriving in Algiers on May 7.
They are joined there by Corcelle and tour the nearby
countryside, which Tocqueville describes in his journal as
a "promised land, if one did not have to farm with a gun."
He visits Oran and Philippeville (Skikda), meets with
General Thomas-Robert Bugeaud, the recently appointed
governor-general and army commander in Algeria, and interviews other senior French officials before falling ill with
dysentery. Tocqueville returns to France on June 11 and
goes to Normandy to recover. During his convalescence
he drafts a long essay on Algeria (*Travail sur l'Algérie*, not
published until 1962) describing its colonization as essential to preserving France as a great power and justifying
the destruction of villages, orchards, and crops in *razzias*
(raids) as a necessary means of crushing Arab resistance.
France joins the four other powers on July 13 in signing a
treaty governing the Turkish straits, a diplomatic move
that restores the *entente cordiale* between France and
Britain. Tocqueville is elected to the Académie Française
on December 23.

1842   In his inaugural speech at the Académie Française,
Tocqueville denounces Napoleon's despotism before an

audience prone to commemoration of the Napoleonic legend. Along with Beaumont, he serves on a royal commission on Algerian colonization but becomes doubtful of its usefulness and withdraws. On July 9 he is reelected to the Chamber, defeating Le Marois, 465–177. Following the accidental death of the Duc d'Orléans, the heir to the throne, Tocqueville addresses the Chamber on August 18 during a debate over provisions for a future regency; in a letter to Marie, he laments that his speech was "horrible" and that he has "no talent for improvisation." To help in a study of modern moral philosophy he is undertaking for the Académie des sciences morales et politiques, Tocqueville recruits late in the year the young writer Arthur de Gobineau as his assistant (the project is never finished). In December he is elected to the Conseil général of his department, the Manche.

1843   In January, Tocqueville publishes in *Le Siècle* six unsigned letters in which he accuses "unprincipled" politicians of killing liberty while speaking in its name. Tocqueville has increasingly come to see Guizot as the leader of a centralizing, manipulative, and corrupt ministry and believes former prime minister Thiers to be equally unscrupulous. ("I despise them," Tocqueville had confided to Royer-Collard in 1841.) In the Chamber he opposes ratification of a treaty on suppressing the slave trade, sponsored by Great Britain and supported by Guizot, that would allow the British navy to stop and search foreign vessels. Tocqueville argues that the treaty is ineffectual, weakens national sovereignty, and permits abuses "in the solitude of the ocean"; as an alternative he advocates an international campaign to close the slave markets in Brazil and Cuba. In March he criticizes Guizot for his failure to support Spanish liberals, who have turned to Britain for help; he also opposes Guizot's support of British efforts to prevent the American annexation of Texas, believing that U.S. territorial expansion will help check British commercial and naval power.

Tocqueville's marriage is often tumultuous, with frequent arguments. He writes Kergorlay in September that he cannot stop his "blood boiling at the sight of a woman" while Marie never accepts "the least deviation on my part." From October to December, Tocqueville publishes another series of six unsigned articles in *Le*

Siècle calling for emancipation in the French colonies. Tocqueville sees the French Caribbean as "the Mediterranean of the New World" and foresees the building of a canal across the Isthmus of Panama. During the fall he works on a study of British rule in India begun in 1840 (it is never finished). Contrasting French agrarian colonization in Algeria with the more flexible rule of the East India Company, Tocqueville is impressed by the British ability to manipulate Indian princes, control the economy by indirect means, and implement a new administrative and legal structure while accommodating local customs.

1844   During a debate in the Chamber over state control of Catholic secondary education, Tocqueville defends the independence of Church schools. The Chamber of Deputies passes a law, introduced by Tocqueville in 1843, instituting the Philadelphia system in French prisons, but the Chamber of Peers acts on it only in 1847 and the law is never implemented. Tocqueville joins with a group of friends in buying *Le Commerce* and establishing it on July 24 as an independent opposition newspaper. As the intense debate between ultramontanists and anticlericals over liberty of teaching continues, he writes in *Le Commerce* warning of the consequences of overturning the intellectual and moral authority provided by religion: "We will need soldiers and prisons if we abolish beliefs." He criticizes *Le Siècle* for its anticlericalism, leading to a sharp polemical exchange between the newspapers and a short, painful dispute with Beaumont, who resigns from the board of *Le Siècle* while praising its editor. Tocqueville publishes articles in *Le Commerce* on the French challenge of combining a "vast" administrative centralization with a "serious representative system," and writes a report for the Conseil général of the Manche advocating the construction of a direct rail line from Paris to Cherbourg.

1845   In June Tocqueville, who had discovered he did not like journalism, ends his involvement with the failing *Le Commerce* and loses his investment — "what amounted to my affluence."

1846   During a debate in the Chamber in June, Tocqueville criticizes Bugeaud and the Guizot ministry for failing to effectively promote agrarian colonization in Algeria. He easily wins reelection to the Chamber on August 1. In October he makes a second trip to Algeria, this time accompanied by Marie. Tocqueville meets again with Bugeaud, travels overland from Algiers to Ténès, and visits Oran, Constantine, and several villages in the interior before returning to France in late December.

1847   In the winter session of the Chamber Tocqueville and a few parliamentary friends fail in their attempt to create a "young left" party of "the really honest men" with a program to end corruption and reduce the burden of taxation on the poor. Tocqueville submits two reports on Algeria to the Chamber in late May criticizing the failure to establish effective political, legal, and administrative institutions in the colony. The reports contribute to Bugeaud's resignation as governor-general that year. Barrot holds a large public banquet in Paris on July 9 in support of enlarging the electorate, but Tocqueville declines to attend and abstains from the subsequent "campaign" of political banquets held by the opposition in public halls and parks throughout the country. Ambivalent about the adoption of universal male suffrage in France, he is also concerned about the potential for disorder. During the fall he drafts proposals for providing assistance to the poor. "There is little doubt," he writes, "that, one day, the political struggle will be between the haves and the have nots. Property will be the great battlefield, and the great political questions will be about how to change property rights and to what extent." Louis-Philippe and Guizot continue to refuse all suggestions of electoral reform.

1848   In a speech to the Chamber on January 27, Tocqueville warns of growing popular discontent. Sensing "the air of revolution," he points to those "opinions and ideas" that "tend not simply to the overthrow of such and such laws, such and such a minister, or even such and such a government, but rather to the overthrow of society." After the government prohibits a political banquet, demonstrations begin in Paris on February 22 that quickly turn into a popular revolution. The king dismisses Guizot on February 23, then abdicates on February 24 in favor of his nine-year-old grandson, the Comte de Paris. Tocqueville hopes that the boy can reign with his mother, the liberal Duchesse d'Orléans, acting as regent, and urges the poet Alphonse de Lamartine, a leading orator in the Chamber, to support this solution. Instead Lamartine declares that he will "join only a Republic," and the Second Republic is proclaimed at the Hôtel de Ville on the evening of February 24.

On March 5 elections are called for a Constituent Assembly to be chosen by universal manhood suffrage, and Tocqueville becomes a candidate in his department of the Manche. (He later writes in his memoir *Souvenirs* that he plunged "headlong into the fray, risking wealth, peace of mind and life to defend, not any particular government, but the laws that hold society together.") At a public banquet held on March 19 in Cherbourg, he calls for an alliance between the French and American republics to free the sea from British domination and praises the American example for the new French regime: "In America, the Republic is not a dictatorship exercised in the name of freedom; the Republic is liberty itself, true and real liberty for all citizens; it is the sincere government of the people by the people; the uncontested domination of the majority, the order of law." While campaigning he writes daily to Marie, describing "the great Democratic revolution now unfolding" as "God's will" one day, while on another day cautiously advising: "we must quietly keep as much money as possible at home, and preferably in coin. For I suspect paper money will soon lose much of its value." On April 24 Tocqueville is elected with 110,704 votes out of the approximately 120,000 cast (voters chose several candidates from various lists).

The Constituent Assembly meets on May 4 with moderate republicans in the majority. Tocqueville, Beaumont, and 16 other members are elected from May 17 to 19 to serve on a commission charged with drafting a new constitution. In June Tocqueville meets George Sand at the home of a mutual friend. Although prejudiced against women writers ("I detest women who write, especially those who systematically disguise the weaknesses of their sex," he writes in *Souvenirs*, "instead of interesting us by displaying them in their true colors"), he listens intently as she provides him with "a detailed and very vivacious picture of the state of the Parisian workers: their organization, numbers, arms, preparations, thoughts, passions and terrible resolves. I thought the picture overloaded, but it was not so, as subsequent events clearly proved." On June

21 the provisional government shuts down the public workshops (*ateliers nationaux*), initiated in March, that employ as many as 120,000 people in Paris. A popular insurrection ensues, June 23–26, in which several thousand people are killed before troops led by General Louis-Eugène Cavaignac finally suppress the uprising. Tocqueville supports the quelling of the "class war" by Cavaignac, who becomes the head of the provisional government. He notes with sorrow the death of Chateaubriand on July 4.

In the constitutional commission, Tocqueville cites American examples and proposes creating a bicameral legislature in order to strengthen the power of local elites, but the commission rejects bicameralism, as well as his repeated attempts to lessen plans for centralized rule. (Tocqueville notes that centralization attracts strong support because "both the government and the enemies of the government love it.") Beaumont advocates limiting the president to one four-year term, a proposal that is adopted. The Assembly begins considering the proposed constitution on September 4 and approves the final version on November 4. During the debate the socialists unsuccessfully attempt to insert the right to work into the constitution's preamble. Tocqueville dismisses their claim to be the heirs of the Revolution of 1789, arguing that its "true heritage" is rather "the incorporation into politics of the divine dogma of charity." In this period, he also serves on a commission that reestablishes work in prisons after it was dispensed with by the provisional government (his last involvement with the penal system). Tocqueville supports Cavaignac in the presidential campaign, while Thiers backs Louis-Napoleon Bonaparte, whom he describes as "this imbecile we will manipulate." On December 10 Louis-Napoleon Bonaparte is elected with 74 percent of the vote.

1849 Confident of winning a seat in the Legislative Assembly established by the new constitution, Tocqueville leaves the Manche before election day to avoid the vexing local quarrels he describes as a "war of chamber pots." On May 13, he is elected with 82,404 votes out of the 94,481 cast. He goes to Frankfurt to understand the failure of the parliament, elected in Germany in 1848 by universal manhood suffrage, to create a federal Germany. Before returning to France he writes to Beaumont, predicting the victory of

the German princes in the revolutionary conflict and observing: " I believe that the king of Prussia has refused the
supremacy the Assembly offered him in the name of the
revolution only with the intention of obtaining it by re-
pressing this revolution."

On June 2 Tocqueville is appointed minister of foreign
affairs in a cabinet presided over by Odilon Barrot.
Tocqueville hires Arthur de Gobineau as his private secretary. While serving as foreign minister, he has his portrait painted by Théodore Chassériau. (It is likely that
because Tocqueville had limited time to sit, Chassériau
used as his model an earlier pencil portrait he had drawn
in 1844.) Tocqueville's major diplomatic challenge is the
restoration to temporal power of Pope Pius IX, who had
been forced to flee Rome in 1848 by the republican coali-
tion led by Giuseppe Mazzini. On July 3 a French expe-
ditionary force occupies Rome. Tocqueville chooses his
friend Francisque de Corcelle, a devout Catholic, as his
envoy to the Pope, with instructions to lead Pius IX
toward democratic reforms in the Papal States, but Corcelle proves unreliable and the pontiff refuses to make significant changes. In Europe, Tocqueville seeks to support
moderate republican regimes throughout the continent
while maintaining friendly relations with the reactionary
powers of Prussia, Austria, and Russia. He helps Pied-
mont negotiate a peace treaty with Austria, and supports
the Ottoman sultan when he refuses to surrender Hun-
garian and Polish revolutionary exiles wanted by the Czar
and the Austrian emperor.

Tocqueville is also involved with affairs in Uruguay
(there is a large French community in Montevideo), where
since 1842 France has supported President José Fructuoso
Rivera against his rival Manuel Oribe, who is backed by
the Argentinean dictator Juan Manuel Rosas. (Although
the French involvement is in contravention to the Monroe
Doctrine, the United States does not intervene.) In October Tocqueville receives a letter from Secretary of State
John Clayton demanding the recall of Guillaume-Tell
Poussin, the French minister to the United States, for allegedly having used offensive language in official commu-
nications. Although Tocqueville dislikes Poussin (who had
been a severe critic of *De la démocratie en Amérique*) and
disapproves of his conduct, he refuses to receive the new
American minister, William Cabell Rives, and writes to

Clayton asking for an explanation. (Poussin is eventually replaced, and the dispute is resolved.) Tocqueville is minister of foreign affairs for only five months. On October 31, Louis-Napoleon Bonaparte, frustrated by the inability of French diplomacy to get the Pope to secularize the government of the Papal States and to acknowledge the French military contribution to the pontifical restoration, and vexed by Barrot's disregard for presidential concerns in the Assembly, dismisses the entire cabinet and replaces them with subservient ministers.

1850   In March Tocqueville is seriously ill and spits blood for the first time, showing symptoms of tuberculosis. He is granted a six-month leave by the Assembly. During the summer in Normandy he begins writing *Souvenirs*, his memoir of the 1848 revolution (published posthumously in 1893). On September 6 Tocqueville, as president of the Conseil général of the Manche, receives Louis-Napoleon Bonaparte in Cherbourg and renews his call for a railroad connecting the port town to Paris. In December the Tocquevilles, seeking a warm climate, rent a house in Sorrento in southern Italy. He continues working on *Souvenirs* and begins conceptualizing a major book on the French Revolution, writing to Kergorlay: "I believe myself in a better condition than I was when I wrote *Democracy* to deal well with a great subject of political literature. . . . For a long time I have had the thought of choosing in this great expanse of time that goes from 1789 to our day, and which I continue to call the French Revolution, the ten years of the Empire, the birth, the development, the decline and the fall of that prodigious enterprise."

1851   In April the increasingly autocratic Louis-Napoleon Bonaparte indirectly approaches Tocqueville about a possible new term as foreign minister, but the overture is rejected. Later in the month the Tocquevilles return to France. Tocqueville serves on an Assembly committee on revising the constitution; its recommendations fail to win approval. In September, he writes the third part of *Souvenirs* in Versailles. Prohibited by the constitution from seeking a second term, Louis-Napoleon stages a military coup d'état on December 2. Tocqueville is arrested along with more than 200 protesting members of the Assembly and is held in jail until December 4. He considers the coup to be "one

of the greatest crimes history has known" and condemns
it in an anonymous article, translated by Henry Reeve, that
appears on December 11 in the *Times* of London.

1852   Hoping that the Comte de Chambord, the grandson of
Charles X and the Bourbon heir, can offer a political alternative to the dictatorship of Louis-Napoleon, Tocqueville
writes to him on January 14 outlining precepts for a constitutional monarchy. He becomes estranged from his
brother Édouard when Édouard runs for office on a platform defending the coup. Tocqueville resigns from the
Conseil général of the Manche to avoid swearing allegiance to the new regime and retires from political life. In
an address to the Académie des sciences morales et politiques on April 12, he underscores the incompatibility of
political science and the art of government, yet points to
the role abstract writers had played in the making of the
French Revolution, a theme he will fully develop in *L'Ancien Régime et la Révolution*. Returning to his château in
the summer, he writes (referring to the events that led to
Napoleon Bonaparte's coup on November 9, 1799, or
18 Brumaire) about how once before "the republic was
ready to receive a master" and describes his country in a
letter to Édouard as "this tired, nervous, half-rotten
France, which asks only to obey whoever will insure its
material well-being." On December 2 Louis-Napoleon
Bonaparte becomes Napoleon III as the Second Empire
is proclaimed.

1853   With his health failing, Tocqueville is advised by his
doctor to avoid the damp climate of Normandy, and in
the late spring he settles in Saint-Cyr-les-Tours in the
Loire Valley. In nearby Tours, he reads the files of the
royal administration of the province of Touraine. After
Gobineau sends him the first two volumes of his *Essai sur
l'inégalité des races humaines*, Tocqueville writes in response: "You speak unceasingly of races that are regener-
ating or deteriorating, which take up or lay aside social
capacities by an *infusion of different blood* (I believe that
these are your own terms). Such a predestination seems
to me, I will confess, a cousin of pure materialism and
be sure that if the crowd, which always takes the great
beaten tracks in matters of reasoning, were to accept your
doctrine, that would lead it straight from the race to the

individual and from social capacities to all kinds of capacities.... I remain situated at the opposite extreme of those doctrines. I believe them to be very probably wrong and very certainly pernicious."

1854   Early in the year Tocqueville decides to devote a full volume to the causes of the Revolution. After learning German, he goes with Marie to Bonn in June to research feudalism in Germany. He finds that feudal dues had survived much longer in Germany than in France, where they were hated most in the very regions where they had already largely disappeared. "I see with a certain satisfaction," Tocqueville writes to Beaumont, "that the ideas I had of Germany without knowing the country, purely from abstract reasoning, attempting to discover why the Revolution had happened among us rather than in Germany, appear to me to be fully confirmed by the factual details." The Tocquevilles return to France in September and spend the winter in Compiègne.

1855   Tocqueville takes an active part in the effort at the Académie des sciences morales et politiques to defeat government-backed candidates for membership. The government retaliates through various administrative measures, but the Académie becomes a symbol of liberal resistance to Napoleonic despotism. Tocqueville returns to Normandy in the summer after a three-year absence. Although he had actively sought his father's advice in the writing of *De la démocratie en Amérique,* he conceals the preparation of his new book from Hervé de Tocqueville, having not thought well of the two volumes his father had written on the reigns of Louis XV and Louis XVI.

1856   In January Tocqueville writes to his friend Madame Swetchine, describing the "moral isolation" he experiences: "to be alone in the desert often strikes me as being less painful than being alone among men." Beaumont helps him proofread the first volume of his book on the Old Regime. Seeing a continuity with the American work, he suggests "Démocratie et liberté en France" to Tocqueville as a possible title. Hervé de Tocqueville dies on June 9. *L'Ancien Régime et la Révolution* is published in Paris on June 16 by Michel Lévy and is given an enthusiastic reception. (*The Old Regime and the Revolution,* translated by Henry Reeve, is published simultaneously in London.) Tocqueville argues that the French Revolution, despite its own rhetoric of breaking with the past, was the outcome of many deep transformations begun in the Old Regime. He sees bureaucratic centralization under royal authority, which killed local liberty, as a long-term agent of destabilization, and argues that the monarchy itself, by depriving the nobility, the Third Estate, and even the royal administration of any real experience with politics, opened the way for inexperienced intellectuals to shape public opinion. The book is understood as a work of liberal opposition to Napoleon III and gives Tocqueville renewed political prominence.

1857   In June Tocqueville travels to London, where he is given authorization to read the diplomatic archives covering the years from 1787 to 1793. He returns to Cherbourg in July on a British naval ship provided by the Admiralty as a special courtesy. The financial panic in the United States worries Tocqueville. Fearing the loss of railroad bonds he had purchased in 1848, he asks Senator Charles Sumner to inquire about the fate of the Central Michigan and the Galena–Chicago railroads. In a letter to Sumner in November, Tocqueville wonders whether the election of James Buchanan in 1856 signaled the triumph of proslavery forces, but notes with pleasure the victory of Free-Soil candidates in the recent election for the Kansas territorial legislature.

1858   Tocqueville goes to Paris in April planning to do extensive research in the libraries for a second volume on the unfolding of the Revolution and the creation of the Empire. By the middle of May he feels so ill that he returns to his château, and in June he spits blood. In August he watches from the roof of his brother Édouard's château at Tourlaville as Napoleon III presides over the official opening of the Cherbourg–Paris railroad line. Tocqueville and Marie move to Cannes in late October, hoping that the Riviera climate will do him good. By this time, Tocqueville has drafted substantial sections of his second volume.

1859   John Stuart Mill sends Tocqueville a copy of *On Liberty*, but he is not able to comment on it as he had promised.

After a brief remission in February, Tocqueville continues to decline as his tuberculosis worsens. Beaumont and Kergorlay visit him. Marie convinces her husband to confess and receive Holy Communion but it is not known whether he recovers his faith. Tocqueville dies on the evening of April 16. As he wished, his body is taken back to Normandy and is buried on May 10 in the village cemetery of Tocqueville

Note on the Texts

Drawn from *Tocqueville: Democracy in America* (Olivier Zunz, editor), volume 147 in the Library of America series, this Library of America Paperback Classic prints the text of volume two of *Democracy in America* (*De la démocratie en Amérique*) by Alexis de Tocqueville in a new translation by Arthur Goldhammer.

From May 9, 1831, to February 20, 1832, Tocqueville and his friend and fellow magistrate Gustave de Beaumont traveled through the United States, inspecting American prisons (the official purpose of their visit), but also conducting interviews with more than 200 informants on American politics, law, mores, and social beliefs. Following the publication in January 1833 of their report *Du Système pénitentiaire aux États-Unis et de son application en France*, which was written primarily by Beaumont, Tocqueville began work in the autumn of 1833 on *De la démocratie en Amérique*. In preparing his book Tocqueville drew on the letters, notebooks, and journals he had written during his American trip, as well as hundreds of books and documents he had collected in the United States and France. The first volume of *De la démocratie en Amérique* was published in Paris on January 23, 1835, by Charles Gosselin in a two-volume edition. Gosselin published six further "editions" between 1835 and 1839 (the 7th "edition" was a reprinting of the 6th). For the sixth, published in 1838, Tocqueville made a number of corrections.

Tocqueville began work on the second volume of *De la démocratie en Amérique* in the fall of 1835 but did not finish it as soon as he had expected for a number of reasons, including the time he devoted to his political career. The second volume of *De la démocratie en Amérique* was published in Paris by Gosselin on April 20, 1840, again in a two-volume edition (this is commonly known as the "8th edition" of the work). In 1842, Gosselin published the 9th, 10th, and 11th "editions," in which the first volume (1835) and second volume (1840) appeared together (the 10th and 11th "editions" were partially, and probably wholly, reprintings of the 9th). For what was called the 12th edition, published by Pagnerre in 1848, Tocqueville added a preface written after the February 1848 revolution in France that overthrew the July monarchy and established the Second Republic, as well as an appendix containing a report he delivered on January 15, 1848, to the Académie des sciences morales et politiques on *De la Démocratie en Suisse* by Élysée Cherbuliez. The new preface and appendix appeared in what was called the 13th edition, published by Pagnerre in 1850, along with an additional appendix printing the text of a speech Tocqueville made in the Chamber of Deputies on January 27, 1848, warning of a possible revolution in France. This was the last printing to appear before Tocqueville's death in 1859.

The translation by Arthur Goldhammer of the first volume of *Democracy in America* is based on the text of the French 1850 text ("13th edition"), and the Goldhammer translation of the second volume of *Democracy in America* is based on the French 1848 text ("12th edition"); these texts have been shown by modern scholarship to be the most accurate ones published during Tocqueville's lifetime. In identifying and correcting typesetting errors in them, the historical-critical edition of *De la démocratie en Amérique* by Eduardo Nolla (Paris: Vrin, 1990), and the Pléiade edition of *De la démocratie en Amérique*, edited by André Jardin, Jean-Claude Lamberti, and James T. Schleifer (Paris: Gallimard, 1992), have been consulted. In the present volume, a new translation of the preface to the 12th "edition" is printed in the notes. The appendices added in the 12th and 13th "editions" have not been included in this volume.

Tocqueville included in his text numerous translated quotations from English-language sources. In cases where his translations are faithful to the English originals, this volume prints the texts of the original English-language sources; but in cases where Tocqueville freely translated or paraphrased the original sources, the quotations are retranslated into English, and the original passages are printed in the notes in this volume.

The translation presented here reproduces the volume, part, and chapter organization, and the sub-chapter headings, of the French texts it is based on, but it does not attempt to reproduce other features of their design. In presenting Tocqueville's footnotes, the present volume uses Arabic superscript numerals, and it numbers the notes continuously within each chapter. Tocqueville's endnotes are printed following the text and are assigned Roman numerals that proceed continuously through both volumes of *Democracy in America*; references to these endnotes are indicated in the text by footnotes using asterisks.

Notes

In the notes below, the reference numbers denote page and line of this volume (the line count includes headings). No note is made for material included in standard desk-reference books. Footnotes in the text are Tocqueville's own. For further biographical background and references to other studies, see André Jardin, *Tocqueville* (New York: Farrar, Straus & Giroux, Inc., 1988); George Wilson Pierson, *Tocqueville and Beaumont in America* (New York: Oxford University Press, 1938); Alexis de Tocqueville, *Journey to America*, edited by J. P. Mayer (London: Faber and Faber, Ltd., 1959); and *The Tocqueville Reader: A Life in Letters and Politics*, edited by Olivier Zunz and Alan S. Kahan (Oxford: Blackwell Publishing, 2002).

23.14   Constituent Assembly and Convention]   The Constituent Assembly met from July 9, 1789, to September 30, 1791; it abolished feudal privileges and adopted the Declaration of the Rights of Man and of the Citizen. The Convention was the supreme legislative and constituent body in France from September 21, 1792, to October 26, 1795; it abolished the monarchy and created the First Republic.

33.11–12   Although they do not . . . productive labor]   In French, *s'ils ne s'associent pas eux-mêmes à l'industrie*. Here *industrie* refers to productive labor in general.

41.16   the civil nations]   In French, *les nations polies*. Here the sense of *poli* is not so much "polite" as "civilized," and using the word allows Tocqueville to avoid repeating the adjective *civilisé*.

43.25   There has recently arisen a sect]   The followers of the French socialist Saint-Simon (1760–1825).

54.25   industrial class]   Tocqueville wrote *classe industrielle*. Throughout this chapter, he uses the word *art* to refer to the skilled labor of an artisan or craftsman; this has sometimes been translated as "trade" or "craft" rather than "art."

64.11–12   the technique of literature]   In French, *l'art littéraire*; here Tocqueville is using *art* as he does elsewhere to refer to trade, craft, or technique.

69.10–11   to the people and even the middle classes]   In French, *au peuple et même aux classes moyennes*.

105.17–18   liberty and equality touch and become one] Tocqueville wrote *la liberté et l'égalité se touchent et se confondent.*

106.8–9   so that equality, . . . the same as liberty,] Tocqueville wrote *que par conséquent l'égalité, dans son degré le plus extrême, se confonde avec la liberté.*

109.8   *egoism*] In the original, *égoïsme*, which can also mean "selfishness" in everyday French.

126.6–7   national lawmakers] In French, *législateurs de l'État*, meaning here not state legislators but national ones.

126.10   in each state] In French, *dans chaque province.*

131.27   private entities] In French, *particuliers*, or private individuals, used here in the sense of legal entities, hence the translation "private entities."

132.31–36   "the freedom . . . master."] Cf. p. 217.29–36 in volume I.

132.37–40   "One . . . close to it."] See p. 219.35–38 in volume I.

135.9   to behave honorably] In French, *d'être honnête*, a phrase that connotes respectability, decency, and, particularly in this context, fairness in dealing with others.

135.13–16   "Should I not . . . most profitable."] From *Essays*, book II, chapter 16, "Of Glory," translated by John Florio.

139.32–34   "In deceiving oneself . . . to be false!"] Cf. *Pensées*, Brunschvicg edition, number 233.

194.32   *lackey*] In French, *laquais.*

212.19–20   allow their children . . . of terms] Tocqueville wrote *qui se faisaient tutoyer par leurs enfants*, literally saying that the children use the familiar form of the second person pronoun, *tu*, in addressing their parents.

219.16   morals] In this chapter and the chapter following (Volume Two, Part III, Chapter 11), the French *mœurs*, translated elsewhere as "mores," is rendered as "morals" because it is being employed in a narrower context.

253.17   Constable of Bourbon] Charles, duc de Bourbon (1490–1527), was made Constable of France by Francis I in 1515. After a protracted dispute with the king, he entered the service of the Holy Roman Emperor Charles V in 1523 and fought against Francis. He was killed while attacking Rome in 1527.

253.20   critical of him] The French text literally refers to the Constable's deeds rather than his person.

264.31–34   "the great advantage . . . without effort."] Cf. Pascal, *Pensées*, Brunschvicg edition, number 322.

305.15–17   "that it is far more . . . prince with slaves."] This is a paraphrase of what Machiavelli wrote, not a quotation.

324.20   pasha who rules Egypt]   Muhammad Ali (1769–1849) was made
Ottoman viceroy of Egypt in 1805 and ruled until his retirement in 1848.

338.37   disciplined]   In French, the word rendered here as "disciplined"
is *policé*.

Index

About the editor:
OLIVIER ZUNZ is Commonwealth Professor of History at the University of Virginia. He is the editor (with Alan S. Kahan) of *The Tocqueville Reader: A Life in Letters and Politics* and *Alexis de Tocqueville and Gustave de Beaumont in America: Their Friendship and Their Travels* and the author of *Why the American Century?* and *Philanthropy in America: A History*, among other works. He has served as the president of The Tocqueville Society / La Société Tocqueville.

About the translator:
ARTHUR GOLDHAMMER has translated more than 120 works from the French, including Tocqueville's *The Ancien Régime and the French Revolution* and *Alexis de Tocqueville and Gustave de Beaumont in America. Their Friendship and Their Travels*. He is an affiliate of the Center for European Studies at Harvard University and a member of the editorial board of *French Politics, Culture and Society*.

The Library of America Paperback Classics Series

American Speeches: Political Oratory from Patrick Henry to Barack Obama (various authors)
Edited and with an introduction by Ted Widmer
ISBN: 978-1-59853-094-0

The Education of Henry Adams by Henry Adams
With an introduction by Leon Wieseltier
ISBN: 978-1-59853-060-5

The Pioneers by James Fenimore Cooper
With an introduction by Alan Taylor
ISBN: 978-1-59853-155-8

The Red Badge of Courage by Stephen Crane
With an introduction by Robert Stone
ISBN: 978-1-59853-061-2

The Souls of Black Folk by W.E.B. Du Bois
With an introduction by John Edgar Wideman
ISBN: 978-1-59853-054-4

Essays: First and Second Series by Ralph Waldo Emerson
With an introduction by Douglas Crase
ISBN: 978-1-59853-084-1

The Autobiography by Benjamin Franklin
With an introduction by Daniel Aaron
ISBN: 978-1-59853-095-7

The Scarlet Letter by Nathaniel Hawthorne
With an introduction by Harold Bloom
ISBN: 978-1-59853-112-1

Indian Summer by William Dean Howells
With an introduction by John Updike
ISBN: 978-1-59853-156-5

The Varieties of Religious Experience by William James
With an introduction by Jaroslav Pelikan
ISBN: 978-1-59853-062-9

Selected Writings by Thomas Jefferson
With an introduction by Tom Wicker
ISBN: 978-1-59853-096-4

The Autobiography of an Ex-Colored Man by James Weldon Johnson
With an introduction by Charles R. Johnson
ISBN: 978-1-59853-113-8

Selected Speeches and Writings by Abraham Lincoln
With an introduction by Gore Vidal
ISBN: 978-1-59853-053-7

The Call of the Wild by Jack London
With an introduction by E. L. Doctorow
ISBN: 978-1-59853-058-2

Moby-Dick by Herman Melville
With an introduction by Edward Said
ISBN: 978-1-59853-085-8

My First Summer in the Sierra and Selected Essays by John Muir
Edited and with an introduction by Bill McKibben
ISBN: 978-1-59853-111-4

Selected Tales, with The Narrative of Arthur Gordon Pym
by Edgar Allan Poe
With an introduction by Diane Johnson
ISBN: 978-1-59853-056-8

Uncle Tom's Cabin by Harriet Beecher Stowe
With an introduction by James M. McPherson
ISBN: 978-1-59853-086-5

Walden by Henry David Thoreau
With an introduction by Edward Hoagland
ISBN: 978-1-59853-063-6

Democracy in America by Alexis de Tocqueville
The Arthur Goldhammer Translation
Edited and with introductions by Olivier Zunz
Volume One ISBN: 978-1-59853-151-0
Volume Two ISBN: 978-1-59853-152-7

The Adventures of Tom Sawyer by Mark Twain
With an introduction by Russell Baker
ISBN: 978-1-59853-087-2

Life on the Mississippi by Mark Twain
With an introduction by Jonathan Raban
ISBN: 978-1-59853-057-5

Selected Writings by George Washington
With an introduction by Ron Chernow
ISBN: 978-1-59853-110-7

The House of Mirth by Edith Wharton
With an introduction by Mary Gordon
ISBN: 978-1-59853-055-1

Leaves of Grass, The Complete 1855 and 1891–92 Editions
by Walt Whitman
With an introduction by John Hollander
ISBN: 978-1-59853-097-1

For more information, please visit www.loa.org/paperbackclassics/

≛ The Library of America

The contents of this Paperback Classic are drawn from *Tocqueville: Democracy in America* (Olivier Zunz, editor), volume number 147 in the Library of America series.

Created with seed funding from the National Endowment for the Humanities and the Ford Foundation, The Library of America is a nonprofit cultural institution that preserves our nation's literary heritage by publishing, and keeping permanently in print, authoritative editions of America's best and most significant writing. Hailed as "the most important book-publishing project in the nation's history" (*Newsweek*), this award-winning series maintains America's most treasured writers in "the finest-looking, longest-lasting edition ever made" (*The New Republic*).

Since 1982, over 220 hardcover volumes have been published in the Library of America series, each containing up to 1600 pages and including a number of works. In many cases, the complete works of a writer are collected in as few as three compact volumes. New volumes are added each year to make all the essential writings of America's foremost novelists, historians, poets, essayists, philosophers, playwrights, journalists, and statesmen part of The Library of America.

Each volume features: authoritative, unabridged texts • a chronology of the author's life, helpful notes, and a brief textual essay • a handsomely designed, easy-to-read page • high-quality, acid-free paper, bound in a cloth cover and sewn to lie flat when opened • a ribbon marker and printed end papers.

For more information, a complete list of titles, tables of contents, and to request a catalogue, please visit www.loa.org.